MW01078423

Emmanuelle, Bianca *and* Venus in Furs

Guido Crepax

EVERGREEN

EVERGREEN is an imprint of Benedikt Taschen Verlag GmbH

© for this edition: 2000 Benedikt Taschen Verlag GmbH
Hohenzollernring 53, D–50672 Köln
© Guido Crepax
© "Emmanuelle", drawings by Guido Crepax, adapted from the novel
"Emmanuelle – la leçon de l'homme" by Emmanuelle Arsan
© lettering of "Bianca": Caterina Crepax
© introduction: Paolo Caneppele and Günter Krenn
Translation (introduction): Chris Miller, Oxford
Design: Lambert & Lambert, Düsseldorf

Printed in Germany
ISBN 3–8228–6301–7

CONTENTS

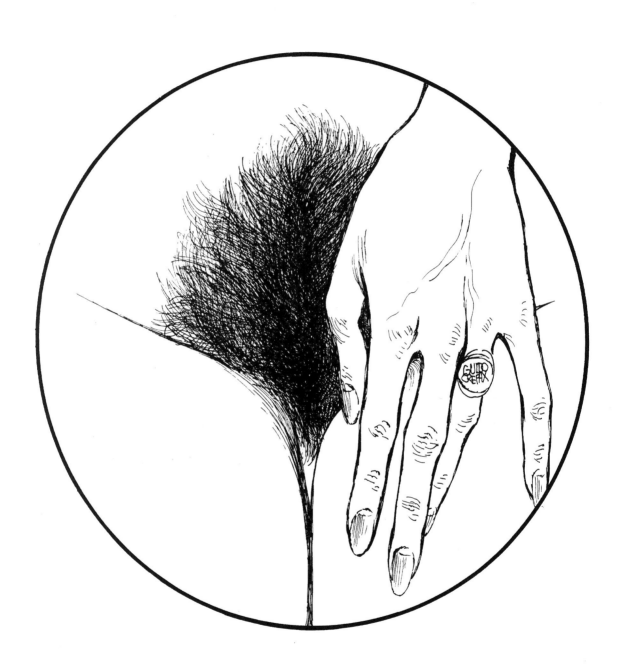

Three Women:
Bianca, Emmanuelle, Venus in Furs

PAOLO CANEPPELE

GÜNTER KRENN

Ineffable as desire may be, it can nonetheless be represented. In his treatment of the erotic, a graphic artist like Guido Crepax has no other recourse, in the face of the Heraclitean flux, than the variable mobility of the individual image. Crepax eliminates commentary in his reduction of the narrative function. The reader must interpret in the author's stead; the illustrator's "language" itself becomes a variable. This has given rise to many misunderstandings, though the essential problem here is the perception of erotic art in our culture. The philosopher Michel Foucault was right to lament the effacement in the 1920s of "ars erotica" in favour of "scientia sexualis". In erotic art, desire is understood in practical terms and harvested as experience. The artistic perspective is not that of some absolute law, proscribing and permitting; criteria of usefulness are irrelevant to it. Art judges the erotic for what it is, in terms of its intensity, quality, duration, and illumination of body and soul. Foucault further points out that a discourse permanently "open" to sexuality does little more than obscure that whereof it speaks. The definition of the erotic is the public, creative, sensitive and therefore palpable humanisation of the libido; pornography we may define as its trivialization.

In traditional comic strips, sexuality was long taboo, and was, at best, represented in highly sublimated forms. However, in the 1920s the "Eight-Pagers" came into existence, and by the 1930s had become a veritable industry, whose salesmen contrived to propagate its products throughout the continent. The anonymous artists working on them borrowed the appearances of their heroes from other comic-strips and from film stars; these were then given a new, bizarre and erotic lease of life. The "Eight-Pagers" soon acquired sixteen and then thirty-two pages, and when they found themselves hard-pressed by competition from pornographic magazines in the 50s, their creators came up with the "Bizarre Comics" to maintain their hold on the market. During the Second World War, Tommies and GIs went to war carrying copies not only of the traditional locker-room pin-ups, but of "Jane" and Milton Caniff's "Male Call".

In Europe, it was not until the 1960s that serious efforts were made to give comic strips an artistic face. In his Le Terrain bookshop in Paris, which sold surrealist writers like André

Breton, Léo Malet and Boris Vian alongside tomes of film theory, Eric Losfeld displayed something quite new: underground comics. Bans and prosecutions quickly ensured their popularity. And they provoked widespread public debate; the attempt to find a enlightened adult market led to a demand for reform of the regulations governing the genre. Jean-Claude Forest's "Barbarella", first published in 1964, belongs to this experimental generation; its nervous and peremptory line, episodic development and lack of linear narrative were at one with its relatively frank handling of the salacious. Later, magazines such as "Jodelle" (1966) and "Pravda" (1968), whose heroines were modelled on the singers Françoise Hardy and Sylvie Vartan, noisily echoed the slogans of their time: mass consumption, rebellion, the cult of the star, and experiments with drugs.

Guido Crepax began his first efforts in the genre in the mid-1960s. At first, his narratives were detective and adventure stories, featuring his superhero Neutron – the art critic Philip Rembrandt in everyday life – and later Rembrandt's lover, Valentina. Erotic scenes at first appeared only incidentally. But Crepax then gave up his linear narrative style and began to mix different planes of reality with dream and fantasy, placing them all on the same footing, and it was at this point that representations of the sexual in his work began to proliferate, culminating in sadomasochistic fantasies. A central feature of Crepax's handling of the sexual is that it is always bound up with dream, and only ever appears in the context of untrammelled and overriding fantasy. Crepax has various methods of demarcating dream from reality; one of them is the use of round-edged framing for dream and traditional orthogonal frames for reality. A subtle interweaving of the two kinds of framing means that the difference between the 'real' and the 'fictive' is often not perceived at first glance, despite the clearly defined code. And thus the stories themselves began to transmute, and the narrative structure, too, ceased to follow traditional patterns. In her daily life, Valentina's sexual life is a fairly normal one, and Crepax has often chosen fairly discreet perspectives on it, in contrast with the note of obsession characteristic of his representation of dream life. His ingenuity in representing the sex-act by neutral details is exemplified in the volume "Diario di Valentina"; Valentina's

Jean Harlow on the cover page of "A Poor Fit" (Eight-Pager)

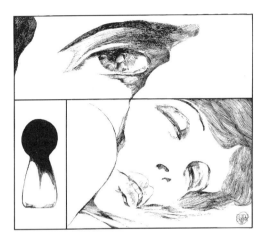

first sexual experience with her professor of history is not recounted via the bodies of the lovers but the objects around them.

"Good taste is a cold thing" the writer and critic Saito Ryoku'u (1867-1904) declared, and his colleague Tanizaki Jun'chiro (1886-1965) added "Good taste is not merely cold but sordid". Crepax's erotic images have sometimes has been criticised for their coldness. Luisa Crepax: "Many people dislike the erotic aspect of his stories because it seems cold to them. The fact is, Guido is a voyeur by nature. He likes to represent erotic scenes without identifying with those he portrays. There are artists in this field who do much more to stimulate the reader's imagination."

The voyeur's stare: keyhole, eye and face from "Venus in Furs"

In comparison with the taut thread of his earlier stories, Crepax has, over the course of his career, tended toward an increasing interplay of dream and reality. The culminating points of this tendency are "Casa matta", whose narrative content is all but indecipherable, and "Lanterna magica", from which all text is excluded. The Valentina stories were first published in "Linus", an anthology of the comic strip, and subsequently in volume form, where they were sometimes supplemented by further drawings. The first comic book by Crepax appeared in 1968: it was a sci-fi story entitled "L'Astronave pirata", and the first volume of Valentina appeared that same year.

How, then, does the master of erotic representation view erotic cinema? Crepax is somewhat negative: "I think cinema rather ill-equipped to contrive an atmosphere of that kind. Only the eroticism of word and idea influences me. My drawings are sometimes lascivious but never vulgar." Crepax never recounts banal love stories; as he says, he detests happy endings and tragic dénouements alike, and prefers to leave the story open-ended.

In homage to Musil's nouvelle, "Drei Frauen", we might entitle this volume "Three Women". The first of these is among the most often-cited protagonists of erotic literature in the world; the second is synonymous with the erotic best-seller; and the third is Crepax's own creation. Their genealogy is as follows: "Initially, I drew only my own stories. Later I began to illustrate other people's stories because I was asked to. To take an example: I created Bianca, and she became popular. Bianca is often naked, in fact she is almost invariably naked. Which is why I got a call from Paris one day, asking me if I would like to illustrate 'Histoire d'O'. At first I refused, because it was not my story, but then I had a think, phoned back, and accepted. And so in 1973 my 'Histoire d'O' came into being. It went on to be my best-selling book worldwide; it came out in the States, in Brazil, in Japan and throughout Europe. Since I took myself to be particularly good at drawing nude women, I agreed to do 'Emmanuelle' by Emmanuelle Arsan. I've never met the author, but I know she likes my work. That was in 1978, since when I have illustrated lots of things, 'Venus in Furs', 'Justine' – almost always erotic stories."

Guido Crepax was born in Milan in 1933; today his books are published in France, Spain (translated into Castilian, Catalan and Basque), Germany, Japan, Finland, Greece, Brazil and the United States. His series of silk-prints, engravings and lithographs, notably "Imitazioni" (1974), "Esitazioni" (introduction by Umberto Eco, 1976), "Casanova" (1976) and "Freud" (1978) are widely admired. "L'Encylopédie di Valentina", Crepax's revision of the illustrations to that great masterpiece of the Enlightenment, the "Encyclopédie ou dictionnaire raisonné des sciences", des arts et des métiers is pre-eminent among these. Both his comic strip drawings and his etchings have featured in exhibitions; the largest of these took place in Venice (22 Feb–31 Mar 1992) at the Museo d'arte moderna di Ca' Pesaro. In a parallel career, Crepax has worked in advertising, with publicity drawings for many product-launches to his credit. Among his most interesting creations in that area are Dunlopella (1969), who strongly resembles his most popular comic strip character, Valentina, and Terry for Terital Textiles.

The revolutions that Crepax brought to the comic book concerned not only style – his innovative viewpoints, with their implications of camera-angle, and his varying of image-size – but also narrative perspective. "I've always been a little arrogant. Which is why, in the 1960s, I told the publisher Gandini that I was going to do comic books that would be completely different. I wanted to prove that I could do one from scratch, without

Dunlopella, Guido Crepax's publicity creation for a tyre company

experience, and still make it better than traditional comics."
And so he developed his preference for disjointed narratives,
in which the image is the vector of thought and all pretence
of verbal logic is abandoned. Crepax stories are often
difficult to follow at first; the architectonic connections are not always clearly conceived or fluently
combined, and their unsystematic deployment yields
no overt plot-line. Eminent semioticians, such as
Crepax's friend Umberto Eco have concluded "You draw

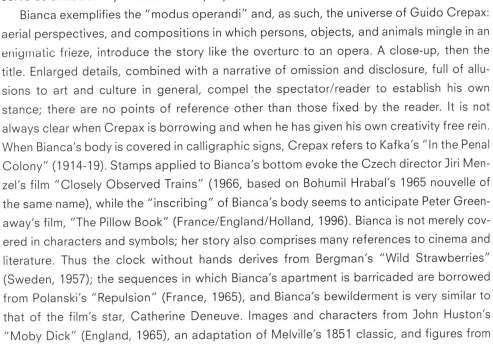

beautifully, but you should find an author to write your stories". He has no young follow-
ers; there is no "Crepax tradition". As he says, "my way of telling stories is so remote from
tradition that young artists – rightly, I confess – choose other models. I have no desire to
serve as a model. My universe is truly my own."

Guido Crepax thinks in images

    Bianca exemplifies the "modus operandi" and, as such, the universe of Guido Crepax:
aerial perspectives, and compositions in which persons, objects, and animals mingle in an
enigmatic frieze, introduce the story like the overture to an opera. A close-up, then the
title. Enlarged details, combined with a narrative of omission and disclosure, full of allu-
sions to art and culture in general, compel the spectator/reader to establish his own
stance; there are no points of reference other than those fixed by the reader. It is not
always clear when Crepax is borrowing and when he has given his own creativity free rein.
When Bianca's body is covered in calligraphic signs, Crepax refers to Kafka's "In the Penal
Colony" (1914-19). Stamps applied to Bianca's bottom evoke the Czech director Jiri Men-
zel's film "Closely Observed Trains" (1966, based on Bohumil Hrabal's 1965 nouvelle of
the same name), while the "inscribing" of Bianca's body seems to anticipate Peter Green-
away's film, "The Pillow Book" (France/England/Holland, 1996). Bianca is not merely covered in characters and symbols; her story also comprises many references to cinema and
literature. Thus the clock without hands derives from Bergman's "Wild Strawberries"
(Sweden, 1957); the sequences in which Bianca's apartment is barricaded are borrowed
from Polanski's "Repulsion" (France, 1965), and Bianca's bewilderment is very similar to
that of the film's star, Catherine Deneuve. Images and characters from John Huston's
"Moby Dick" (England, 1965), an adaptation of Melville's 1851 classic, and figures from

"Pinocchio" and Edgar Allan Poe also make an appearance. The Marquis de Sade's Juliette is a central figure, and there is a cameo role for the film-director Erich von Stroheim, who appears as a circus director named after a character he portrayed in his own film "Foolish Wives" (USA, 1922).

One of the few incidents in which a clear temporal and spatial unity prevails amid the chaos of "Bianca's" 'plot' is the series of games that she plays against a chimpanzee (dominos, nine men's morris, chequers and chess); four nights follow the four days in which the games take place. Otherwise, the only limits to Bianca's life are the frames of the drawings. These are rectangular like dominos and, like them, could theoretically be realigned and recombined in an infinite game; the frames/dominos of "Bianca" can be rearranged at random by the reader/player. Like dominos, the framed drawings of "Bianca" are black and white. The alignment of the pieces is akin to the montage of these images, though the sequences of the latter, like the series taken by that pioneer of the cinema, Eadweard Muybridge, suggest a sequence of movements. Similarly, the infinite series of images in the Bianca stories evoke the infinite profusion of images in experimental cinema.

In this way, though she has no literary or cinematic forebears, Bianca might be said to star in the only cinematic story that Crepax has ever written. In the cutting-room, the film-director decides the rhythm, meaning and structure of the film. Crepax performs this function, and the variability of the medium is more in evidence in "Bianca" than anywhere else in his work.

One of Crepax's favourite occupations is the invention of games, of which he has produced a great number. Playfulness is integral to his personality, and it inflects the more dramatic moments of his stories with humour. A free, artful and ludic form of representation is the ability he cherishes above all others. Crepax emphasizes this in the subtitle he chose for "Bianca: A Story of Excess." The title under which an earlier German edition

The infinite combinations possible in game-playing occupy a central role in Crepax's poetics

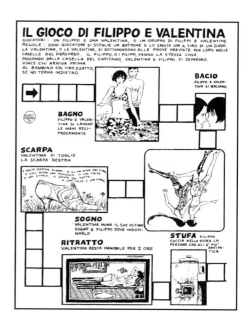

of the work was published – "Bianca torturata" – is, therefore, somewhat misleading: "What I like about 'Bianca' is the unrealistic structure that I have given her stories. Compared to Valentina, whose adventures belong to a particular reality (so real she even has an identity card), I had fun making Bianca a completely free character. She has no profession; she could, perhaps, be a student. I created her to give myself a little more freedom. My friend Giovanni Gandini, the editor of 'Linus', often made life difficult for me in the early 1960s because, at least at first, he didn't want me drawing Valentina nude. I created Bianca precisely so that I could draw her nude. I first published the stories in the men's magazine,

Crepax's heroine as a female Gulliver in "I Viaggi di Bianca"

'Kent', a rather successful imitation of 'Playboy'. The structure of the Bianca stories is not homogenous, there is no real beginning and no real end. Without my ever intending it, it eventually became a big book. I just made image after image, put them one after another, and all of a sudden I had some two hundred pages."

Bianca was thus conceived as entirely free and unfettered; she stands outside any moral order as an incarnation of the unlimited powers of nature. She seems about nineteen, but she is, in theory, ageless. The name "Bianca" suggests blankness and white, and in this respect suits her better than "Candida", as she was first christened. Crepax is very fond of Voltaire's "Candide", but "Candida" would have suggested the whiteness of purity. In his "Valentina nel metrò", Crepax has Valentina meet many famous characters from comics; while doing so, he alludes to Bianca's original name. Each episode of the Valentina volume is a homage to the great masters of comic books; the gallery features, among others, Hugo Pratt, Milton Caniff, Harold Foster, Burne Hogarth, Wolinski and Pichard, Jean-Claude Forest, Alex Raymond, Chester Gould, Stan Lee, John Willie, Winsor McCay, with their most important creations. Crepax has, rightly, introduced his own characters into this parade, and among them is Bianca. When the deputy-head of a girls' boarding school asks "Dov'è Candida? – Where's Candida?", Valentina replies "Candida? Ma non si chiama Bianca? – Candida? Isn't she called Bianca?"

Bianca incarnates a blank white surface, a screen onto which first Crepax and then the

13

reader can project his fantasies. The lack of biographical detail is both to the advantage and the detriment of Bianca; she is at once everyone and no one. She is the female incarnation of that "óutis" ("no one") that Odysseus claimed to be during his sojourn with the Cyclops. While Valentina personifies the actress Louise Brooks, Bianca has no model in real life. Her creator defines her as an amusing distraction, a pure product of the imagination, and a representation of his own artistic freedom. This is what enabled him to use her in the illustration of other authors' stories, for example in "I Viaggi di Bianca" (1983), which is based on Jonathan Swift's "Gulliver's Travels" (1726).

In contrast with Bianca, Crepax finds "the 'Emmanuelle' stories very simple in construction. Everything leads to sensual pleasure. Malice and sadism are completely lacking. Their author, Emmanuelle Arsan, never speaks of philosophy or morality, her stories are simply 'erotic games'. As ever, I remained faithful to the text in my adaptation. I know that Madame Arsan has written other books, but I have no desire to adapt them. On the other hand, I felt great while I was doing 'Emmanuelle', it's perhaps the most light-hearted of my erotic stories."

The origin of Bianca's name in "Valentina nel metrò"

Emmanuelle Arsan's novel featured on the erotic best-seller list for several years; it owed some part of its success to the rumour that it was the true story of the life of the author, who is the wife of a French diplomat then working in Thailand. "Emmanuelle" was adapted for the screen in 1973; the director Just Jaeckin chose Sylvia Kristel as his first lady and made an erotic classic, which was featured for twelve successive years by a major Parisian cinema in Montmartre. Four million spectators came to see it at that cinema alone. "Emmanuelle" package tours to Paris, including a cinema ticket, were organised from countries where the film was banned. Jaeckin, who also adapted "Histoire d'O" for the cinema, was given a large budget, and made a film of unusual aesthetic subtlety for the genre; this contributed to its positive image, and distinguished it from the many feeble imitations that it spawned.

Crepax presented his "Emmanuelle" volumes in a variety of different ways; these include extreme contrasts of black and white, pages

with minimal shadow and exotic framing, and near-grisaille. In the bath-room scene of the second volume, Crepax returned to a device he had first used in one of the frames of "Diario di Valentina". The device is similar to that used by Hitchcock in his silent, "The Lodger" (England, 1926). In the "Diario", Valentina, the Countess Geschwitz (a character from Wedekind/Pabst's "Lulu") and a man in an armchair are viewed from below, as if through a glass floor. The characters in this scene are seen both through a similarly transparent floor and from an overhead perspective.

In contrast with the film of "Emmanuelle", whose aesthetic was essentially that of fashion photography, Crepax remained faithful to his style of cinematic framing and montage, expressive details and narrative inflected by the varying size of image. His version of Emmanuelle, almost of necessity, retained the legendary wicker peacock-chair featured in the poster, but is otherwise quite uninfluenced by the iconic status of the film.

The contrast between Crepax's "Bianca" and "Emmanuelle" and his "Venus in Furs" is striking. Here, for once, Crepax does not faithfully accommodate the text, but presents a highly individual perspective on it. He wholly omits Sacher-Masoch's introductory description of the situation, and reduces the text to a case-study, in which the visual clearly predominates. The images specify what Sacher-Masoch can only imply: "'Venus in Furs' documents pain, but pain that was desired." Crepax began his version in 1983, and the first publication was in 1994, but the theme had preoccupied his best-known creation, Valentina, since 1976. As a fashion photographer, she is looking for a theme for a photo session; she selects a spectacularly beautiful model who must not be exposed to cold. For this purpose, she orders a vintage car and entitles the sequence "Venus in Furs". It seems, then, that it was only a matter of time before Crepax took up the original text.

No other work by Alexander Sacher-Masoch (1836-1895) has attained similar renown, and the "Venus in Furs" has, over the years, been the victim of a number of erroneous interpretations. It was widely acclaimed by his contemporaries, notably by Émile Zola,

Homage to Alfred Hitchcock: Valentina seen through an imaginary glass floor in "Diario di Valentina"

Henrik Ibsen and Victor Hugo, and was never censored. But Sacher-Masoch's posthumous fame is largely the result of a categorisation made by the psychiatrist Richard Krafft-Ebing (1840-1902) in his "Psychopathia Sexualis" (1886), in which he labels a particular perversion as "masochism". It was not until Gilles Deleuze's famous study, "Présentation de Sacher-Masoch", that the necessary distinctions were made and the largely unjustified stigmatization which this once popular author had suffered was finally removed. Deleuze points out that neither Sade nor Sacher-Masoch are pornographers; they are, rather, 'pornologists'; he adds that a knowledge of both bodies of work is indispensable if one is to grasp how completely different are their literary powers. Their worlds are unconnected and their works distinct.

This is a point that Crepax has clearly intuited. Our first view of Wanda, the Venus in Furs, is that of a voyeur: we see her through a keyhole. Severin/Gregor observes the object of his desire, then serves tea at her command. Crepax's women have the sensuality of a model from a Klimt painting; by contrast, the gestures and behaviour of his men have something of the over-embellished Jugendstil "objet d'art": they are themselves merely ornamental. The novel is set in Florence, but the city that Crepax illustrates is a compound of Prague and Vienna. Crepax eliminates the introductory material and begins "in medias res". Large images predominate, and the many close-ups place the reader at the centre of the action. The links between the frames of the drawings are closer than in other Crepax works. In "Bianca", Crepax lavishes images on the story; his "Venus in Furs" is both static and sparing. The impression of spatial confinement given by this technique illustrates the cramped nature of masochistic love. The flow of the narrative is curbed by the insertion of blank pages. The most striking innovation, which underpins all the others, comes at the end of the book; Crepax sends Severin off to Sigmund Freud (rather than the logical but less popular choice: Krafft-Ebing) to recount his case. In doing so he illustrates the psychiatric practice of citing examples from literature, whether it be Oedipus, the Marquis de Sade or Sacher-Masoch. Indeed, what Crepax has done throughout is to place himself in the role of the psychiatrist, presenting the case history and illustrating all that the patient seeks, in his own narrative, to hide; this is interpretation as projection. This addition also confirms Crepax's preference for open endings; it forces the reader to re-examine the entire story. At the close of the circle, 'The End' marks a new beginning.

Here then are Crepax's "Drei Frauen" – three women who have little or nothing in common. Bianca personifies the liberty of the unbounded woman; her adventures are puzzles with multiple solutions. Wanda, the Venus in furs, is also an incarnation of absolute sovereignty, but her absolutism is exercised in the form of bondage inflicted on others. She liberates herself by sacrificing the liberty of others; victim of an obsession, she is the prisoner of the game for which she longs. Emmanuelle represents a third extreme, as she wanders unscathed through a jungle of erotic experience without ever encountering moral conflict. A 1960s outlook is integral to her heedless freedom.

il piccolo Hans

Sigmund Freud and "Little Hans"

"Bianca" exemplifies the fertility of Crepax's imagination, "Venus in Furs" its discipline, and "Emmanuelle" the fluidity of his narrative technique at its most peaceful and disengaged. All three seem to have emerged from the inexhaustible universe of images that is Crepax's imagination. Crepax thinks in images. He records them with his eyes and elaborates them in his mind. They leave his body through the agency of his pen in the form of some new image. But this image is incomplete; for its completion, it requires the complicity of our own imagination. And this is what raises Guido Crepax to the pantheon of art.

Emmanuelle

Unicorn in Flight

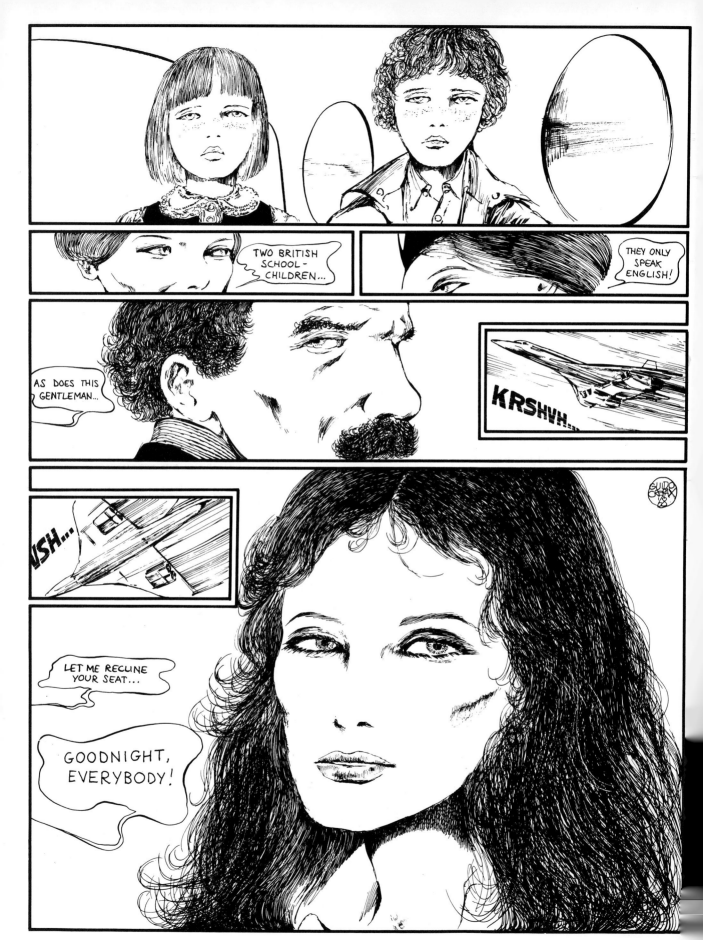

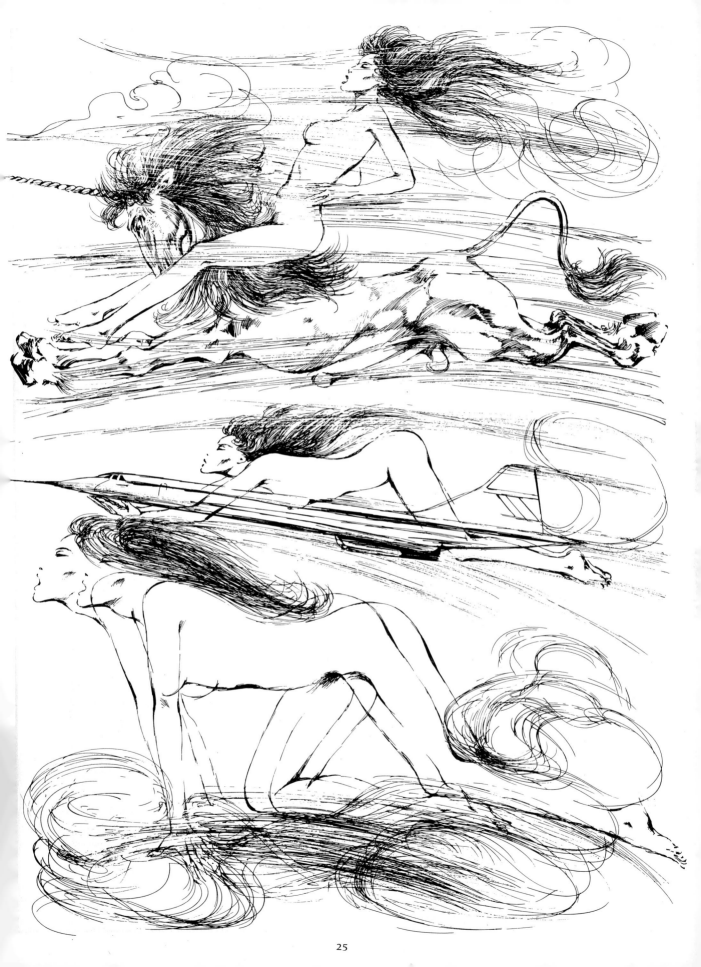

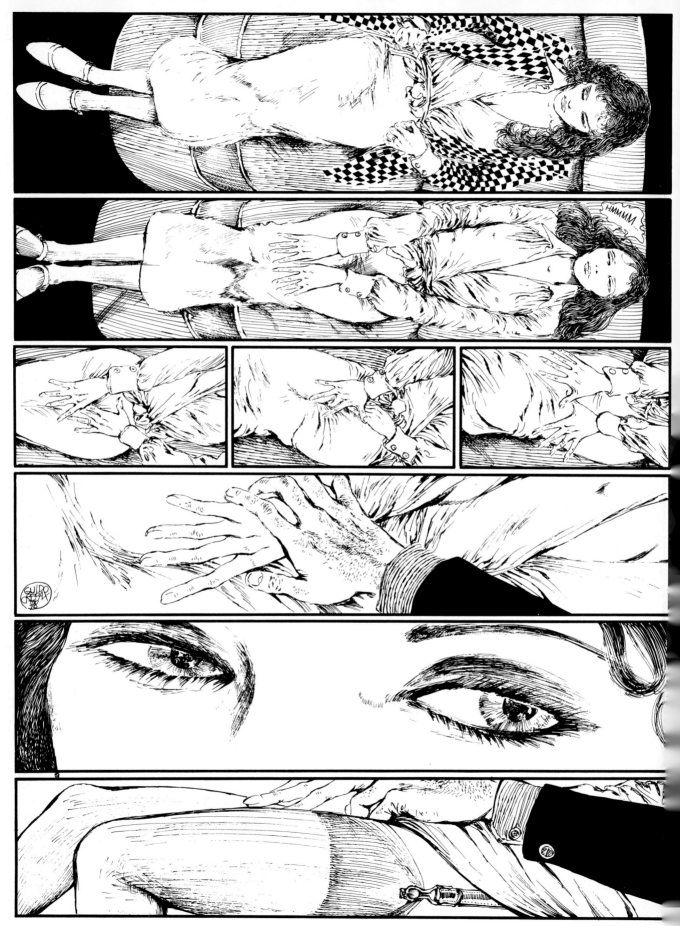

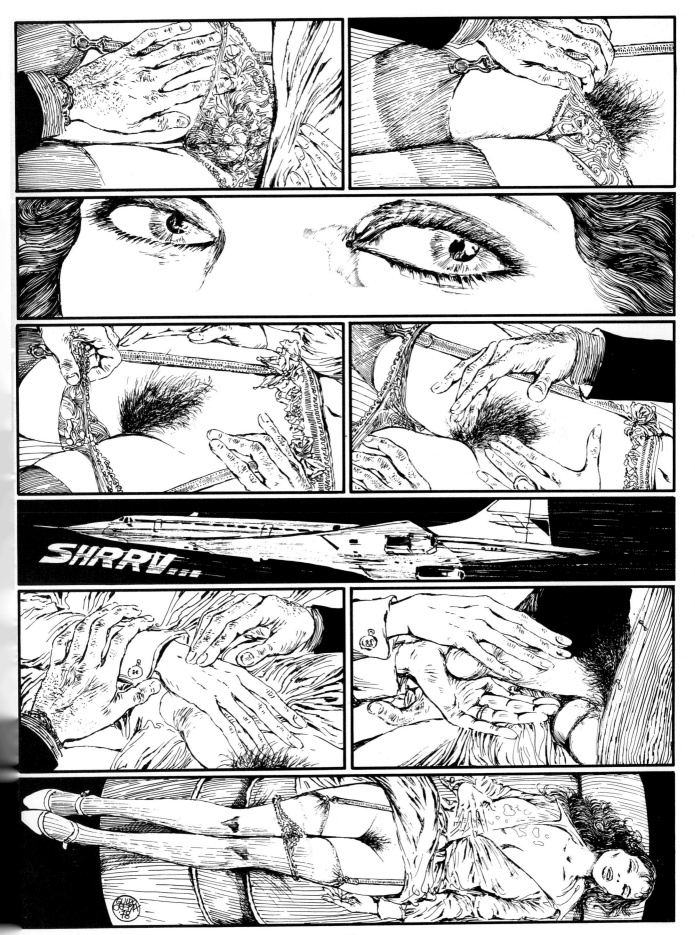

SHRRV...

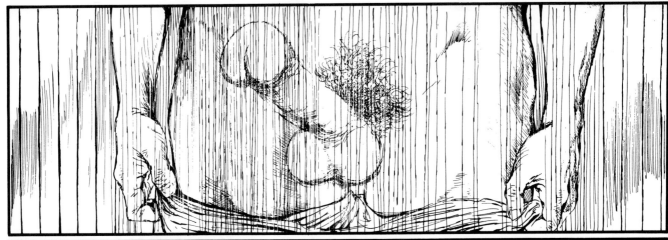

SHRRRR...

AHH! AHHHH... HN...HN HN...HN AHH

AHH... AHHH... AHNNN... HNNN...

HMMM... HMMMM... AHHH...

AAH!

HHHHHH... HHH!!

I LOVE YOU! ...TAKE ME AGAIN?

SOON... I'LL BE BACK! NOW GET DRESSED...

...ADONIS, AIRBORNE
...ARES...WAS IT A DREAM?
...IT COULDN'T BE REAL
...AND YET...
HE TOOK ME...
FILLED ME...WITH
THAT...IMPOSSIBLY...
LONG...STAFF
OF HIS...

IT WAS
WONDERFUL!
HH...HHHH...
WONDER-
FUL...

YES...
WONDERFUL!
AND I FEEL
WONDER-
FUL....!

WHILE I'M WAITING FOR
MY DREAM-GOD TO RETURN...
I'LL TAKE A SHOWER!

IT MUST BE LATE...
CAN'T GET MY HAIR WET...

YOUR
ATTENTION,
PLEASE! WE'RE
APPROACHING
BANGKOK!

HMM...I SHOULD
DRESS...HE DIDN'T
COME BACK...
TOO BAD!...I'LL
GO TO MY SEAT...

34

Green Paradise

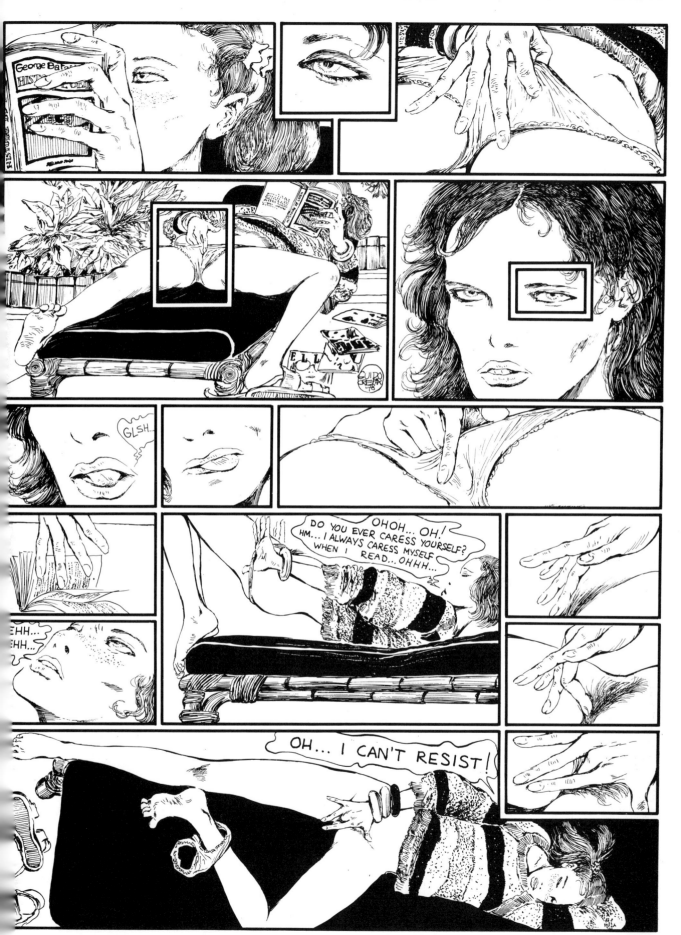

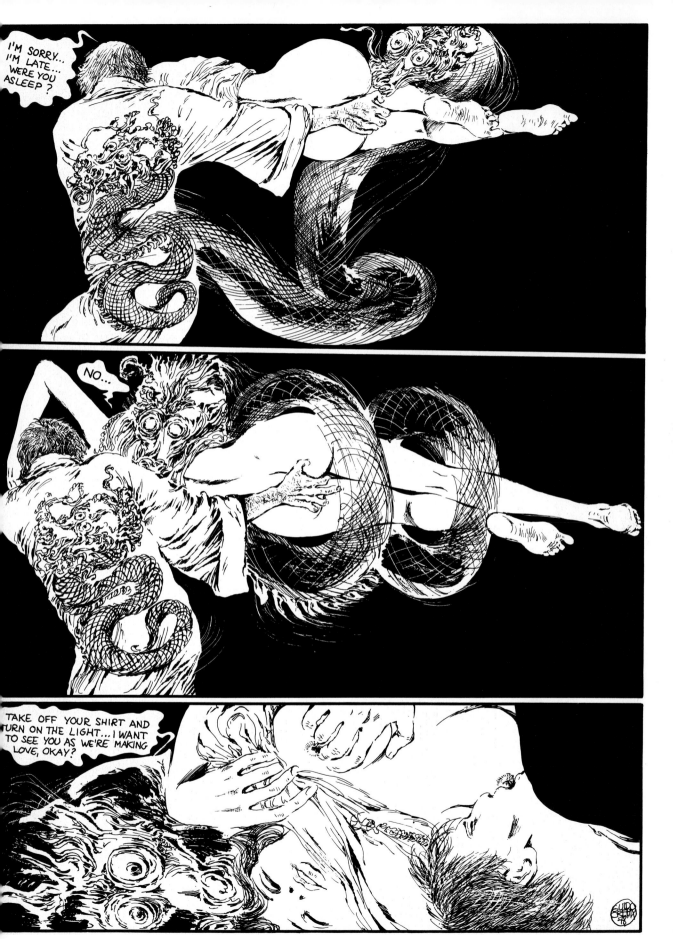

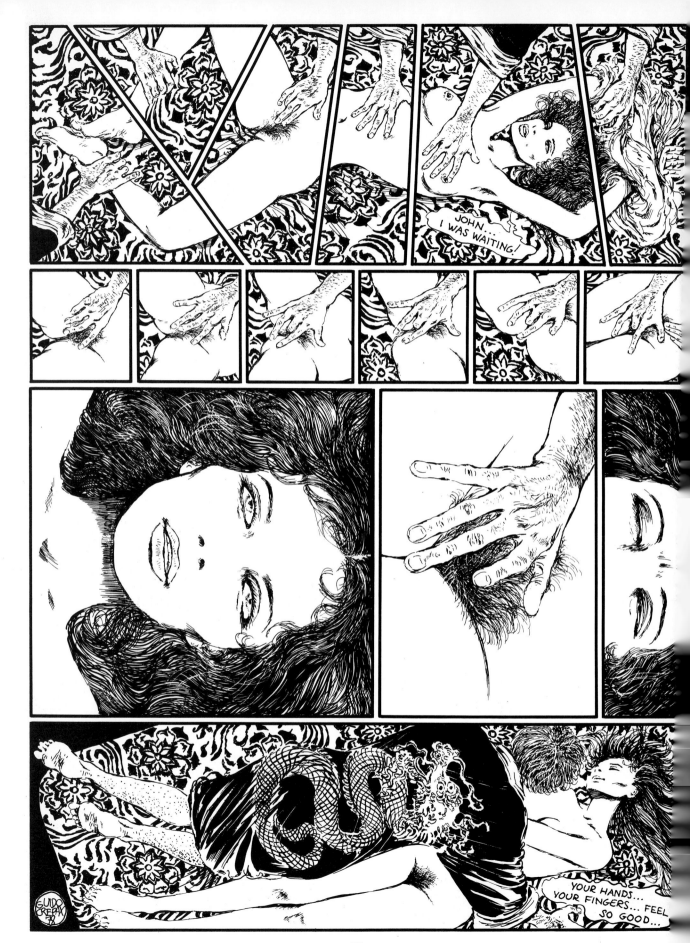

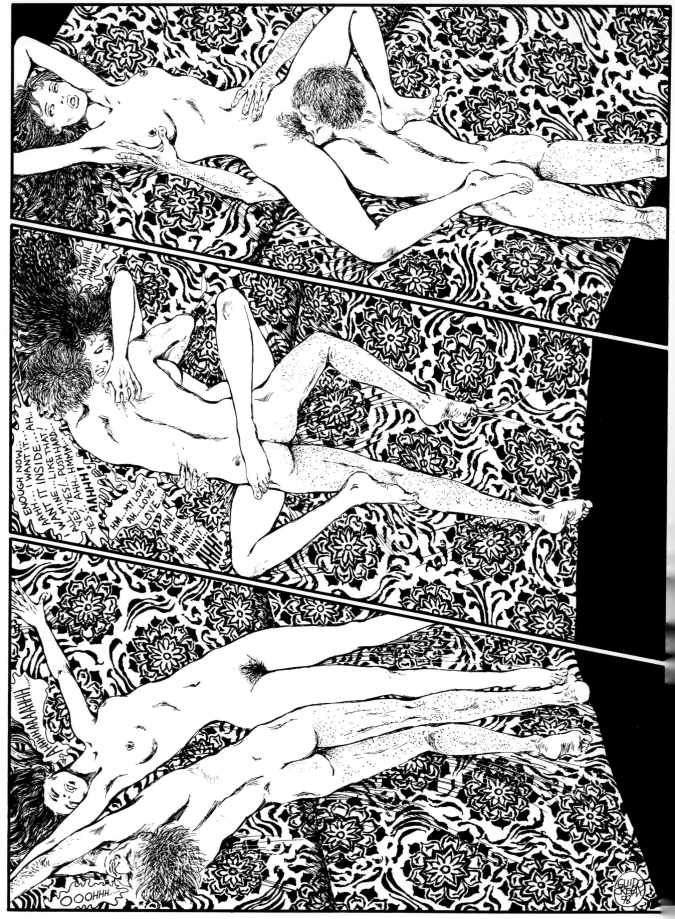

60

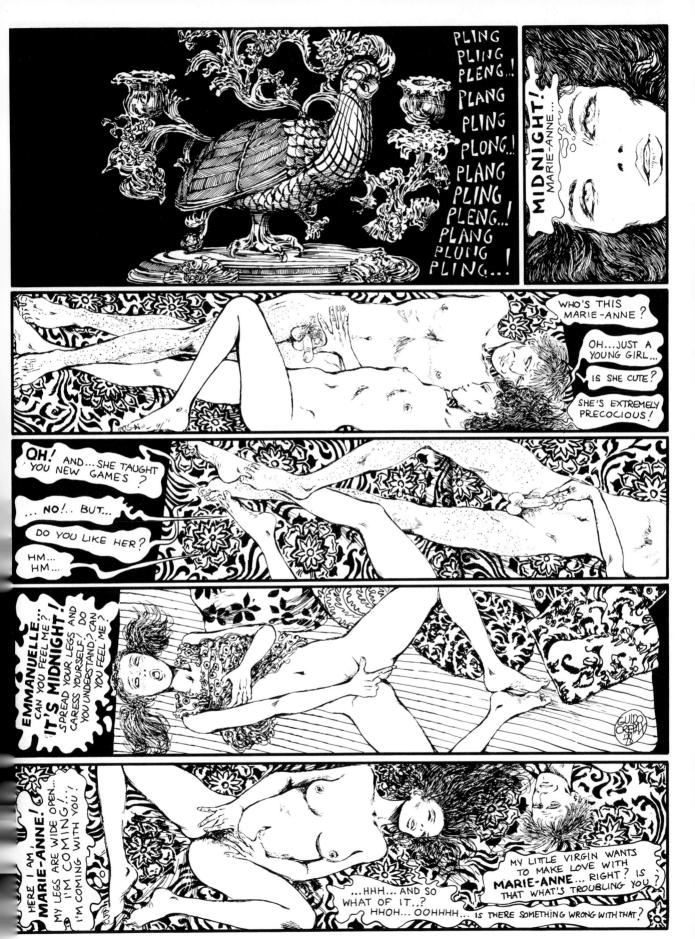

Of Flesh, Gods, and Roses

FFFHHH!...

AHHHH...

OOOOF...HHHH... I'M EXHAUSTED!

OH...THE COUNTESS!...

UP!...

YOU LOOK WONDERFUL, MY DEAR!

THANK YOU!...

HELLO!..

WHAT DO THOSE TWO WANT?

HM...

FORGET IT. LET'S GO ON THE DIVING BOARD!

HA, HA! GOTTA GET PAST ME!

HUFFF!!..... WHAT FUN! MARIE-ANNE IS SO STUBBORN... INTRODUCING ME TO HER MOTHER... HAVING TEA AND PASTRIES...

STUFFY OLD LADIES!..

IH...IH...IH... OH...OH... AH! AH! IHHH... OOOOH!?

OOHHH... BUT WHO'S THAT? SHE'S INCREDIBLY STRIKING! ...I SHOULD...

MARIE-ANNE!

I'M HERE!.. LISTEN... I FOUND A MAN FOR YOU...AN ITALIAN... AN ARTIST, YOU KNOW? THIS GUY'S FANTASTIC!

THAT'S NICE! BUT TELL ME SOMETHING...

WHO'S THAT STUNNING GIRL?

A STUNNING GIRL? WHERE?

THERE... IN FRONT OF YOU.

YOU MEAN BEE?

HER NAME IS BEE?/... WHAT KIND OF A NAME IS THAT?

WELL... ACTUALLY IT'S AN ITALIAN NICKNAME... BI... SPELLED WITH AN I... BUT THEY PRONOUNCE IT BEE...

BEE...

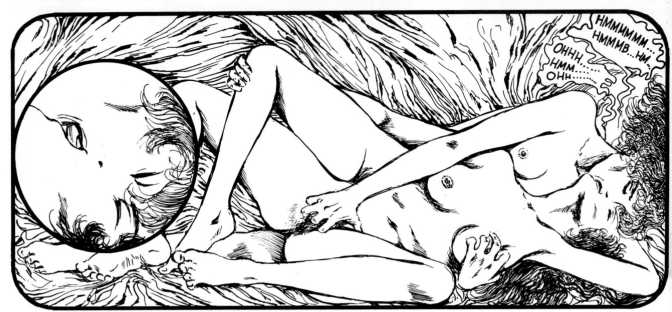

SHE WANTED TO FEEL THE
BODY OF A WOMAN, NAKED
OVER HER OWN...

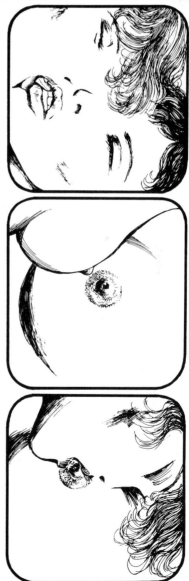

Bee's Love

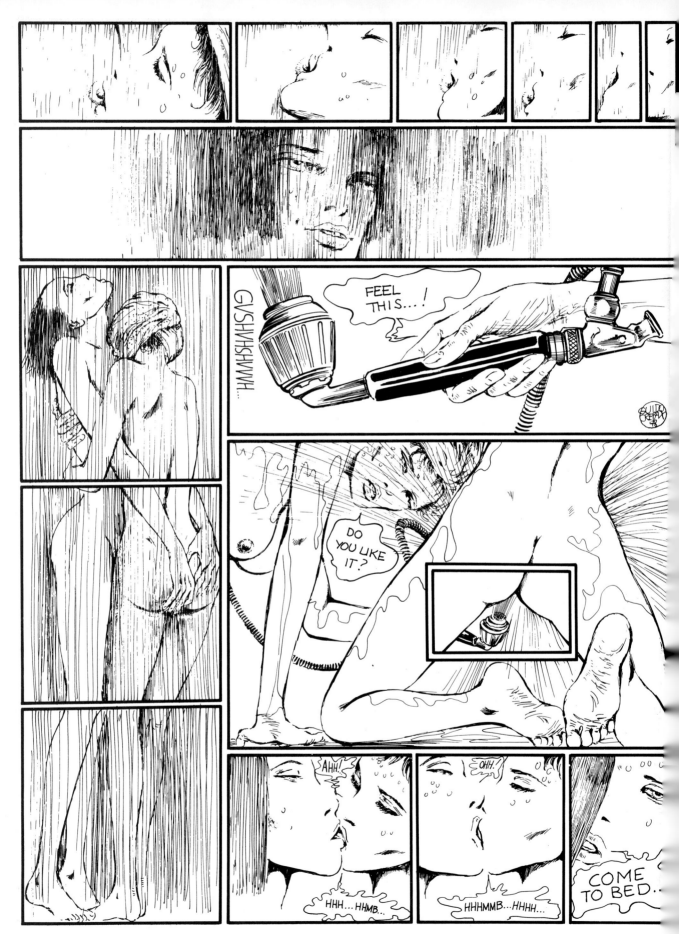

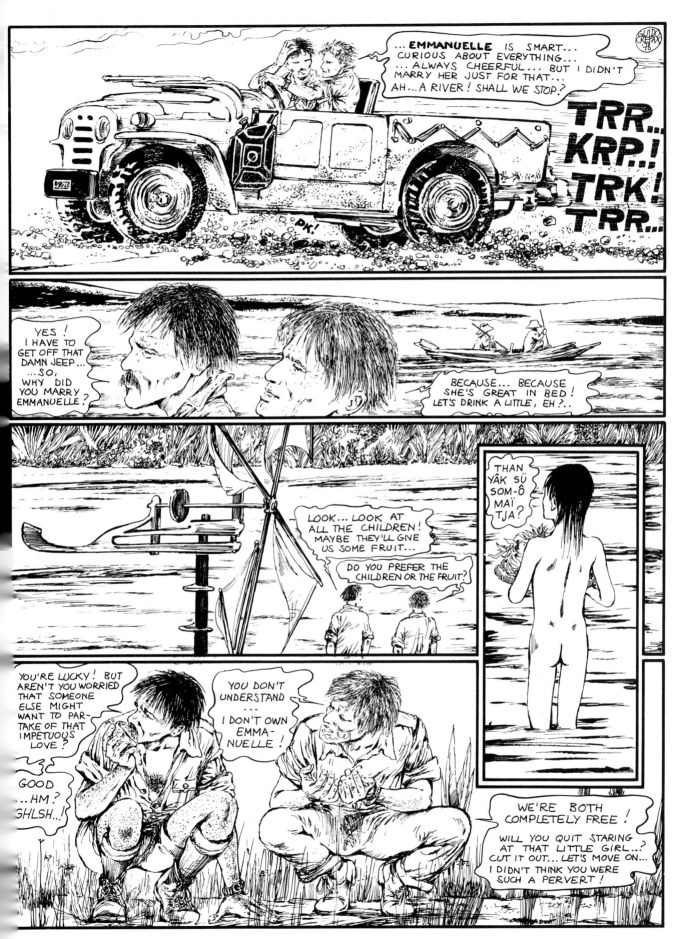

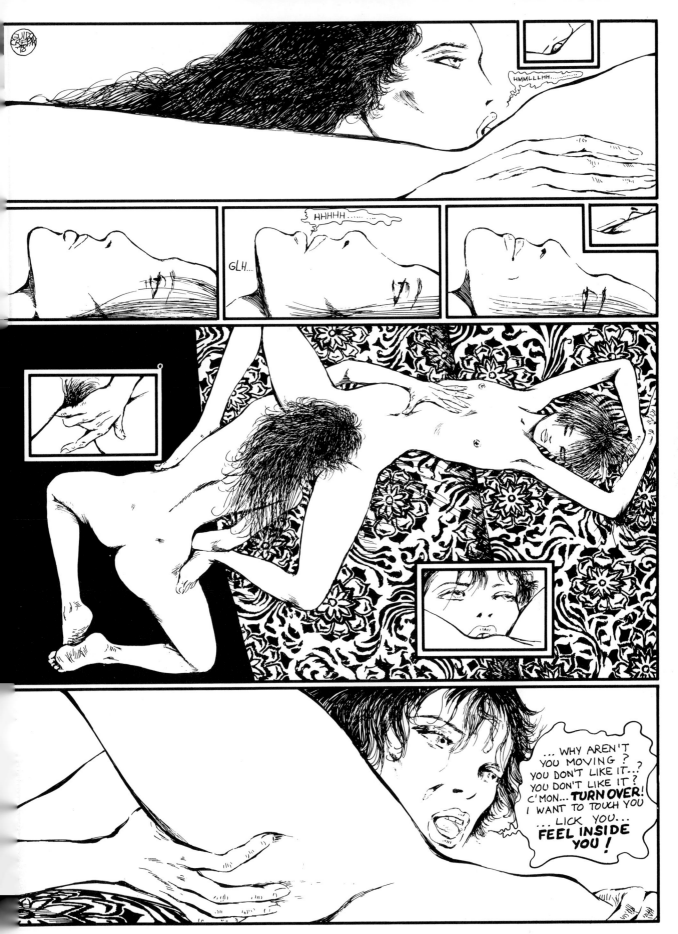

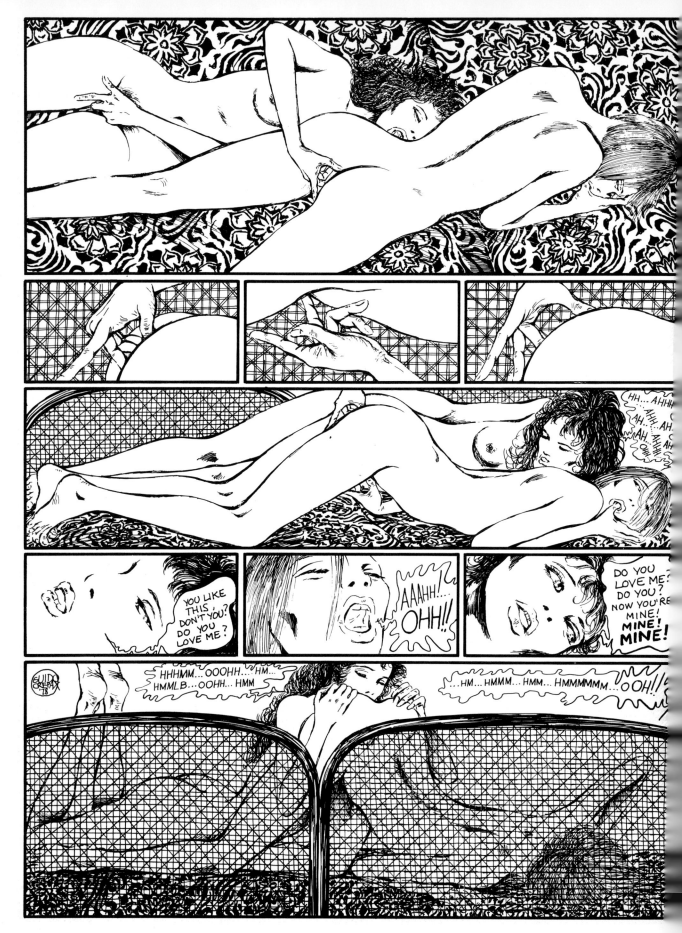

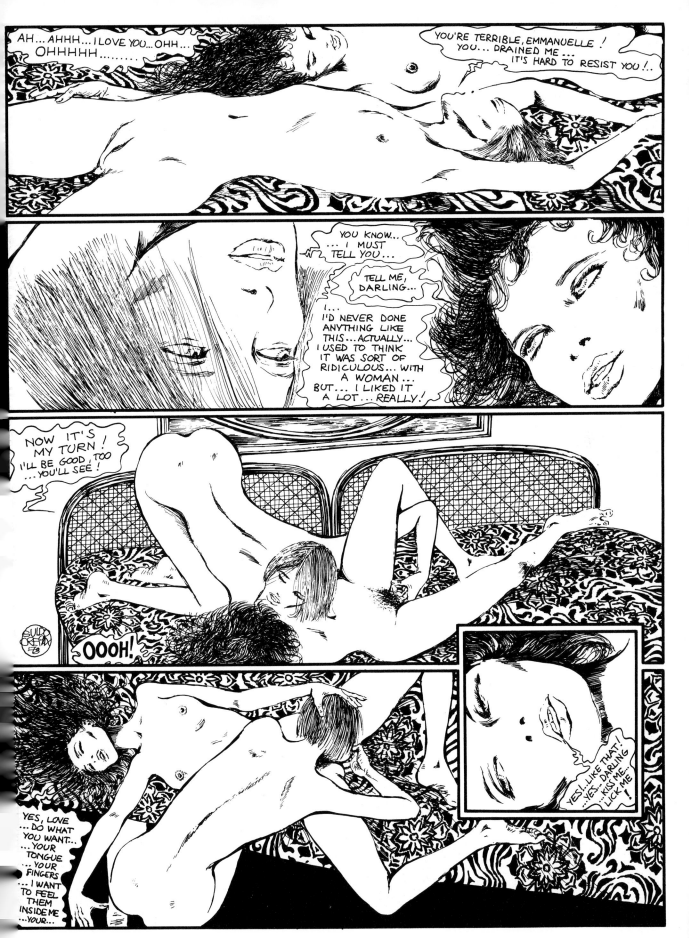

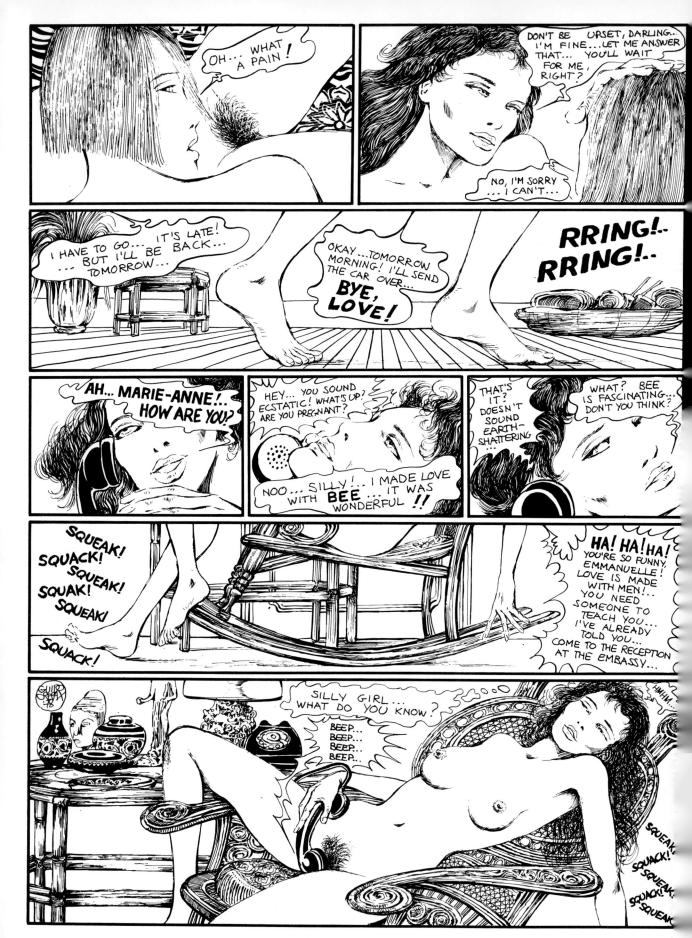

OH!
THE RHINOS
DANCING WITH
THE CRANES...
THE IBIS...
THE FLAMINGOS...
THE EGRET...
THE HERONS...
THE PEACOCKS...
THE AIGRETTES...!

..I'LL LEARN MORE LOVE GAMES...

Laws of Free Love

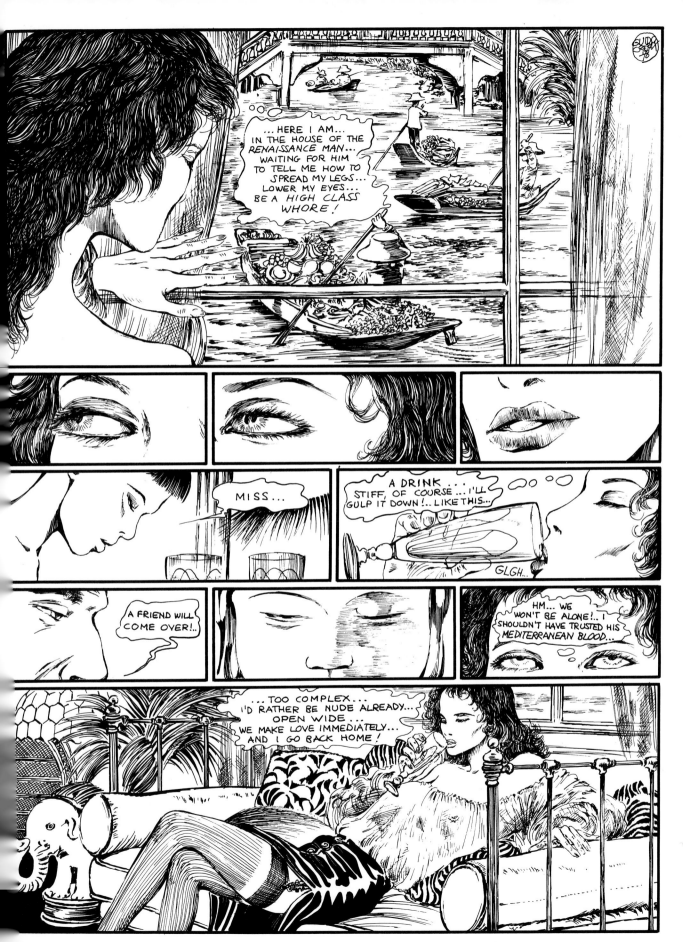

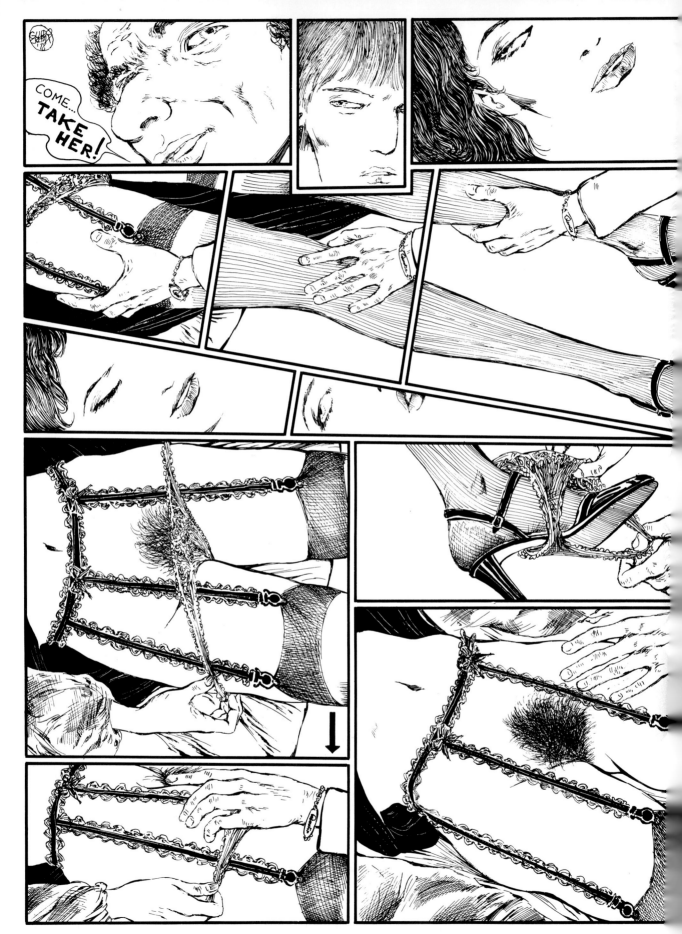

113

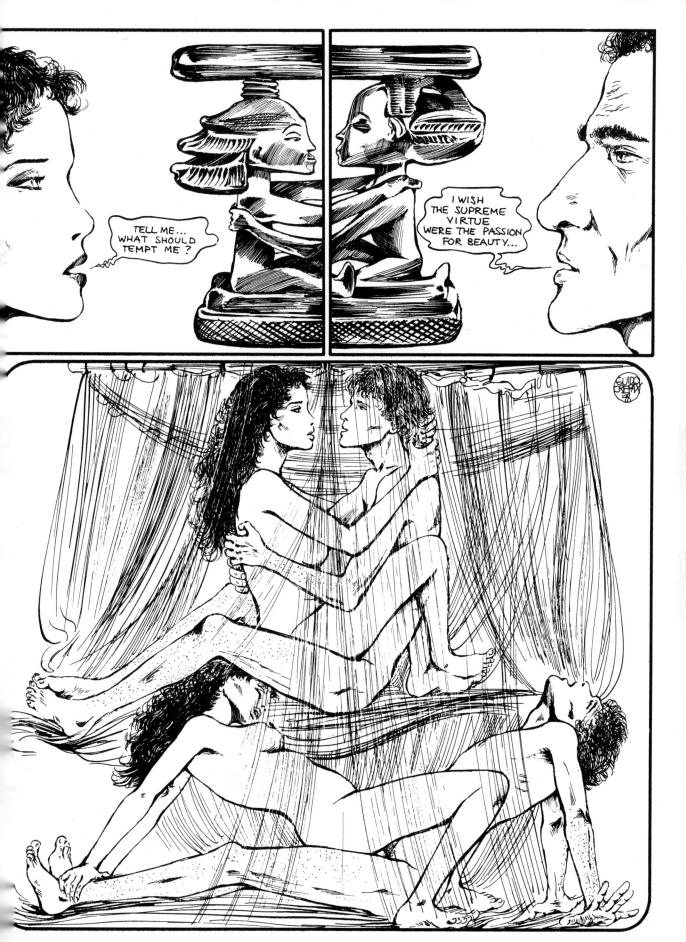

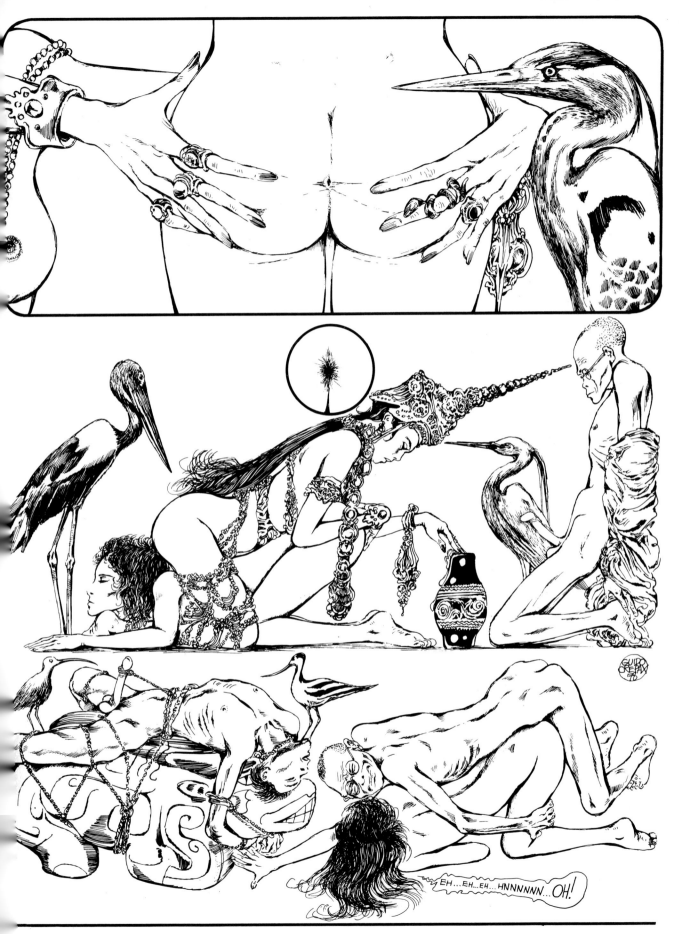

EH...EH...EH...HNNNNNNN...OH!

117

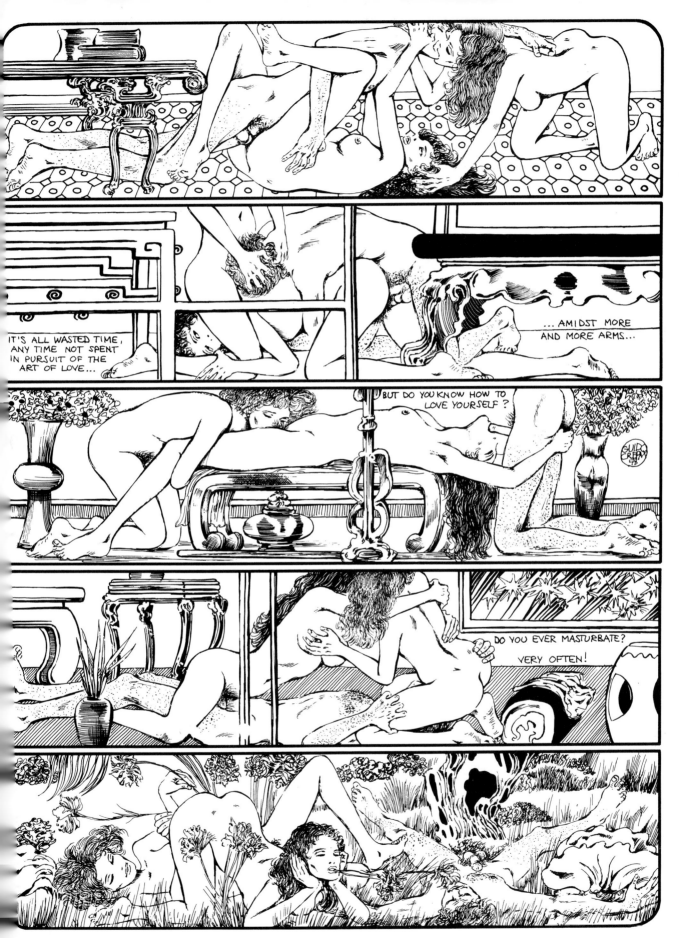

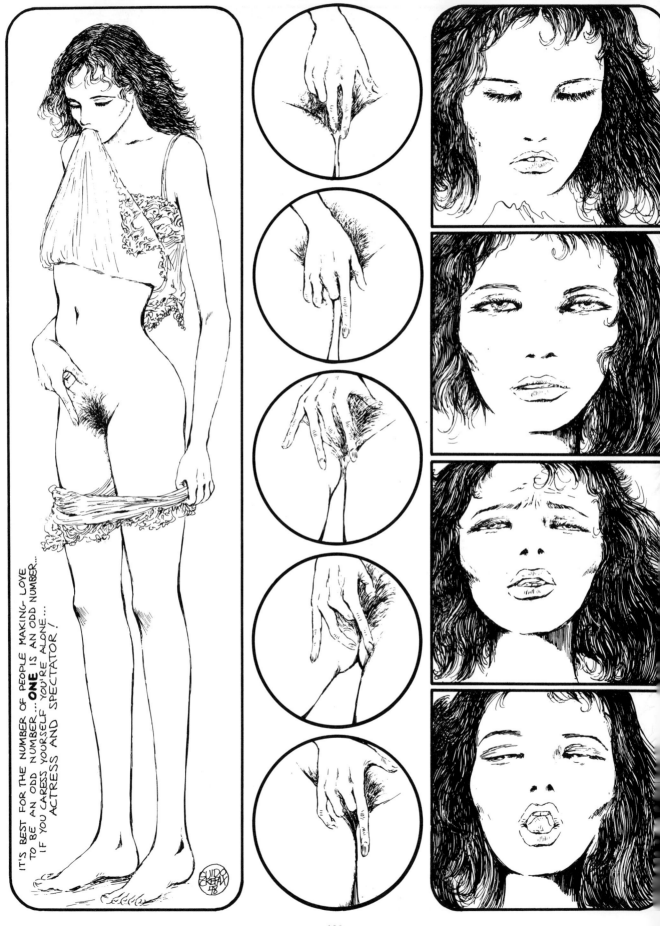

IT'S BEST FOR THE NUMBER OF PEOPLE MAKING LOVE TO BE AN ODD NUMBER... **ONE** IS AN ODD NUMBER... IF YOU CARESS YOURSELF YOU'RE ALONE... ACTRESS AND SPECTATOR!

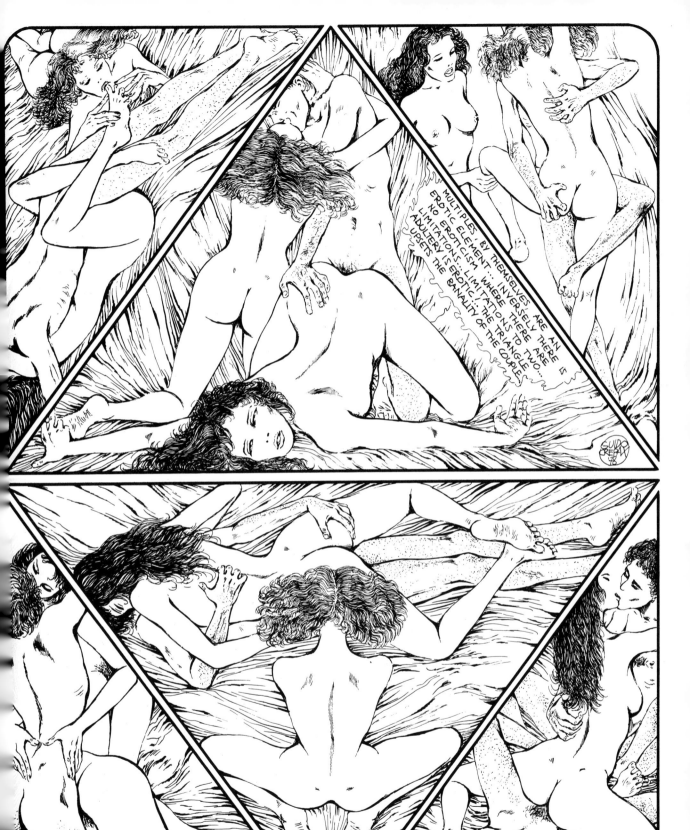

MULTIPLES, BY THEMSELVES, ARE AN EROTIC ELEMENT... INVERSELY, THERE IS NO EROTICISM... WHERE THERE ARE LIMITATIONS: LIMITATIONS TO TWO... LIMITATIONS IS EROTIC: THE TRIANGLE, ADULTERY IS EROTIC... THE TRIANGLE UPSETS THE BANALITY OF THE COUPLE...

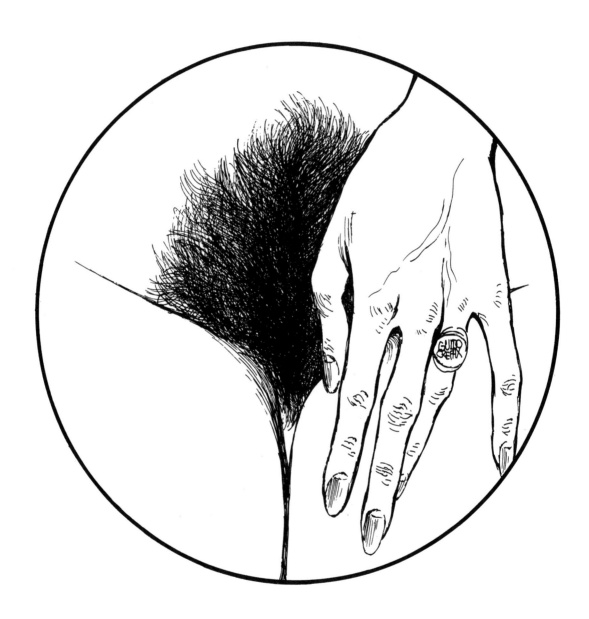

Sam-Lo

129

OH!

MY GOD!! WHAT IS THAT..?!

DON'T BE AFRAID!... IT'S KING KONG, BUT IT'S FAKE... JUST LIKE THE DAMSEL IN DISTRESS. WE'RE NEAR A STORAGE SITE FOR MOVIE PRODUCTIONS...

COME ON... UP AHEAD YOU CAN MEET CASANOVA... OR THE LAST WOMAN, IF YOU PREFER...

A TEMPLE? IF A PRIEST SAW ME LIKE THIS...!

IT WOULD SEEM APPROPRIATE...IN THE SANCTUARY OF **PRIAPUS** ...THE PHALLUS!

YOU SEE... SIZE IS PROPORTIONATE TO THE WEALTH OF THE DONOR...

I HOPE I WON'T BE IMPIOUS IF ... TAKE THIS! IT'S THE RIGHT SIZE, NO?

TAKE IT !

BUT... WHAT FOR?

WE HAVE A WONDERFUL AUDIENCE!... WHAT SHALL WE DO? WHAT SORT OF MALICE WILL YOUR SWEET HANDS SUGGEST?

HM... HE'D BETTER NOT EXPECT ME TO PUT IT IN...

I WILL TREAT IT AS AN IDOL ... SHOULD I WORSHIP IT ?

EXCELLENT! BUT NOW IT'S TIME TO SUBSTITUTE FANTASY WITH REALITY...

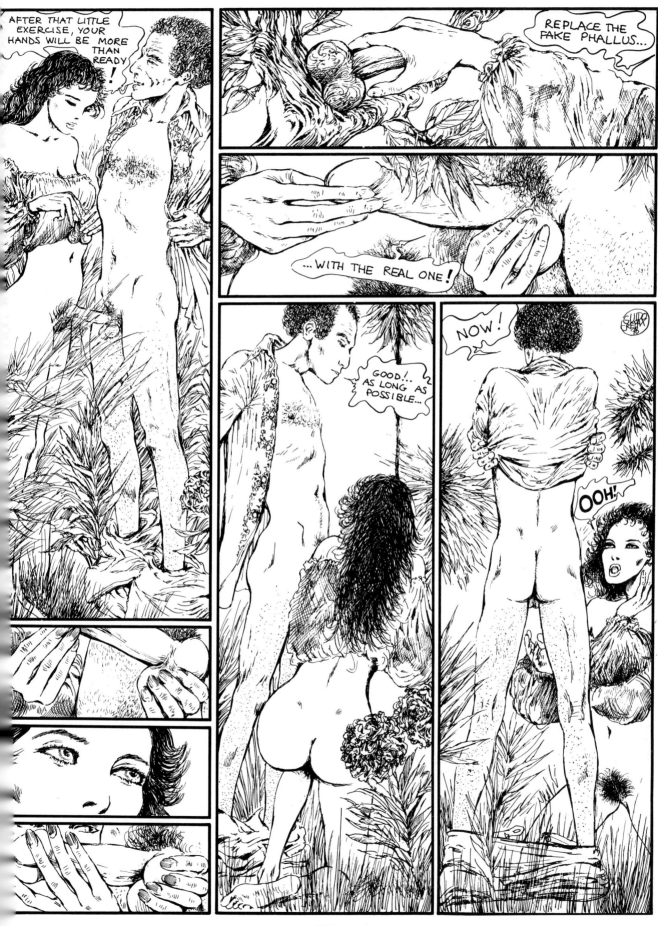

143

149

150

PEPPER-MINT ON THE ROCKS!

...OOOF...SOMEONE ELSE IS INVOLVED THIS TIME TOO? I THOUGHT... ...WHY WON'T HE JUST TAKE ME?.. WHY ALL THESE INTRICACIES?.. ... DOES HE LIKE TO TORMENT ME... ...OR NOT LIKE ME AT ALL..? HERE... I'LL SPREAD MY LEGS... I'M TIRED OF HIS BRIGHT IDEAS... IF ONLY HE WERE A BIT MORE NORMAL!

NOW I'LL COME INSIDE YOU...

...THROUGH...

...THIS PRETTY LITTLE SHEPHERD... AND I MEAN THAT LITERALLY!

DO WHATEVER YOU WANT WITH ME!

Bianca
A Story of Excess

The Madhouse

BIANCA!

MA PETITE BLANCHE...

PST...PST... IN THE CAGE... HEE...HEE...IMPERCEPTIBLE ...PST... STOPPED HER... HEE!HEE!

IT WAS YOU!

NO... NO! IT'S NOT TRUE!

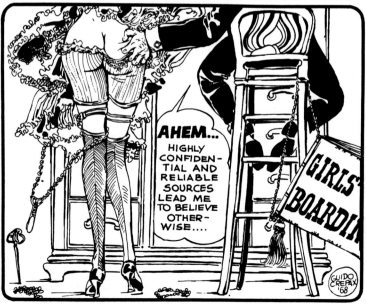

AHEM... HIGHLY CONFIDENTIAL AND RELIABLE SOURCES LEAD ME TO BELIEVE OTHERWISE....

GIRLS' BOARDI...

...UNE BEAUTÉ DE QUINZE ANS ENFANTINE... ...YOU WON'T BE ANGRY IF I'M FORCED TO TAKE THE APPROPRIATE DISCIPLINARY MEASURES... HHM?

I WAS SURE OF IT, ANGE DIVIN! ... HMM... JULIETTE, WOULD YOU CALL MADEMOISELLE SQUE-LETTE?

AT ONCE, SIR!

NO! WHY?

MY DEAR, YOU KNOW THE RULES OF THE INSTITUTE, DON'T YOU?

... I'LL SEE TO IT IMMEDIATELY! 135 MINUTES?

OF COURSE... BE VERY GENTLE WITH THE LITTLE LADY ...HMM... UN FRONT DE ROSE... ...UNE VERTU DE TELLE BEAUTÉ DIGNE... HMM...UN COL DE NEIGE... UNE GORGE DE LAIT! ...

OH!...OH!...

CREAK!

CREAK!

... PLACE A MATTRESS AGAINST THE DOOR ... ABSURD! WHY DO THEY BOTHER WITH THESE FORMALITIES!

... JULIETTE, WIND UP THE GRAMOPHONE!

YOU, BIANCA, DRAW DOWN THE LAMP!

HORSE LEADS DONKEY UP THE HILL UPHILL TO THE RUINED MILL THE MILLER'S HANGING FROM THE SILL...

LEAVE IT, LEAVE IT, I'LL DO IT ... BIANCA, WHAT ARE YOU WAITING FOR?

THERE YOU GO... THESE MATTRESSES JUST WON'T STAND UP! WELL, ARE YOU READY?

GUIDO CREPAX '68

...HUNG HIMSELF FROM A RAFTER HIS WIFE IS MAKING SUPPER...

SDRSH!

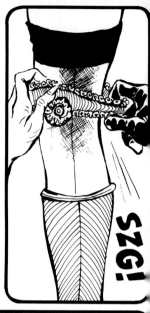

SZG!

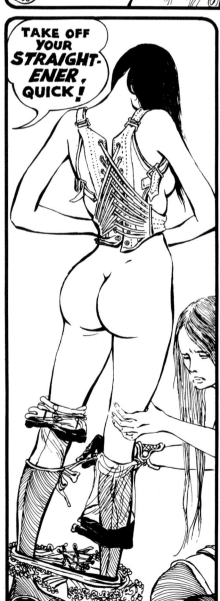

TAKE OFF YOUR STRAIGHT-ENER, QUICK!

WELL? HAVE I GOT TO DO EVERYTHING MYSELF?

Ss..

THERE! JULIETTE, GIVE ME THE ALARM, HURRY!!

...SNIP

SNAP

SNIP

STRRZ!

SCREK... SCREK...

SCREK...

WHIP! WHIP!

Tic

Tic

Tic

164

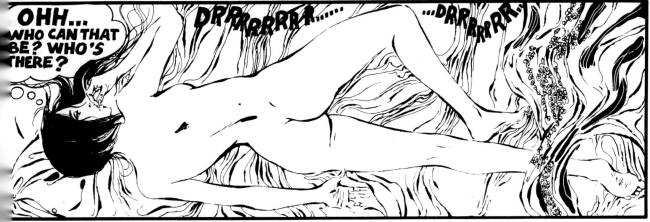

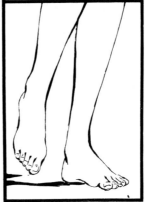

BUT WHO?

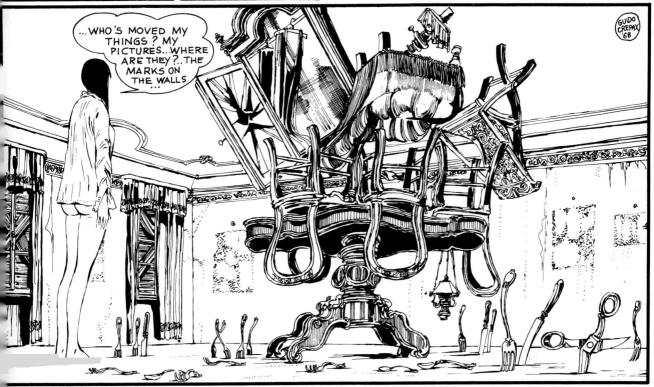

...WHO'S MOVED MY THINGS? MY PICTURES...WHERE ARE THEY?..THE MARKS ON THE WALLS...

GUIDO CREPAX '68

...THE FORKS ARE GROWING IN HERE TOO..OW THEY'RE BITING!

THEY'RE BITING!

UGH...

AARGH!

171

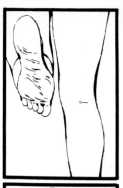

...THEY WANT TO EAT ME... I'M NOT GOING BACK IN THERE...

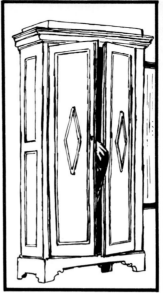

GZGH...

AHHH

GZH...

GZSHGH...

GUIDO CREPAX '68

GET UP, BIANCA, YOU SLUT!... YOUR MASSAGE, FATSO ...YOU'RE DISGUSTING!

EAT, BIANCA INDULGE YOURSELF, SPINDLE-SHANK!

GO AWAY! ALL OF YOU! I'M NOT LIKE THAT... I DON'T WANT YOU...

WHAT CAN I DO? THE WATER KEEPS RISING...

RISING...

RISING...

GRLSH!

...THE WHOLE BATHROOM'S FILLING UP... I CAN'T MAKE IT TO THE CORRIDOR... THE DOOR WON'T OPEN... BUT IN THE CABINET THERE'S **A MASK!**

GSH!

...THERE, I CAN GET OUT NOW... I CAN GO THROUGH THE CORRIDOR... ...YES, BUT HOW AM I GOING TO GET THE BOARDS OFF THE FRONT DOOR?

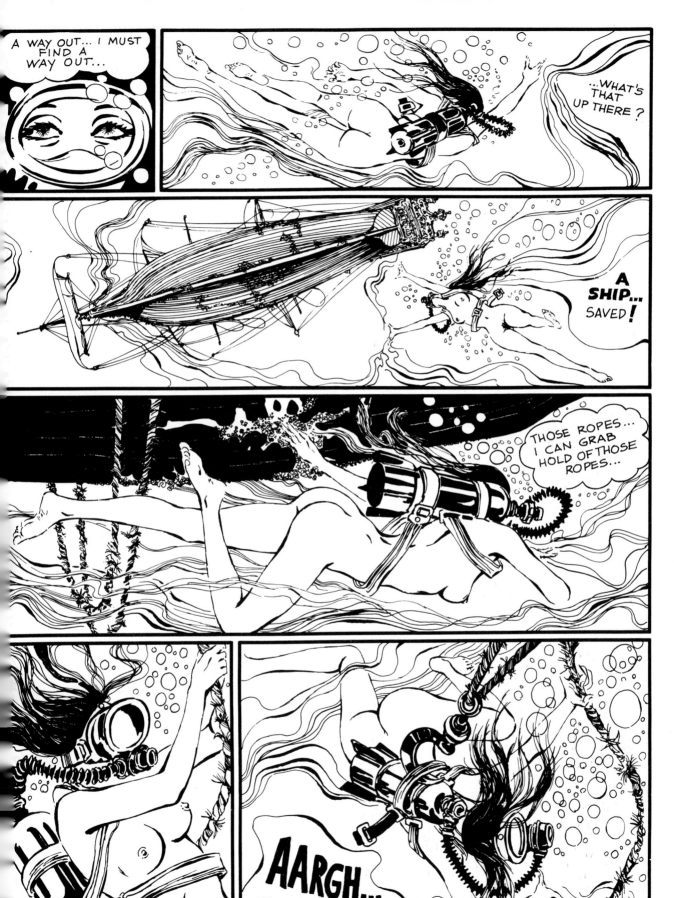

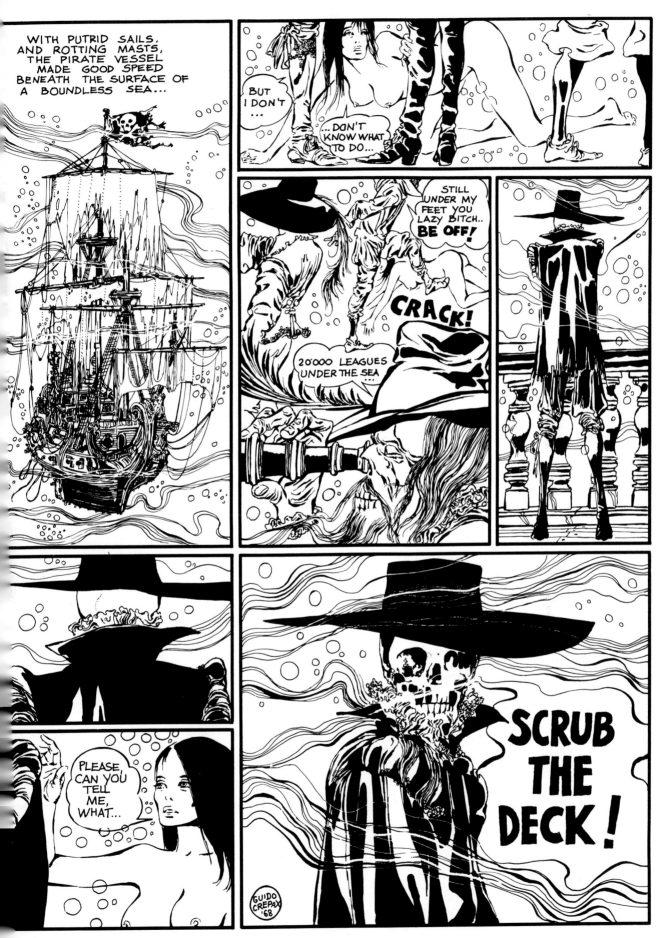

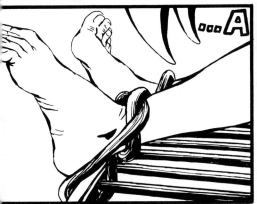

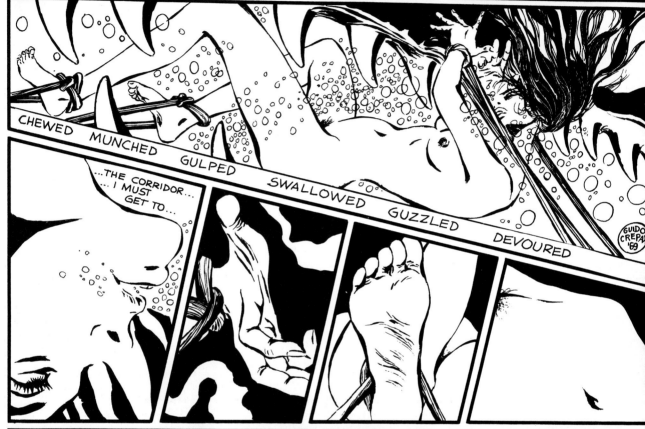

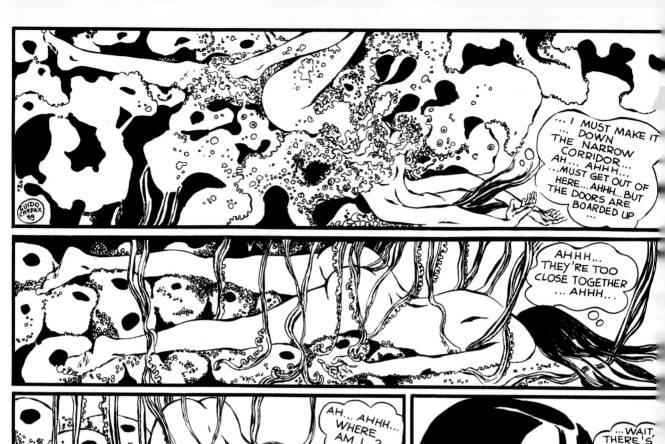

I'LL BREAK YOUR RIBS, MOBY DICK, I'LL STAVE YOUR CARCASS IN, CREATURE OF SATAN!

HEY, YOU, SIR!

GUIDO CREPAX '69

WHAT DO YOU WANT OF ME? INFERNAL DELUSION! DEVIL'S MINION!

NO... NO... I JUST WANT YOU TO HELP ME OUT OF HERE...

OH... POOR LITTLE GIRL. I WANT OUT TOO. FOR 117 YEARS, I'VE WANTED OUT OF THIS DARK WOMB! BUT NOW, PUT SOME CLOTHES ON...

...LET'S SEE, WHAT WOULD SUIT YOU... THE COUNTESS TARNOWSKA'S... NO. PERHAPS ISADORA DUNCAN'S... THERE, HAVE THIS! IT'S A LITTLE THREADBARE, BUT IT WILL DO...

HOWEVER FIRST YOU MUST PUT THIS BELT ON!

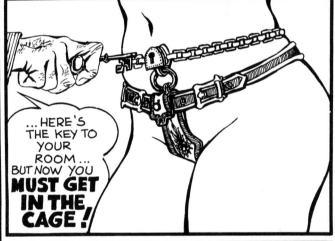

...HERE'S THE KEY TO YOUR ROOM... BUT NOW YOU **MUST GET IN THE CAGE!**

GET IN THE CAGE? **WHY?**

THAT'S NOT FOR ME TO KNOW...

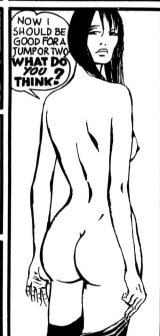

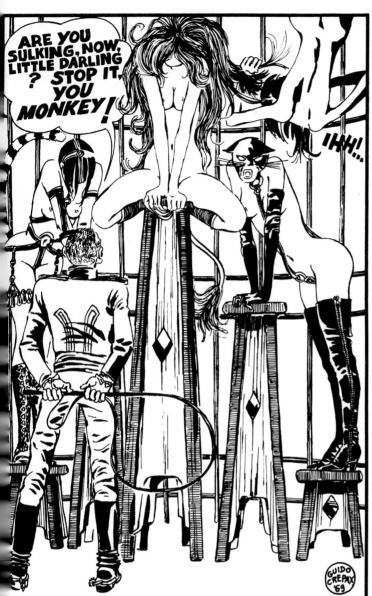

INTO THE LION'S MOUTH

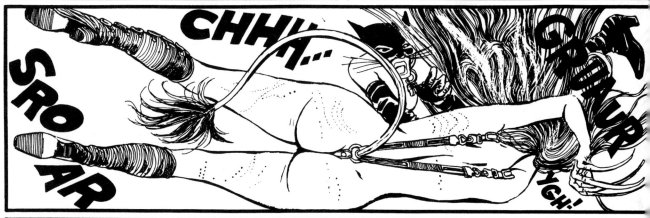

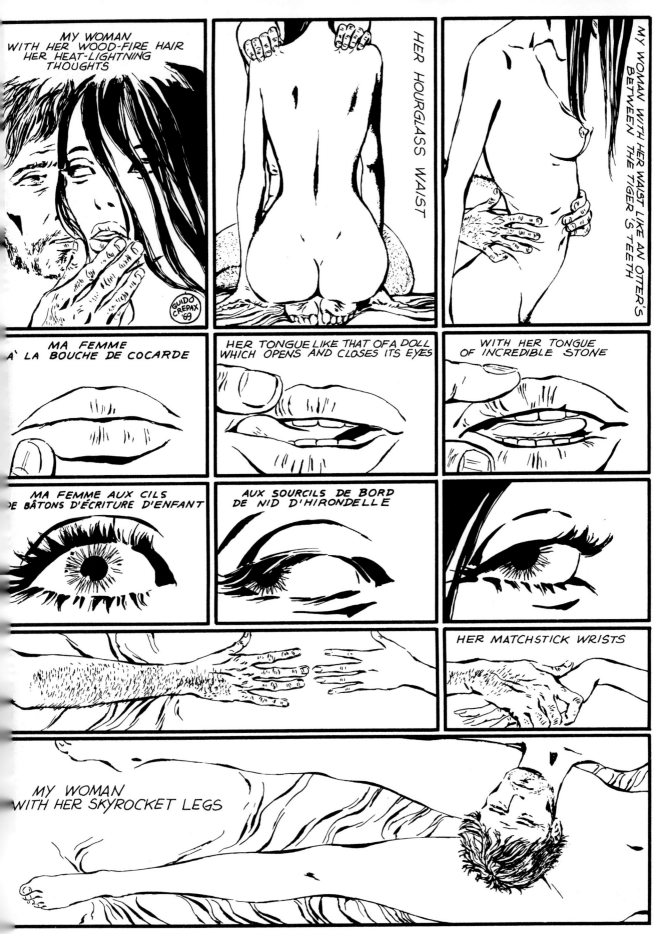

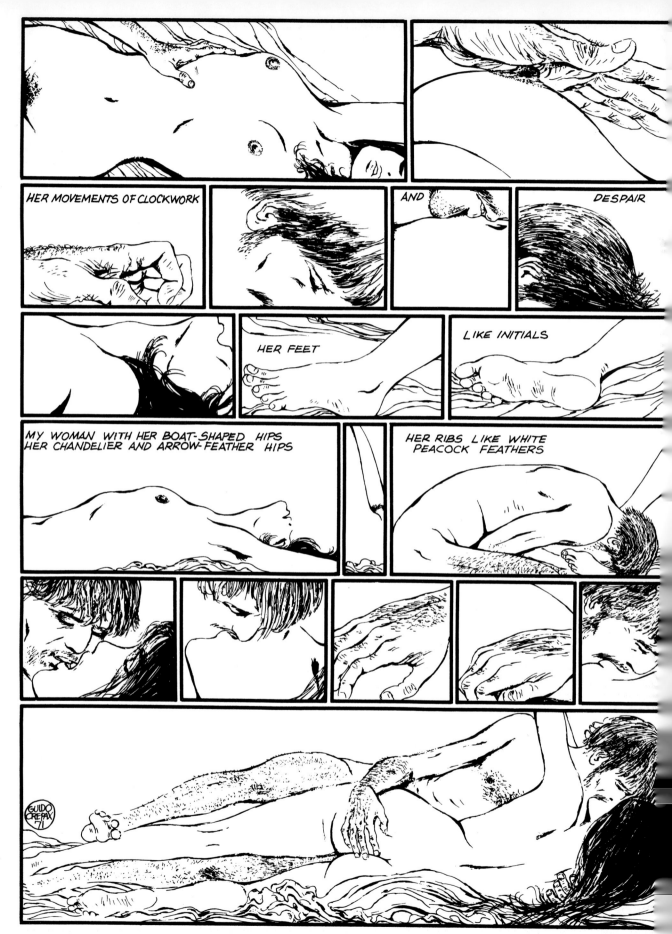

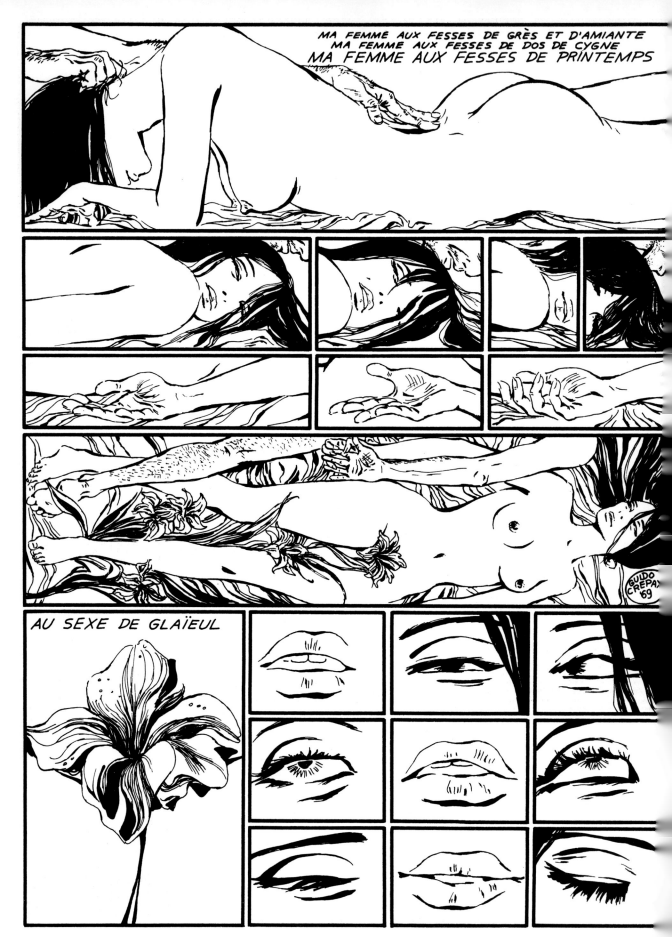

MA FEMME AUX FESSES DE GRÈS ET D'AMIANTE
MA FEMME AUX FESSES DE DOS DE CYGNE
MA FEMME AUX FESSES DE PRINTEMPS

AU SEXE DE GLAÏEUL

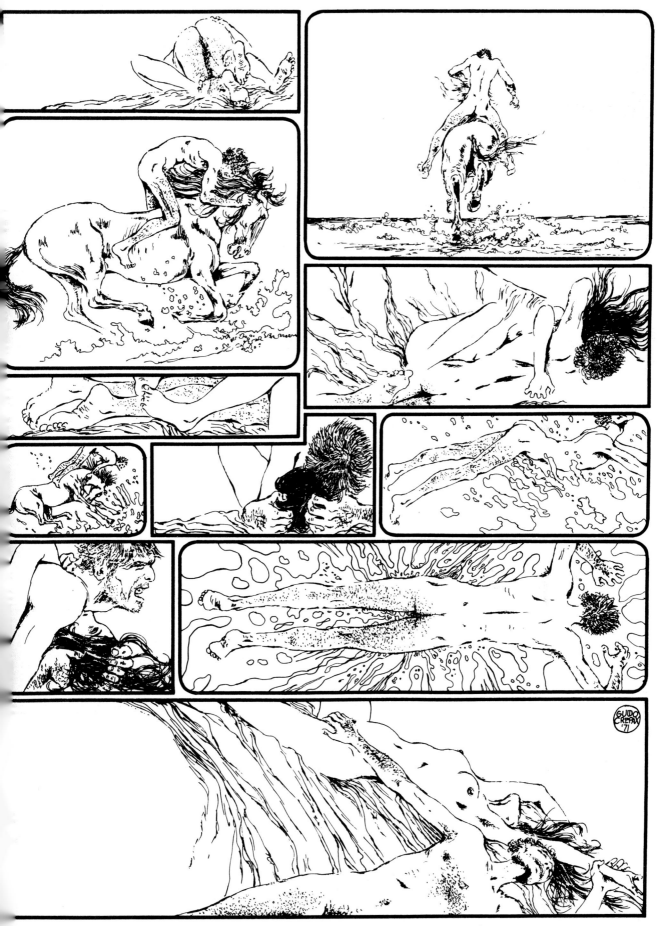

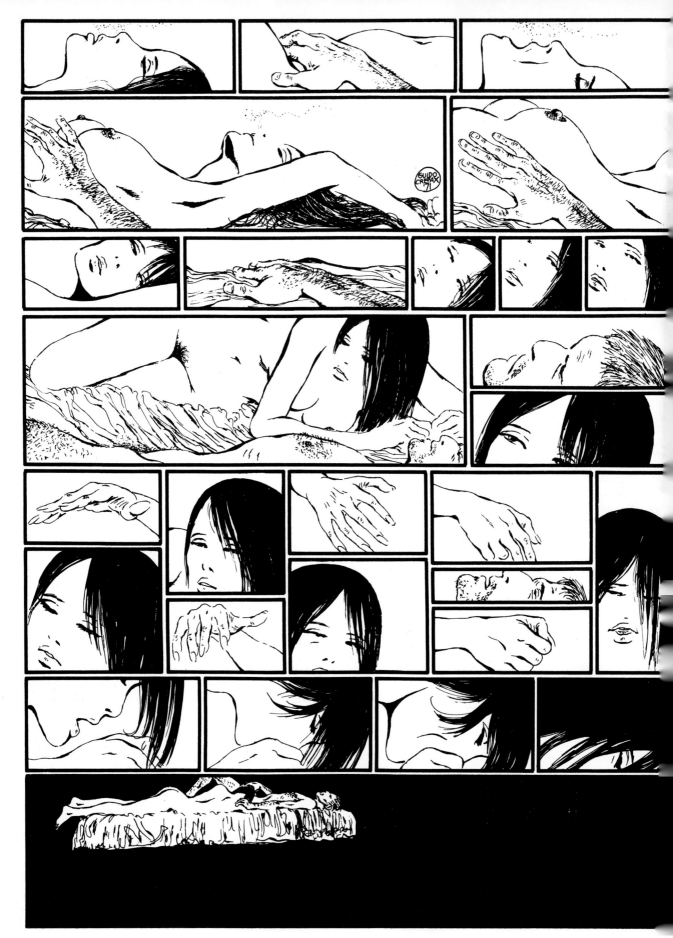

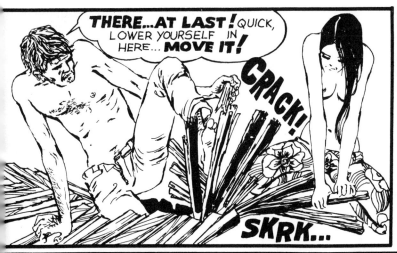

SO! PREPARE HER...

LEAVE THE HAT, GLOVES, STOCKINGS AND SHOES... THAT'S IT... NOW GO!

BUT... WHERE DO I GO?

QUIET!

GUIDO CREPAX '69

YOU LOT! HAVEN'T YOU FINISHED? GET A MOVE ON!

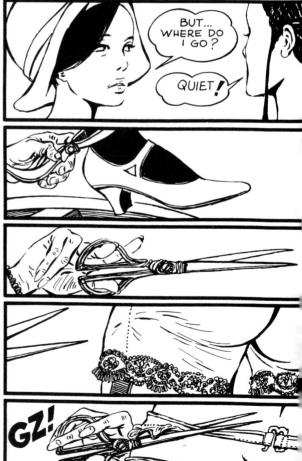

GZ!

FIRST NIGHT

COPTOLABRUS ANTHAEUS

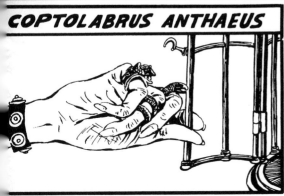

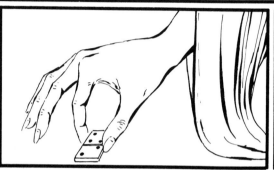

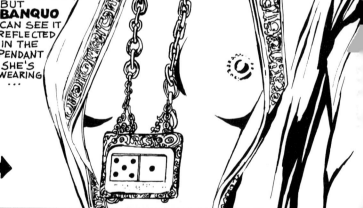

SECOND NIGHT

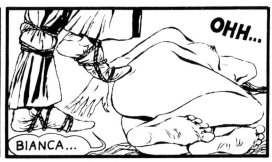

ANTINEA'S **SPINNING MACHINE**

HMM...THAT'S DREADFUL, IT'S ALL RAVELLED! TOO BAD, EH ?...

OH, NO! BUT I...

TAKE HER, CALIBAN!

AH!

I AM CURIOUS →

NO! NOT THERE... DON'T LOCK ME IN!

HHH... HHM...

GAME TWO

228

ARTEMISIA NEEDLES, COMPLETELY PAINLESS!

HMM... AND THIS? THIS... AH, YES!

DRAW THE CHINGS ON THE HIPS AND LOINS CLEARLY...

WE'VE FOUND A PERFECT YUNGRAK ON HER THIGHS!

YOU CAN GO AND SLEEP NOW, BIANCA!

229

233

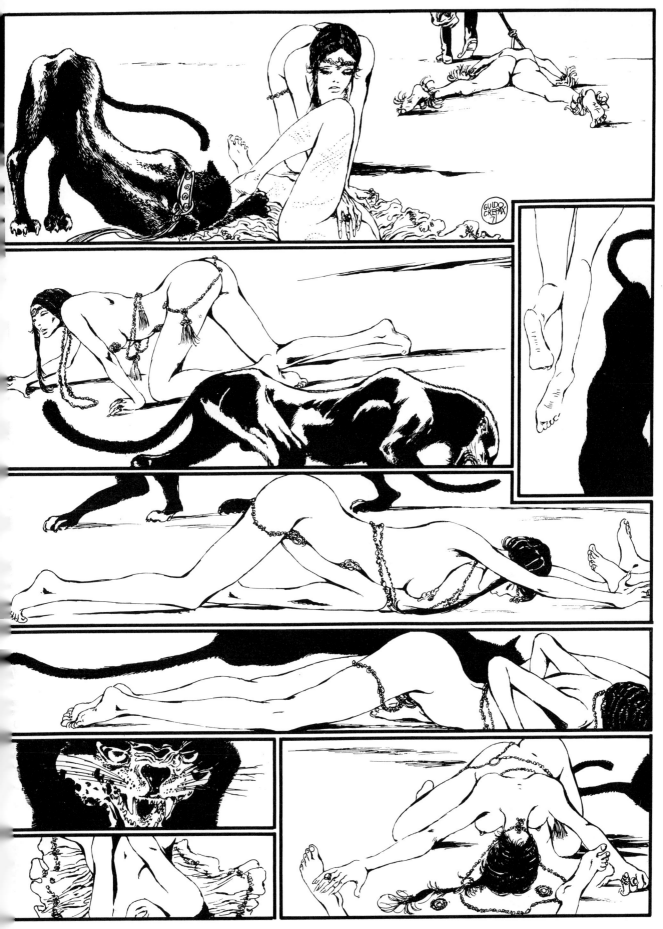

OH... I'D FORGOTTEN **THE EXAMINATION!**..

HM..HM...

JULIETTE!!...

JULIETTE, TAKE HER AWAY!

COME ON, UP...ON YOUR FEET! COME AND GET DRESSED ...OBEY!

TOUTE NUE, ONDULEUSE ET LE TORSE VIBRANT... ...BOUCLAIT NONCHALAMMENT SES JARRETIÈRES ROUGES SUR DE TRÈS LONG BAS BLANCHES D'UN TISSU TRANSPARENT...

237

239

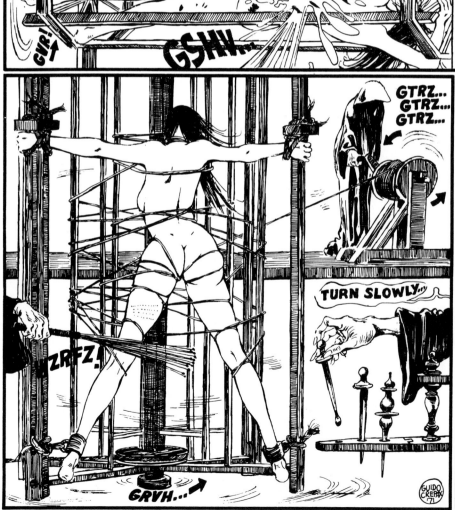

240

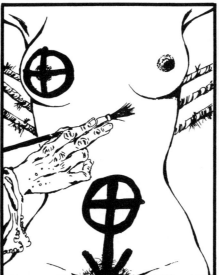

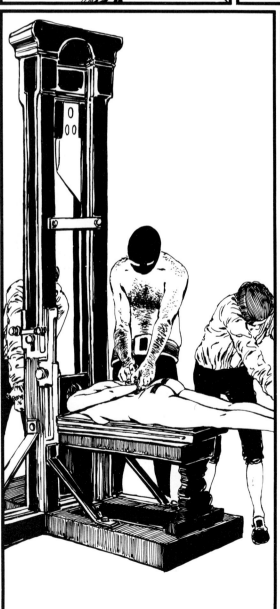

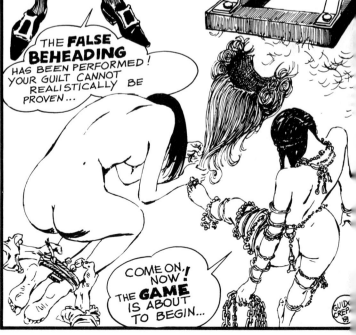

GAME FOUR

TAC...
TAC... TAC...

TAC...

COME ON, MOVE, **BIANCA!** YOU'RE FREE TO MAKE ANY MOVE YOU LIKE...

ON THE ELEVENTH MOVE...

THUD!

!?

AH, A PIECE TOUCHED IS A PIECE PLAYED, BANQUO!

GARF!

IT'S YOUR MOVE, BIANCA...

...ANTINEA (INADVERTENTLY?) KNOCKS OVER A **BLACK KNIGHT** WITH HER **FOOT!**

TAC...
TAC... TAC...
TAC... TAC...

...TAC...TAC

CHECKMATE! WHITE QUEEN **BIANCA** MATES IN TWELVE MOVES!

SO YOU WON, DID YOU?! NOW YOU'RE COMING TO **HUNT!** WITH ME, HAPPY?

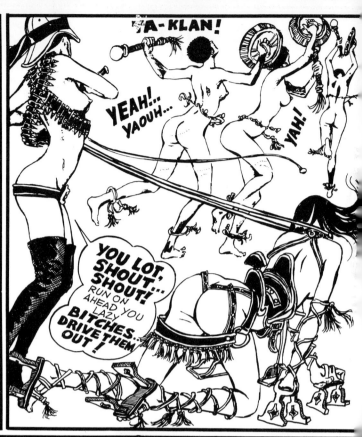

SHHH... QUIET! DOWN, BITCHES ... AND DON'T MOVE!

COME OUT!

KWA- -SHVVV...

AHAUGH...

AH... AGH!

AH...HA GOT HIM! HEE...HEE...

THIS ONE'S FOR *BIANCA*! TAKE HIM AWAY...

MY TURN, NOW ... OVER THERE PERHAPS...

CLICK!

ANTINEA!

ANTINEA... THE *MIGRATORY LOCUSTS*! THERE ARE MILLIONS OF THEM... WHAT SHALL WE DO?

WE NEED BAIT, NATURALLY! THIS LITTLE *BRUNETTE* ...IT'S A SHAME, THOUGH, MY SWEET LITTLE HORSE...

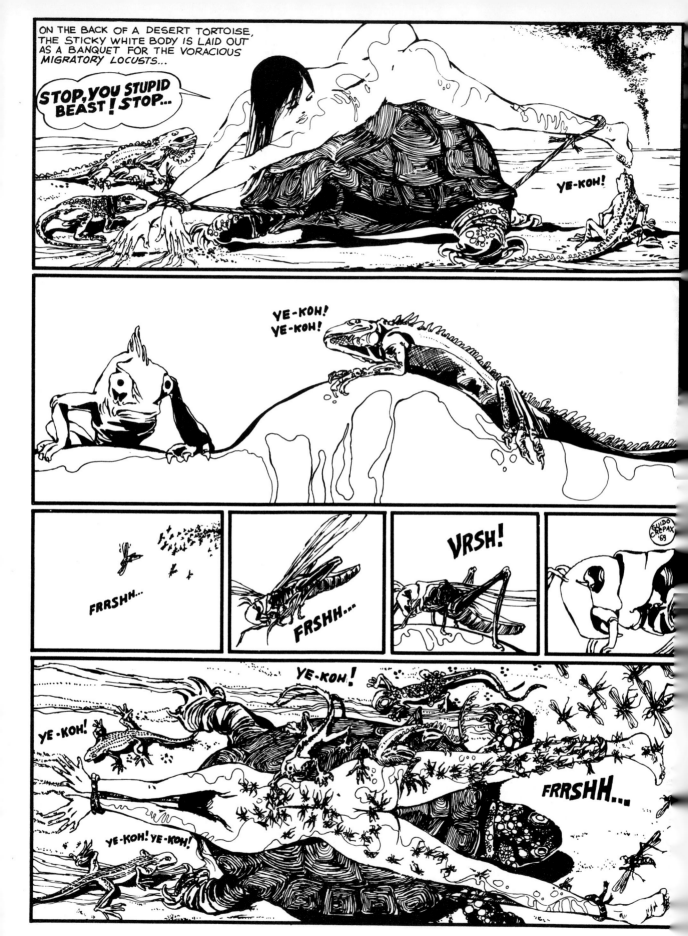

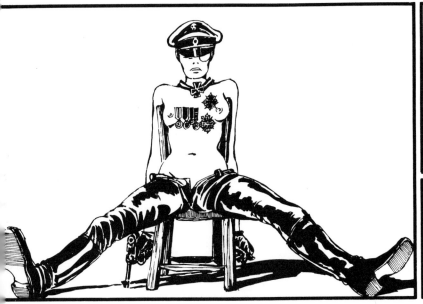

LEFT··· LEFT!

BANG!

BANG ·····SHVVVV

BANG ·····SHVVVV

VROOO...

KRAT- -RAT- -TAT

VROARR...

NO. 11, MISSED! NO. 2 ....

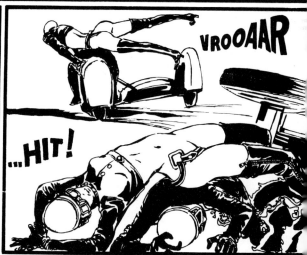

VROOAAR

...HIT!

...IT'LL BE BIANCA'S TURN NEXT LAP...

LISTEN ··· WE'LL FOLLOW NO. 9. THEN...

GUIDO CREPAX '69

NO.6 HAS FAILED AT 25 CENTIMETRES

ELIMINATED! COME FORWARD NO.15... LOWER IT TO 23 CENTIMETRES!

THIS ONE JUMPS FRENCH-STYLE... SHE'S MAGNIFICENT! IN TRAINING WITH ME SHE JUMPED 18 CENTIMETRES... COURAGE, PUTAIN!

WELL DONE! TOTAL CONCENTRATION, NOW...

TZ!.. TZ!.. TZ!..

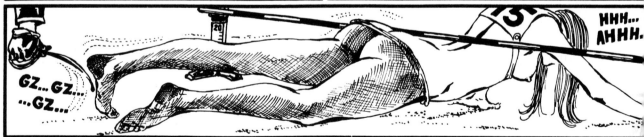

GZ... GZ... ...GZ...

HHH... AHHH.

15 AH!

SHE BROUGHT THE BAR DOWN... ELIMINATED!

TRRR... TA-TA-TA!

WHIP.. WHIP..

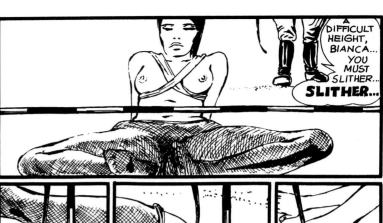

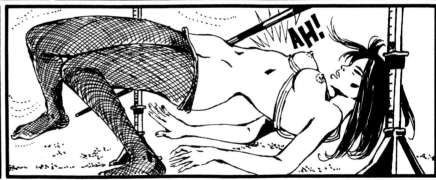

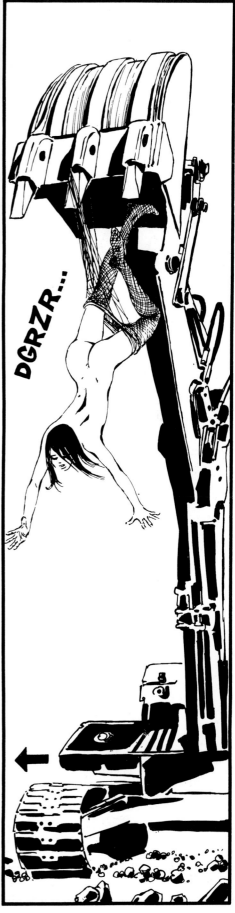

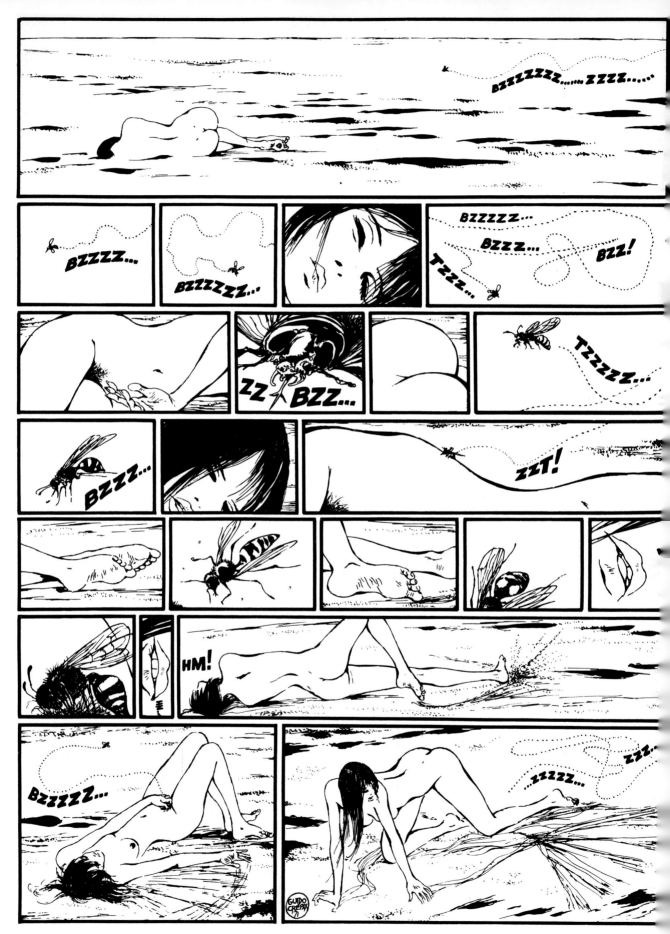

268

8 ¼

8 ½

273

YOU'RE BACK...

HANG HER BY THE WRIST- AND ANKLE-RINGS, THEN CALL **JULIETTE**...

SKRKR

KRK

WHIP... WHIP...

HIGHER!

RAISE HER LEGS...

SKRKR...

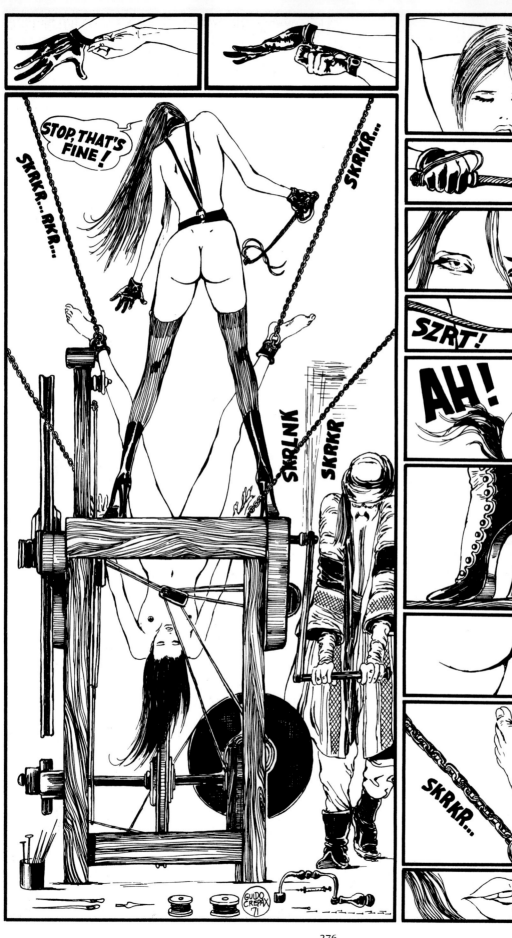

Odessa 1905

283

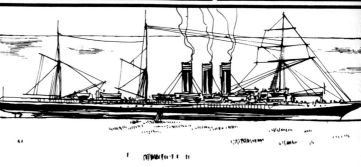

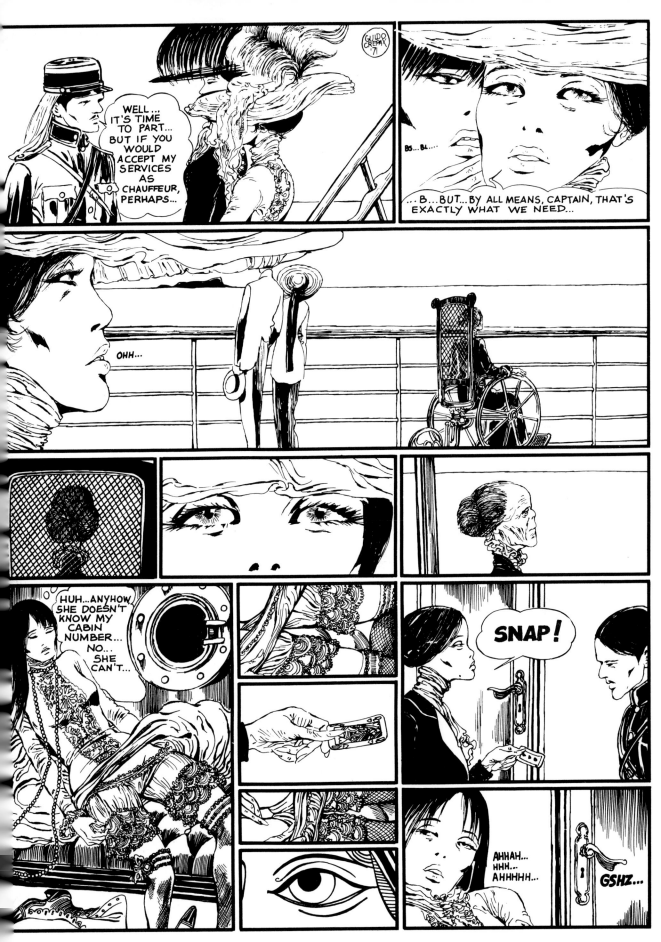

ODESSA 1905

COME, MADAM! WE MUST LEAVE AT ONCE!

BE QUICK, NOW! BRING YOUR CLOTHES...

YES... JUST A MOMENT!

THERE ISN'T TIME!

TOC
TOC
TOC
TOC

BIANCA...

MADAM... WAKE UP!

HMM.... AHH...

MADAM...

THERE'S...

A LITTLE HIGHER ...

PERFECT!

WHIP!... WHIP!...

A BRUTAL CRIME WAS COMMITTED LAST NIGHT... THEY KILLED AND ROBBED A MAN CALLED **STOLYPIN**, A STOCKBROKER... HE WAS STRUCK WITH A BRONZE LAMP...

...SO HEAVY THAT EVEN A **WOMAN** ...

...COULD HAVE KILLED HIM WITH A SINGLE BLOW!

THE POLICE THINK IT MUST BE **DENTED** ...

293

THE BROKEN BOTTLES OF ESSENTIAL OILS FILLED THE ROOM WITH THEIR PERFUME AND MAY ALSO HAVE SPILT ON THE ASSASSIN'S CLOTHES ...

NFH... NFH... NFH...

AMINA, I'D LIKE TO CHANGE... I HAVE TO GO OUT... HELP ME! I DON'T LIKE THIS OUTFIT ...

I DON'T THINK MADAM SHOULD GO OUT... IF THERE REALLY IS EVIDENCE THAT MIGHT INCRIMINATE HER...

SHE MIGHT BE FOLLOWED...

IN FACT... SHE MIGHT DO WELL TO HIDE!

MADAM, YOUR BATH IS READY!

AHH... IT'S SO HOT! AHH... TOO HOT ... AAAH... AHH...

HMMMM... ...HMHHH...

HH...

AHH..!

295

...YOU KNOW HOW THEY FOUND THAT BALLERINA? **ALEXANDRA FEDOROVNA**...SHE'D BEEN HUNG FROM THE CEILING LIGHT, USING A SILK STOCKING AS A NOOSE...JUST LIKE THIS ONE OF MADAM'S

...I WONDER **WHERE THE OTHER ONE IS?**

BUT I HAVEN'T BEEN OUT OF THE ROOM! **AMINA** KNOWS THAT!

MY TESTIMONY WOULDN'T BE ACCEPTED...

THE **MANAGER WANTS TO QUESTION MADAM**...

THEY HAVEN'T STARTED AN OFFICIAL INQUIRY YET... BUT IT WOULD BE BEST IF THEY COULDN'T LAY HANDS ON HER...

WE COULD SAY SHE ISN'T HERE... LET'S HIDE HER

YES, GOOD IDEA. IN THE WARDROBE!

THERE...COME ON, IN WITH YOU!

298

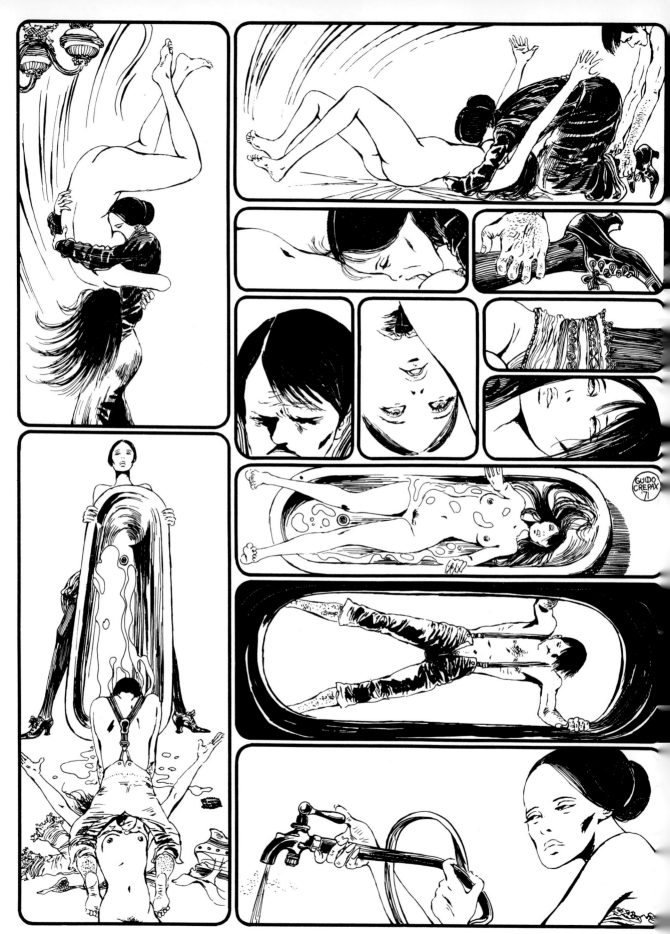

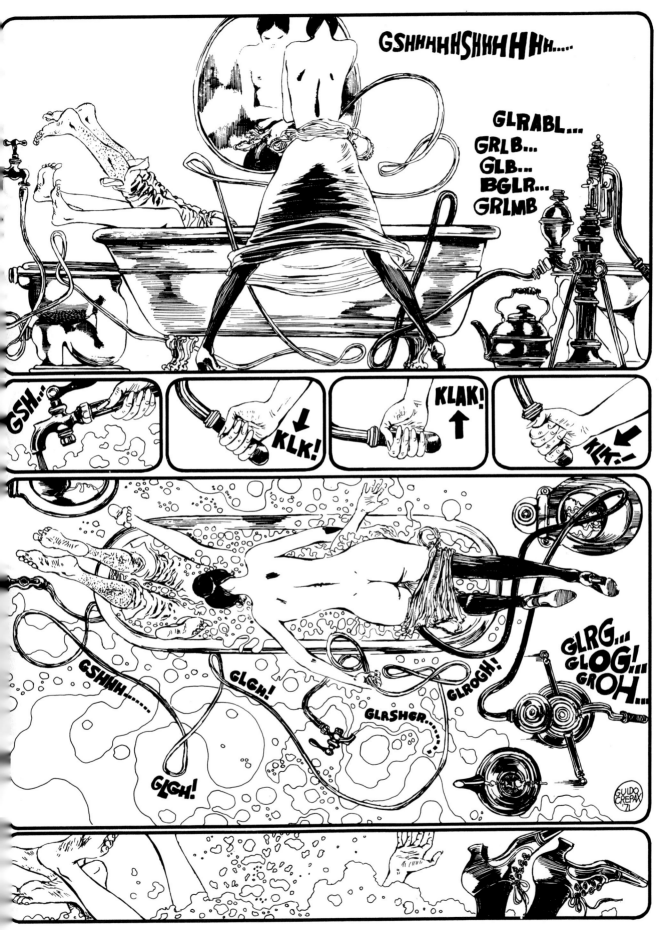

...EXCUSE ME... I JUST WANTED TO GO THROUGH...

...COULD I JUST GO THROUGH TO THE...

...CORRIDOR...

...IT WAS JUST TO...

AHH...

YES..!

BUT THERE'S NO ONE ELSE...

IN THE MIRROR!

HHH... AHHHHH......
HHH... AHHHHH...

THERE'S NO REFLECTION IN THE MIRROR!

SO I COULD HAVE...

ON THE DESK!

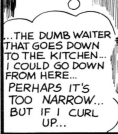

SDRRRG.....

NICE AND HARD! THE GRAND DUKE IS VERY DISCRIMINATING!

GUIDO CREPAX '71

WRAGZ!

ZT!ZT!..

GOOD, **RODZIANKO**, THAT'S TENDER ENOUGH...NOW WE CAN SEASON HER!

FLK!

YOU DON'T KNOW WHAT YOU'RE TALKING ABOUT **KORNILOV**, YOU'RE JUST THE HEAD WAITER ...FLING HER DOWN ON THAT MARBLE SLAB AND LEAVE IT TO ME!I'M THE HEAD-COOK...TAKE OFF HER SHOES, STOCKINGS AND KNICKERS...

THERE! NOW TURN HER OVER AND SERVE HER!

PAONNE À LA PRINCESSE...

VITELLA BELVEDERE AND MARINATED BOAR...

GOLDEN PLOVER IN CHAUD-FROID SAUCE...

STOP! GRAND DUKE MICHAEL HAS CANCELLED THE BANQUET!

NOW WHAT? ALL THAT WORK FOR NOTHING... THROW IT ALL IN THE GARBAGE!

ACH...IT WON'T GO IN ANY FURTHER!

GO ON, SHOVE!

STRUBH! SKRUK!

HERE!...STUFF THESE RAGS IN TOO!

THUNG!

BONG

MADAM, WE WERE SO WORRIED ABOUT YOU!

WHAT A STATE YOU'RE IN! NOW I'LL HAVE TO GET THE STAINS OUT OF THAT DRESS... THEY'LL NEVER COME OUT...AN ELEGANT LADY LIKE YOU SHOULDN'T DO SUCH THINGS!

AND YOU MUST TIDY YOURSELF UP AT ONCE. THE MANAGER WANTS TO TALK TO YOU...

THUN

KRUNK!

CRASH

SKRMB

THUN.

BOING!

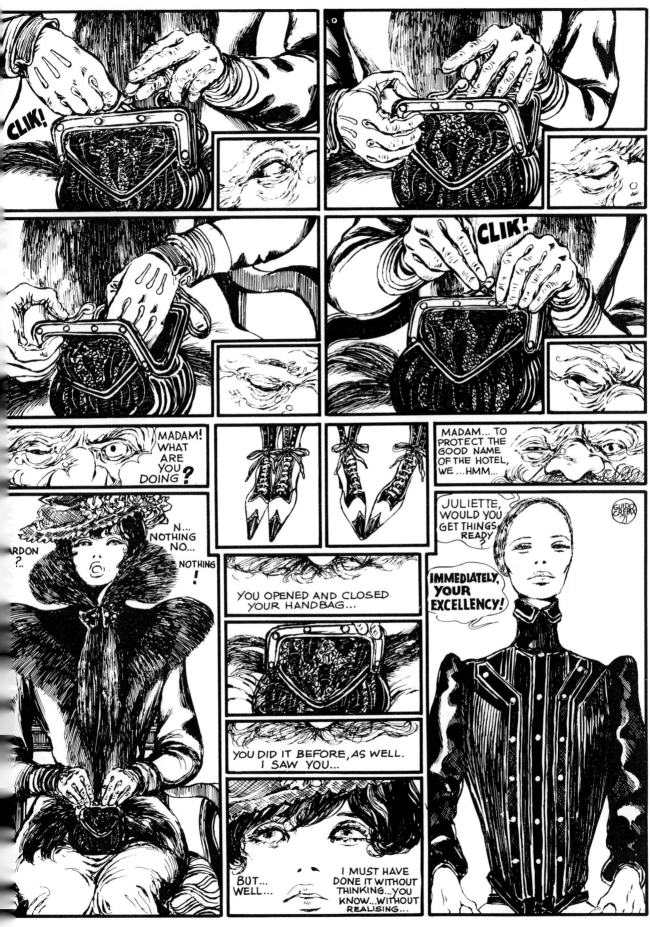

CLIK!

CLIK!

MADAM! WHAT ARE YOU DOING?

MADAM... TO PROTECT THE GOOD NAME OF THE HOTEL, WE...HMM...

ARDON...?...

N... NOTHING NO...

NOTHING!

YOU OPENED AND CLOSED YOUR HANDBAG...

JULIETTE, WOULD YOU GET THINGS READY?

IMMEDIATELY, YOUR EXCELLENCY!

YOU DID IT BEFORE, AS WELL. I SAW YOU...

BUT... WELL...

I MUST HAVE DONE IT WITHOUT THINKING...YOU KNOW...WITHOUT REALISING...

REMOVE
THAT
TABLECLOTH
...

...AND
TAKE THE
FOURTH
FROM
THE
TOP
...

YOU CAN KEEP YOUR HAT
AND BOA ON ...JUST RAISE
YOUR SKIRT A LITTLE...
COME ON, GET ON

BUT... WHY?

DO THE STRAPS UP TIGHTLY AT THE
WRISTS AND BELOW THE KNEES
...THEN UNDO
THE KNICKER
RIBBONS
...

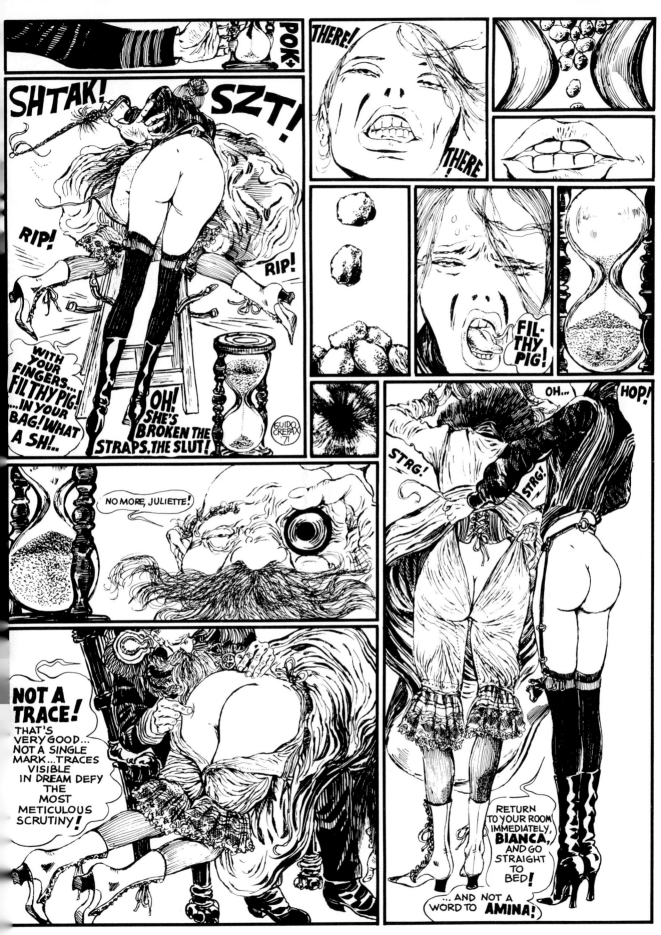

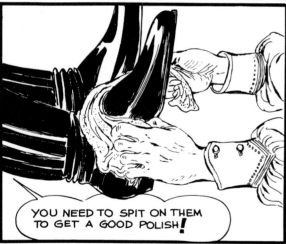

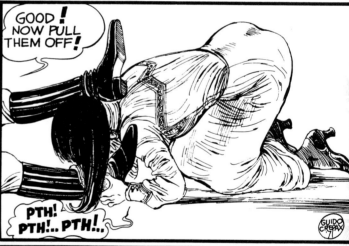

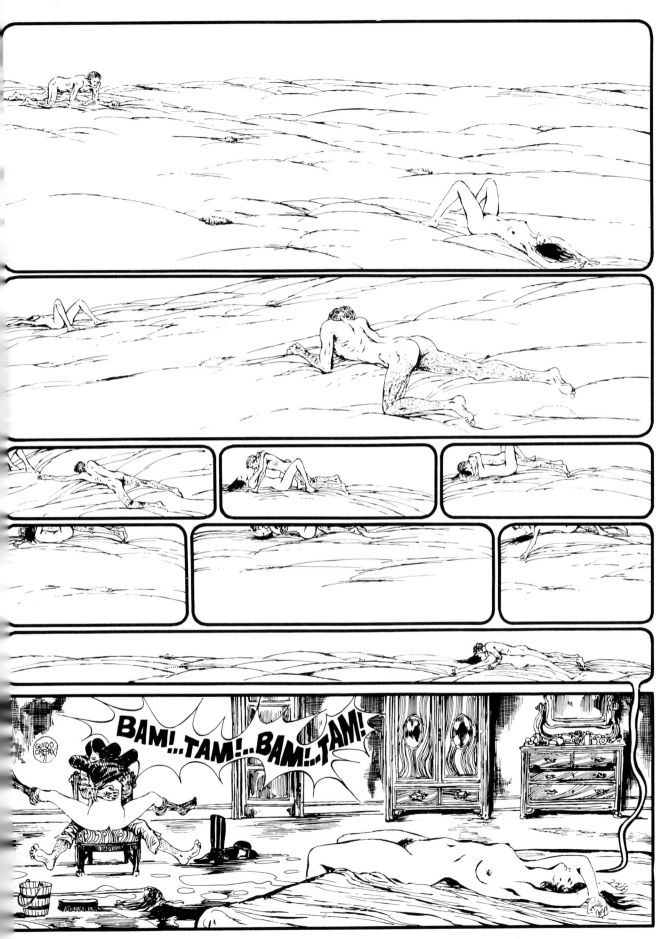

317

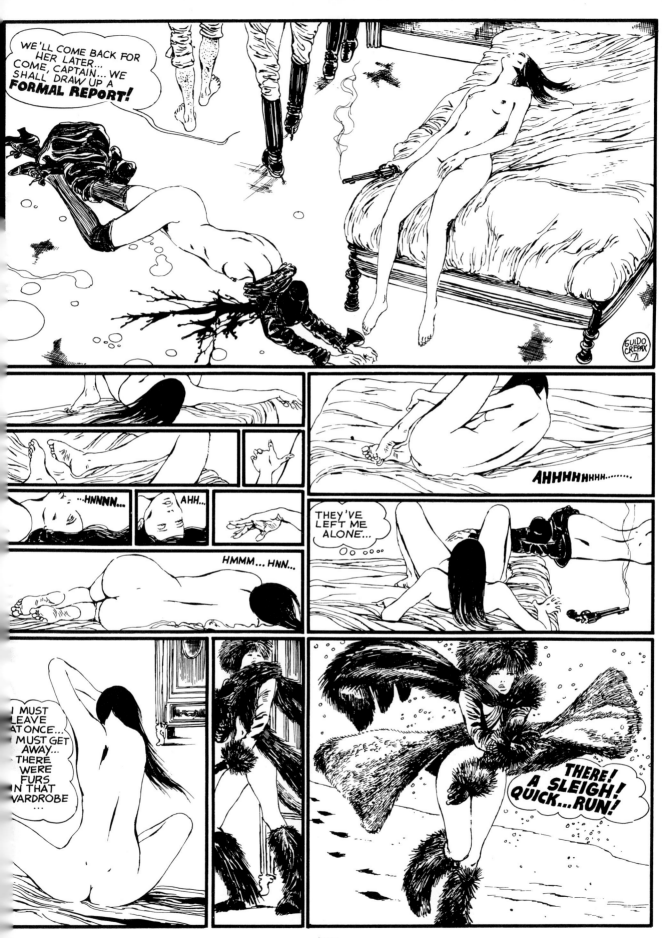

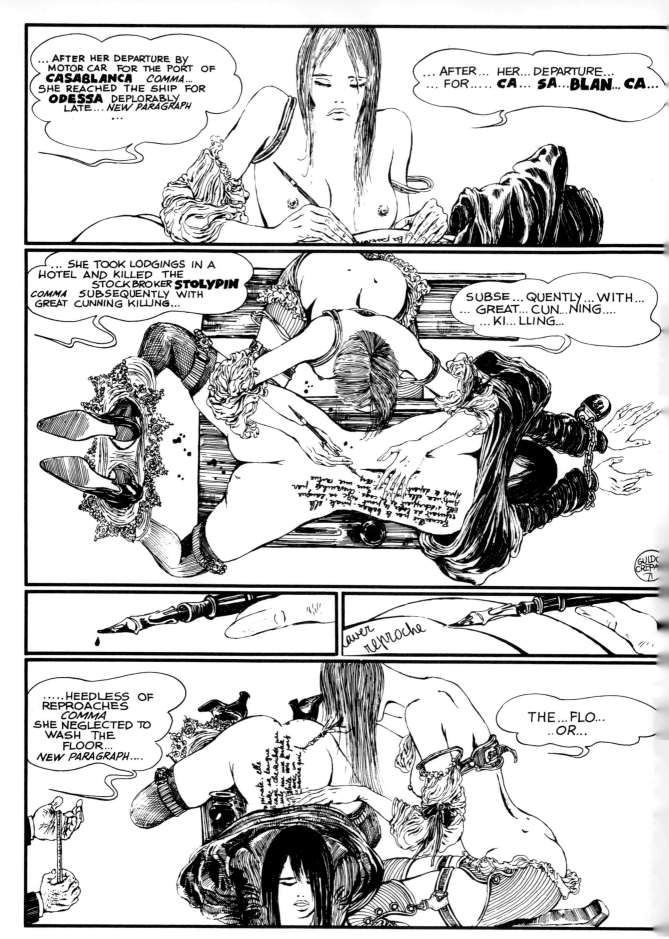

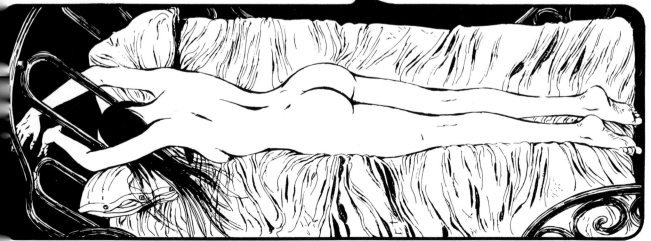

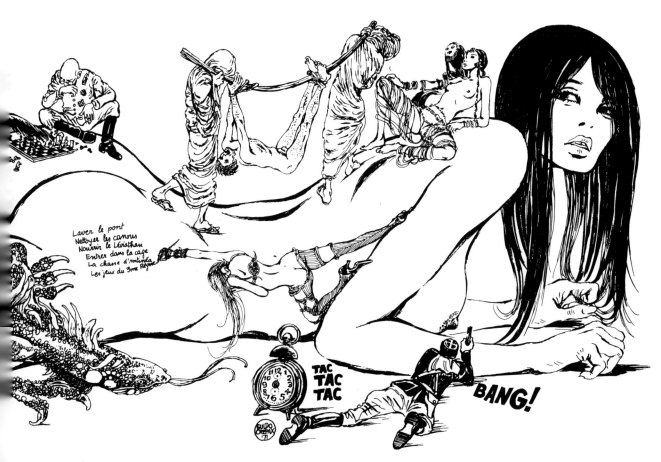

Girls' Boarding School
(reality, before)

Extraordinary Visions
(reality, afterwards)

OH...IT'S YOU. I'M BUSY TODAY...

NO! LET HER STAY... YOU WERE GOING TO DO THE *BLACK CAT*, NO? COME ON, GET IN THERE

GO ON!... BEND YOUR KNEES...LIKE THAT! LEAN AGAINST THE BACK

FOR THE MOST WILD, YET MOST HOMELY NARRATIVE WHICH I AM ABOUT TO PEN... I NEITHER EXPECT NOR SOLICIT BELIEF...

COME OUT!

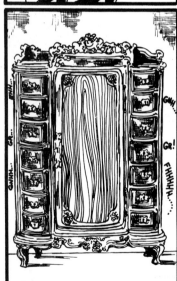

GRGNGR...

GAHH...FHHH!

FHG...

GNAUHH...

GNAUH... MRR.....GAH... GRGNAHH... FHHH...

NOW, LET ME DRAW!

354

TODAY WE'RE DOING LADY **LIGEIA** !

...**LIGEIA** TOOK ILL... HER WILD EYES BLAZED WITH A TOO-TOO GLORIOUS EFFULGENCE... THE FAIR-HAIRED **LADY ROWENA** WAS TO BE HER SUCCESSOR...

NO... NOT THESE ...THOSE ...YES!

THE FULL, AND THE BLACK, AND THE WILD EYES OF THE **LADY LIGEIA**

HUGE MASSES OF LONG AND DISHEVELLED HAIR... BLACKER THAN THE RAVEN WINGS OF MIDNIGHT

...TOTTERING, WITH FEEBLE STEPS, WITH CLOSED EYES... THE THING ADVANCED BOLDLY AND PALPABLY INTO THE MIDDLE OF THE APARTMENT ...

ROWENA WAS ATTACKED WITH SUDDEN ILLNESS ...

BUT HAD SHE THEN GROWN TALLER SINCE HER MALADY? WHAT INEXPRESSIBLE MADNESS SEIZED ME WITH THAT THOUGHT!

I'LL BE THE SAILOR

I'LL BE MADAME D'ESPANAYE

I'LL BE HER DAUGHTER

SOFT-ORANG-OUTANG...

THE DAUGHTER LAY PROSTRATE AND MOTION-LESS; SHE HAD SWOONED...

THE SCREAMS AND STRUGGLES OF THE OLD LADY HAD CHANGED THE... PURPOSES OF THE OURANG-OUTANG...

IT FLEW UPON THE BODY OF THE GIRL, AND IMBEDDED ITS FEARFUL TALONS IN HER THROAT...

CONSCIOUS OF HAVING DESERVED PUNISHMENT, IT SEEMED DESIROUS OF CONCEALING ITS BLOODY DEEDS, AND SKIPPED ABOUT THE CHAMBER IN AN AGONY OF NERVOUS AGITATION ... IN CONCLUSION, IT SEIZED THE CORPSE OF THE DAUGHTER, AND THRUST IT UP THE CHIMNEY, HEAD DOWNWARD...

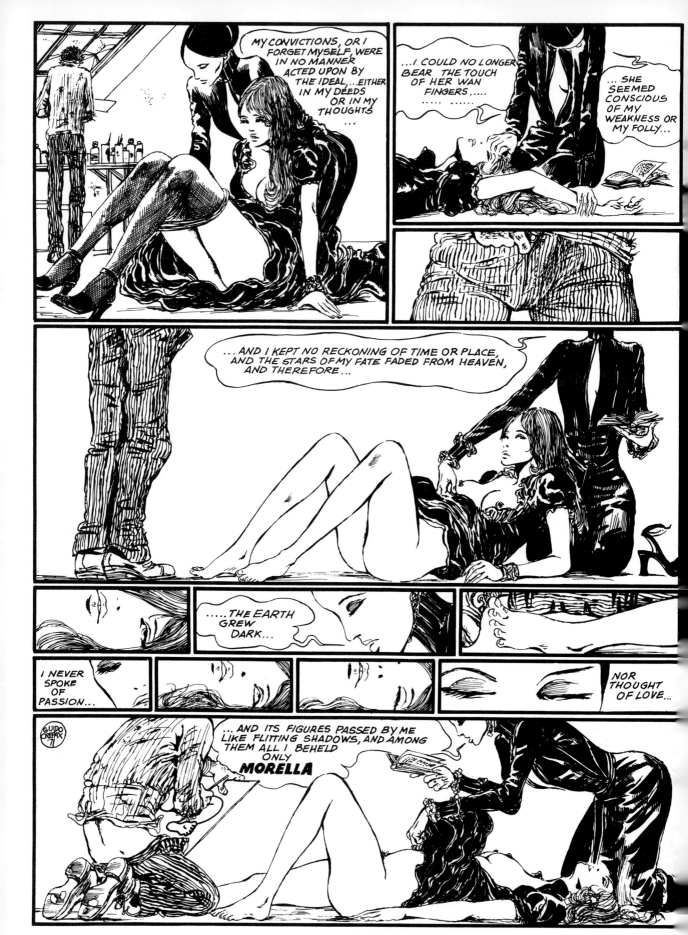

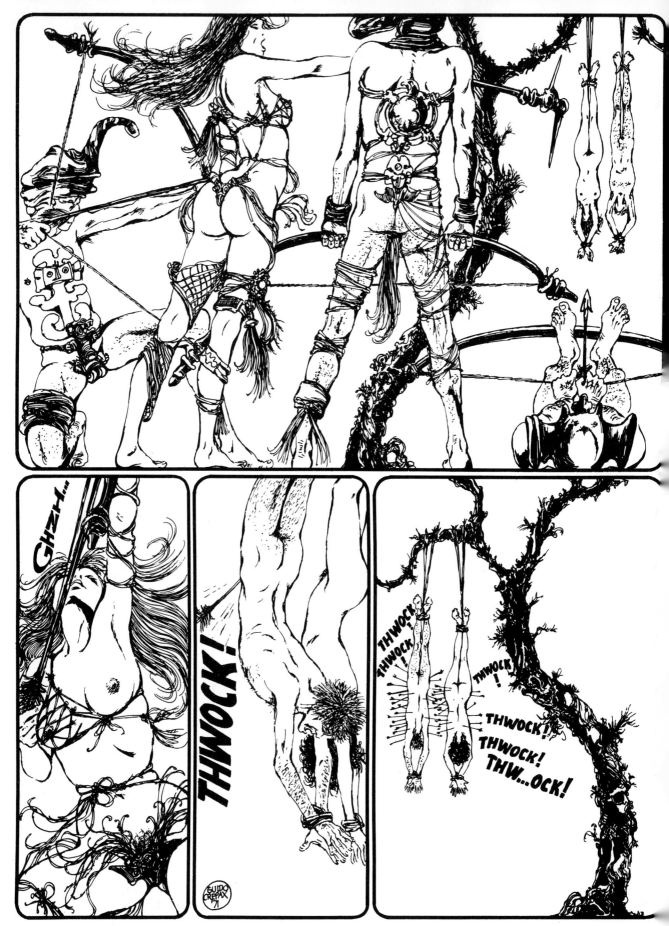

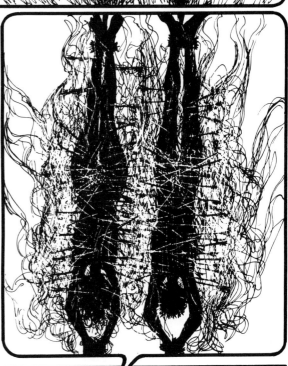

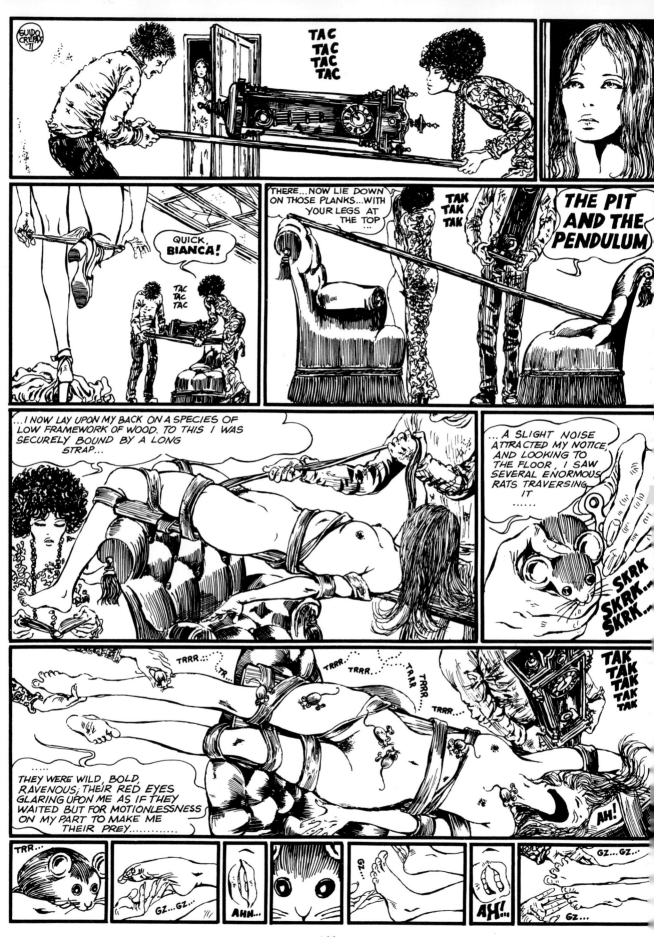

Venus in Furs

Wanda

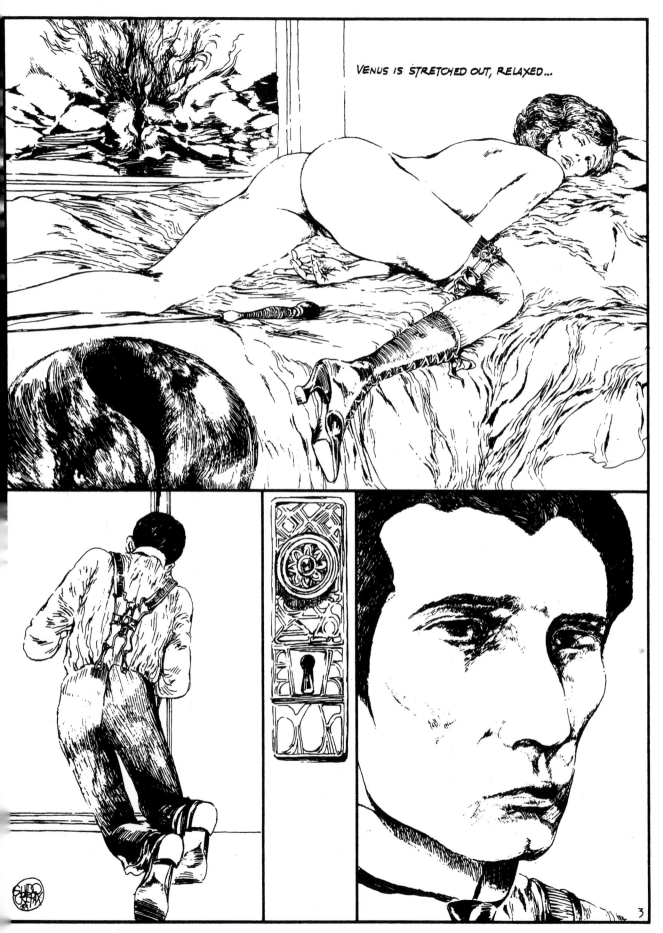

VENUS IS STRETCHED OUT, RELAXED...

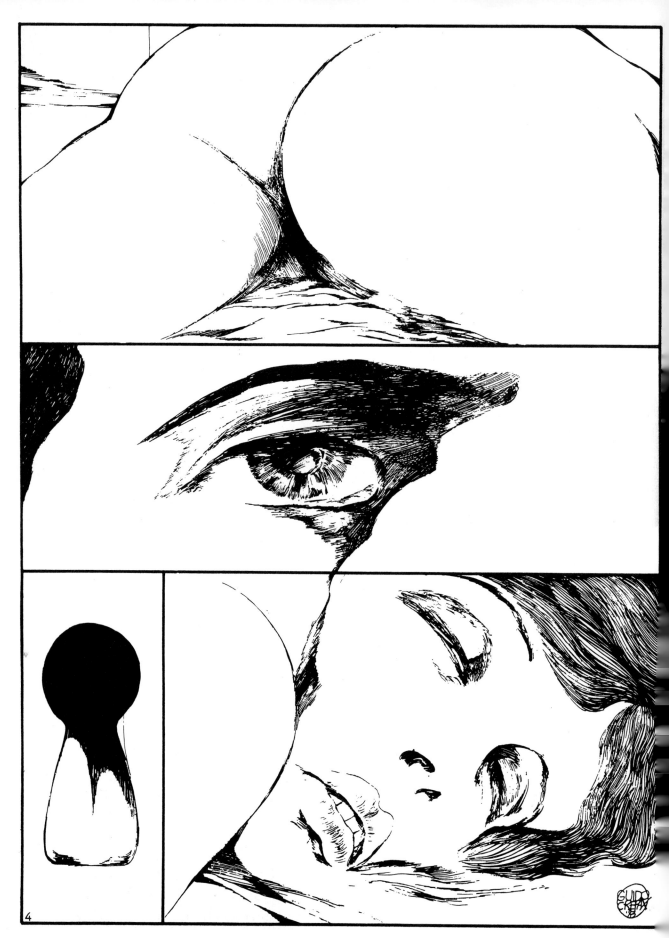

"GREGOR, TEA!"

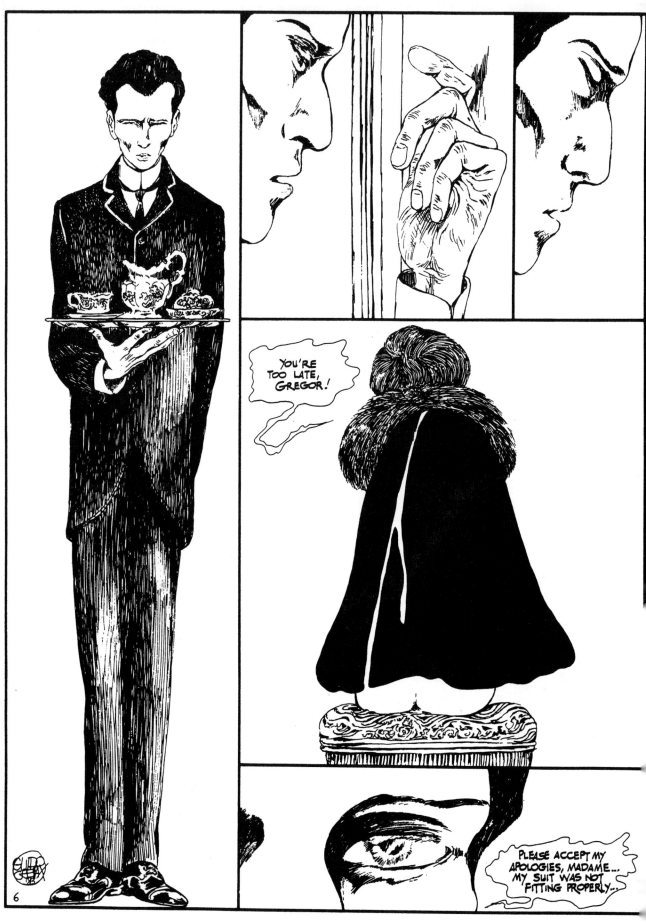

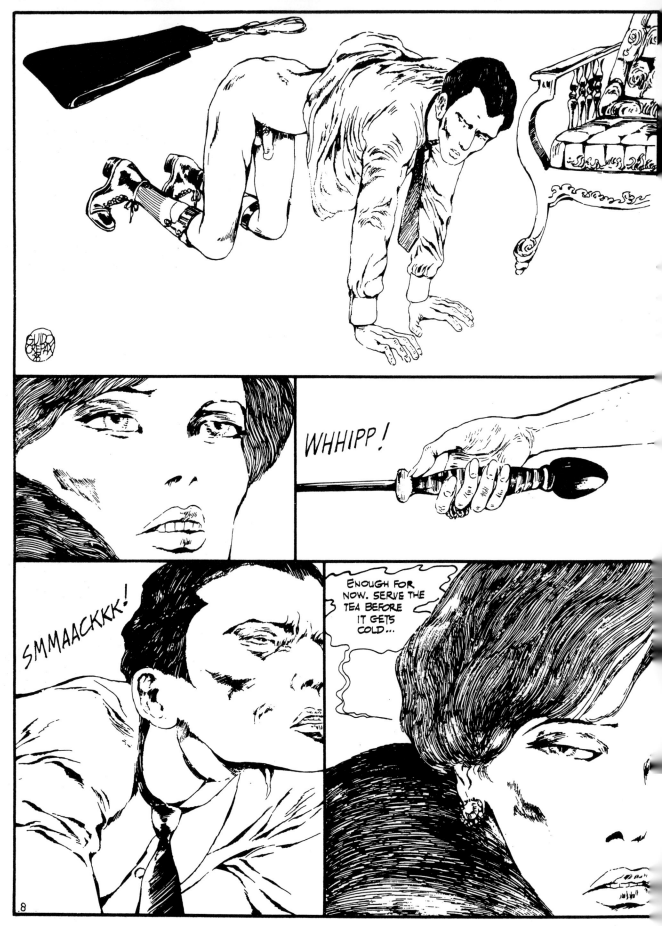

The Baron

Haffedah, Zorah, Sahadia

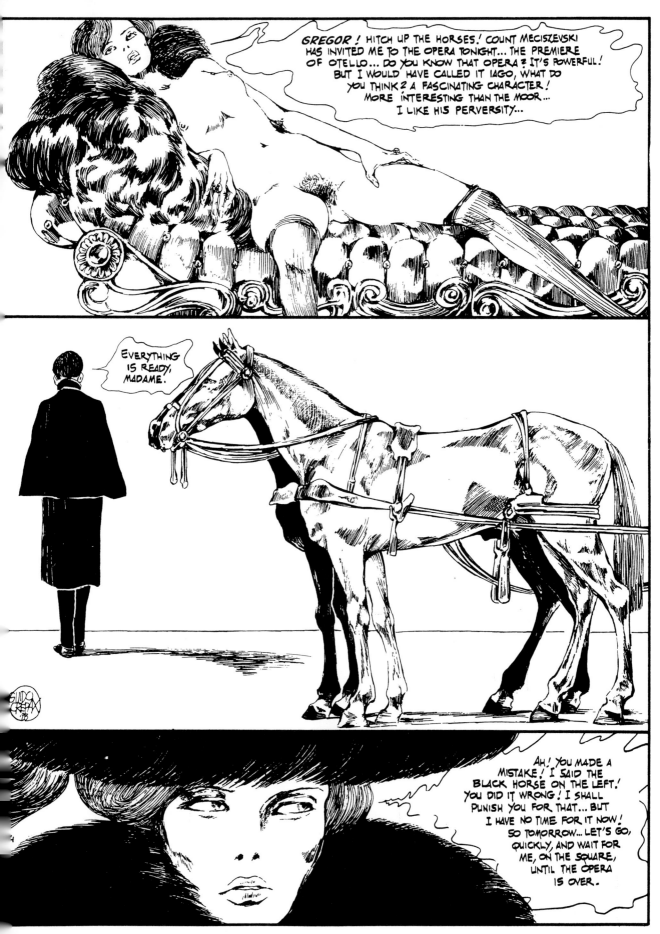

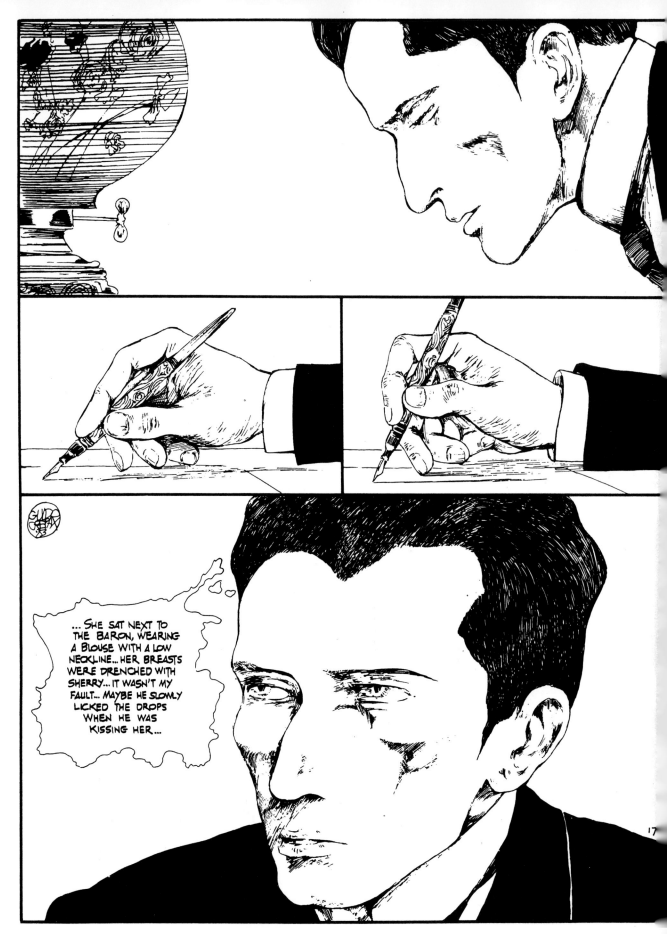

...SHE SAT NEXT TO THE BARON, WEARING A BLOUSE WITH A LOW NECKLINE... HER BREASTS WERE DRENCHED WITH SHERRY... IT WASN'T MY FAULT... MAYBE HE SLOWLY LICKED THE DROPS WHEN HE WAS KISSING HER...

17

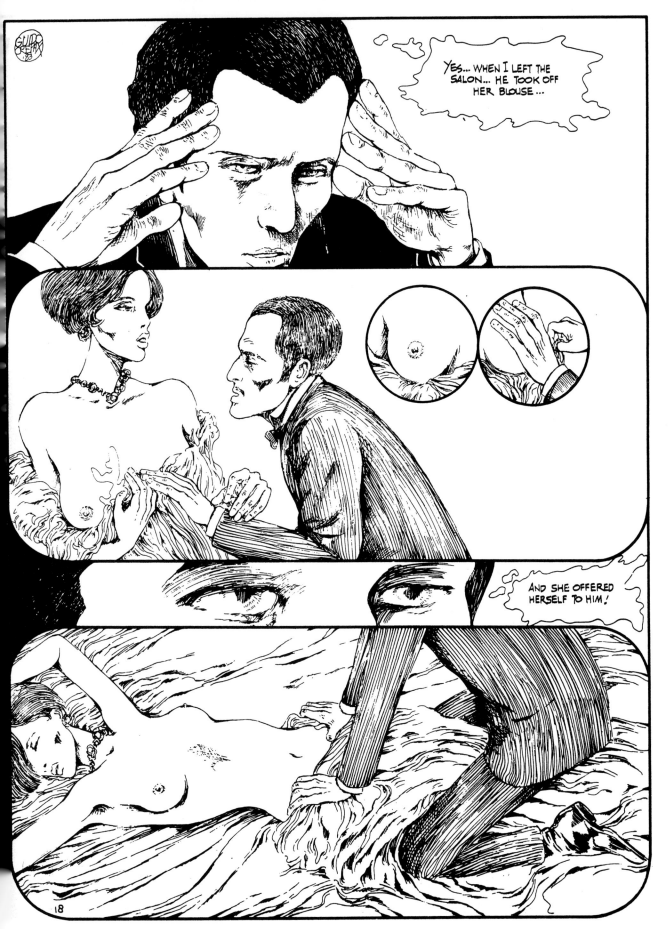

... I WAS UNABLE TO LOVE HER ...

NOW I WANT TO BE PUNISHED! SHE HAS TO WHIP ME! BEAT ME!

19

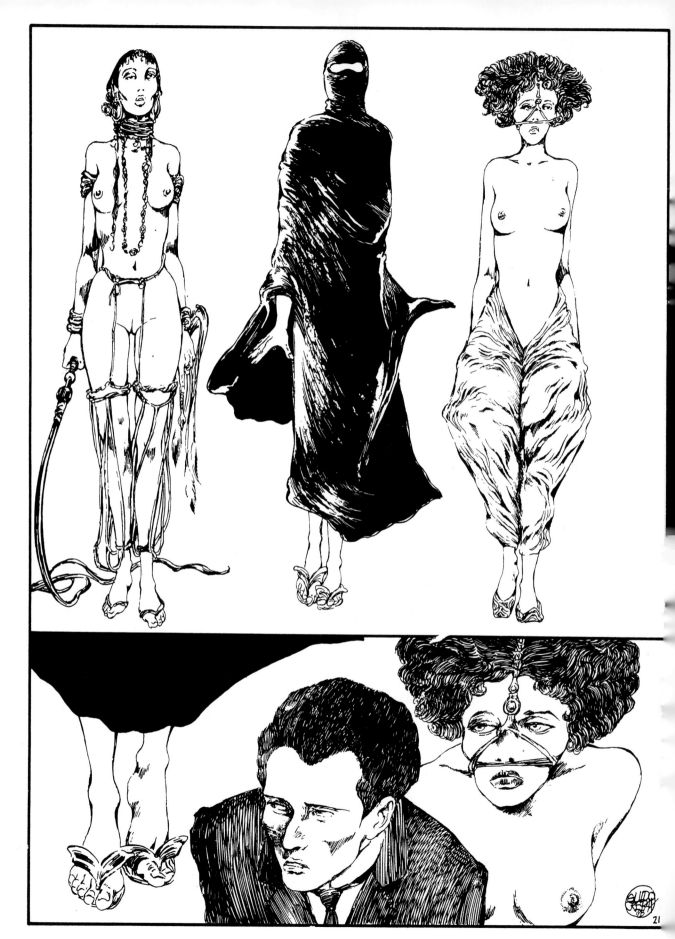

YOU HAVE ADEQUATELY PROVEN YOUR INSOLENCE. YOU WILL BE PUNISHED...

22

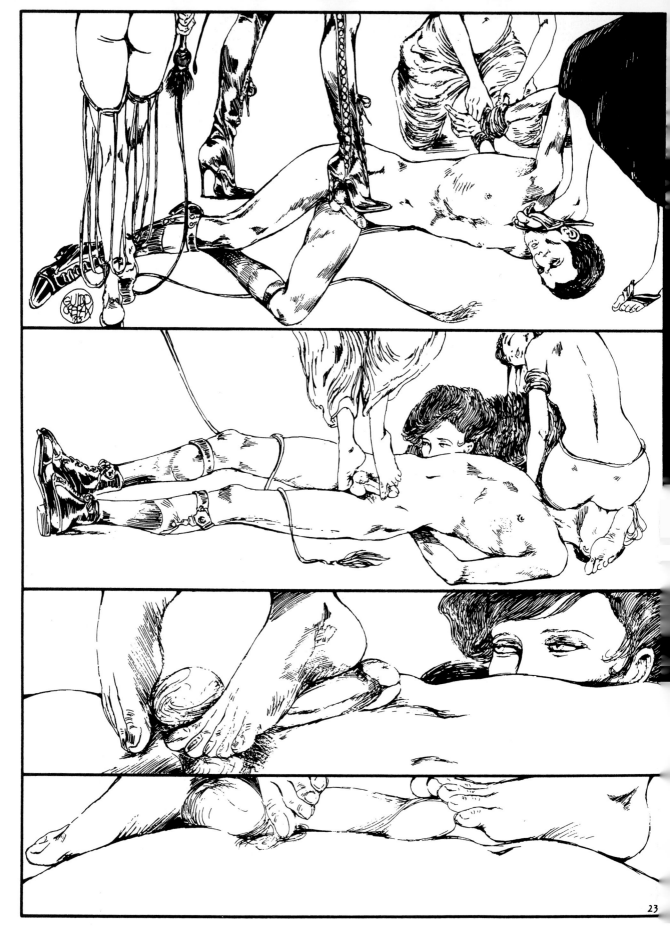

SEVERIN...
THESE WOMEN ARE
FOR YOU... THEY WILL
DO WHAT YOU WANT TO DO
WITH ME, BUT I CANNOT
HUMILIATE YOU
THAT WAY.

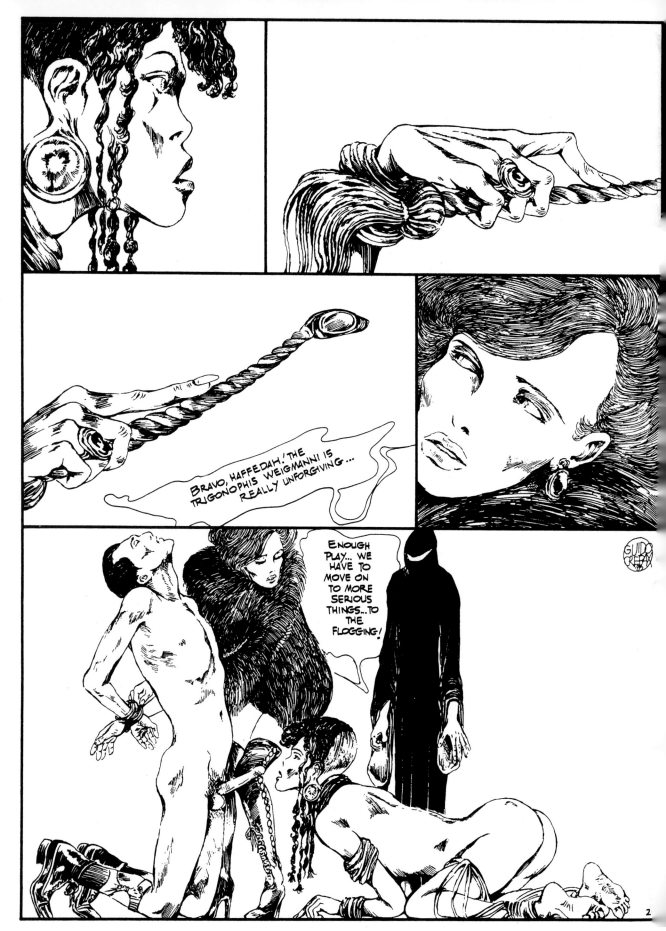

YES... I WANT HIM STRETCHED OUT! ZORRAH, TIE HIM TO THE CHANDELIER.

AND YOU, SAHADIA, TIGHTEN THE ROPE.

WHHOOOSSHHHH!

GET AWAY FROM HIM, HAFFEDAH, YOU'VE SUCKED HIM ENOUGH...

Severin

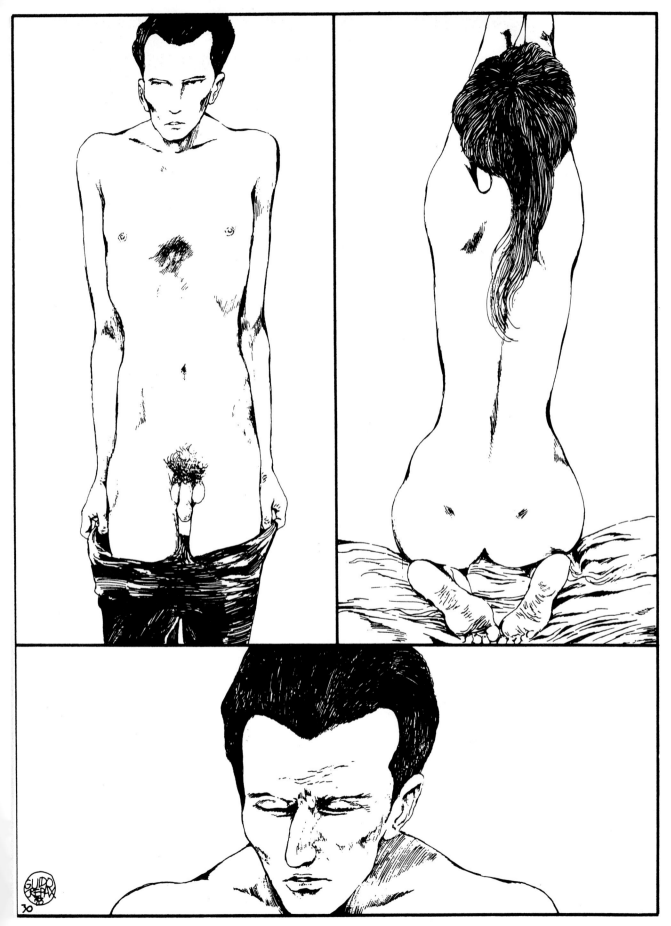

The Concert

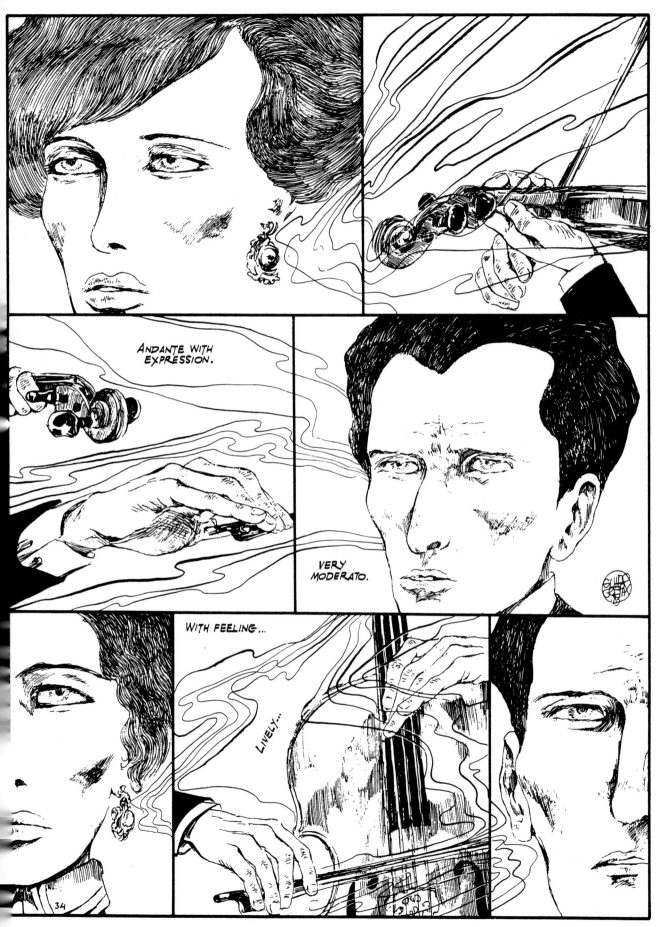

The Major

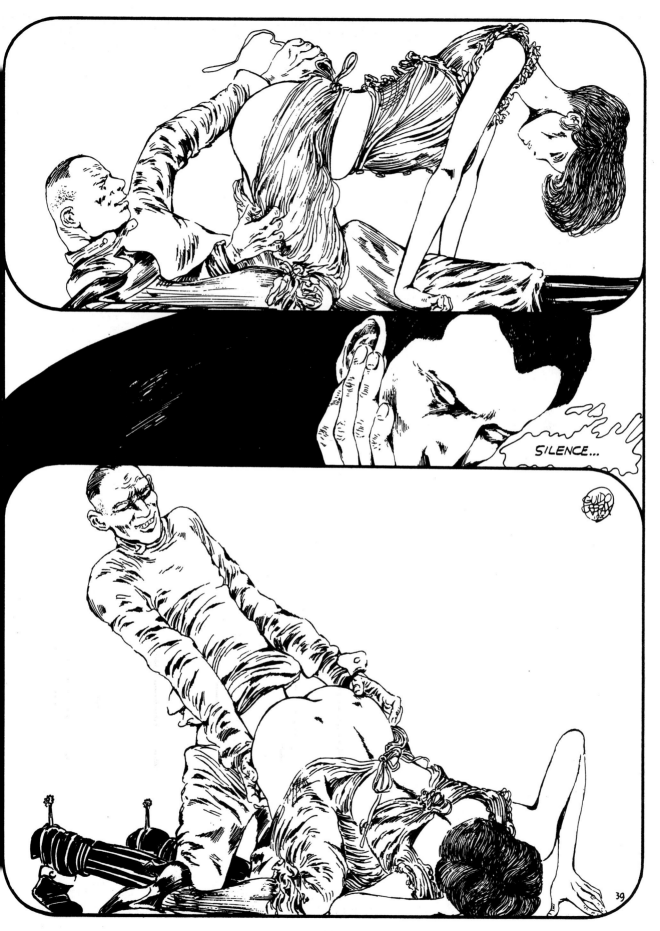

SILENCE...

40

Gregor

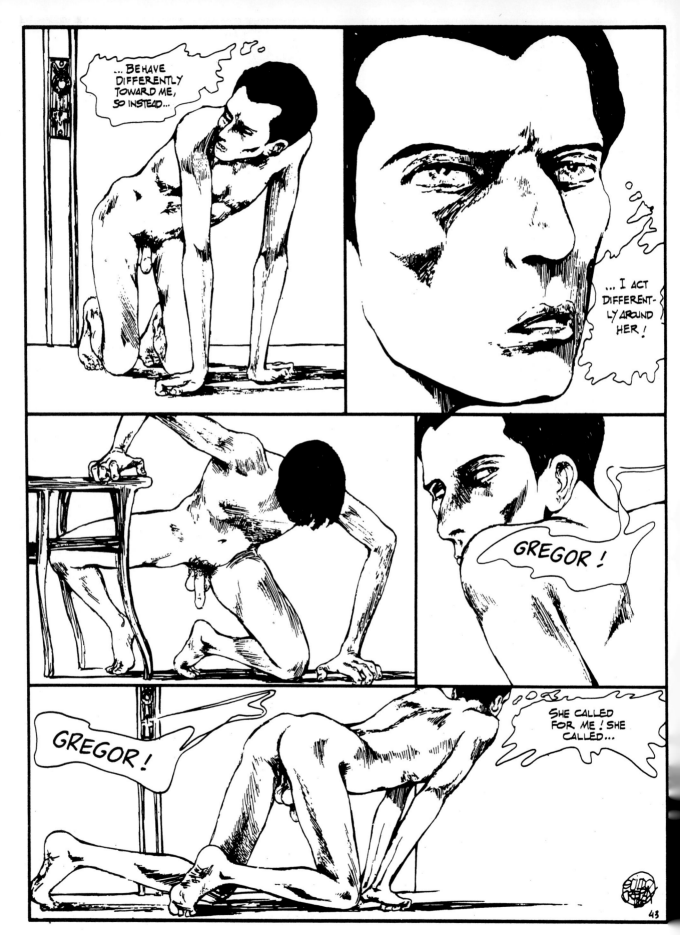

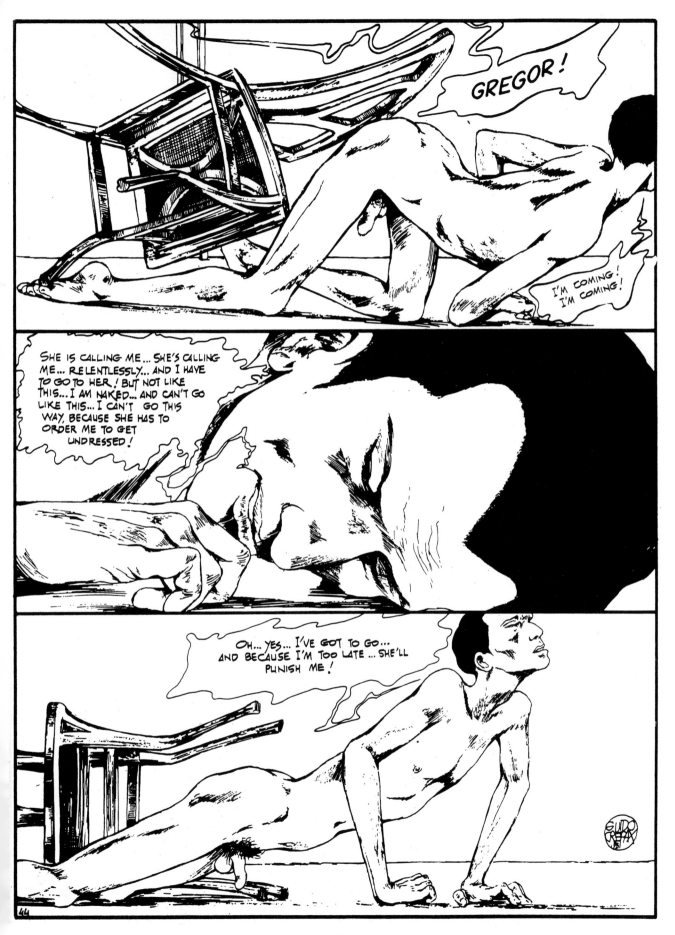

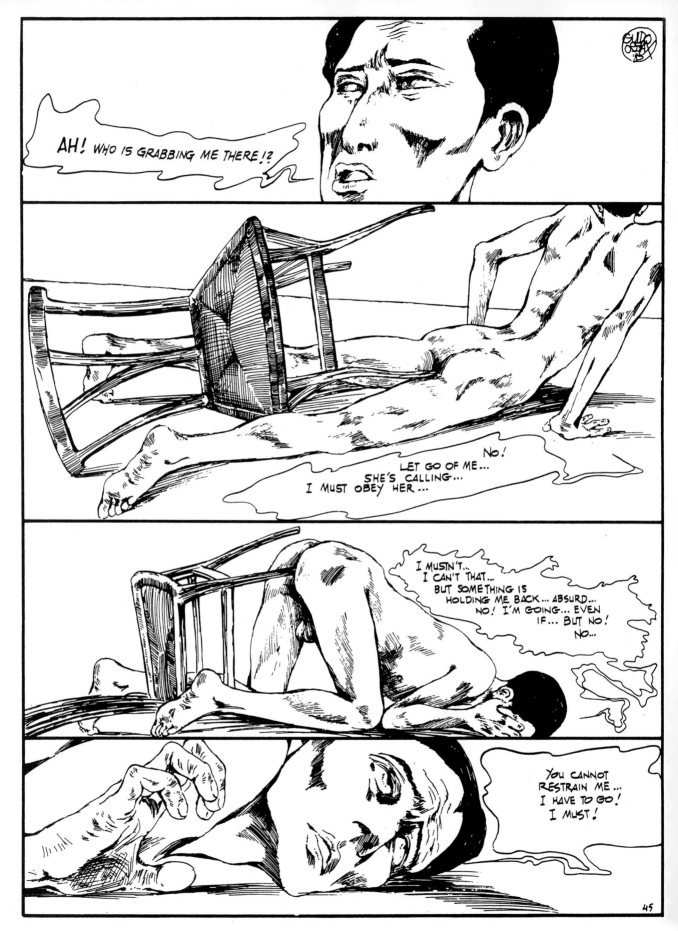

Venus in Furs

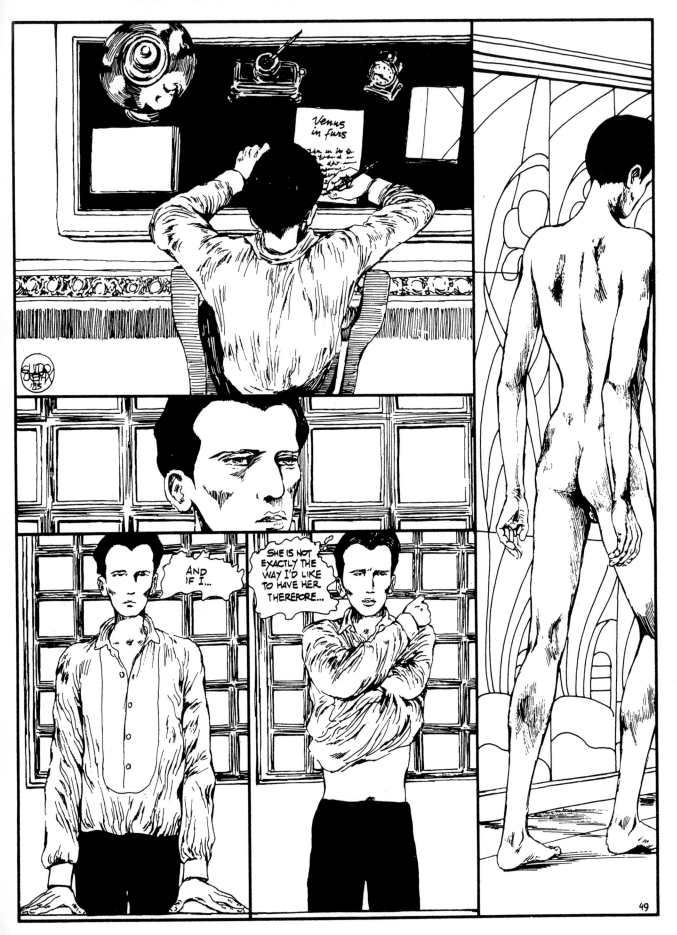

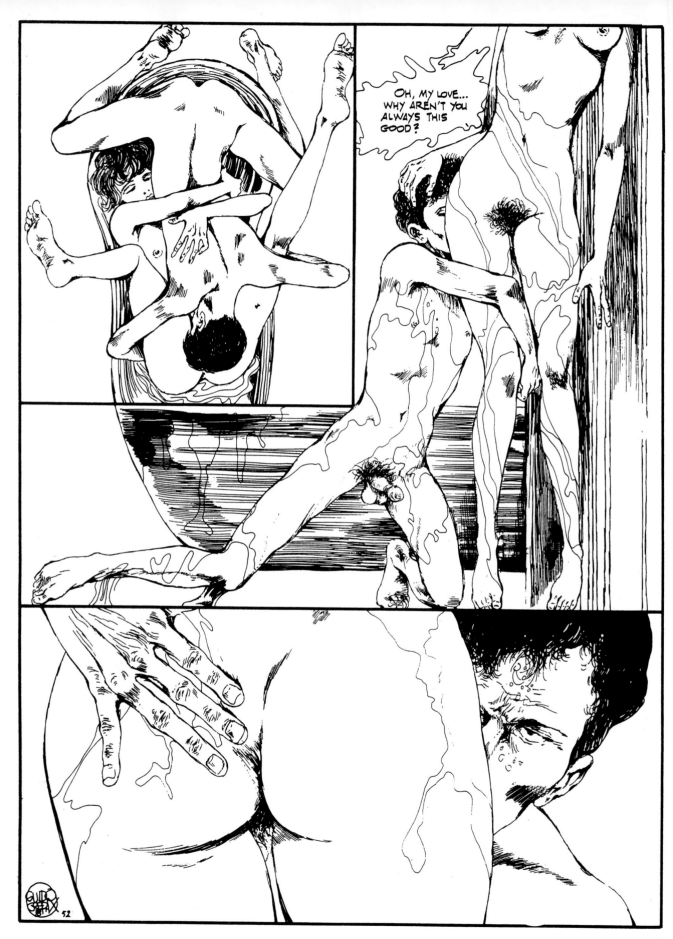

The Contract

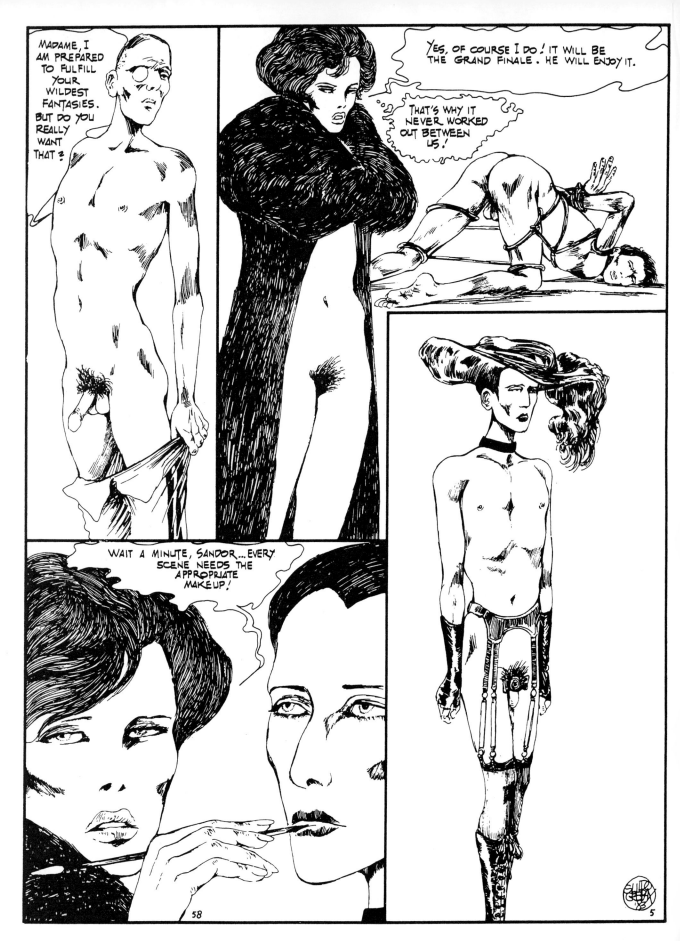

Dr Freud

In the same series:

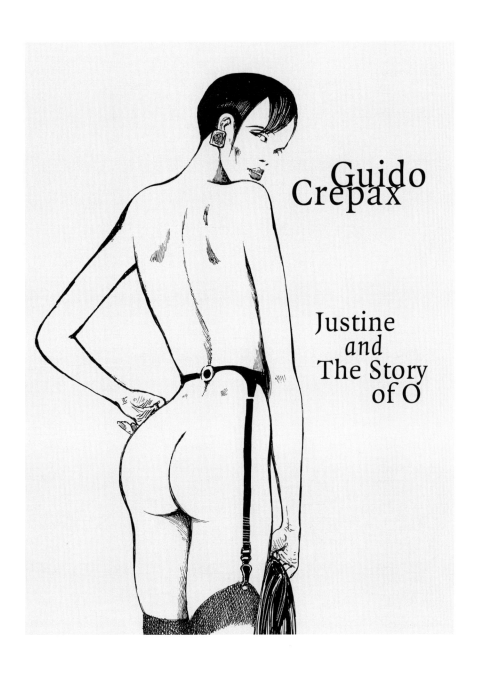

Guido Crepax

Justine and The Story of O

UPON
A
FROSTED
STAR

SIGNED BY THE AUTHOR
M.A. Kuzniar

PUBLISHED BY HQ
SEPTEMBER 2023

UPON
A
FROSTED
STAR

M.A. Kuzniar spent six years living in Spain, teaching English and travelling the world, which inspired her children's series *The Ship of Shadows*. Her adult debut, *Midnight in Everwood*, was a bestseller and a love letter to ballet and fairy tales. When she is not planning her next adventure, she can be found at her cosy home in Nottingham, where she lives with her husband, and spends her days reading and writing.

Visit her online at mariakuzniar.co.uk or @cosyreads on Instagram.

Also by M.A. Kuzniar
Midnight in Everwood

UPON A FROSTED STAR

A

FROSTED STAR

M.A. Kuzniar

ONE PLACE. MANY STORIES

This novel is entirely a work of fiction. The names, characters and incidents portrayed in it are the work of the author's imagination. Any resemblance to actual persons, living or dead, events or localities is entirely coincidental.

HQ
An imprint of HarperCollins*Publishers* Ltd
1 London Bridge Street
London SE1 9GF

www.harpercollins.co.uk

HarperCollins*Publishers*
Macken House, 39/40 Mayor Street Upper,
Dublin 1, D01 C9W8, Ireland

This edition 2023

1
First published in Great Britain by
HQ, an imprint of HarperCollins*Publishers* Ltd 2023

Copyright © M.A. Kuzniar 2023

M.A. Kuzniar asserts the moral right to be identified as the author of this work. A catalogue record for this book is available from the British Library.

HB ISBN: 9780008450717
Special edition HB ISBN: 9780008643348
TPB ISBN: 9780008450724

MIX
Paper | Supporting
responsible forestry
FSC www.fsc.org **FSC™ C007454**

This book is produced from independently certified FSC™ paper to ensure responsible forest management.

For more information visit: www.harpercollins.co.uk/green

This book is set in 11.5/15.5 pt. Centaur by Type-it AS, Norway

Printed and Bound in the UK using 100% Renewable Electricity at CPI Group (UK) Ltd, Croydon, CR0 4YY

All rights reserved. No part of this publication may be reproduced, stored in a retrieval system, or transmitted, in any form or by any means, electronic, mechanical, photocopying, recording or otherwise, without the prior permission of the publishers.

This book is sold subject to the condition that it shall not, by way of trade or otherwise, be lent, re-sold, hired out or otherwise circulated without the publisher's prior consent in any form of binding or cover other than that in which it is published and without a similar condition including this condition being imposed on the subsequent purchaser.

For my husband, Michael Brothwood, whom I will love until the moon falls from the sky and the stars no longer glitter.

Prologue

The parties always started the same way.

When the nights deepened, swallowing daylight by the hour. When winter whispered its frozen song across the land. When the promise of snow could be tasted in the air.

Then, and only then, would the grand doors to the manor house on the cliff be flung open to the night.

The invitations bore no address. No notice was given in the nearby sleepy town. The date changed each year. And yet the glamorous and rich and curious would wander through those doors.

It began with a murmur of delicious excitement, a champagne-fizz of anticipation, a tickle of imagination. It took mere hours to spread to the city, ensnaring all who heard the rumours of a night like none other with a compulsion to witness it for themselves. It ended with dawn staining the sky like wine, leaving the revellers stunned at the realm of decadence into which they had stumbled.

And the very next day? Not a minute eclipsed between the last reveller dragging their feet through the doors before they shut, locking out the world once more.

The parties were a thing of legend. An extravagance borne out of lavish dreams and wondrous delight.

And sometimes, an obsession.

PART ONE

1922

'The moment you doubt whether you can fly, you cease for ever to be able to do it.'

—J. M. BARRIE, *Peter Pan*

Chapter One

It was a late November night when the wind was blowing like Father Frost and the Thames was near frozen solid that Forster wondered if he had been cursed.

He had begun the day sitting in his kitchen sink. His sketchpad propped awkwardly upon one knee, he'd been attempting to capture the mellow sunshine seeping down into their basement window and setting the whisky glasses from last night aglow. Like melted butter. Only, halfway through committing ink to paper, the light had shifted, leading Forster to abandon his efforts. He'd started and grown bored of another five sketches until the late afternoon ushered in a deep darkness that suited his sense of ennui. Not long after, the little mantel clock had chimed six, reminding him of his longstanding evening walk with his flatmate, and he had hurried out into the bracing temperature.

November had whirled into London like a storm, frosting the spires and domes, and leaving Forster with a childlike longing for snow. This was heightened by the scent of roasted chestnuts drifting along the Embankment. He set off in search of the cart and parted with a few coins for a bag. The paper warmed his hands as he made his way to a bench overlooking the river. Beside him, the light from a solitary streetlamp puddled on the cobblestones as he stared out at the boats drifting past like his thoughts. They set the river aglow with their cosy lanternlight and he wished one would anchor. Perhaps he ought to learn how to sail? Then he could purchase a small boat that was in some disarray and spend time learning how to fix it, polishing it until it gleamed on the water like a pearl, and sleeping out on deck, watching the stars spattered over the roof of the world. But – what of his decision to dedicate his life to art? He'd spent the better part of this year attempting to search out a lone spark of inspiration, but the muses had turned their faces from him and his sketchbooks were filled with half-formed pictures. Perhaps he had been cursed by some hidden malevolence, leaving him destined never to finish them. Sometimes they became flesh and slipped into his nightmares. A woman that had no face, a city never finished, and a man that was not whole. These nightmares had intensified now he had entered the final year of his twenties last month. Twenty-nine. Another decade near completed without him making his mark on the world.

'If you think any harder, your brain will catch fire,' came a familiar voice.

Forster was lifted from his musings to find his flatmate, Marvin, standing beside him. 'Do you ever feel dissatisfied with your life?' Forster asked.

Marvin regarded him through murky blue eyes, the tip of his long nose turning a delicate pink as he exhaled a plume of frozen air. 'What is it now? Penning the next great novel? Becoming a chef? Or—' Marvin pinched a roast chestnut from the paper, twirling it in his fingers as if searching for inspiration. His gaze alighted on the river with a lick of mischief. 'Or running away on a boat?'

'Nothing of the sort,' Forster lied, filling his mouth with another butter-soft chestnut that tasted like Christmas. He ignored the sudden whisper of temptation that echoed Marvin's words, picturing himself painting with ingredients and writing recipes like poems. 'I just seem to be suffering from a lack of inspiration lately, that's all.'

Marvin's sigh was deep, filled with the same bone-ache of tiredness Forster felt. 'You and me both, old chap. Arthur dismissed every idea I proposed to him today. I need something brilliant to cover, something that will make him wish he hadn't overlooked me. But every idea that comes to me, someone else has already thought of, written it better, had a closer source. I'm tired of chasing after scraps.'

Forster commiserated with him. The two men had first made each other's acquaintance when Forster had relocated to London from his native Northampton and was in search of decent rooms with a flatmate that might stretch his stipend enough to live comfortably while he decided what he wished to do with his life. When he was younger, his dreams had been stuffed with a hundred possibilities, from wearing freshly starched uniforms with polished boots and marching into war fearlessly, to living amongst bohemians in Paris, painting scenes that would hang in gallery walls, to buying a grand manor and filling it with family who would smile each time he walked into a room. Now he had reached the final years of his twenties with a fresh sense of horror of what war truly entailed, though he had not been permitted to fight, and dozens of abandoned pastimes. With Forster being estranged from his flesh and blood relatives, Marvin was the closest thing to family he had. An old friend from Forster's schooldays had made the necessary introductions between the pair last January. Almost two years ago, now. Marvin shared Forster's deep-seated desire to make a name for himself and it hadn't taken long for the would-be reporter and aspiring artist to strike up a firm friendship.

Now, as per their evening custom, the pair wandered down Embankment together. A thick fog had descended along the river and was slithering through the streets, winding around streetlamps and blotting out their flicker.

'How frightfully gothic.' Marvin pulled his thick woollen collar up, shivering under his pork pie hat that he fancied made him look like Buster Keaton, a regular man about town.

The Houses of Parliament loomed before them, imposing in their perpendicular Gothic style and decaying stonework. The pair were careful to maintain a little distance, lest another large stone crashed down from its walls, like one had a couple of years earlier from Victoria Tower. When Forster glanced up at the illuminated clock face, something white whispered past his ear. Too small and soft and light to be stone, he exclaimed, 'Why, it's snowing.'

Yet, like so many other times this year, Forster was wrong.

He took his hat off and squinted through the fog. Hundreds of paper twists were twirling through the air. Each one elegant as a swan. 'They're scrolls,' he realised aloud. 'Tied with ribbon.'

'Well, don't just stand there staring at them . . . catch one.' Marvin held onto his hat and attempted to jump and take one but they fluttered away into the night, much to his frustration.

Forster laughed, reaching up and grasping one with very little effort. Marvin scowled, and gestured impatiently for him to read the contents. But Forster enjoyed curating little pockets of contentment within his days. He took his time untying the black ribbon, noting the softness of the velvet, before unrolling the parchment. The paper was thick, luxurious, his interest piqued. He read its contents aloud:

Second star to the right and straight on 'til morning.

'How curious,' he murmured to himself. 'I wonder if they all bear the same quote.' He began hunting down scrolls and untying them faster, ceasing when he'd read another four. They were all of a likeness. 'What can this mean?' he asked, turning to his flatmate. 'Is it an advertisement for the play? Or novel? It's been some time since I read *Peter Pan* . . . ' he trailed off.

Marvin was staring at a scroll, deep in thought and uncharacteristically silent. 'Oh, I know *exactly* what this means.'

Chapter Two

'I told you this would be good, old chap,' Marvin crowed like the Lost Boy he was costumed as. Passing through the doors of the manor house, they were at once swept along in the tidal path of the crowd.

Forster craned his neck to take in the vaulted ceilings, where aerial artists glittered and dazzled in five-pointed star costumes, dancing high above. Now and then, one swung across a trapeze like a shooting star. 'I still don't understand how you found this. The scrolls didn't have an address nor any other clue on them.'

Marvin leant closer. 'Two years ago, I heard rumours of a party in a mysterious manor on a cliff. That the invitations had been painted onto shells that were discovered floating in all the fountains in London. They simply said, "Come to the Sea Queen's Ball" but those were accompanied by an address. To this very manor.'

Forster was fascinated. 'And people came?'

'There were so many in attendance that last November, when the clue was stamped onto paper bags filled with gingerbread, given out from carts on Regent Street, there was no accompanying address. That was the first party I attended. Now, everybody who's anybody will be seen here tonight.' Marvin paused as a waiter painted in olive-green with a crocodile mask protruding from his face offered them a tray of cocktails. Marvin took two with a nod of thanks, presenting Forster with one of them. He accepted it, frowning. 'Where was I when you came last year then?'

Marvin hesitated, and in a low whisper explained. 'It was during all that business with your family.'

'Ah.' That familiar pain and regret surged up Forster's throat, a visceral reaction he suffered each time that particular memory resurfaced. Diverting himself, Forster sipped from his glass. A palm leaf was secured around it with gold thread and a scrap of parchment dangling from the stem proclaimed that the golden confection was 'fairy dust'. 'But we only found the clue earlier this evening. How did everyone here learn this event is taking place tonight?' As he raked his gaze through the crowds, he saw few faces he recognised despite Marvin having dragged him along to as many of the fashionable restaurants and clubs in London as he could wrangle an invitation to in the name of his career. *The City Star* was an up-and-coming tabloid that hungered to make a name for itself. As did half of London, it seemed. The war was over and fortunes were to be made. And celebrations wanted to dazzle. Perhaps if they shone bright enough, hard enough, they'd drown the shadowed trenches of their collective memory in light.

'Whoever stumbles upon one of the clues ensures that the relevant people are told. Word spreads fast.'

'Indeed,' Forster commented, the crowds pressing tighter against them as people grew impatient to gain entry. 'And who is responsible for these parties?'

One of Marvin's shoulders rose in a half-hearted shrug, his attention already wandering onto a cluster of fairies nearby, their wings shimmering as an arctic breeze rippled through the hall. 'Nobody knows. I heard that the first few parties were smaller gatherings that started sometime during the war but you know what it's like, half the people claim one thing, others spin another story altogether. The whole affair is bound up in too much rumour to unravel. Anyhow, it's high time you lose that serious countenance you've been sporting lately. Lighten up. Drink, dance, live. Tonight's a night in a million, Forster.' Marvin held his arms up high, spreading them with a battle cry as they entered the ballroom.

The crowds parted and Forster set eyes on the beating heart of the party. A large recreation of the *Jolly Roger* pirate ship sat in a champagne lagoon, drums beat wildly, jungle ferns clustered around the edges of the ballroom, hiding little huts where people congregated, and more stars swung across the ceiling. The sight rendered him speechless for a moment. In the space of a single, solitary night, Forster had been plucked from unrelenting boredom and dropped into a world that fizzed with magic. His heart beat harder, sending electricity coursing through his veins. He had been sleepwalking through his own life, a life that was a canvas devoid of colour, and at last, he had awoken to a dazzling reality.

'A night in a million!' Marvin downed the rest of his fairy dust and reached out for a fresh glass in one swoop, passing Forster a second glass, too.

Forster pushed up his glasses and drank deeply. Tonight, he would be one of the Lost Boys. His patched, ragged clothes and mud-green face paint would not be a costume but a reflection of his inner wildness. The cocktail was velvet-smooth with a hint of sweetness and some tropical fruit he could not identify, and the party roared louder after his glass was emptied. The air was humid inside, as if a patch of tropical rainforest had been smuggled into the manor. Tiny lights flitted through palm trees and, for a moment, Forster wondered if they were fairies, sprinkling their magic dust over the party and dissolving his worries, his fears. Setting him free. He exchanged a grin with Marvin.

Nothing captured the senses like this. Forster might have worried that he was dreaming had he never felt this alive before. Something buried deep within him was rousing itself, cracking an eye open after a deep slumber.

A Captain Hook shouted with laughter as a group of Lost Girls bound him in a net-trap dangling from a nearby palm and stole his hook. Ramshackle wooden rafts glided across the champagne lagoon towards the pirate ship, the deck of which formed the dance floor. And women and men in shimmering pixie wings darted by. Faint snatches of their conversation trailed after them:

'Have you seen the host?'

'No, where is he?'

'I heard it was an obscenely rich heiress—'

'Really? Someone informed me that it was a foreign prince—'

Outside, snow was falling. It had not been snowing in London but here, a mere hour's drive away into the countryside, the world was held firmly in winter's grasp. A thick blanket of white was now coating the grounds. Here, he was forever young. Peter Pan in the flesh.

Forster continued to wander through the party, pausing to watch a fire-eater write with flames – *never grow up. I won't*, he thought to himself, seizing another cocktail. *I shall live in this moment for an eternity, until the world ceases to bleed time and—*

A pixie with wings dipped in moonlight thrust a parchment into his hands. 'Good luck,' she said, and winked at him.

It was a tea-stained pirate map with rugged edges. And *x* marked the spot. Forster let out a delighted laugh and began to follow it. He was soon joined in his quest by a fellow Lost Girl, whose warm brown face and honeyed eyes disguised a fierce competitive streak. They chased one another through the debauchery as the hour grew later and the fairy dust cocktails worked their magic, until Forster took a stumbling running jump onto one of the wooden rafts. It bobbed on the champagne lagoon, threatening to throw him off but he clung tight. The revellers on the neighbouring rafts cheered, dipping their emptied glasses into the fizzing lagoon to replenish them.

'That was terribly ungallant of you.' The Lost Girl laughed from the lagoon shore.

When Forster leant forward on his knees, he noticed a square at the centre of the raft was outlined. It was a trapdoor. With an exclamation, he opened it. 'I do apologise,' he called back, reaching into the little cubby hole. 'But it seems that I was struck by gold fever.' He held up the golden ingots he'd found.

The Lost Girl leapt into the champagne lagoon and waded over. Further investigations revealed that the ingots concealed thick dark chocolate beneath their golden trappings. A group of pixies abandoned another raft to swim in the lagoon, and, with a sound like an errant cannon firing, a firework shot up. It was joined by a second, then a third, until the ballroom turned incandescent and for a heartbeat, Forster quite believed he had fallen inside a magic potion.

As a grandfather clock chimed ever later, Forster drank and danced and danced and drank into the early hours. Spinning down from the ceiling in a costume that glittered brighter than the sun he glimpsed a fallen star, landing on the helm of the *Jolly Roger* as fireworks exploded behind her.

That was the last thing he remembered from the evening's revelries.

✳ ✳ ✳

Champagne flowed in lagoons, Peter Pans and Wendy Darlings clattered across the deck of the Jolly Roger, *and Lost Girls in fur-lined capes brushed up against the secrets of the night. My manor was haunted with memories of youth and stolen kisses, a heart-shattering dream of an affair. For one brief spell of a night, the world lay before our feet, enchanting and hope-bright, sparkling with possibility.*

And who was I?

I was a woman strung together with glitter and wishes. A midnight apparition, cast in the coldest winters. I would not be here tomorrow. But tonight I would drink champagne until my veins ran in golden, bubbling streams. I would dance until the ice in my heart melted. Kiss until my lips bruised. And I would live until it hurt.

Chapter Three

Four weeks later and Christmas had settled over London like a festive cape. The streets sparkled with strings of electric lights and each pocket of the city hummed with cheer. Wagons of evergreen trees were trundled into Covent Garden for sale, great sacks of Christmas mail arrived at Paddington station, and parents queued outside Gamages Department Store in Holborn for its Christmas Bazaar, to purchase toys and games that their little ones had wished for.

'Where are we heading again?' Forster rubbed a hand over his neck, easing the corkscrew of muscles that had tightened as he'd spent another day confronting a blank page, dreaming of fallen stars and a face that had shimmered in and out of his dreams like a mirage.

Marvin lit a Turkish cigarette. Its pack had been scented with Habanita, sweet and smoky with a bite of earthiness, as if they were standing in a souk in Morocco, admiring leather slippers and sunset-spices instead of strolling downstairs, into the underbelly of the city. Here, the air was hot and stale and alive with the rumbles of distant trains, hurtling through their warren of tunnels. With a start, Forster realised Marvin had been speaking for some time. 'You saw the hold that party had on people last month,' Marvin was saying. 'People are drawn to excitement like that—' he pointed with his cigarette '—and do you know why?'

'Why?' Forster wondered.

'Because they're as much interested in *who* might be attending as the event itself. Think about it, everyone's shedding their inhibitions, spilling their souls over cocktails. All those dark little secrets coming out to play. It's becoming more and more apparent that people are hungering for details of these events . . . no, for the details of the *people* that attend these events. I suppose it's only natural; after all, that's why the boxes in theatres face the audience rather than the stage.'

'I suppose they're like the gods of modern society.' Forster considered if that could be a potent painting before dismissing the notion. 'So, what are you suggesting? Becoming a well-placed confidant to the rich and famous? That's bold, even for you, and would evaporate the instant you wrote about them in the paper. Besides, I thought you were more interested in covering politics? Why this sudden sidestep?'

A train screeched to a halt and they boarded, leaning closer together to continue their conversation.

Marvin's tone turned to exasperation. 'The paper seems to be moving away from its political roots. The way it's headed, I'd be better served becoming a society columnist while I establish my name. I'll garner morsels of gossip from well-placed sources and attend fashionable society events to write them up. It'll be a mutually beneficial arrangement, I'll choose those that crave the spotlight, until I can work my way up enough to write what I truly care about.'

Forster nodded. 'That sounds like an agreeable solution to me.' Although he was glad Marvin had a clear path, he couldn't help but be envious of his sense of purpose and certainty. The party had stirred something deep within Forster and he had hoped it would mark a shift in direction for him. Inspiration. The first page of a new story. Alas, he had been naive. Since leaving the party, his life had been reduced to its monochrome palette and not a single of his canvasses bore a streak of the wild, bright colour he longed to saturate his life with. 'Then tonight's mission has a purpose to serve?'

'Mary Pickford and Douglas Fairbanks almost caused a riot amongst their fans when they were spotted in the city last week,' Marvin whispered excitedly. 'I happen to have it on good authority that the couple plans to make an appearance at Rector's Club tonight.'

They disembarked at Tottenham Court Road, where Rose was leaning against a lamppost, awaiting them. The pair had first made the acquaintance of the self-proclaimed society beauty at a charity fundraiser in Claridge's ballroom that the paper had sent Marvin to cover last year. Rose Wright was charmingly fun and always keen for a night out. She surveyed them both with wide amber eyes, her chocolate-coloured hair fashionably pinned up. Marvin's gaze dipped to take in her robe de style dress in a shade of sultry indigo that Forster longed to bottle.

Rose gave them a pretty smile. 'I'm glad you like it,' she said as she spun around, giving the ballgown skirt of her dress enough shape that a strong gust might have lifted her into the air and up above the rooftops of London. 'I cabled for it from Paris and it arrived today, can you believe; such perfect timing.' Her smile widened and she held out both of her arms. Forster and Marvin took one arm each and escorted her inside the nightclub.

They claimed a little table with a starched white tablecloth, tucked into a corner at the back. The band was raucous and brassy – jazz, Forster suddenly realised. It had recently arrived in London's night-clubs from the sultry American South, by way of the speakeasies of New York and Chicago. He craned his neck to watch them play but their table was at a disadvantaged position. 'All the better to observe,' Marvin informed them with a sly twinkle. 'People always look forwards; they never suppose that someone might be watching them from behind.'

'How positively thrilling, darling, it's like we're secret agents.' Rose giggled and adjusted her hair. 'Shall we order some drinks?'

Marvin lurched to his feet. 'I'll fetch them. What would you like?'

Forster hid a smile. Marvin's admiring glances at Rose were becoming more transparent this winter and he could not decide if Rose was simply oblivious to them or playing coy.

Two rounds of gin cobblers later and they were out of their seats and dancing. But for Forster, it held none of the crackle of electricity that the night of the party had brought him. He returned to their table, sinking deeper into melancholia. Soon it would be Christmas. Another one to spend in Marvin's company since matters with his own family had come to a head the previous year. Estranged. The process in which your closest kin became a stranger to you. And then there were the other, worse thoughts. The ones that once dwelled on, filled him with pain until he near suffocated.

He was lost in his own life.

His maudlin thoughts were interrupted by Marvin pushing another cocktail into his hand. 'Forget them——' he leant closer over the table, speaking over the swelling jazz '——you're worth a hundred of them and if they can't see you for who you are, then more fool them. You deserve better.'

Forster's throat filled. 'Thank you.' He took a long drink then gestured with his glass at the dance floor, where Rose was tossing her hair and shimmying. 'Have you set eyes on the famous couple yet?'

'No. It seems my source was incorrect. Or maybe they had a change of plans. But it's of no consequence; sooner or later I'll dig up something to write about.'

Forster nodded, his eyes glazing over. Perhaps he should have stayed home, painting festive scenes of London he could sell on the streets. Of cosy Georgian houses with wreaths on their red-painted doors, windows beaming light onto passers-by. Of children pressing their hands and noses against toyshops to better see inside, and chubby robins perched in frosted trees. Yet deep down, in that dark place where the only sound was the beating of his heart, Forster knew he would have done nothing of the sort. No, he would have stayed home and hurried to sleep so that he might dream of that night again. Of glittering stars and champagne lagoons and the wild beat of the drums. Of a night where it did not matter that he was a Lost Boy, where his directionless amblings were celebrated and occasionally rewarded with a treasure map to follow. Of a night touched with magic that had lingered on, seeping into his waking thoughts until he was haunted.

For perhaps in one of those dreams, he would remember her face.

PART TWO

1923–1924

'But magic must hurry on, and the lovers remain . . .'
—F. SCOTT FITZGERALD, *The Beautiful and Damned*

Chapter Four

Rose tapped her cigarette holder out of the window at the same time as she wrenched the wheel to one side, veering around a thin, curved lane.

'Steady on, woman.' Marvin held onto his fedora as he was flung across the backseat. Forster, sitting beside Rose at the front, laughed.

Rose winked at Marvin in the mirror. 'Sorry, fellows, I drive like I drink.'

Forster was glad to escape London. Autumn had arrived, gilding the world overnight. Here, in the countryside, the trees bloomed in gold and the air tasted like wild berries. Forster gulped down deep breaths of it, closing his eyes as the breeze streamed through his smoothed-back curls. It was perhaps too chilly to drive with the top of Rose's Model T down but the glorious crisp apple of a day had proved too irresistible not to. A steamer trunk of necessities for Forster's upcoming birthday celebrations was strapped to the back of the motor. Alongside a picnic basket from Fortnum & Mason that Rose had forbidden them to peek inside. Marvin had sat beside it on the pretence of guarding it but now and then the scent of a French boulangerie crept out, and Forster harboured suspicions that Marvin was sneaking a bite.

A line of trees appeared. A thick wall of forest that Rose slowed to enter. Painted with autumn's fiery palette, the leaves were agleam in burnt orange, saffron yellow, and russet red. The air turned thicker, mossier. Time seemed to slow and if it wasn't for the motor chuntering along the dirt road, seeking to enter the forest's secret beating heart, Forster would have sworn they had slipped through some crack in time. Fallen into an ancient world. The canopy grew thicker, ferns brushing against the wheels, the day darkening. The breeze showed its teeth and Forster shivered, pulling his woollen jacket tighter around himself to ward off its nips. 'Where are we again?' he asked. Rose beamed at him and he winced as she looked away from the road. 'Watch out for that fallen trunk,' he added in a hurry.

Rose was unaffected as ever and swerved violently. 'Dreadfully macabre, isn't it? Just wait until you see it for the first time. We should be there any minute now— Ah. There it is.'

At the end of a sweeping driveway stood the old hunting lodge that belonged to the Wright family.

Marvin leant forwards from the back, slinging an arm over the top of Forster's seat as both men took in the estate. Eighteenth-century redbrick with three ogee gables that rose from the surrounding trees like turrets from a fairy-tale castle. The forest had crept closer over the centuries and now seemed on the verge of gobbling up the lodge altogether; thick roots wandered over the cracked courtyard and branches tapped against windowpanes.

'It's the perfect spot for our celebratory weekend,' Rose declared. 'We shall have the entire place to ourselves and it's as deliciously melancholy as our own dear Forster.' She blew him a kiss and Marvin snorted.

'Let's take a look inside.' Forster jumped out, heaving down the steamer trunk, leaving Marvin to tug the roof back over the Ford and carry the picnic hamper.

Inside, the lodge was smaller than Forster had been expecting, and colder, as if a spirit was lurking within the crumbling stone walls. Rose set about lighting candles as Forster wandered about, admiring the dark-green painted walls and old-fashioned framed pictures. 'It's filled with character,' he told Rose, wondering if he ought to have brought his sketchbook. He had so seldom finished a piece this year that his sketchbook was becoming a relic, haunting him from his bedside table with its untouched pages as Forster frittered the days away until he had suddenly realised the year was near over. And tomorrow morning, when he awoke, he would be thirty. 'Thirty, with nothing to show for it,' he had complained to Marvin only last week. That had been the catalyst for his and Rose's scheming. Forster had let them whisper their plans together, hoping that he'd at least get a bottle of decent champagne out of it. He hadn't expected the hunting lodge and ensuing excitement from the pair of them, and for the first time this year, his interest stirred. Good friends were like starlight on the blackest nights, filling his heart with gratitude.

'You haven't seen the best part yet,' Rose announced when Marvin joined them. She flitted away, her crimson ribbon sash trailing along a dim corridor and up several winding staircases, their steps worn smooth with age. Up to the highest point, where the lodge fell away to ruins and suddenly Forster was standing at the top of the forest, the sky above him molten fire. A glorious autumnal sunset. 'Surprise!' Rose clapped her hands together. 'We shall dine up here and toast the last night of your twenties.'

In a flight of fancy, they dressed in warm pyjamas and top hats before sitting down on a carpet to eat thick slices of bread with equally thick slices of salted butter, sharp aged cheddar and creamy Somerset brie, tomatoes with herbed stuffing followed by a large golden apple tart with lashings of clotted cream. They washed it all down with bottles of vintage champagne until the sky was black.

Forster lay back, nursing his glass as he traced the constellations, each star jewel-bright from their perch in the treetops.

'I wish I could dance among the stars.' Rose's sigh was affected; she often took pains to represent herself as romantic, frivolous yet wise, and Forster adored her for it. Her personality was as cultivated as the aesthetics of his unfinished pieces but beneath it all beat the kindest, truest heart he'd ever encountered.

Marvin offered a hand but she flapped it away. 'Oh no, darling, I've eaten far too much to prance about a rooftop. What if I fell to my death?'

'Then you will have to haunt me forever lest I miss you too much.' Marvin spread his arms dramatically as Rose's eyes widened with delight and Forster almost choked on his champagne.

'Do you believe in those kinds of preternatural phenomena?' Forster asked. 'Spirits, I mean.' An image of his father's war grave rose, unbidden, before he banished it. He wondered if his mother had remembered it was his birthday tomorrow. If he would be in her thoughts. If he still held a place in her heart. He drank deeper into his glass, hoping the bubbles would erode the lump in his throat as he pictured her face, twisted with cruelty and grief as she had turned against him all those months ago. It had been a slow hardening, culminating in a cruel blow he still had not recovered from. Perhaps he never would. Her words had injured the deepest, softest parts of himself, her betrayal seeping into his very soul. He set his glass down with a trembling hand, forcing himself to push those memories to the back of his mind and focus on what Rose was saying.

'My dear friend Letitia visited a medium last month and she was positively convinced she heard her late brother's voice speaking from the medium's mouth.' Rose sat up and poured herself another glass.

'Charlatans, the lot of them.' Marvin swept the champagne away from Rose to refill his own glass and top up Forster's.

Rose sipped thoughtfully. 'I'm not so certain, Marvin. She hadn't told this woman one jot of information about poor David; how would the medium have known to start speaking in a west country accent?'

'Perhaps she heard Letitia speak and hazarded a guess,' Marvin said wryly.

Forster looked back to the stars. 'Sometimes I feel like there has to be more.' He was tired of waiting for something to happen, of not being where he'd always assumed he would be by this point.

'Feeling morose about the big birthday, old chap?' Marvin nudged him. 'It's not as bad as you think, just look at me, thirty-two and as handsome as ever!'

Rose laughed and Forster smiled. Marvin and Rose were the family he had chosen, the family that had insisted on celebrating this milestone and supported him fiercely, no matter which way the wind blew his thoughts.

On the turn of midnight, Rose produced a lavish cake. Chocolate cream with three candles that flickered like tiny fireworks. When Forster blew them out, she and Marvin cheered. 'Now make a wish, darling,' she instructed.

Forster watched the smoke curl into the velvet night. The champagne was fizzing through his veins, making him float through the night as if he were on the back of one of the moths that flitted by, with feather-light wings and not a care in the world. It was October and he'd spent nearly an entire year dreaming of a face he couldn't quite remember, from a single night that had happened eleven months ago that he couldn't let go of. And he did not know why.

Deep in a forest, under a star-swollen witching hour, Forster turned thirty, wondering if he'd been bespelled. He closed his eyes and thought of the wish he'd just made – to see that face again.

Chapter Five

November was a strange month. As the anniversary of the party grew near then passed, Forster became increasingly restless. Each day, at the point when the afternoon yawned and tipped into evening and the streetlamps were lit, he ventured out into the streets of London for a walk. To begin with, Marvin had found it a fine game, keen to find the first invitation of the year, to be the ones who would spread the word, who would arrive first. As the third week of November drizzled by, then the fourth, he soon begged off their customary walk as the Society calendar of events began to request his attendance more often.

But Forster continued to wander the canals and fountains, the streets and parks. Repeating the stories he'd heard of previous invitations like an old legend. One that, if he only repeated enough, would come true. Shells floating along fountains, paper bags sold from gingerbread carts, and the scrolls falling from Big Ben which they had stumbled across themselves. Perhaps there were even earlier clues, for smaller affairs that he had not yet heard of. Each evening he did not give up his pursuit until the darkness grew so thick you could cut it with a knife and it was evident no invitation would appear. Then, he would hurry home, often around the same time as Marvin had returned from some party or club opening, to see Marvin's shake of his head. *No. No news tonight.*

'So, it's not an annual event then,' Forster had said on the final day of the month. 'It doesn't mark November in any way.'

'No,' Marvin had replied, frowning at their calendar. 'It doesn't seem that way.'

November exited much as it had arrived; with rain that trickled down their windowpanes, the sky an unending sea of grey.

But on the first of December, the world froze over.

Frost crunched underfoot like sugar, painting beautiful patterns on leaves and grass, and feathering everyone's breath. It was a cut-glass day. Sharp and clear. And though it was a Saturday, both Rose and Marvin were free to accompany Forster on his daily wandering that eve. They were ambling around St James's Park Lake, searching for clues and members of the resident colony of pelicans as it grew dark. The trees, which had been looking rather bare and spindly of late, were iced in white, and the old royal park seemed to be holding its breath, awaiting the first snowfall.

'If we walk any further, I'm going to need sustenance,' Rose was complaining when Forster noticed a little kiosk selling pink champagne, tucked beneath a fig tree.

'Allow me.' Marvin jogged over to buy one for Rose as she and Forster continued their slow stroll along the perimeter of the lake.

'Are you ever going to put him out of his misery?' Forster's glance at Rose was replete with meaning.

Rose plucked at the fur cuffs on her coat. Sapphire-blue, it was the latest fashion with a side wrap and dropped, belted waist. Falling to her calves, it revealed her laced boots and was altogether fetching with her peach complexion and amber eyes. It had not escaped Forster's notice that Marvin's gaze had lingered on her several times this evening already.

Rose turned coy. 'Whatever are you referring to?'

'Don't play games, Rose, not with him.' Forster turned to her, lowering his voice. 'He's in serious danger of losing his heart to you.'

She softened. 'I know.'

Forster looked at her, at her pinkened cheeks, her gaze that evaded his, her fidgeting fingers, and could not tell in which direction her feelings lay. Before their confidence might deepen, it began to snow.

'Oh,' Rose said softly as she and Forster looked to the skies. As they had walked, it had clouded over, and endless flurries of snow were descending upon them. Forster grinned at Rose, something about snow always made him feel like he was seven years old again, waking up on Christmas morning and rushing to peer out the window.

Marvin returned with three saucers. 'They were giving them out for free.' He shrugged, handing one to Rose.

Rose's answering smile was tender, sweet, and Marvin's grin widened to see it. Forster's black leather gloves squeaked against the glass as he drank his, granting the pair a little privacy by turning and leaning against a lamppost to watch the water darken like wet silk. Night fell earlier day by day as they plummeted towards the winter solstice.

'Oh.' Rose suddenly soured. 'I think this is the temperance movement at work again.' She showed the men the bottom of her glass. There was a tiny masquerade mask there and on it, a single word was engraved. *Damned.*

Marvin launched into a diatribe against the movement but Forster didn't hear a word of it. Something was tickling his heart, his soul flaring alive with hope and he just *knew.* Tossing his champagne into the lake, he looked for the mask at the bottom of his glass. And just like he knew it would be, there it was. His was inscribed with: *Beautiful.* Forster laughed and laughed and the other two stared at him with not a little concern. 'I shall go on shining as a brilliantly meaningless figure in a meaningless world,' he quoted, watching the knowledge dawn on Rose's face.

'*The Beautiful and Damned*,' she gasped with realisation.

Marvin squinted at his own glass. 'Whatever did they put in these?'

Rose laughed too then. 'You silly fool, we've happened upon this year's clue! Don't you ever read?' she teased.

Marvin swatted at her but she paid him no attention, absorbed in re-examining her glass. 'The mask must be a clue, too. I believe we're to conceal our identities. A masquerade party, what fun.'

But Forster was now gazing at the frosted night. At the first snowfall of the season. 'Marvin, it was snowing in Wuthercliffe when we found those scrolls falling from Big Ben last year.'

Marvin frowned in thought. 'Yes—'

'We were wrong!' Forster exclaimed. 'The parties were never at the same time each year, that's why it wasn't in November again. The invitations appear when the snow falls. The party marks the start of winter.' Now that he'd been struck by the realisation, Forster didn't know how he hadn't seen it before. Of course such a bewitching event would not follow the calendar but be beholden to the turn of the seasons and the wild magic of the first snowfall.

'How curious,' Marvin began. 'Perhaps they're intended as a diversion from the cold, dark nights setting in.'

'Let's not deliberate on all that now, we need to get ready,' Rose said, her patience melting away. She started marching back along the path they'd come from. 'This is going to be positively decadent and *I'll* be damned if we don't dress the part.'

Chapter Six

Just as he had wished for, Forster entered the doors of the manor house once more. Tonight, it was dripping with strings of electric lights and filled with jazz, the night rich with the promise of a bustling dance floor and brassy music.

Masks spilled out of tall vases set along the sides of the hall, a couturier's delight in silks and satins, glittering with sequins and bursting with colour. A thousand tales yet to be told. Thanks to Rose, their trio had arrived already masked. Beside him, Marvin's murky blue eyes peered out of his russet fox mask, his whiskered mouth twitching as he plucked a saucer of champagne from a passing waiter's tray. It gleamed and bubbled, as golden as the waiter's mask. Rose had favoured her namesake, her face blooming in delicate pink petals. Forster waved off her offer of champagne in favour of retaining a clear head this year. Not only did he wish to sketch some of the finer details before they eluded him in the morning – the moon-shine of pearls gracing a slender neck, snow whispering past the leaded windows, lights that twinkled like a thousand stars – he wanted to find *her*. The face that had been resigned to his dreams. Forster frowned beneath his midnight satin mask. He adjusted its fit around his round, black-rimmed glasses to disguise the worry he wore on his face. Everyone was masked. It dawned on him that he might not remember her face if it was hidden from view. His heart matched the erratic beat of the jazz as all of his wishing and wondering fell away. Leaving only the truth: she might not be here tonight.

'Are you feeling quite well, darling?' Rose laid a concerned hand on his arm.

Forster nodded, forcing a smile as they were granted access to the ballroom. Here, the masquerade ball was in full swing. Jesters danced the foxtrot with cats, a trio of butterflies flitted by in turquoise and violet chiffon beaded dresses, their arms bare, silk shawls slipping down their shoulders as they moved to the rhythm of that sultry jazz. One would never have known that outside, snow painted the world white.

'Oh, how marvellous. Look.' Rose's hand tightened on Forster's arm as she glanced up. Tonight, the vaulted ceiling played host to a beautiful garden. Manicured hedges, flowering bushes, and ornamental trees flourished above them. Performers in angel wings perched on branches, pouring down champagne as people flocked to catch the sparkling drops in their glasses and mouths below.

With a theatrical flourish, an angel suddenly plummeted from his branch. Rose gasped and Forster's heart stuttered. Before the angel hit the marble, he spread his wings, revealing the wires that slowed his fall until he was standing in the ballroom. Those same wires ripped the wings from his back as the angel smiled wickedly at the guests congregating around him, slipped on a pair of horns, and started to dance. Forster snorted with amusement.

'I say let's join him.' Marvin downed his champagne in one and backed into a gaggle of dancing girls, their ostrich feather headdresses prancing in tune to the music. 'Come, Rose, let's dance.'

Rose's laugh fluttered out of her. She followed him, blowing a kiss to Forster. 'Don't forget to have some fun,' she called out as Marvin ushered her into the fray. They were swept from sight by a melee of feathers belonging to masked revellers and towers of champagne saucers that flowed like fountains.

Before Forster could remove himself from the scene, silken-gloved fingers ensnared his arm. 'Dance with me.' The golden-haired flapper standing before him lifted a perfectly plucked eyebrow above her mask. A challenge.

Forster ruminated on the sketchpad tucked in his jacket pocket. Both he and Marvin had attended this party with the sole purpose of stealing its secrets. While Marvin was determined to hunt down a juicy scoop, Forster craved something deeper, truer. He longed to capture its essence, distil the night's magic into graphite. This night could be the key to unlocking his imagination. But the flapper took his silence as acquiescence, leading him to the centre of the crowd, where dancers moved as one to the jazz flooding their veins like honey. His feet moved before his mind, caught up in the foxtrot. The golden-haired flapper grinned at him as they danced, her filigreed lace mask wound around hazel eyes, her mouth a bright slash of scarlet. She wore a pair of gossamer wings in dusky lavender that fluttered like petals. As he bent to ask her name, he caught a glimpse of Marvin's russet-brown mask, his crude gesture of approval. It twisted something inside his stomach, spiked his thoughts with guilt. For deep within Forster's chest beat the heart of a romantic. 'Do excuse me,' he demurred, taking his leave. He filtered across the ballroom, silently searching for *her*. Tonight he would allow nothing to distract him from his quest.

Past the women dancing inside oversized champagne saucers, past a fountain of melted chocolate that people were dipping hothouse strawberries into and feeding each other, he heard the whispers:

'I hear she's the lost Russian Grand Duchess.' One flapper sighed.

'No, she's an heiress that was set to marry one winter before her love tragically perished,' another said, running her fingers dreamily through her pearls.

'You're both wrong,' a third, dressed in a ripple of emerald silk, announced. 'Someone informed me that she was merely hired to perform a role, that the entire event is a charade.'

Forster ignored them and kept walking. Yet still, the gossip wound through the party, a ribbon that kept unravelling.

'Well, I heard that the previous owners of this manor died, leaving it to be inherited by their second cousin, who never visits though they pay for a custodian – perhaps that's who your mysterious ballerina is,' a woman with a tarnished halo declared.

'Who, the second cousin or the custodian?' her partner asked and the pair dissolved into giggles.

Forster lifted his eyes in silent exasperation as he exited the ballroom. And there, he saw them. A pair of blue-grey eyes, watching him from across the great hall. Framed by a white mask, their gaze was deep as an ocean, vast and ancient. For a moment, he stared back, losing himself within them. Then he blinked and like a distant memory, they vanished. But he remembered them. In a flash, he was standing here one year earlier, watching as a fallen star spun to earth, landing on the deck of the *Jolly Roger* in ballet slippers. Those blue-grey eyes regarding him with amusement before she began to dance and the night slipped away from him.

He cut a path through the hall, weaving amongst couples in amorous exchanges, lovers' words coated with chocolate and the anonymity of the night. The jazz rhythms quickened, growing more seductive, urging Forster on. But as he battled the tide, more and more dancers crowded in, pushing him back. Just as he was about to wrench his mask from his face, overwhelmed with frustration, the ballroom was cast into shadow.

The garden was being lowered from above. Great emerald hedges were being guided into position. A saxophone rasped as the jazz band rearranged themselves, drawing in tighter on their stage, though they did not cease their playing. Dancers swept out of the way, revealing that the marble flooring bore several markings – it was a maze, Forster realised, as the verdant hedges suddenly surrounded him, meeting the marble with a dull thud.

The jazz was hushed by thick greenery. Forster looked up, gauging his position by the ceiling. Parts of the garden remained up there, the inverse of the maze, and his brain whirled, calculating his escape.

This year, he would not lose her again.

Chapter Seven

Forster was weary. It had taken longer than he'd imagined to exit the maze. Its lush corners harboured a myriad of secrets; devils that presented him with riddles he must solve if he wished to pass; dead ends and tunnels that he had crawled through; the giant champagne saucers that now presented obstacles to clamber past as the dancers inside fluttered their feathers and blew kisses.

He was craving a respite.

Which was why he was stealing up the staircase.

Whispering couples crept past him, their masks askew, drawn to vacant rooms and shadowed corners. Downstairs, the air was hot with jazz, punctured by shrieks from those lost in the maze. As Forster made his bid for escape, it transpired that the sweeping staircase led to a balcony which surveyed both the hall and ballroom, overlooking the entire party and the maze. The perfect viewpoint.

On the far side of the ballroom, a wall of French panelled doors were flung open, the manor spilling its secrets into the velveteen night. Snowflakes whirled inside. They danced over the maze, past the angels sitting in the ceiling garden, who were awaiting their turn to join the damned below, and settled onto the balcony. Forster reached out and caught one on his jacket sleeve. It settled there, its intricate pattern melting away as he considered which paints he'd blend to conjure it back to life. Creamy ivory and Chantilly lace and pale dove feather-grey. All too soon, it vanished.

'Beautiful, aren't they?' a teasing voice sounded from behind. Forster turned. 'They say that each one is utterly unique.' The woman to whom the blue-grey eyes belonged was reclining on a velvet chaise longue at the far back of the balcony, which retreated into a recess Forster had missed. His breath caught in his throat at the sight of her. She wore a midnight-blue gown embroidered with silver crystals, each a spark of stolen moonlight, and a pearl headpiece that, try as it might, could not quite contain the whisky-coloured curls that poured down to her shoulders. And those eyes. Framed by her white feathered mask, they called to mind a forest wreathed in mist, the luminescence of an evening sky after rain, a lake shrouded in mystery. Deep and compelling. For the first time in longer than he could recall, Forster's fingers itched. Forgetting the snowflake, he longed to immortalise her in paint and canvas. Suddenly, his thoughts bloomed in colour.

'I find the world changed when it snows. Sometimes I wonder if it's the closest thing to magic I shall ever experience.' The moment the words tumbled from Forster's mouth, he regretted them. It was her. He had been dwelling on how to find her amid such chaos before he'd stumbled upon her and now her sudden presence had bewitched him, confounded his tongue.

'Be careful what you wish for; not all magic is a delight,' she replied with a shiver. It was delicate yet for Foster, who could not tear his eyes from her, unmissable.

'Forgive me but you speak as if you had knowledge of the fact,' he said. She merely offered him a smile, deepening his intrigue.

'Are you enjoying the event tonight?' she asked.

'I'm enjoying it a great deal more now,' Forster confessed. She did not look away from him as she stood up and the air between them seemed to thin and heat and fizz. Her proximity was headier than a magnum of champagne and their gaze remained locked on each other. Was this prolonged moment having the same effect upon her? He hardly dared dream it so. 'Funnily enough, so am I,' she murmured and his stomach tightened. Yet before Forster might amuse her with some witty anecdote or charming remark he had yet to think of, the grandfather clock in the hall chimed. 'I am certain we shall meet again,' she told him, her smile rich with meaning, which turned his mouth dry. She made past him to the staircase.

This broke the spell. 'Wait,' Forster called after her, rushing to the balcony. 'I don't even know your name.'

She glanced back at him, impish. 'Now that would be telling.'

His hands tightened on the balcony as he watched her descend the staircase, her back arched, fingers trailing on the polished handrail.

'Well, she looked like an interesting prospect.' Marvin's voice materialised from behind, sending Forster's heart lurching for the second time that evening.

'Must you appear like that? Where have you been?'

'Rose and I have been searching for you.'

Forster's gaze rested on the woman as she walked downstairs with unusual liquidity, her gown a river of silk. 'My apologies. Did you happen upon anything interesting tonight?'

'Only the event itself, which was far more diverting than anything else I could have uncovered.' Marvin jerked his head at the woman as she cleared the foot of the stairs and halted in the centre of the black-and-white checked marble hall. 'But tell me, who is *she*?'

'I don't have an inkling of an idea.' He sighed, unable to subdue his disappointment.

Marvin laughed. 'Well, she seems to have quite turned your

head. Tell me you at least managed to learn her name, her address, something?'

'Sorry to disappoint.' Forster leant over the banister, watching the woman's gleaming curls as she spun in a languorous circle, her arms caressing the air in a lover's embrace with the music that softened and slowed.

Marvin grasped Forster's arm. 'Look at the crowd.'

The revellers below had retreated, allowing a ring of space around the mysterious woman. She stretched a single leg behind, her spangled dress a midnight sky that rippled up her calves, revealing her matching ballet slippers. Embroidered silver feathers echoed her mask and, for a moment, Forster expected her to take flight.

'Who is she?' he murmured as she stepped up onto her toes, her arms fluttering up beside her head, raising those smoky eyes to where he stood. She pirouetted en pointe, holding his gaze. With each step she took, she wove her spell and he was powerless to look away. As the jazz quietened, a violinist stepped forward.

Beside him, Marvin inhaled sharply. 'Don't you remember? There was a ballerina at the party last year. She must be someone of note. Forster, I have to interview her.'

Forster paid him no heed. Witnessing this woman dance was like peering inside her soul; her face was taut with yearning, a surprising grief pooled in her eyes. As the lone musician continued to accompany her, she surrendered herself to the sweet strains of their single violin. She floated across the hall in tiny pitter-patter steps and elongated balances on one leg, her dress as silken as she, as if they had both been spun from moonlight. When the music grew, becoming a grander, greater force, she danced more fiercely, matching the allegro as it hit passionate crescendos. In the rising and falling notes, spinning and soaring, she lost herself, one twirl, one leap at a time, raw longing carved into her body, cast in her face.

In a shimmer of light, thousands of tiny silver stars started drifting down from the ceiling. They fell on the delighted guests like snow and collected in the ballerina's curls as she painted the night with beauty.

'Why — taste one! They're sugar-stars,' one reveller exclaimed. In a flurry, hands reached up to sample the confectionary floating down.

'How marvellous,' Marvin whispered, collecting them from his jacket. Yet Forster didn't move to dislodge the sugar-stars that clung to his hair. For nothing could match her and he was utterly enchanted. She danced how he wished he painted, with naked emotion and dark feeling. In a place where strength and vulnerability twined together and beauty and sadness met in a collision that threatened to shake the moon from the sky.

'Her performance is winding down, let's see if she'll agree to an interview.' Marvin pushed Forster towards the uppermost step, his expression edged with something hard. Hungry. Yet it was not for him that Forster ran down the stairs, taking them two at a time, eager to ensure the woman couldn't slip away again. Turning round in a facsimile of one of her pirouettes, he searched for her as the shift in music registered. Soft jazz was now filtering through from the ballroom maze, accompanied by sugared laughter and conversation as the revellers returned to their own frivolities.

The ballerina was nowhere to be seen.

Catching up with him, Marvin cursed. 'Tell me you saw where she went?' he demanded of the nearest person. Her shingled hair swung as she shook her head, inching away. He turned to question another as Forster caught a glimpse of midnight-blue silk sweeping out of the front doors. He ran outside.

The circular path held a cluster of motor cars and a couple of carriages. A woman shrieked as she ran through a statuesque fountain, the icy water rippling in blackcurrant hues, already reflecting the first hint of dawn. The frosted land resembled icing on a cake until it reached the clifftop, where the world seemed to end. Forster squinted but couldn't make out anyone promenading along that edge. A little further along, the road held a cacophony of guests departing in various inebriated states. There was nothing else, save for a deep thicket through which Forster glimpsed a distant lake, glowing with the last vestiges of starlight.

She had vanished like a whisper in the night.

* * *

Rumours clung to me like the silk of my dress, as numerous as the crystals sewn onto my bodice. That I was a lost princess. A Russian heiress. That my family had fled the war. Some claimed that I was an imposter, a charlatan. Others, that I was a spectral figure, from the pages of a Dickens novel, hosting sparkling affairs each year on the very date that would have marked my wedding day. Clearly the latter did not pay attention to when I hosted my parties.

Once, I had craved attention, longed to dance beneath bright spotlights, watched by hundreds. Now, I feel their eyes on me, seeking, searching, prying, and it suffocates me. Sometimes I fear I've set myself a trap. But then the snow falls and I cannot resist throwing another event. Party. The word is too little. They're a performance, a production. One that shines a thousand times brighter than any he could have hosted. My events shall be grander, vaster, more spectacular than his. For I refuse to be trapped in the cage of his legacy.

I walked out into a tumble of snowflakes. Stalked deeper into the frozen night, fleeing the revelry with half a smile. Many of these rumours I had seeded myself. These strangers' minds are so pliable, easy to lead in whatever direction I desire. The hunt for gossip eclipses truth, and so I feed them a fantasy. A tasty morsel to share and devour. And thus these rumours spread, becoming a little changed with each telling until I myself no longer recognise the seeds. But this is good, for they are nothing but a story. They are not me.

And nobody can be allowed to glimpse the monstrous reality lurking beneath the glitter, champagne, and stars.

Chapter Eight

'Come on, hurry up, Rose will wake up soon and wonder where we've gone,' Forster urged in a hushed tone.

'I'm just having a quick look,' Marvin whispered back, examining the bolted manor door. 'Besides, with the amount of champagne she drank tonight I don't think she'll be waking any time soon.'

Forster bounced on the balls of his feet, blowing into his hands, numb from the night's cold bite.

They'd returned to the manor, where the atmosphere had shattered like a glass bauble. Morning had arrived in a wash of bleak mist, casting a pall over the glitter and glamour. They had observed from Rose's motor as several vans and wagons had departed, overstuffed with all the props and décor they'd swiftly disassembled and removed from the manor. Marvin had attempted to speak with one of the fallen angels, who was smoking as he oversaw the packing of the hedges, but the angel had known nothing of note. Not long after, several burly men bolted the main doors and left in a van, the side of which was printed with: *Watchers Private Security Est. 1884.*

The manor was now deserted.

But Forster and Marvin had shared a curious glance, which had led to Rose yawning, 'I shall leave you to your usual capers, come and find me afterwards,' and promptly falling asleep, stretched out in the back.

Marvin resumed his examination of the padlock as Forster wandered further away, circumnavigating the manor. Something called to him, luring him inside the manor to peel back its secrets. There was a mystery at play here. He suddenly thought back on the rumours that had swirled through the night as thick as snow. Perhaps he had been wrong to dismiss them as idle gossip.

Mist hung around the walls of the manor, rendering the trees spectral figures. Sneaking tendrils found their way through Forster's shirt and jacket, a light-fingered thief, robbing him of warmth. The manor was Jacobean, an imposing pile that perched on a high bluff with honey-coloured stone that the elements had laid siege to over the years, and grand, mullioned windows. One of which had been left ajar. Forster examined it. The wood was warped, no longer capable of closing. Prising his fingers into the opening, he pulled. It refused to budge. The manor was holding onto its secrets. But Forster was determined. Bracing a foot against the stone, he pulled and pulled until it eventually succumbed to his efforts with a screeching whine of protest. Grinning, Forster gave a low whistle in Marvin's direction and climbed through. He emerged on the far side of the great hall.

It was impossible to comprehend that the manor had played host to a roaring, decadent affair mere hours earlier. He'd expected a carpet of crushed sugar-stars, a hundred faces staring up at him, all those masks discarded as their owners peeled back to their own identities at the end of the night. Instead, the floors had already been swept clean and the furniture covered. As if the party had been nothing but a beautiful dream. A fancy of imagination. Forster walked through the great hall and ran a hand over a generous mantel.

The manor's old bones appeared to have been refurbished during the late Georgian period and played host to delicate Palladian features and stucco work. The owner had been sympathetic to its Regency gildings, with walls painted in the shades of spring's first blush; dreamy blues, pale yellows, lavender blossom, and lashings of creamy white.

With a grunt, Marvin clambered through the window behind him. He straightened his jacket as they walked through the great hall together in silence, hawkishly observing their surroundings.

Ascending the staircase, they discovered the upper rooms had now been closed and, in the pale morning light, were thick with dust. Forster stepped out of the study where Marvin was looking around and into a drawing room. Doubt was pewter-grey, a dark, obscuring cloud. This had not seemed of such great consequence when they'd first sneaked back inside – getting up to their usual high jinks, what a lark! But within the manor, its walls were steeped in loneliness, and he wondered what could have happened to lend it this air of sadness.

The drawing room had once been a confection in pistachio-green, trimmed with gold. Now the chandelier was cobwebbed and when he pulled a sheet down, he discovered a bookcase shrouded in dust. It was a manor that time had forgotten. A relic from a Gothic novel that Austen's Catherine Morland might have devoured. When he glimpsed one of the titles, he smiled to himself. Plucked it from the shelf and blew the dust from it. A newspaper clipping fell from its pages. Forster picked it up. It was a local paper from the nearby small town, Wurthercliffe, dated 15 April 1912, with the headline:

UNSINKABLE SHIP HIT BY ICEBERG

An estimated 1,800 lives have been lost on the ill-fated vessel *Titanic*'s maiden voyage. Included in that number are Wurthercliffe's own Lord and Lady Lakely and their daughter, Odette Lakely.

A small photograph was printed at the bottom of the page of the young family, perhaps the final one before they had boarded the doomed ship. A deep crease marked it. Yet even through the black-and-white image, the girl's eyes retained their luminescence as she stared out from the paper, the manor house behind her parents the very same one Forster stood in now.

His heartbeat a moth-wing flutter, Forster stared at the girl who would grow up to become the ballerina that had eluded him tonight. He'd spent over a year dreaming of those eyes; he'd recognise them anywhere. *Odette.* 'So that's your name,' he murmured, thrilled to discover a detail about the woman at last. He shook himself; this was impossible. He had to learn who she had been. And why the paper proclaimed her dead. Unless a spectre had appeared to him. He laughed nervously, unsure what to believe, only knowing that Odette had breathed life into him and he had to see her again.

Footsteps echoed in the hall. Refolding the clipping, Forster returned it to its original resting place seconds before Marvin entered the drawing room.

'Found anything of interest?'

Forster shelved *Northanger Abbey*, his heart still beating with unusual ferocity. 'Nothing. Save for a proclivity for Gothic literature. Rather fitting, considering the circumstances,' he added wryly. He'd never lied to Marvin before and fretted that he wore the lie on his face like a signpost. But real or not, he did not think it fair to share this ballerina's secrets. He yearned to paint her, to learn why her dance had stormed with waves of longing, passion, and grief. Were they for her former life? Were these glittering parties held each year when winter seized the manor with ice, freezing its halls, allowing its ghosts to roam free?

As he followed Marvin back downstairs, his flatmate grumbling at having learnt nothing, Forster suffered a peculiar sensation: His fingers were itching for a pencil, his mind whirring with ideas that had flown into his head on light-silvered wings of inspiration. He wanted to create something with meaning. For the first time in years, he ached for a blank page.

Chapter Nine

An abandoned manor, a girl purported to be dead, and an annual party that was notorious for its dream-like world and debauchery. Together they formed a recipe for the most engrossing of mysteries. And Forster was intrigued.

His imagination had been ignited, the fires of his creativity stoked into insatiable flames that licked higher and higher, devouring the daylight as he painted deep into the night. His canvasses began to steal past the boundaries of his bedroom and into their shared living quarter, stacked against walls and bursting with textured recreations of that seminal night. A masquerade ball that captured the decadence of this bright new decade Fitzgerald was writing about. A ballerina lost amongst the living. A mist-coated dawn slithering through a suddenly desolated manor. It was February 1924 now, two months later and still those blue-grey eyes stared at him through one dream to the next until he woke shaking, fingers itching for a pencil, a paintbrush, a palette knife. It continued until one morning Marvin tripped over a canvas and spilt his mug of coffee on their wireless. At once their crystal set began warbling over Marion Harris crooning that she *ain't got nobody*.

'For god's sake, Forster, will you get rid of some of these,' Marvin had snapped, rushing over with a cloth.

Later that same day, Forster struggled onto an omnibus with

a stack of canvasses, the holes in his boots taking on melted ice. By the time he arrived in Bloomsbury, his curls had turned wild, his glasses slipping down his nose as he disembarked, sweating beneath his navy woollen coat.

'Well, this is most unexpected.' Vivian Blake puffed on her silver cigarette holder as she surveyed his paintings. Forster glanced around the living room in an attempt to quell his gathering nerves, which were currently a rather noxious shade of arsenic, poisoning his confidence.

Vivian, a seventy-five-year-old art dealer who claimed to be fifty, resided in a smart flat that overlooked the leafy Russell Square, and flew through life on wings of art and colour. Her hair was swept up in a violet turban that matched her walls, her flat a dragon's cave of treasures, cluttered with pieces from the various artists she had selected to nurture throughout her long and influential life. Forster was an outlier as he did not possess any formal training yet thanks to a decent monthly stipend, bequeathed from his late grandfather, he had been fortunate to pay for that most costly of tuition: time. And so he had studied and learnt and practised until he'd honed his raw-cut talent into something that gleamed like a gem. Promise. His first year living in London, he had been sat in Russell Square one autumnal afternoon, sketching under the buttery light, when a shadow had fallen over his sketchpad. Vivian Blake had added him to her roster of talent and Forster had had the first stirrings of hope. A daffodil-yellow that had settled over him like warm sunshine. Being a prolific patron of the arts, she was solely responsible for the establishment of many an acclaimed artist, whom she now counted among her dearest friends. Legend had it that the woman had even been recruited for a spot of espionage during the Great War but Forster would not have been surprised to learn that she had cultivated that rumour herself.

Now, Vivian was surveying him. Forster faltered under her direct gaze.

'It's been well over a year since you have brought me anything new. I was beginning to consider that I might never see you again. I have always known that you were technically gifted, but these—' she prodded a canvas with her cigarette holder '—these are exciting, Forster.' Her expression gleamed. 'You've finally painted something with emotion. A spark. I am gladdened to see that you have taken my advice and summoned some spirit.' Vivian tapped a finger against her deep-brown cheek and nodded. 'I do believe I ought to be able to sell these. I have a collector in mind – darling fellow, though a tad eccentric,' she muttered to herself, 'who has been searching for something like these. Yes, I must arrange to pay him a visit at once.'

Forster's chest hitched. Though his monthly stipend stretched to cover the cost of his rent, he often had to choose between dining on bread and butter or the kind of paint that spread like satin. With the sale of a painting or, dare he be bold enough to dream, two, he'd be able to pay Marvin back for all those gin cobblers and invest in a new pair of boots that would withstand all the rain and ice that February had brought to the streets of London. Perhaps this was what ambition felt like, the driving force that had settled inside, tantalising him with what may be within his grasp.

Vivian swivelled to study him, her chandelier earrings swinging. 'I had been certain you had given up your artistic pursuits. What changed?'

Forster gave a guilty shrug. 'Inspiration's a fickle muse,' he dismissed wryly.

'Not so fickle of late, it seems. Tell me, what inspired these?' She tapped a painting of a ballerina reclining on a velvet chaise, her smoky eyes appearing to follow the viewer. 'Have you sought out a muse? Taken a new lover?'

Forster cleared his throat. 'Nothing quite so scandalous, I am afraid.' How peculiar. Lying was becoming easier. He banished all thought of the ballerina that twirled through his dreams. *Odette Lakely.* When he rested his head on his pillow, he fell asleep determined to awake and learn more of her. Yet, each day, he rose with a desperate ache to make, to create, to paint. He was greedy to fill each blank page with life, to paint meaning into his world, and he fretted that he might perish before he'd told all the stories he desired to. His heartbeat was a clock, counting down the hours, days, weeks that remained, locked inside his chest.

'Hmm—' Vivian seemed to peer straight through him '—how disappointing; I am positively starved for a titillating morsel of gossip.' She let out an exaggerated sigh. Then, a smile. Deep and true. 'I strongly suggest you return to the source of your inspiration for these. I wouldn't have taken you on if I hadn't suspected you harboured some gifts but the past few years—' she tutted at him '—I had second-guessed myself. And now?' She tapped the ballerina once more. 'Now I have learnt my lesson. I'll never question my judgement again.'

'Thank you,' Forster said earnestly, pondering how he might track down a ghost. For Odette was more than a mystery; she was his inspiration, the answer to his dreams, his muse.

'I shall be expecting to see more like this at your soonest convenience. Now do hurry along, I have places to be, people to see.' Vivian shrugged on a floor-length ermine coat as she ushered him out of the door. With a kiss on the cheek, she bid him adieu and marched off in the opposite direction, leaving him a little stunned in her wake.

As Forster strolled down the street, he wondered how he might find Odette again.

Chapter Ten

Marvin claimed the second leather chair in their cramped flat and poured two glasses of gin from the decanter on the rickety side table. He handed a glass to Forster before rubbing his forehead as if he could erase the weary lines that traipsed across it. 'It's been a hell of a day.'

'Arthur again?' Forster knocked back the gin and held his glass out for a refill. A headache was nestling above his eyes and the evening had been a long time coming after the frustrations of the day.

'He didn't run my story on the tram and bus strike.'

Forster shook his head. 'Sorry, Marv.'

Marvin refilled their glasses. 'It's fine. I knew I'd have to bide my time as a society columnist first, but I had hoped I'd be able to sneak in the odd story of note. I was naive. Anyway, Rose stopped by the office at lunchtime, apparently the usual crowd will be attending The 43 in Soho tonight. What do you say? Fancy a couple of sidecars? A spot of dancing? Perhaps you'll find a pretty distraction from her.' Marvin nodded at the nearest painting, where a ballerina watched them with a curious longing.

'I presume you've informed Rose that there are less dingy night-clubs that happen to be closer and serve better cocktails?'

Marvin snorted. 'Not when rumour has it Rudolph Valentino will be in attendance tonight.'

Forster couldn't help grinning at this. Along with half of London, Rose had fallen madly in love with the film star following the screening of *The Sheik* a few years ago. Much to the vexation of Marvin. 'You go. Valentino could be a story. Give Arthur what he wants and perhaps he'll be more amenable to your next idea. Besides, I gave Vivian my word that I would have another collection for her to see shortly and I'm struggling.'

'Yes, I noticed your period of manic painting had slowed to a crawl.' Marvin considered Forster over his rim. 'Everything all right, old chap?'

Forster drained the contents of his second glass, set it down on the end table and stood. 'Probably just in need of some fresh inspiration.' He warmed his hands before the fire, working out the tight coils of tension that gnarled around his wrists. Between the draughty window in his bedroom and the damp that gleefully clung onto the walls, it was a miracle he hadn't succumbed to illness this winter. Though it was March, spring felt a far-fetched notion as, day after day, he awoke to a lamp-black sky, swollen with storm. Vivian's voice echoed through his head: *I strongly suggest you return to the source of your inspiration.* Yet he hadn't. He had been standing on the platform, on the verge of bordering a train when he had been struck with a sudden fear. What if he was to return to the manor in the middle of the day, only to find it mundane? Its hold upon him would thus be weakened and his inspiration fade away. He left the train station at once, unable to bear being robbed of the magic.

His thoughts were drowned out by the sudden onslaught of rain sheeting down their living room window.

'What devilish weather.' Marvin stared out into the night. 'I suggest we pay it no heed and go and join Rose. You can spare a night and you ought to celebrate your good news. Three paintings sold in the past month! You're on the up and up now, Forster.'

Forster smiled. 'All right, you've convinced me. I wasn't getting much done here anyway. Let's accompany Rose in her star-spotting tonight. It seems we could both use a change in scenery.'

Marvin narrowed his eyes at him.

'And you were right, I ought to celebrate,' Forster hastily tacked on.

Marvin leapt to his feet. 'Superlative. Let me find my hat.'

'Darlings, you came!' Rose clapped her hands together as Forster and Marvin arrived at 43 Gerrard Street. 'What do you think?' She lifted a hand to her newly bobbed chocolate-coloured hair. A kiss curl rested against each rosy cheek and her wide amber eyes searched for their approval.

'Why, you're a regular flapper now,' Marvin declared, resting an arm around her shoulders and guiding her into the club.

She paused inside the entrance and looked up at Forster from beneath darkened and curled eyelashes.

'Beautiful,' Forster pronounced.

Rose blushed.

They made their way downstairs, to the dance hall in the basement, peeling off woollen winter coats. Rose dashed off at once to another friend, her jet-beaded dress clinking with each step. The air was heavy with smoke and jazz and everywhere Forster looked, he spotted another person of interest; The 43 was home to celebrities, gangsters, and royalty alike. Ripe pickings for reporters, indeed. Marvin cheered as he glanced around before raising his eyebrows at Forster. 'Drinks?'

They had situated themselves at one of the only vacant tables in the hall with a couple of sidecars when Rose materialised through the glittering throng of dancers. 'You'll never guess what just happened, Tallulah Bankhead offered me some naughty salt in the lavatories!'

'Did you take any?' Marvin asked, amused, scanning the crowd for a glimpse of the American actress. Material for tomorrow's papers perhaps.

'Only a tiny sniff, darling. Well, it would have been rude not to!' She looked aghast at the very notion of refusing Hollywoodland royalty.

Marvin laughed. 'Oh, you do tickle me, Rose.'

Forster almost choked on his cocktail. 'Precisely when did you start speaking like an ageing grandmother?'

Rose's laugh pealed out. Sweet and high and entirely addictive. 'You can drink those later, let's dance while the jazz is hot.' She turned and whirled towards the dance floor, pearls clacking around her neck. 'I hope you can keep up, boys,' she teased.

As they danced deeper into the night, Forster's thoughts grew cognac-hazed, dipping into the waters of his imagination. Of girls that pirouetted until they vanished in thin air. Of bathing in blue-grey eyes, fathoms deep. He blinked hard, rousing himself back to the present. 'Say, where is everyone? I thought the usual crowd were meeting us here?' he called out over the brassy music to Rose.

'Ethel and Margaret left before you arrived, this godforsaken weather is making everyone terribly tiresome,' Rose said. 'Why, did you fancy seeing someone in particular?' She gave him a curious look.

'Who could fail to be charmed by your company?' Marvin made as if to stroke her kiss curl before he thought better of it, his fingers closing in the air.

At once, Forster determined to leave the pair alone. Yet before he could voice words to that effect, a sudden screeching of whistles and heavy tread of boots erupted on the floor above them.

Rose gasped. 'I do believe it's a raid; how positively *thrilling*.'

Marvin's cigarette almost fell from his mouth. 'Indeed.' He frowned. 'Say, what time is it?' he asked Forster.

Forster glanced at his watch. 'I make it a half past two,' he said, ignoring the twinge that came with looking at his grandfather's watch. It had been gifted to him upon his twenty-first birthday and was one of the few reminders of home he had brought with him to London. A few weeks after he had moved in with Marvin, he learnt of his grandfather's passing with great regret, a regret that had festered and turned bitter, yet still he did not venture to visit his family. Not since the argument that had cleaved him from them. Home was the place where his heart might rest easy; it was not the battleground of his birthplace.

Marvin cursed. 'Damn licensing laws. We'd better make a swift exit.' He knocked their glasses onto the floor where they smashed, the last of their cocktails seeping into the floor.

Rose darted to fetch their coats as Forster yanked Marvin away from the scene. 'Was that really necessary?'

'Got to hide the evidence, cover our tracks now, haven't we?' Marvin grinned as they fled through the broken glass and other nightclubbers forcing their way out as the policemen streamed into the dance hall, whistles blowing.

They fell out of the club in a gaggle of laughter.

'Oh—' Rose suddenly looked crestfallen '—I never did see Rudolph Valentino.'

✿

Two days later, the story of the raid made the front page of *The City Star*, cementing Marvin in his new appointment as a regular society columnist. 'It's not the story I would have wanted to write but the tides are turning now and one day it will be,' Marvin said, showing off his by-line to Forster as Rose cracked open the champagne. 'I'm finally moving up in the world.' His grin was wide enough to devour the world and Forster imagined him gobbling up his dreams, one by one.

The very next morning, Forster caught the first train out of London. For Marvin was not the only one who nurtured a fierce ambition. And the answer to Forster's dreams lay in Wurthercliffe.

Chapter Eleven

As the little train chuntered towards Wurthercliffe, its clacking rhythm sent Forster to sleep. The ballerina pirouetted through his dreams, haunting him from afar, drawing him closer and closer. He awoke with a start before he missed his stop. Though the manor was at most an hour's drive from London, it was double that on the old train that puffed and rattled along, and Forster couldn't help imagining that when it stopped, he would step down into a different world.

Hopping down from the train, he proceeded from Wurthercliffe's single platform on foot. It was a crisp blue day in the sleepy town. He walked through it and farther, to where the sea roared against the cliffs and the manor perched on top of the world. Forster stared up at it for a moment. Far removed from the bustle of the city he'd left that morning, it appeared to belong to another era altogether. A lost moment in time. He had the sudden inclination to meander around the perimeter of the lake, nestled between the grassy expanse that led to the manor and wild woodland. It was charming. Reminiscent of a bucolic painting by the likes of Boddington. A sudden contentment in warm butterscotch-yellow, like a toffee melting on your tongue, swept over Forster, and he smiled to himself, pushing his glasses up his nose.

At once a painting presented itself to him: the manor as glimpsed from the far side of the lake, looming up in the distance. Its honey-stone peeping between blossoming bluebells, their silken petals peeling open, scenting the air for spring. Though it was late March, out here there was a bite of frost in the air that had the wildflowers shivering. It was far colder than the city, even colder than Wurthercliffe. And since he had departed the train, the bright blue wash of sky had mottled into grey. Rose would have declared that he was treading a spectral path, that this was a sign that the manor was certainly haunted. In London, he might have dismissed her. But here, here where his inspiration had bloomed like the fields of wildflowers, here he might believe in the impossible. When he glanced back at the manor, its windows gave him a hollow stare. What ghosts prowled through those silent halls?

Forster walked on. Crunching along the stones bordering the lake, he traced the water's edge. It reflected the grey gloom of the day back at him as the water sighed and nibbled at the ground. As he watched, something wet touched the back of his neck. Reaching back to feel it, he realised it was snowing very lightly. The slightest flurry, refusing to stick to the grass, the stones, but melting away at once.

Yes, this would work with the painting: the mysterious manor peeping through a riot of wildflowers as a soft snowfall pattered down. A scene not of winter, not yet spring but some liminal place between them. The kind of place where secrets ran deeper than lake water, and girls refused to die.

Mulling this over, Forster reached the treeline when he heard something. A deep, shuddering gasp. The sound of a drowning person piercing the surface at last, their starving lungs swelling to suck in as much air as possible. Forster whirled back to look at the lake. Its surface was still; not a soul had emerged from its cloud-speckled depths. A softer inhalation followed, one that he would not have heard had he not been straining his ears for something out of place. This time, he located it.

It was coming from the woodland.

✿ ✿ ✿

The snow fell on me, softly coating me with consciousness. Scattered remnants of my thoughts, my mind collected once more. Awareness stirred within me like an ancient entity, dragging me back into my own skin.

Feathers rippled back, revealing paleness below. A long, curved neck that weighed heavy, matted hair cascading down my back, my newfound limbs rubbery and unfeeling with cold.

I took a deep, shuddering gasp to anchor myself, the weight of recollection sitting heavy in my lungs, drowning me with the knowledge of who I am, of what is happening to me. For my life has been steeped in fairy tales and I am cursed down to the bone.

Chapter Twelve

Forster raced into the tangle of trees and bracken. Branches arched high above him, meeting in a conspiracy to blot out the sun. Inside the woods, it was a dark hinterland. Phantoms stalked through Forster's imagination, ancient tales of what might inhabit woods as old as these. The force of that historic fear threatened to still his feet and he shivered as he stopped, listening, knowing with an instinctive force that something was wrong in this place. The sound came once more. It could not be ignored. He ran. Skidded over a patch of muddied moss, weaving through trees, until he broke through into a small clearing.

There, sat a woman.

She was unclothed, her head buried in her knees, arms looped around her legs. He halted at once, startled by the intimate view, the slope of her spine. The snow melting on her pale skin.

He shucked his jacket as he stepped towards her, gaze averted. 'Excuse me, I heard you call out . . .' he trailed off, knowing that she had not called out for him, nor anyone. 'Are you quite well?' he asked instead, taking care to keep his voice soft, to minimise the intrusion.

She started and whirled around. Her light blue-grey eyes were winter moons, her hair wild and knotted. He inhaled sharply as she pinned her gaze on him. 'It's you,' he whispered. 'Are you real?' Her feet were bare in the mud and moss and melting snow. He held out his jacket, afraid to touch her. He didn't fear her but he had crossed paths with a vision, a spectre, and he feared brushing against her and discovering – what? That she was not real? Or, that she was very much real, a flesh-and-blood woman with a different kind of secret than the one he had been imagining.

She licked her lips, her breath catching in her lungs. 'You attended my party.' Her voice was scarcely more than a whisper, rough and scratching. 'I remember you.'

She had ignored his coat. Still, Forster held it out, not certain what he was hoping for, numbed with shock at finding her here, sitting like this. 'You died on the *Titanic*.'

Her laugh was hoarse, disused. 'I am no ghost.'

With that, Forster closed the distance between them. He wrapped his jacket around her shoulders as she watched, tracking his every movement. Her frame was real, solid. Disappointment lasted a moment before it washed over him, receding like the ripples on the lake. Then, foolishness. 'Of course, you're not.'

'I am something worse.'

Forster hesitated. Why was she here, unclothed? A fierce protectiveness surged within him. 'Do you need me to fetch you help?' He disliked the notion of leaving to fetch help, pondered if he ought to sweep her up into his arms like one of the heroes in an Austen novel, and carry her to safety and warmth. Whatever she needed, he was willing to do.

She suddenly whipped her head up, staring at the slashes of sky visible between the canopy. 'It is no longer snowing.' She trailed one hand through the mud at her feet. 'And no snow remains on the ground.' Her expression contorted. 'No. No, it is too soon!'

'Your name is Odette, is it not?' She was panicking now and

though Forster did not wish to alarm her by picking her up, the sight of her bare feet in the cold set his jaw tight. He bent down to unlace his boots. One at a time, he pulled them off, standing in the frozen patchwork of leaves and moss in his socks. One needed darning and he caught himself hoping that she would not notice.

Odette's gaze swung wildly. Between the sky and the trees and him. Her breathing turned fast and shallow. 'Detta. But you must leave at once. The snow is melting as quickly as it fell and I—' her voice caught '—I am out of time.'

'Please, if you'll only allow me to accompany you, I can find you some help. Do you live nearby? In Wurthercliffe?' Forster held his boots out to her. 'There is no need to panic, I can take you home.' She had been photographed standing before the manor in that newspaper clipping he had found but the manor was bolted shut and devoid of inhabitants.

'The manor is mine.' She closed her eyes. A single tear fell from her lashes. 'Now you must leave. Leave before I do.'

'Then you are the host of those parties,' Forster realised. His realisation was followed by relief; they were close. He reached to lift her into his arms to carry her home, remove her from this cold and wet, and light a roaring fire to chase the chill from her bones.

But Detta began to tremble.

'I assure you, there is no need to fear me,' Forster said kindly, pausing. 'I won't share your secret if you don't want me to. I only wish to take you home.' Yet her trembling turned fiercer and she fell to the ground, shaking before him. 'What's happening? What do you need me to do?' Forster's panic intensified as she convulsed. He'd never seen someone fit before and his helplessness was terrifying. His grandfather had founded a doctor's surgery in Northampton but though Forster wore the man's watch, he had not an inkling of his medical knowledge. Before he could think what to do, her skin mottled. Turned dove-grey. He gasped, watching her pale to snow-white. It was as if winter was claiming her fairest maiden, reaching out with frost-fingers to encase Detta in ice. *I am something worse*, she had warned him. He had not believed her. *The manor is deserted*, people had said. Was this why she kept it closed most of the year? This . . . secret he was on the verge of? He reached a hand towards her but something was happening to her neck. Something that he could not quite understand, no matter how much he grasped for that knowledge. It was a secret that belonged in this ancient woodland. The great yews and oaks around them whispered of impossible things, furling their branches around their secret, sharing it only with the shining orb of a moon by night, and the sighing lake she adored to peer in by day.

And now Forster had stumbled upon that secret.

Detta turned to stare at him.

And as he saw, Forster gasped and staggered back under the weight of it.

Her neck, impossibly elongated, her luminescent eyes darkening to a maw. Within them, he sighted that endless galaxy of grief and sadness and yearning, robbed of a single star to light her way. As he watched, she shrank away before him, losing herself. Her whisky-coloured curls blanched, coating her neck in a silken wave. Ivory feathers rippled out along her skin.

Before his own eyes, she was now a swan.

Chapter Thirteen

Forster had no recollection of how he had made it back to London that day. His last memory was of watching the woman who had transformed into a swan glide across the lake and behave as if she had never been anything but a swan. He wondered if he'd hallucinated the whole episode. It had been a frozen day that he had not dressed for, the cold a malignant force that had seeped through his skin, his bones. Perhaps hypothermia had set in. His memories were hazy. Each time he tried to piece together what had truly happened, he lost himself in the fog. The first thing he could remember was sitting up in bed as Marvin brought him soup and checked his temperature like a mother hen. He could not stop picturing people as birds. Marvin, clucking with concern as he read the thermometer. Rose, a cherubic nightingale with a song as sweet as her disposition, urging him to stay in bed to rest. But people were not birds and he had witnessed something extraordinary, something that could not be real. He had not told Marvin the story of the woman whose skin had become a blanket of downy feathers, whose arms had unfurled into wings, an impossible fairy tale that had stolen into reality. Nor had he told him that the ballerina was the mysterious host of these parties; a revelation his conjured imagination could be responsible for. 'But that part could have been real, couldn't it?' he asked Rose, who had suddenly appeared in his bedroom, pressing a glass to his lips.

'Shhh, do not vex yourself with these worries now, darling.' She removed the glass and placed something cool over his eyes. 'Try to relax and get some sleep.'

He fell into a dream of stolen breaths and moonbeams. Of melting snow that trickled into a lake, deeper than an ocean and rippling with magic. And a woman with blue-grey eyes and great feathered wings. Try as she might, she could not soar up into the clouds and as the lake grew deeper, her wings sodden and drooping, she drowned in its midnight depths.

He woke with a start. A single lamp was burning in the hall. His legs wobbly as a newborn faun, he stumbled into the living room. Marvin leapt up, tossing the newspaper he was reading aside. 'You damn near gave me a heart attack.' He rushed over to support Forster into a comfortable settee. 'I didn't expect to see you up and about so soon; you've had a raging fever.'

'How . . . long?' Forster croaked.

Marvin went into the kitchen and returned with a glass of water. 'You've been bed-bound for the past two weeks. I came home from work and you were delirious, muttering some nonsense about birds.'

Two whole weeks? Forster gratefully sipped from the glass and rubbed his face, more bewildered than ever at what had happened to him over the past few weeks.

✿

Spring ripened to its peak, bursting into a summer that speckled the streets with blush-pink cherry blossom. Pavements frothed with petals under the gentle warmth of the sunshine. Until the sun beamed brighter and London grew stifled.

Society papers filled with photographs of the wealthy decamping to glamorous coastal destinations, where one could idle beside turquoise waters, and drink late into moonlit nights. Forster's fever-ravaged delusions continued to trouble him over what he had seen in the woods that day. But surely it had been the delirious onset of his illness, festering within him on his countryside jaunt that had provoked such hallucinations. He tried to dismiss them.

'That's it,' Rose announced, letting herself into their flat one morning. 'Everybody who's anybody has fled the city and I refuse to stay here a day longer in this infernal heatwave merely because of your insufferable pride, Marvin.'

Marvin, who was sitting opposite Forster in their little living room, looked taken aback. 'Are you referring to me refusing your charity—' he began.

'It is not charity—' Rose planted her hands firmly on her hips '—it is my own selfish wants so therefore it cannot be charity. Now pack your bags, boys; our boat leaves at dusk.' With a devilish grin, she fanned herself with three tickets. 'We're taking a little sojourn to my darling great-aunt's house in the South of France, and I've already informed her of our impending arrival so you can't possibly disappoint an elderly lady.'

Forster couldn't help grinning back at her. Rose made precious little mention of her inheritance but from what he'd learnt from the snippets she had shared and what the papers had covered, he knew that she was extremely wealthy, being the daughter of a shipping magnate, and the thought of clear blue waters and all the charms of the Continent were too appealing to resist.

Marvin groaned. 'Rose—'

'It'll be just the tonic for Forster's convalescence,' she added. 'Don't worry, you can be as vexed with me in France as you like!'

Chapter Fourteen

Rose's elderly great-aunt turned out to be an effortlessly sophisticated woman in her sixties who lived with another woman in a nineteenth-century Belle Epoque villa perched on the tip of Cap d'Antibes.

'Do make yourselves at home,' Elsie informed them when they arrived, their travelling clothes rumpled and stomachs empty from the journey. 'I've had your rooms freshened up and dinner shall be at eight.'

Forster's guest room was light and airy in shades of lemon and cream, with a stone balcony that offered sweeping views of the coast and a gentle clime that was already softening the cough that had laid siege to his lungs following his fever. He lay down for a rest and did not wake until a soft knock on the door roused him. 'Come and join us for dinner, darling,' Rose called through the door. He dressed in a linen suit, planting a fedora atop his head as he set out to find the others.

They were all sat around a table on a large terrace overlooking the sea, sparkling beneath the lazy evening sun. Elsie, whose silver hair threatened to escape from her silk headscarf, gestured for him to sit. She introduced him to her beau, Sylvie, a Frenchwoman somewhere in her forties, with a twist of dark hair and a philosophical gaze, as a bottle of rosé was poured with an aperitif of tapenades and fresh bread.

'Forster, you shall never guess what Sylvie has just informed us.' Rose turned to him in a haze of excitement. 'It seems the beautiful Hotel Du Cap is hosting a select group of guests holidaying here.'

'I cannot say I blame them—' Forster idly reached for his glass '—I could live here year-round.'

'Ah, but wait until you hear who our new neighbour is.' Marvin's gleam of interest intrigued Forster.

'Picasso!' Rose beamed. 'How perfectly thrilling, perhaps you might make his acquaintance, Forster. Oh, do let us try and wrangle an invite to one of their parties, darlings.' She turned her imploring stare onto Marvin, who looked dazzled and cleared his throat hastily. 'Of course,' he told her. But not before Elsie noted his initial reaction.

'There are other artists and writers among them, I believe,' Sylvie added. 'Hemmingway, too, though he is often found at the bar, of course.'

Possibility was as bright as the blue basin of sky. And Forster was giddy with it. Perhaps he did not need to concern himself with what may or may not be occurring in that windswept manor back in England. Perhaps he might find inspiration elsewhere. And where better than a summer spent neighbouring the founder of Cubism himself?

The South of France was scented with pine trees and herbs and a salted breeze that swept in across limestone hills. Forster painted the landscape as Rose and Marvin enjoyed languorous strolls, arm in arm, along the beach.

'You're quite a painter,' Elsie commented one day, wandering out to the terrace with an extra cup of coffee that Forster took gratefully. 'Very pretty indeed.' She smiled at the painting of her view.

'I am glad you think so as I painted it for you. A small token of my appreciation for inviting me into your home,' Forster said.

'Oh, how lovely.' Elsie's smile widened with delight. 'Now, what do you make of those two?' She indicated Rose and Marvin, on the sand below, Rose's distant shrieks echoing up as Marvin splashed her.

'He's been in love with her since the day they met.' Forster laid his brushes down and joined Elsie in her observation. 'She appears more reticent.'

Elsie pursed her perfectly red-painted lips. 'She once confided in me that she would never marry. I wonder if he shall be the one to change her mind.'

Forster fretted for Marvin's heart. 'Does her father wish her to wed some titled or befortuned man?' After all, she was an heiress.

'Oh no, nothing of the sort.' Elsie took a measured sip of coffee. 'If you had not noticed by now, we are not the kind of family that pays heed to inane societal rules. No, we're new money, darling.' She smiled with a glint in her eye and Forster laughed, delighted by her before sobering once more as Elsie turned to him, serious. 'Rose's mother died birthing her and her father never recovered. She is his only child and they are uncommonly close. I have never witnessed another father cherish his daughter as Ernest does her and she adores him in turn. It will take a great love for her to leave her father's home.'

'I had no idea,' Forster murmured, drinking his own coffee as he glanced at the pair below.

Forster's cough soon lessened then vanished altogether as the endless summer days meandered by. He grew strong enough to join Marvin and Rose in their long walks, picnicking on crusty baguettes, a wedge of sea-blue-veined Roquefort and ripe pears that spilled syrup down his fingers. One evening, they sat on the sand together, watching the moonlight dance on the retreating tides. High above, an eagle whorled through the air. Forster watched it lay siege to the sky before hurtling down, hunting something in the piney shrubs and wild grasses that rose behind them. 'It's heavenly here.' Rose sighed. 'Perhaps I too shall live here one day. Did you know that Edith Wharton has a house nearby? I just adored *The Age of Innocence*.'

Marvin reached for a couple of madeleines. 'I've never read it. You know I much prefer a rip-roaring adventure or crafty little mystery.' He paused, watching Rose lie back under the star-bright sky.

Forster was on the verge of excusing himself to leave the pair to themselves, hoping the charming evening would work its magic on them, when Sylvie called out from the terrace above. 'We have an invitation, *mes chéries!*'

Their party of five wandered over to La Garoupe beach, a pretty little northeast-facing shore with crystal-clear waters, where a large group of people, mostly Americans, had congregated, mixing cocktails on the lantern-lit sand.

'That's the Murphys,' Rose whispered, her eyes darting all over the place before she absconded with Elsie to introduce themselves.

Forster had already spotted Picasso and Olga, his young Russian wife and muse, but a swift surge of imposter syndrome had rooted his feet to the beach. 'This will help.' Marvin handed him a Manhattan. Forster drank the entire cocktail in one heady gulp. He handed the glass back to Marvin and marched over before his newfound bravado evaporated. Picasso glanced up and Forster swerved back to Marvin. 'I cannot, I simply cannot speak to him.' He took a second Manhattan from Marvin, who was regarding him with no little amusement. 'Well, you'd better think of something to say and quickly, because he's coming over.'

'What?' Forster whirled around.

'You are a painter, too?' Picasso gestured at Forster's hands. Paint was embedded beneath his nails, staining his fingers.

Words failed Forster. 'Yes.' Marvin cleared his throat, stepping in. 'Yes, he is. And a damn good one, too. He's painted many fine landscapes since we arrived.'

'Landscapes.' Picasso lit a cigarette and inhaled deeply. His face was dynamic, his expression enthusiastic enough to convey what his limited English could not. The man was a legend and Forster was struggling to believe that he stood before him now. Picasso had been a child prodigy and now was at the forefront of entire new movements. He was more than a painter; he was a lifeforce of art itself. A revolutionary. 'And this is your passion?'

'Hmm, I wouldn't say so,' Marvin continued. 'There is a woman . . . ' he trailed off, with a sidled glance at Forster that leaked mischief.

'Ah, a woman.' Picasso gestured with his cigarette. He exchanged a knowing look with Marvin, who smirked. Picasso's mannerisms were irreverent, often fun-seeking, and Forster found him deeply compelling, unable to look away from his enigmatic stare, his eyes so dark they were almost black. 'She is your muse?'

'Perhaps.' Forster thought hard. 'Though I cannot tell if she is inspiring me or haunting me.'

His face cracked into a mirthful smile. 'Do you dream of her?'

Forster's thoughts turned to last night's dream, of a ballerina who pirouetted until she sprouted wings and flew towards a swollen pearl of a moon.

'Does she make you want to paint?'

'Well, yes—' Forster hesitated. He had awoken with twitching fingers, desiring nothing more than to shape creamy paint into feathers, yet he had resisted. Painted another view from the terrace instead. It did him no good to fill his head with delusions of women turning into swans, he needed to move on.

But Picasso laughed. 'Then you do not let her go.' He ambled off, shaking his head and calling out for another drink, more music, the party roaring louder as he returned to it.

'I think I need to rest a moment.' Forster sat on the beach, away from the chairs and blankets and candles of the party. He curled his fingers into the sand, concentrating on the ebb and flow of the sea. Perhaps if he stared long enough at the moonlight sparkling on the water, he would not have to admit to himself what he already knew, what Picasso had pointed out. That painting landscapes had never been for him; they did not set his soul alight. And this was reflected in Forster's latest works – Vivian would have been disappointed by their lack of meaning.

Marvin joined him. 'He's right, you know. Your landscapes are beautiful, striking even, but when I look at them, I cannot tell what you felt when you painted them. I am sorry to say that they don't have that spark you've been chasing lately.'

Forster lay back and closed his eyes.

'You've been recovering from your illness, you'll find your way back to it,' Marvin added confidently before falling silent beside him.

The sounds of the party settled into the background, clinking glasses, chatter and laughter across several languages, the receding waves. Forster had just met one of the greatest artists of his time; he ought to have been fizzing with inspiration, not this unending restlessness that had set in since his fever had waned.

Though he was not certain what he had seen that day a few months earlier, he had seen *something*. It was growing harder and harder to ignore that fact of late. He wanted to be a great artist himself and a great artist did not hide away from that which inspired him.

They chased it. Welcomed it into their lives, and if it snagged them with hidden thorns, if it summoned pain, they painted until they understood it better. Now that Forster was strong enough to confront that, a fresh decisiveness settled into his bones. He was determined to understand exactly what had happened in those woods. And uncover the mystery of Odette Lakely.

'Perhaps I am simply ready to return to London.'

Chapter Fifteen

After they had returned from the French Riviera, Forster had scarcely unpacked before departing for Wurthercliffe, determined to reveal the secret the lake and woodlands held in their gnarled branches.

The country air was sweet with peach honeysuckle, the estate in summer's full bloom, perfumed with bushels of lavender and an abundance of hydrangea that tickled the manor pink. Forster strolled past the fountain, its pool of stagnant water greening over, and into the trees. There, the highest branches were alive with birdsong, the lowest furred with moss. Daisies and wild geraniums blossomed in pockets of sunshine, buttercups gleamed yellow like hidden yolks, and beneath the thickest parts of the canopy, where the shadows rustled and crept closer, troops of glistening inkcaps sprouted. Forster picked a path through it all until he spotted water shimmering ahead.

The lake was empty, save for a few ducks sunning themselves on the shore and though he waited, Odette did not appear. Neither in human form nor swan, leaving him wondering if the entire event had indeed been a feverish delusion. *The manor is mine*, she had informed him. In a sudden fit of curiosity that seized his imagination in dazzling yellow, Forster strode towards the manor, set on seeking out the mysteries hidden within its honeyed stonework. After knocking on the grand front doors and peeking into windows, he arrived at the same conclusion as the gossips: it was as vacant as the last time he and Marvin had trespassed.

Forster wandered around the back.

A window on the second floor was ajar.

Perhaps he'd left it open on his last visit. He tried to remember but nothing grasped his attention the way the lake did. The way *she* had. She was like the sun, moon, and stars, and he was helplessly bewitched by her. A lacework of ivy twined up to the window and Forster gave it an experimental tug. Before he could assess whether he was being foolish, he was already clambering up the side of the manor and reaching for the open window. Pulling himself through, his glasses escaping down his nose with the effort, he found himself in what appeared to be a drawing room he had not seen before. Standing slowly, he examined his surroundings.

This room had been decorated and recently, too. It was light and fresh in shades of pink and cream, with an antique French mirror above a mantelpiece still carrying the scent of polish. And something else, too. Half a sheet of torn paper was resting there, tickling the mirror with its edges. Forster picked it up. It was the remnants of a faded poster in red and gold, and for a moment it felt as if it had been left there for him to find, like the first breadcrumb that marked a path through the deepest, darkest woods.

It had been torn straight through the middle and read:

of Enchantments
nd wonder you shall never forget!
n sale now.

Half an aerialist swung from a trapeze at the top corner, dark firs encroached along the bottom but — *there*. In the very centre of the golden stage that had been torn clean in half, he found her. Odette. She appeared near the same age as she'd been in the *Titanic* article. Though it was only half of the photograph, she was unmistakable. Her blue-grey gaze haunted Forster and he could not look away. He was locked in her enchantment. She wore a simple white tulle that gave her a strangely vulnerable appearance against the darkness of the forest, and he was brought rushing back to that day in the woods, four months ago, when she had sat there in the mud and roots and moss, before white feathers had sailed down her back, her limbs, and snatched her away into a different realm. The memory shimmered before him, intact and powerful, and his disbelief shattered. Surely, he could not have imagined such a thing. 'Who are you?' he whispered.

Something creaked outside the door.

Forster slipped the crumpled poster into his jacket pocket. 'Odette?' he called out, reaching for the doorknob, yanking it open hopefully.

The hallway outside was dark and silent. Eerily so. Dust motes flitted through a single shaft of light. A shiver danced down his spine. 'Odette?' he called again, quieter this time. No answer came and, unwilling to pry any longer, he climbed back down from the window, convincing himself that the manor had just been settling its old bones.

Chapter Sixteen

Marvin's silence was thick and unyielding.

Forster frowned at his latest painting, trying to see why it had disturbed his flatmate. 'I take it you don't much care for it?' he asked, giving up.

'On the contrary, I'm relieved to see you painting with feeling again.' Marvin lit a cigarette, sending the scent of spiced tobacco coursing through the flat. 'But I am a little uneasy that you've fixed this woman in your mind as your muse though you've only met her once.'

Forster's frown deepened. 'These are street performers in Covent Garden.' He glanced at the canvas once more. It was inspired by a lively street scene he'd happened upon last week. Musicians played to an enraptured crowd and several acrobatic dancers soared against a darkly mysterious backdrop of horses and carts, motors and bustling shops in tones of bronzed reds and burnished coffee-browns. It was moody and atmospheric and he had not expected Marvin to take a dislike to it.

'This girl, right here.' Marvin tapped the side of the painting. Where a woman was observing the performance, expressing her glee as she turned to the man on whose arm her hand rested. Marvin exhaled a plume of smoke. 'Look at the peculiar quality of her eyes.

Familiar, no? You've also transposed them onto this woman.' He strode over to where a stack of canvasses were propped against a wall, hoarding valuable space in their cramped flat. 'Here, you have painted the ballerina's curls onto another woman; this one features a corps de ballet performing *Swan Lake*, and look — why, it's her eyes again, this time staring out from a bloody swan of all things.' He let the canvasses thud back against the wall.

Forster watched a puff of plaster dust float down to rest on the topmost painting. It resembled a solitary snowflake and he had an acute pang of longing for another time, another night.

'Your source of inspiration has become an obsession,' Marvin continued. 'And it concerns me that if you were not to meet her again then this recent success you've been enjoying might fade.'

'What would you have me do?' Forster braced his arms against the fireplace. Stared down into its ashy pit. Last week he had visited Foyles on Charing Cross Road, leaving with two new purchases: *A Study of Swans in the British Isles* and *A Complete Natural History of Swans*. They were hidden beneath his bed. But he could not conceal his thoughts, his dreams and memories. They leaked out through the bristles of his paintbrushes and crept onto canvasses like a thief in the night. Though he remembered the woman transforming into a swan with great clarity, his logical mind still urged him to dismiss it as a fevered vision. Thus, he had not told Marvin of what he thought he'd seen that day, nor that this ballerina was most likely the owner of the grand, dusty manor, the host of those great, roaring affairs each winter. The secret, the lie by omittance, was a hard kernel inside him. Each conversation they had rubbed against it, leaving him raw. Still, he thought of Odette, stripped bare of clothes, of her humanity, in the woods. Of her younger self, dancing through a sinister treescape on that torn poster he stared at each night, wondering at the secrets that twisted and twined through her life, and he knew he could never tell.

'Just . . . be careful,' Marvin was saying. 'I've put my feelers out about this ballerina – I've heard she dances at each winter party but no one seems to know her—'

Forster's hands tightened against the mantelpiece.

'—you'll be the first I come to if I happen to dig up anything but until then, take care that you do not spend so much time idolising one woman, one muse, that you forget to look to your own happiness. When was the last time you took a girl dancing?'

Forster thought back. 'Julia, the spring after I moved to London. Almost two years ago now.' She'd been a pretty nurse with a droll sense of humour who had amused him at first, until she grew frustrated with Forster's aimless drifting through life. After a couple of months, they had amicably parted ways.

Marvin fixed him with an arched look. 'And since then? Are you swearing off all women until you happen to cross paths with this ballerina again?'

But Forster could not answer him. And as the silence stretched tighter and tighter, he grabbed his hat and keys and left.

Marvin came chasing after him on the street, hat sliding off his Vaseline-slicked-back hair. 'Forster, wait. I apologise. I pretend to know nothing about art and if this woman is your muse—' he spread his arms '—who am I to tell you how to feel about her? Besides which, I'm hopelessly besotted with another woman who has no notion of the fact. I did not wish to see you suffer the same fate as mine.' He wrapped an arm around Forster. 'Brothers?'

'Brothers,' Forster repeated, promised, the kernel of his secret swelling, toughening until it would be impossible to crack without hurting.

'Rose, Charles, and Nancy have invited us to some new club tonight; what do you say? I need some fresh material for the column this week and you haven't been out in an age.'

It was true. He was a man obsessed. For who would not be, having witnessed what he had? 'Count me in, I'll catch up with you later.'

Forster hopped on the Piccadilly line for a few stops, disembarking at Green Park and making his way over to The London Library in St James's Square, where he was a member. Just after he had joined the library, a seven-storey bookstack had been added onto the Jacobethan building, and when Forster remembered his membership, he enjoyed perusing the labyrinthine book stacks, losing himself in the hushed world of literature and occasionally stumbling across something that inspired. Until something else distracted him and he didn't visit again for months. Though today, he was on the hunt for answers.

'Of enchantments, of enchantments,' he muttered to himself, raking his hands through his hair until his curls were dishevelled. He'd guessed that the poster's *n sale now* referred to tickets but tickets for what? It was precious little to go off.

'It looks like a circus to me,' the librarian advised. She tapped the soaring aerialist with a clean, polished nail.

'I don't suppose you know of any Circus of Enchantments? It would have been touring sometime around the years nineteen twelve to fourteen by my estimation.'

She leant a cheek on one hand as she moved closer for a second look, her ink-black hair escaping across her face. She pushed it back behind her ears, then held up a finger and exited the polished counter she had been working behind when Forster had approached her. 'One moment please, I shall look it up for you.' The faint traces of a southern Indian accent lent her words a hint of musicality.

Forster leant against the counter and glanced around the Reading Room. It was a grand affair, with tall windows and taller columns, giving the impression that you were entering a revered place of knowledge. Forster drummed his fingers against the wood, restless to move on, to discover the answers that eluded him.

When the librarian returned, she gave a shake of her head. 'No Circus of Enchantments, I'm afraid. Plenty of spectacles and dazzlings though.' She offered him a wry smile. 'Are you sure I can't interest you in one of those?'

'Not magical enough for me, I'm afraid.' Forster smiled through the disappointment. Odette continued to dance through his fingertips. 'Any idea where I ought to look next?'

She considered for a moment. Her hair had fallen forwards again and she tucked it back by rote. 'Well, it's entirely possible that this was a touring circus, perhaps on a smaller, more local scale? If I were you, I'd try speaking to people who are interested in that sort of thing, perhaps another company of performers who are well versed in the history of circuses?'

'I'll try that, thank you.' Forster set his hat back on his head, tipped it at her, and exited.

✿

As time continued to trickle by like warm honey, turning days to weeks, weeks to months, Forster searched for a circus of enchantments. Asking other performers, librarians, archivists, until he began questioning if he would ever learn the answers. If he would ever set eyes on her again. In the meantime, he painted.

Beautiful maidens with moonbeam-bright eyes and whisky curls spooling down their backs. Swans as demi-gods and goddesses, ruling land and sky on silvered wings. Wondrous palaces of snow and ice with all the delicacy of lace, where the impossible might become possible if you only dared to dream it so. Feathers that granted wishes and a man who longed not to be alone.

The paintings had begun as memory transposed onto canvas as Forster dredged the images of a woman re-shaped into swan from the crooked recesses of his mind. Slowly giving himself permission to believe in the impossible. Yet something peculiar happens in the journey of creation that oft results in the finished product inhaling its first breath, taking a look at the world, and deciding that it shall be something quite other than what you initially intended it to be. So it was with Forster's art. What had started as a means to process his thoughts had transcended. For him, they now represented the potential for income, a career, a path to making a name for himself. For his art dealer, they were an indication that she ought to pay more attention to him. And for his buyers, they were a fantasy. An enchanted dream. A sprinkle of magic that you might dust over your everyday life until it glittered like starshine. For Forster had glimpsed magic in its wildest form that day and it had torched him down to the marrow. He would never see the world in the same way again and this truth infused each of his canvasses. Through his art, he shared his secret, and though not one person might guess it, buried beneath the brushstrokes, they shared in his wonder. And just like that, they began to sell. For who does not wish to bring home their very own piece of magic?

Chapter Seventeen

'Careful now,' Rose cautioned, her lace gloves fluttering near the steering wheel like moth wings.

Forster flapped her away. A grin seeped across his face as he sped up to forty miles per hour, the high speed afforded by the smoother, paved roads surrounding the capital. It was the first time he had driven to Rose's hunting lodge and he was in good spirits.

'Don't distract the man,' Marvin said, sprawled across the back seat of the Tin Lizzie. His feet were propped up on Rose's Fortnum & Mason picnic hamper and now and then there was a surreptitious rustle. Forster suspected their provisions were dwindling fast. 'It was your idea to sell the motor to him.'

'I know—' Rose patted its side '—but she's still my baby.'

'I bet the new Rolls-Royce Daddy bought you helped though,' Marvin muttered under his breath.

Forster's hands tensed on the wheel as Rose whipped around, demanding, 'What did you just say to me?'

'Just teasing.' Marvin offered a box of fresh chocolate truffles in contrition.

Rose snatched the entire box from him. 'And stop eating those, they're for Forster's birthday.'

Forster hid his smile. He'd spent the past few months painting fiercer than ever before, enough that he was beginning to earn something close to a proper wage. But his newfound focus had been at the sacrifice of nights out with Marvin and Rose and he had missed those dearly. He was glad that Rose had decided throwing a birthday supper for Forster at her hunting lodge should become an annual tradition; they hadn't spent an entire weekend in each other's company since their holiday in the French Riviera a few months ago. He glanced back at Marvin but his hat was resting atop his face as he pretended to sleep rather than face the brewing tension between him and Rose. The sky was thick with cloud and tattered sunlight, as textured as a Renaissance painting. In the distance, rain was falling like a painted veil.

Sometime later, they entered the forest.

At once the day darkened and the air richened with the scent of petrichor. Then, the familiar three-gabled turrets rose from the treeline. Forster slowed to a crawl, parking his new motor outside the redbrick hunting lodge. Roots snaked through the courtyard and he watched his step as he and Marvin carried the picnic hamper inside.

'Shall I carry this up to the roof?' Marvin asked.

A deafening crash shook the lodge to its foundations. The two men jumped as seconds later, the front door slammed open as Rose ran back inside. 'Blimey,' Marvin exclaimed, 'was that thunder?'

'It's louder out here, isn't it?' Rose said. 'I always think that it makes you all too aware that we're alone in the middle of a forest with only the crumbling ruins between us and the raw power of nature.' Her mouth curved into a dagger of a smile. 'Shall we amuse ourselves with some ghost stories?'

Forster shivered. 'Let's light some candles first.'

Soon the old lodge glowed with crackling amber light. Thick church candles warmed them, their flames sending shadows darting around the sage-green-painted walls and skittering up the dim corridors. Outside, the storm raged through the forest and pelted the ramshackle stone walls with rain, but inside they painted a cosy, familiar scene. Rose had lowered her voice into a chilling tone, telling a tale of Spring-Heeled Jack, clambering over the rooftops of London in search of prey to devour with his metal-clawed hands and burning red devilish eyes. Forster and Marvin were toasting thick slices of crusty bread on the fire they'd managed to coax to life as they listened, melting cheese over the toast until it bubbled and turned golden. They ate entirely too much, washing it all down with a fine bottle of champagne that Rose had packed for the occasion, and Forster could not remember a more first-class meal.

'And then he vanished with a whirl of his cloak, his blue flames crackling and sputtering on the street,' Rose whispered, bringing her story to a dramatic finish.

'Superlative,' Forster said, grinning as Marvin applauded from where he was reclining beside the fire.

'Why thank you, gentlemen.' Rose took a deep, swooping bow. 'Now, close your eyes, Forster, and no peeking.'

He obeyed, stifling his amusement as he sat, listening to Rose and Marvin's scurrying about and the flare of a match.

'Make it a good one this year,' Marvin told him as Forster reopened his eyes to a large chocolate cake, iced with delicate cream swirls and candles blazing on top. When he blew the candles out, he wished to see Odette one more time. Smoke curled up, and as Forster stared into it, her face seemed to flicker before him for a heartbeat.

'What did you wish for?' Marvin asked, with a curious look.

Rose slapped his hand. 'You cannot ask him that or it shan't come true,' she admonished. 'Shall we do presents before we open another bottle?' She rooted through the hamper.

'Well, what would you have wished for?'

Rose paused, glancing up at Marvin. 'Oh, I don't know.' She laughed lightly. 'Some silly trinket perhaps.'

Marvin quirked an eyebrow at her. 'You mean to tell me that the fearless Rose who just entertained us with tales of Spring-Heeled Jack is afraid of sharing her greatest wish with us?'

'Marvin,' Forster cautioned.

'Fine,' Rose said hotly. 'I would wish for a charming little townhouse on the same street as my father's, with an equally charming husband with whom I would have a bunch of darling little girls, all named after flowers, like myself. Happy now?'

Marvin gave her a terse nod. His throat bobbed up and down. Rubbing the back of his neck he sheepishly began to apologise but Rose waved it away. 'That's all right,' she said awkwardly.

Forster reached for the bottle of champagne before the night spiralled down a different path than the one he had been anticipating. Popping it open, he poured each of them a saucer as Rose busied herself with cutting the cake.

'This is for you.' Marvin handed him a parcel, wrapped in brown paper.

'You needn't have done this.' Forster pushed his glasses up, touched. When he opened the gift, he found a beautifully illustrated book about swans.

'I noticed that you've been painting them of late and thought you might enjoy reading about them,' Marvin told him.

The thoughtful gesture made Forster feel guilty that he had not shared his secrets with Marvin, but then it was not his secret to share, no matter how much Marvin had demonstrated that he cared. Forster's divided loyalties were warring, filling him with remorse. He opened the book to a picture of a lake touched by moonlight with a single swan resting on its dappled surface. *Mute swans mate for life*, the caption informed him. *It has oft been observed in nature that if one of a pair succumbs to death, the remaining swan shall grieve its loss as humans do.*

Forster traced the words with his fingers, willing the weather to turn and paint the world white with snow so that he might attend Odette's party once more. Where they would finally meet again.

Chapter Eighteen

Forster slung his bag into the passenger seat of his Tin Lizzie. With greater care, he placed his camera bag on top. It contained his brand-new Leica One, along with spare rolls of thirty-five-millimetre film. A birthday gift to himself.

He drove out of London in high spirits, the smog lifting from his lungs as he headed towards Wurthercliffe. Soon the air crispened and more and more trees appeared. Each one aglow in autumn's golden cape. Forster slowed to take it all in. He'd spent the past week poring over the book about swans Marvin had gifted him with a singular question: could it truly be possible that a woman might become swan?

Perhaps today might be the day he stumbled across Odette once more. Why, this very moment she might be strolling along the clifftops, the wind tugging at her dress, her beautiful hair. He accelerated, his anticipation thrumming along with the engine. When salted air swept in from the sea, he knew he was close. It was early November and autumn was teetering at its peak before its bronzed decline into winter.

Marvin had been chasing another headline when Forster had taken leave, the temptation to drive to the manor twitching in his limbs. His head was a swirl of mysteries and puzzles he could not solve. Of a forgotten theatre, an abandoned manor, and that freezing evening seven months ago in the dark woodland that curved around the lake. The night he could not stop painting in a thousand different ways. But no matter how he told her story, it ended the same way. With the desperate grief pooling in her darkening eyes as the feathers claimed her. He wished he could steal the stars to light her way. Surround her with starshine until she smiled once more.

The lake was forever unchanged.

Sun-dappled water, algaed breeze, and ducks gliding across the mirrored surface, basking in the honeyed warmth of the afternoon. Lifting his Leica, Forster walked through the grassy overgrowth, spilling over with weeds and a last, late burst of forget-me-nots that might have been planted by a wild sprite. Perching beside the lake, he scanned it with bated breath. Nothing. Save for a rising swell of disappointment that caught him unawares. Lowering his camera, he sat there in the undergrowth. A dragonfly meandered past, its wings iridescent blue, and he idly twisted a blade of grass, considering how to recreate that spark of colour that appeared lit from within.

He whiled away the afternoon by the lakeside. Photographing the scenery and drawing in charcoal against the rich cream of his sketchbook. Pausing to luncheon on the bread and cheese he'd packed earlier that morning, he chased it with handfuls of sticky-sweet blackberries, lingering on the briar, their juice staining his fingertips a happy heliotrope-purple. Yet still he awaited something which he did not care to articulate, even to himself. There had been several mute swans lazing across the waterways along his drive but here, not a single swan. He lay back, watching the rustle of golden leaves above. Now and then, one fell to earth, twirling and pirouetting in tandem with the wind.

He hadn't realised that the pleasant hum of the country had lulled him into a siesta until he woke with a start, the late afternoon having already fallen away to eve. Still submerged in a dreamlike state, he had not the wits to subdue the lemon-sharp hope that seized him. He sat up to survey the lake. Nothing. Perhaps he was allowing his foolish fancies to sweep him away like a child who dreams of magic carpets and fairies frolicking at the bottom of their garden.

The night sky was clear, the full moon suspended like an orb, surrounded by a glittering envoy of stars. A second moon beamed up from the centre of the lake. A flash of white diverted Forster's attention. He stood, searching it out. It had originated from the far side of the lake. There, it was long overgrown with towering weeds, nettles, and all manner of wild thorns and briars, buzzing with pollen-drunk bees and gleaming beetles. But amid it all, something white glowed. Forster fought his way through the tangle, cognisant of his intrusion with each nettle sting, each thorn-bite, until he found it. A swan. His heart juddered. Its way back to the lake had been severed. Possibly during the thunderstorms that had started raging across the south on his birthday last week. 'How long have you been trapped here?' Forster murmured as he pulled at the branches blocking its path. One by one they surrendered to him. At last, the swan swam back into the lake in a grateful flurry. Forster dropped the last branch and stared after it. Could it be?

Circling the lake edge as if under a bewitchment, he observed the swan's peregrinations across the water. His fingers itched to photograph it but he'd left his Leica on the other side of the lake. Instead, he committed each detail to memory, determined to immortalise it on a canvas he would never sell. Its tapered orange beak that looked as if it had been dipped in ink, the creamy white of its feathers. It was a creature of molten moonlight and elegance and though he could never paint such a thing of beauty as it deserved to be painted, he would never stop trying.

When the swan approached him, he stilled, becoming one with the night. *Could it truly be her?* As the bird reached the shore, it paused. They were on the verge of touching, the moment strangely intimate, man and swan, alone together beneath a starlit sky. Forster's breaths were whisper-soft as he reached his hand towards the swan. It turned its slender neck, bowing its head towards him.

With the softest touch, he laid his hand on its soft down.

Chapter Nineteen

'Wake up.'

Forster lurched through his dreams towards the voice shaking him awake. 'What is it?' he mumbled, still fogged with sleep. He'd been dreaming of silvered wings and Ophelia, drowning in a lake of feathers.

'Rose is outside. It's tonight. We must drive up at once.' Marvin opened Forster's rickety wardrobe and began searching through it. 'Apparently she heard it from Margaret, who heard it from her distant cousin Edgar, who claimed that several trees in Hyde Park bore hundreds of petit fours tied onto their branches with ribbon. Each one was iced with the words *let them eat cake*.' He tossed a white shirt onto the bed before contemplating a pair of ink-black tapered trousers. 'Do you happen to have a pair of scissors handy?'

Forster sat upright. 'No. And hold off, I shall not let you mutilate my best trousers.'

Marvin shrugged. 'Have it your way.' He handed them over. 'I suppose you might tuck them into a pair of high socks, that ought to do.'

'Did you say something about cake?' Forster reached for his glasses on his bedside table. Through the lenses, Marvin's grin grew clearer and sharper. 'Buck up old chap, pay attention. The party is tonight.'

'Tonight?' Forster leapt out of bed. 'But I have been searching for the invitation since the weather turned icy last week.' He began to dress in a hurry, vexation turning him clumsy as he shoved both feet through the same trouser leg. 'Dammit!' He righted himself. 'Since the streets frosted over, I've been out hunting for it. Every evening!'

'I know—' Marvin made a sympathetic noise '—but one man cannot search an entire city by himself in a single night. We were fortunate to have been early to find it the past two years in a row. But it's of no consequence now; it has been found and we are to leave at once. Perhaps your ballerina shall be in attendance tonight.'

They raced against the night. The purring engine roared along the dark roads under a vast inky sky; its constellations masked beneath an endless flurry of snow. It was December the seventeenth. Between searching for the invitation, he had been lost in an unexpected wave of inspiration, painting a series of tragic heroines in alternative situations as if by doing so, he might swoop down into their stories, plucking them free from the words that held them there, trapped on the pages, and save them from their fates: Ophelia, wild swimming in a brook; Juliet, in her own apothecary, mixing glass bottles of violet spells and apple-green curses; Lavinia, a general in the Roman army.

Marvin lit a cigarette and offered one to Rose, who sat in a cloud of pale-pink satin, taking up both rear seats with her pannier, claiming her elaborate costume rendered her quite unable to drive her shining new yellow Rolls. She had brought brocaded jackets in holly-green and gold for both men, along with several powdered wigs that had seen better days, which Forster imagined had been rotting away in a corner of the hunting lodge.

'I say, did you remember to bring your Leica?'

Forster shook his head.

Marvin swore. Smoke curled around the word, hanging in the tight space between the two men. 'Why the devil not?'

'You roused me at an ungodly hour; forgive me for not possessing my wits,' Forster said curtly and Marvin held his hands up in suppliance. If truth be told, he had considered bringing it to capture a memory he might return to time after time. Yet he understood why Odette lived shrouded in mystery and he held no desire to rob her of that protection. He would hold her secret close. Tonight promised to be their third meeting.

'Oh, let us not squabble,' Rose said from the back, interrupting Forster's thoughts. 'And do drive faster! At this rate everyone shall reach the party before us.'

Marvin tapped his cigarette against the open window. 'I should hardly think so. Forster is keener than you to arrive.'

Rose leant forwards, pausing in her endeavour to affix a beauty spot upon a pale cheek. Her kiss curl brushed against it. 'Oh? And why might that be?'

'Why, have I not told you?' Marvin gave Forster a peculiar look. 'Forster is harbouring a hidden devotion to the ballerina that seems to dance at each and every one of these events. In fact—' his tone tightened '—some say that she might be our mysterious annual host.'

The air was hot inside the motor. Forster tugged at his shirt collar to better breathe. 'Whatever has gotten into you tonight?' he asked Marvin. 'You seem in a foul temper.'

'Marvin, do not be ridiculous, you cannot love someone you have never spoken to.' Rose's laugh was pitched a note too high, a sure sign that she was discomfited. Not for the first time, Forster wondered if something had transpired between the pair of them, their moods seemed inextricably linked these days, and whatever had riled Marvin had apparently shaken Rose as well.

'Unless,' Marvin said, turning to Rose in an approximation of sharing a delicious titbit of gossip, 'he already has and has chosen to not share the conversation with us for reasons I can only imagine.'

'You were there that night I spoke to her,' Forster reminded Marvin, frustration biting into his tone. 'And apparently I am not the only one who desires to speak with her tonight. Why don't you secure an interview with her instead of sniping at me?'

'Is this all true?' Rose demanded, her hand shaking a little when Forster glanced back at her. 'I thought you told me everything.'

'Pay him no heed,' Forster told her. 'You know well how Marvin lives to embellish the truth.'

The atmosphere within the car was a tinderbox, what with Forster's excitement battling his need for secrecy, and whatever had occurred between Rose and Marvin leaving the pair dangerously on edge.

Setting his jaw, Forster accelerated down the winding lanes.

✳ ✳ ✳

I returned to the manor to discover that another year has eclipsed me. Nine months since he witnessed me shedding my humanity. Surrendering to something rawer, wilder.

Night is darkening around me, my fears gathering in the shadows. Yet the skies are white with the promise of a thick blanket of snow. It is time to dream in music and champagne and petit fours until those shadows melt away.

As I made the necessary arrangements, I wondered if he would attend. Has my secret spilt from his lips or has it been locked inside his memories all these months? Perhaps he has written off my very existence as hallucinatory in nature and I need not concern myself a moment longer. I tasted the lie in a sudden recollection of moon-dappled water and blackberry-stained fingers reaching towards my cursed cape of feathers.

He has been searching for me.

Chapter Twenty

Walking into the manor was like entering a patisserie on the Rue Royale. The ballroom was bedecked in pastel silks and satins and adorned with elaborately wrought candied creations. The air was warm with vanilla, the music a jangling minuet. Dancers twirled through the crowd like spun sugar. Velvet curtains created dark pockets around the edges where, much to his amusement, Forster spotted a Napoleon Bonaparte sipping smoking goblets of absinthe with a Louis XVI, the pair reclining on crimson silk cushions. The Tour D'Eiffel had been recreated in pistachio macarons, chocolate-coated hothouse berries were stacked high on golden platters and croquembouche towers rose to impossible heights.

'Ah, I spy Charles and Nancy.' Rose waved to a couple wearing matching champagne-coloured bouffant wigs.

Forster's gaze wandered past them, searching for Odette.

'Nancy is Charles's beau, which you would know if you were to make an appearance on our nights out every now and then.' Rose rested a hand on Forster's arm, dragging him back into their conversation. 'I feel as if I've barely seen you the past few months,' she chided, looking up at him.

'We shall have to make amends for that soon,' he promised. 'I have missed you both dearly.' He was rewarded with her smile. 'And that's not the only thing I have missed,' he added quickly. 'Whatever is happening between you and Marvin?'

Rose's smile grew pinched. 'Ah, that. Well, I asked if one of my suitors might join us on the drive tonight but Marvin refused.'

Forster hid his amusement. 'I'm sure he did.'

Rose swatted at him. 'It's not funny, Forster! I have always known that Marvin was sweet on me but I was not certain if his affections would prove to be long lasting or but a passing infatuation—'

'Rose,' Forster began but she carried on, 'Yes, I know that was terrible of me but all that waiting has made it clear that he is the one for me. Only now it's been months since I told him I wished to marry and he has said nothing. Perhaps he is not the marrying kind after all.'

Marvin reappeared at that timely moment and passed Rose a smoking goblet.

'Ah, there you are.' She eyed him. 'Have you come to your senses yet?'

'Yes. No. Can I speak to you for a moment?' He glanced at Forster. 'You don't mind do you, old chap?'

'Of course not.' Forster watched them head off together, seized with hope that Marvin would finally unburden his heart. He had watched his friend silently pine for Rose for years but Rose had always been more guarded with her heart and he had not known for whom it beat until tonight. More selfishly, he also hoped that this turn of events would distract Marvin from Forster's own search. He did not know how Marvin had discovered that Odette was responsible for these parties, only that he must find her first.

He wandered deeper into the manor, enamoured with the violet-bright spirit of bon vivants unspooling around him in the rustle of silks and forbidden flashes of stockings in dim corners. After ascending the grand swoop of the Georgian staircase, he had a bird's-eye view over the entire French affair sparkling below. His gaze drifted through the party until he spotted Rose and Marvin, deep in conversation in one of the velveted pockets, sitting closely together. Smiling to himself, he continued to scan the crowd. An elaborate confection of a Marie Antoinette costume stole his focus. For a beat he remained unsure if it was due to her duck egg–blue gown shimmering beneath the chandeliers or her powdered wig, whorled up into a coiffure light as candyfloss and flecked with tiny, jewelled birds. Then she moved and he caught a glimpse of those blue-grey eyes, as unforgettable as ever. She was dancing with a string of young men and women, all of them drawn to her. His breath caught in his throat. She was magnetic.

He leant on the balcony, watching her. She tossed a coy look here, an irreverent smile there that almost brought a man to his knees. He awaited the moment when she took to the centre, to perform her customary solo yet it never came. Instead, Odette swanned through the crowd, every bit as royal as the French queen she had dressed the part of. He longed to speak with her, to unravel the mystery of her life, to seek an explanation for the swan form she had dissolved into. Each night he rested his head upon his pillow, she filled his dreams until he awoke with more questions, yet he did not know how one could broach the subject when the very notion of its existence was impossible.

Odette lifted her head. Her gaze collided with his. In an instant, the party between them melted away until there was only him and her and this pull between them.

She carved a path towards the French doors at the far side of the ballroom. As he watched, she turned and slowly beckoned to him with a curl of her ivory silk gloves before vanishing into the snow outside.

He followed.

Chapter Twenty-One

Fairy tales oft followed the rule of three, whether that pertains to bears or mice or number of sisters attempting to slide their foot into a glass slipper. And so, as Forster exited the ball, he could not help but imagine himself walking through the pages of a storybook. The third time he would speak to her. A white garden, glittering with snow. Inside, the Versailles-themed ball carried the heat of an illicit embrace but the instant he stepped outside, snow settled on his wig, his glasses, stole beneath the neck of his collar.

'It is you.' The words unfurled from her pink painted lips. 'You saw me.'

Forster inhaled sharply. He had been right to trust what he had seen; it had been no mere delusion. Yet how could it be possible? The very notion of a woman turning into a swan was dizzying, impossible to conceive. 'Yes.' Forster watched fear darken her expression. He stepped closer in a hurry, lowered his voice. 'Though rest assured that I have not uttered a word to another soul and nor will I.'

She tilted her head to one side in consideration and Forster found himself searching for swan-like vestiges in her movement, the lilt to her head, the way in which she comported herself. Though it was not a great surprise that a ballerina also carried herself with such grace. 'You were watching me that day on the lake,' she said with hesitation.

Her feathered back glowing in the moonlight, her silent, ink-dipped beak was seared into his memory. That evening now worlds away from this iced night and the snow that continued to softly fall. He had known it was her. There was something about her that called to him. Even as he stood there in the snow with her, he felt it. As if he had been tethered to her. 'In autumn, yes.'

'Autumn,' she repeated softly.

How cognisant could she be in her swan-form? 'It's my pleasure to make your acquaintance at last,' he said, feeling too formal, foolish after that day in the woods when she had shed her skin before him. He remembered how vulnerable she had been, the curve of her back, her shoulders bared to him. Her skin so pale and smooth he had longed to lift her into his arms and carry her away. 'I'm Forster Sylvan.'

She raised a lilac-painted eyebrow. 'And somehow you already knew my name. How?'

Forster cleared his throat, self-consciousness creeping across his skin as he considered how much to divulge, walking a tightrope of truth and deceit. 'I must confess, I did a little detective work after our first meeting.'

Odette stared at him for a moment and he tensed, concerned that he had spooked her but she merely laughed instead. 'How perfectly thrilling. I feel rather as if I'm in a novel.'

'Forgive me for asking but I happen to have visited your lake several times over the past year yet I only saw you the once. As yourself, I mean. Where I could speak to you.' Even in the frozen air, Forster grew hot beneath his wig.

Odette plucked his unfinished glass from his hands, startling him from his thoughts as she replaced it with her emptied one. 'Tell me, Forster, why have you been searching for me?'

His name in her mouth was rich and earthy. It unrooted him.

'Well, it doesn't tend to be a common occurrence to witness a woman turning into a swan.'

Her lips twisted into a wry smile. She drank her purloined champagne rather than offering an explanation.

Something about her unsettled him. He wished he might ask her how she changed, what could have possibly occurred in her life to cause such a phenomenon, why the world believed she had drowned in the aftermath of the *Titanic*. He had sought her out with the intention of assuring her of his discretion. But he was also seeking answers to the questions that had pursued him from the frost-enlaced mystery of the precious winter to the world reawakening in the spring, through the blossom-burst of summer, and the golden breath of autumn's sigh as snow once more reclaimed the land. Yet now he found those same questions paled before another, stronger desire. He wanted to linger in her presence.

He held out his hand instead. 'Would you care to dance with me?'

She laughed then. 'In the snow?'

Forster tipped his head back. The world spun on its axis as the sky fell towards him in an infinite swirl of snowflakes. 'Whyever not?'

She stepped forward in a whisper of silk on snow. 'Very well then. But you must call me Detta,' she said, placing her hand in his.

'Detta,' he echoed, holding her hand. It was warm beneath the glove, and small within his. When he glanced up, her lips parted. They were full and bow-shaped and he had a sudden longing to pull her towards him, test if they were as soft as they appeared. Slowly, he moved closer. He took her in his arms. Forster took a deep breath, struck with the terrible realisation that she was more than a mystery. More than a muse. He placed his hand on her back, feeling her shiver at his touch.

They began to dance. Moving together as one in a manner that made Forster ache for more. 'Your garden looks like a fairy tale,' he told her in a bid to distract himself as they danced over the moon-drenched snow. Flowering pink viburnum and dogwood shrub stems in vibrant crimson burst from the snow in large arrangements. Winter pansies bloomed in splashes of yellow and purple. This was not a garden that slumbered through winter.

'Perhaps I shall make that my next theme,' Detta mused, arching back as he dipped her. He looked down at her, close enough to fall into her gaze. Imagined leaning down and kissing her, his mind spinning wildly out of control, wondering if she would taste like snow and champagne and the delicate perfume that frolicked over her neck.

Aware that he had been holding her there a beat too long, he raised her, his arms falling from her waist, her back, as she pirouetted to a finish, her eighteenth-century-style gown flaring. 'This dress is ridiculously dramatic. Can you picture having to don one every day?' She laughed with him before taking his arm and guiding him further into the garden. 'You're a far better dancer than I was expecting.'

'Ah, all down to my mother. She made me take lessons.' A lifetime ago, when he had played escort to his older sister at parties before she had married. Before his mother had uttered those final words that had torn straight through their relationship, leaving it with jagged ends that bit into him. They wandered past the frozen drapery of a great weeping willow. Snow pattered down onto its branches, lending it a sparkling blanket for the night.

'Why haven't you asked me why I am the way I am?' Detta whispered into his thoughts.

'Though I'm deeply curious, it isn't my place to ask. If you ever wish to confide in me then you have my ears, my silence even. But I have no desire to plague you with questions.' Forster gestured at the ball, twinkling in the distance. 'Especially not on a night that you've taken great effort to orchestrate.'

Detta's answering smile was luminous. 'How very chivalrous of you,' she said teasingly.

Forster grinned at her. 'One tries.'

They fell into a companionable silence, strolling beneath an ancient oak tree, its branches bent over them, shielding them from the snow. A small lantern had been left beneath, its candle almost spent. It was a pocket of magic. Forster turned to Detta, her eyes searching his as he closed the space between them. In the distance he heard the faint strains of the string quartet playing something unbearably romantic, the snow falling around the tree leaving them untouched. Detta's chest rose and fell faster as his gaze dipped to her mouth. 'It's terribly unfair that you're wandering around with lips like those,' he uttered, reaching out and softly running his thumb along her bottom lip.

'And why might that be?' Detta murmured, watching him.

'They have been driving me to distraction since I stepped outside with you. All I can think of is—' He swallowed, his hand falling away.

Detta rested her fingers on his chest. 'Yes?'

His heart beat harder. With a sudden courage, he claimed her mouth with his. He kissed her like a man come home from war. Held her tightly as she responded, sweet and soft and tender, her hands running up into his hair.

They parted as suddenly as they had come together, as if they did not, they might have lost an eternity in a single kiss. It stirred something within Forster, urged him to breathlessly confess, 'I wish this night would never end.'

Candlelight flickered over Detta's face. 'I am cursed, Forster.

Chances are, I shall not be here in the morning.' They both glanced at the snow, icing the garden like a Christmas cake.

Forster shook his head. 'I don't understand. What are you saying?'

'It is the snow,' Detta said simply. 'I am only human in the snow. When it melts away, so too do I, for then I am cursed to be a swan.'

Forster staggered back, the cruel twist of fate resounding through his bones, his heart. 'No,' he whispered in disbelief. Most of her days were stolen away as she swam through one season to the next. He struggled to comprehend it. Searched for the right words but there weren't any.

She smiled. It was touched with sadness that he yearned to reach out and brush away. 'The funny thing is, the more people I surround myself with, the lonelier I feel. I could be dancing in a sea of people and still be completely alone. You may be the very first person at one of these parties to see *me*.' She caught her lip between her teeth. 'If you wish to know the truth, look to Rothbart's Theatre of Enchantments.' He started at this reveal, not a circus but a *theatre*, but she was already speaking on. 'Do say you will return? Then we might speak properly, without all of this—' she waved an arm back at the Versailles ball glittering in the distance '—as a distraction.'

'The very next time it snows,' Forster vowed.

'Until then, Forster Sylvan.' With that, she ducked beneath the oak's branches and danced away over the snow in light steps, her shoes not making a print. Forster watched her leave, suddenly believing in the wild magic that swept through the world like a winter's gale.

'Do not disappoint me now,' she tossed over her shoulder. Her accompanying laugh was airy, as if it belonged to creatures that flew on gossamer wings and drank vials of moonbeams. Something not of this world. And he was utterly beneath her spell.

PART THREE

1925

'Snow-White longed for the beautiful apple, and when she saw that the peasant woman was eating part of it she could no longer resist, and she stuck her hand out and took the poisoned half. She barely had a bite in her mouth when she fell to the ground dead.'

—JACOB AND WILHELM GRIMM, *Little Snow-White*

Chapter Twenty-Two

Forster crumpled the letter in his fist at the same time as Rose shrieked. 'Do not even think about it,' she warned Marvin, who was advancing on her with a devilish grin and a spoonful of batter dripping all over their flat. 'This is hand-embroidered French silk from the House of Chanel!' She stroked the asymmetrical black dress that fluttered around her calves as she backed away.

Marvin cast it an appreciative look. 'It's beautiful. Though it pales in comparison to you.' Reaching for Rose's wrist, he gathered her towards him, forgetting his spoon, which dripped all over Forster's letter.

Forster made to throw it into the fire. 'That's all it was fit for anyway.'

Rose broke free of Marvin's arms to intercept it. 'This is your older sister who wrote this? Beatrice?' She glanced at Forster, all puckered brow and pursed lips and righteous indignation.

Forster nodded confirmation. Having just returned from celebrating Christmas with Marvin's family, it had cheered him to find evidence of his own family having remembered him. Until he had read the contents. Rose wiped it free of batter and unfolded it.

'I am sorry to say that I have attempted to broach the subject with Mother on several occasions yet still she refuses to speak on it.

Though it pains me to tell you, you must maintain your distance as she is in poor health and the very mention of your name sullies her mood,' Rose read aloud before scoffing and handing it to Forster, who tossed it into the fire. She placed her hands on Forster's cheeks, surveying him seriously. 'You have done nothing wrong, darling, I do hope you know that? Your mother is clearly addled with grief and you cannot reason with such a devastating emotion.'

'I know,' Forster choked out over the lump in his throat. He pretended to miss the pitying look that passed between Rose and Marvin, instead stealing a piece of gingerbread cooling from the oven.

Rose gave him a mock glare. 'You just ate our chimney.'

Their tiny kitchen was clouded with the sweet spice of gingerbread. It had turned out in misshapen pieces but Rose still vowed they would assemble to form a darling little house. Forster and Marvin harboured misgivings about this since Rose couldn't tell what any of the pieces were meant to be.

As Forster reached for a nibble of what was either designated to be half of the roof or perhaps the door, Rose playfully batted his hands away and ushered both men into the living room. There, a little fir was standing in a corner, next to a box of decorations that Rose had brought over. 'If you cannot keep your hands off my gingerbread then we shall have to trim the tree until you can be trusted.' She offered a shimmering glass bauble to Forster. It was painted with frost. His memories snow-stormed back to a few weeks ago, standing beneath a great oak and kissing Detta as if the world were ending around them. *I am only human in the snow.* His heart gave a painful thump each time he remembered her words. Sleep eluded him as he lay in bed, staring up at his basement window and the sky beyond, wishing for snow that never came, aching to return to Wurthercliffe. To hold her tightly and take in a deep breath of her hair, all soft and curly, scented with jasmine and the woods and the lake. That bite of wildness rippling under her skin. One glance at the living room window confirmed the weather's utter refusal to grant Forster's wish. It was the first of January and the sky had not shed one flake of snow since the night of the party. Christmas had whirled by with Forster spending it with Marvin's rambunctious family of seven siblings and Marvin's mother, who had fed him extra platefuls of everything until he was sure he would burst like a Christmas cracker. Since Rose had escorted her father to Paris for the holiday, the three friends were determined to celebrate the festive season together upon her return. For there was no finer family than the one you had chosen yourself.

Forster gently hung the bauble on the tree.

'Splendid,' Rose declared, admiring their efforts. Their fir tree reached Forster's waist and it had scented their entire flat with its pine needles. That and the gingerbread made it smell like Christmas, and with Lewis James crooning 'When Christmas Chimes Are Ringing' on the wireless, Forster quite forgot it was not Christmas Eve once again. Marvin hung a sprig of mistletoe and pounced on Rose as Forster looked away, turning his attention to tying red velvet bows on the branches.

They whiled away the afternoon covering themselves in icing as the panes of gingerbread slid over each other and refused to resemble anything close to Rose's darling little house she'd promised. As she grew more and more frustrated, Forster and Marvin found it harder to conceal their laughter, especially once they'd mixed a jug of eggnog together.

Finally, Rose managed to place the roof atop her house without it slipping. 'There!' she crowed. 'I told you it would work.'

'Can we eat it now?' Marvin reached for the chimney.

'You most certainly may not!' Rose swatted his hand. 'First it must set and then we can decorate it.' Marvin looked horrified and glanced at the clock on the mantel as if wagering how long all of that would take. Forster laughed so hard his eggnog went down the wrong way.

Later that evening, Marvin placed his black bowler hat on his head before hesitating. 'You are welcome to join us.'

'And watch you spend the entire evening staring into each other's eyes?' Forster laughed as Marvin struggled to contain his pride at the fact. 'No, you go and enjoy your time together. I'm certain you will make a good impression on Rose's father,' Forster added as Marvin grimaced, looking nervous. It was to be their first meeting and Rose had arranged for the three of them to dine together at the Café de Paris, a fashionable cabaret spot over on Coventry Street.

Yet still, Marvin lingered. Even as Rose sounded the horn on her yellow Rolls-Royce, the envy of their street each time she visited. 'Are you quite certain? What will you do?'

'I shall paint. Though I cannot promise that you will return to an intact house.' Forster jerked his chin at the gingerbread house, dripping icing and the Parisian chocolate truffles Rose had come bearing.

Marvin tapped the brim of his hat. 'Have at it.' He chuckled.

Forster waved them off before returning to the empty flat. Slowly, he gathered his materials and began prepping a fresh canvas. Yet when it was ready, the only thing he could think to paint was snow. A sky filled with titanium white snow and blue-casted shadows. A street slowly took shape, forming behind the feathery white. And in the centre focus, a building. Its doors open, puddling light, it bore a glowing sign: *The Theatre of Enchantments*.

Chapter Twenty-Three

The early January day was as crisp as honeycomb as Forster walked through the winding streets of York. It had been some time since he had ventured this far north. Though he was unsure what he might find amid the butterscotch-stone buildings, according to folklore, York was a city of ghosts. And Forster was haunted. His dreams swimming with a woman that disappeared into feathers. Perhaps here he would find some answers to the questions he did not know how to frame. It had not snowed in weeks. Eventually he had grown tired of watching the skies and taken it upon himself to address the second startling revelation that Detta had made. To look to Rothbart's Theatre of Enchantments.

He wandered up and down Clifford Street several times before he found the large redbrick exterior that had seen better days. Halting, mid-step, he stared up at it. It was smaller than he had been expecting, less assuming, and yet there was something inexplicable about it. Perhaps this was the root of Detta's curse. The building hummed with an odd energy and, as he listened closer, it raised a trail of goose bumps up Forster's arms.

'Can you believe it?' An older woman with milky eyes and a wisp of grey hair idled on the street beside Forster. 'Once this was the greatest theatre in Europe. I had the good fortune myself to see one of their performances once. *Snow White*. I've never seen the like since . . . '

'What happened to it? I'd never heard mention of it until recently.' Forster scanned the dilapidated façade. A faded sign declared it as *Rothbart's Theatre of Enchantments*. Once, it must have been glittering and grand.

The woman let out a melancholic sigh. Rose would have appreciated her; they shared the same sense of theatricality. Her voice lowered to a whisper as she leant in closer. 'Not many folk know this but it happens that there was an investigation. Performers kept disappearing in the night, never to be seen again. The police took an interest in Rothbart, the great showrunner himself, but it was too late.' She trailed off, fixing him with a stare that invited reaction.

'Why? What became of him?' Forster asked. As he studied the woman, a deep curiosity settled into his bones.

'Well, one day he just upped and left, same as the vanished girls. Then the war came and I daresay he was forgotten. Much like his theatre. Fell into disgrace, it did. Folk didn't like to talk of it after that.' She gave an exaggerated shudder. 'Chills my bones, it does, to think of him still out there somewhere.'

Forster's mind whirred faster over this latest mystery as he tried to decipher whether the two were tangled together. 'Does nobody have an inkling of where he might be?'

The woman shrugged. 'It's been a long decade, I doubt anyone's still looking.' Hefting her shopping bag more firmly on her shoulder, she began to trundle away. 'Such a shame,' she muttered before she was out of earshot.

Forster proceeded to the rear of the theatre. Marvin would have made for excellent company on this excursion but Forster had risen before dawn had crowned and motored north to York, leaving Marvin in slumber, dreaming of Rose. Forster had not told him of his plans. Each time he was tempted to confide a little of that secret in Marvin, his thoughts trespassed to Odette. Detta. And the way she had trembled and shaken and fallen apart in that frozen copse.

The back door of the theatre was sitting off its hinges. Doubtless it had been plundered if it had sat abandoned since before the Great War, its gilded sign promising untold riches within.

Forster stepped inside. Treading through these corridors was like walking through someone else's memory. He wanted to paint Detta floating by, her pointe shoes barely touching the worn carpets, her tutu a lustrous satin, gleaming against the dim walls. An angel flitting through the mortal world. He understood now why Degas had painted and sculpted and drawn more than a thousand ballerinas. After navigating his way to the stage, Forster stood in the audience and closed his eyes, picturing her there. Sparkling with youth and talent, bringing the audience to a standing ovation as the prima ballerina who had been painted on the poster which had led him here. His world darkened to bitter charcoal as he reopened his eyes to the stage, cast in shadows. What had happened during those missing years between Detta dancing upon this stage to her grand parties in that abandoned manor house and her curious existence as half-woman, half-swan? Turning on his heel, he marched back down the central corridor, on the hunt for clues.

There was an office at the end of the corridor. A bronze nameplate stamped Rothbart's ownership on the door. Forster hesitated, dwelling on the stranger and her story. *Girls vanished.* Had Detta brushed against tragedy at every corner of her life? She'd sailed on the ill-fated *Titanic*, danced for a man suspected of grave crimes, and encountered some dark and powerful force he could not yet comprehend. If Forster dared to dream, he would have hoped he could be her rescuer. But the darker, nightmare-ridden crevices of his mind whispered that perhaps he too was marked now. After all, he had never been a hero, and if this situation was anything like the one he endured with his family, his involvement could make everything worse.

Swallowing his self-doubt, Forster pushed the door open. The office was in disarray with drawers yanked from the desk and emptied, files and folders bereft of their documents. Debris littered the Persian carpet which suggested either it had been abandoned in a hurry or had since been emptied by opportunists. It was the walls that captured Forster's attention. Posters of Rothbart's Theatre of Enchantments lined them, each one framed. A handful showed Detta in the trappings of various ballets and fairy tales. *Snow White. Rapunzel. The Snow Queen.* More featured another woman, a little older, with an angular face and eyes in woodland shades of green and brown. Forster dug through the debris yet found nothing of interest. Some old tickets, a receipt, bits and pieces from another life, another world. This was a useless endeavour; he had no notion of what he was looking for. Still, the mysteries he had happened upon gnawed away at him, leaving him restless and on the hunt.

When he was younger, both he and his older sister, Beatrice, had been avid fans of Sherlock Holmes, battling to be first to read his stories in *The Strand Magazine*. Beatrice, being the eldest, had recruited a rather too compliant Forster to the position of Watson, and would sit and muse and pretend to smoke their father's pipe while Forster hunted around for clues. He felt like that young boy again now. Desperate to land on an excellent clue that would make his sister pout, his mother smile, his father ruffle his hair. He slumped to the carpet, overpowered by nostalgia and the sharp jaws of grief that had suddenly closed over him. His father was gone, his mother refusing to see him, and Beatrice, once a firm ally, now instructing him to stay away. To remain estranged. He cast his gaze for a distraction. A tiny spark of inspiration seized him. The hearth. If Rothbart had known that he had invited suspicion upon himself . . . Forster scrambled over to look. The last fire had sputtered ash everywhere like a belligerent dragon. Lifting an iron fire poker from the wall, he poked amongst the charred remains.

And, like the brightest jewel in a dragon's cave, he found something. Several old photographs that had refused to burn: one of Detta with an abundance of ringlets that called to mind princesses and witches and towers; an ancient castle, crumbling down its mountain-perch; and a man with silver-white hair and ice-cold eyes.

Chapter Twenty-Four

January closed in a curtain of snow. Forster awoke to a world painted in feathered white and silhouetted in ice. A crystalline canvas. He pulled on a knitted jumper and his navy woollen coat and leapt in his Tin Lizzie before Marvin had yet departed the land of dreams.

The roads were barren but perilous with ice. Each minute he lost, he cursed and raised his eyes to the sky, the weather a fickle beast he did not trust to hold steady.

Upon reaching his destination, he parked out of sight behind the manor, took a woollen blanket from the back seat and strode down to the lakeside, hoping that Detta would be there still. Would still be *her*.

Though the lake was snow-speckled, the woodland donning a lacy white cape, he sighted not swan nor woman. Retracing his steps in greater urgency, he discovered that the manor door had been left unlocked.

'It seems you are a man of your word.' Detta's voice echoed down the stairs as she descended. She wore wide-legged flowing trousers and a velvet jacket in cabernet-red, her whisky-coloured curls dancing free around her shoulders.

Forster's chest tightened. There was no party, no revellers dancing in a champagne-haze, just the two of them, alone in the vast manor. Their togetherness stark in the pale morning light. Before he might respond, Detta waved a hand airily. 'Would you care for some breakfast?' She padded past him on bare feet, back into the depths of the manor. She did not glance back, assured that he would follow. If Orpheus had possessed her belief then Eurydice would not have vanished back into the underworld, he thought, following her through a shadowed corridor, past closed doors, unsettling motes of dust in their passage, and into a kitchen beaming with light and warmth.

To his great astonishment, there was already a woman cooking at the range. Detta seated herself at a table laid for three and frowned at her nails. They were torn and jagged. A visceral reminder that she had returned from the wilderness.

Forster slowly sat opposite her. 'It would seem you were expecting me.'

'So it would.' Detta's tone was teasing. She gestured at the woman who was studying him intently. 'Mrs Fischer was once my nanny and is the last of the staff who still reside in the manor. I am fortunate that she oversees it in my absence.'

Mrs Fischer wore a long burgundy dress with a high neck and long sleeves which was undoubtedly a Victorian relic. Her grey hair was pinned up and her dark grey eyes were steely in a narrow, olive-skinned face.

'Good morning, Mr Sylvan,' she said, before turning her attention back to a ceramic bowl. Fiercely whisking it, she nodded to herself as if she had completed her evaluation of him. Forster wondered what she had been searching for in him. Whether she had found it or discovered him to be lacking. 'I do hope crêpes are to your liking?'

Detta glanced across at him with a youthful spark. 'I used to accompany my parents on their various trips to Paris when I was young. If I was quiet and well behaved while my mother visited the couturiers, she would indulge me with a visit to my favourite crêperie.'

Her smile set Forster aglow. He could not keep from dwelling on their passionate exchange, from wondering why she had invited him here to speak with her. 'To this day, whenever I taste crêpes, I am back there. The spring air teasing my curls free as I run alongside the Seine. My mother with a sugar-smudge on her usually perfect nose.' Her lips parted as she sighed and something deep down tugged at Forster.

As the stack of delicate crêpes rose higher, a sweet cloud of sugar powdered the air. Mrs Fischer squeezed a lemon rind over them, like liquid sunshine, before arranging them onto plates.

'I unearthed an article about your parents,' Forster admitted. Mrs Fischer's spine stiffened, a lioness keeping a fierce guard. 'You must miss them dearly.'

Detta toyed with a starched napkin, unfolding it onto her lap. 'My father thought sea voyages romantic. I believe some part of him once wished to be a great explorer.' Mrs Fischer averted her attention back to the stove. 'Though we rarely accomplish what we most desire in our heart of hearts, I found his death cruel. As if the Fates were laughing when they threaded his path through life.'

'It was a great tragedy. Unthinkable that it should ever had happened. You were fortunate to have survived such an ordeal,' Forster said gently.

Detta's laugh was short, harsh. 'I never left this manor. I had the misfortune – or so I believed at the time – of quarrelling with my mother. And though there already existed a ticket under my name, I threw the weight of young stubbornness behind my argument and refused to accompany them. They left without me. That ticket bought in my name and undoubtedly my mother's unwillingness to admit a most unseemly rebellion on her daughter's part led to why I was presumed dead. Or—' She swallowed.

'Or?' Forster echoed.

'Or she went to her watery grave believing I would change my mind and meet them at the dock,' she whispered. 'Forever waiting for a reconciliation that never came.'

Forster reached a hand out and gently laid it on top of hers. 'You cannot think such thoughts,' he whispered back. Detta turned her hand palm side up, her fingers seeking his. With a secret thrill, Forster interlaced their fingers. Her skin against his tingled. He had never been as acutely aware of his hand before yet now it was all he could think of . . . look at . . . feel.

Mrs Fischer slid three warmed plates onto the heavy oak table, startling them apart. She seated herself, grimacing at her stiffness. 'Eat up.' Her gaze rested fondly on Detta, though not without a pinch of concern. 'You're thinner than the last time I saw you.'

Detta inhaled, her breath ragged. 'Not all of the bodies were recovered from those dark waters,' she shuddered, continuing their conversation, haunted by glimpses of the fate that might have befallen her. 'And at seventeen, burning brightly with dreams of stardom, it suited me better to be dead. It removed me from Society's spotlight, leaving me free to claim my life as my own. To pursue a career in dancing.'

'Miss Lakely is a beautiful ballerina.' Mrs Fischer beamed. 'Though her mother was concerned at the thought of her living alone at such a tender age, each time she danced, she welcomed magic and life and beauty into the manor.' Her eyes grew damp and she blinked the tears away. 'They would have been proud of her.'

'Only dear Mrs Fischer and our trusted family lawyer knew I had not perished, so I took myself to York under my mother's maiden name and danced in Rothbart's Theatre of Enchantments. My dreams soon came true and I was elevated to the position of prima ballerina for a time.' Detta lifted her fork and pierced her crêpes. Curlicues of steam rose. The scent of lemon bit the air. 'Needless to say, it did not end well.' Her knife scraped the china plate in a high-pitched screech.

Forster did not press her for details, even as his curiosity swelled.

'Now I take care of Miss Lakely.' Mrs Fischer watched her eat affectionately. The crease between her eyebrows deepened. 'But I am growing older with each year that passes by and—'

'I am positively certain that you shall outlive me, Mrs Fischer,' Detta interrupted brightly.

Mrs Fischer exchanged a loaded glance with Forster.

He turned his attention onto his crêpes, attempting to banish the concern that had flooded him on hearing Detta's statement. As swans did not live as long as humans did, she was in more danger than he had realised.

After breakfast, Detta embarked on giving him a tour of the manor. They left Mrs Fischer pottering and humming along to the wireless in the kitchen. 'She's an old dear,' said Detta fondly. 'I would simply perish without her.'

She took to the role of tour guide with great enthusiasm, her stories conjuring the manor to life. 'These old Great Houses, they're the hallmark of a dying era. A glimpse into the echoes of the past. I've borne no heirs that might inherit it so it shall pass down to some third cousin, twice removed or some such, and they will eventually be forced to sell.' She let out a dusty sigh before a spark inflamed her, setting her aglow. 'But first I plan on going out with a bang. I shall not go quietly into that long, deep, endless night, Forster.'

Forster suddenly found it hard to breathe, the thought of the world being robbed of Detta was too cruel, but her eyes were clamped on his, her tone fierce and bright enough to burn down worlds, and he could not look away as she told him, 'I want to firework through it.'

✿

'This is my favourite place you've shown me so far,' Forster said sometime later, when they stood in an oak-walled library, surveying the leather-bound tomes shelved up to the painted ceiling with Georgian embellishments – medallions encircled the chandelier as sculpted leaves of plaster crept towards it, mimicking the trees that stood like sentries around the frozen lake. A reminder that though the snow continued to fall, it would not do so forever.

Detta ran a finger along a dusted shelf. 'Tell me, what drew you to art?'

Forster paused, attempting to distil thought and feeling into explanation. 'For me, it's the moment when it becomes real. When a collection of brushstrokes cease to be marks upon canvas and suddenly come to life. Art is like alchemy; the right formula sparks something magical.'

Detta sat down on a chaise and curled her legs up beneath her to make room for Forster. He sat beside her, all too aware of her proximity, suppressing the urge to draw her closer, to taste her lips once more, to hold her in his arms and never let go. Her gaze dusk-blue in the weak afternoon sunlight, she softly uttered, 'Go on.'

Mindful of all the intimate moments and history she had shared with him, he spoke from a deep and truthful place. 'When I'm painting, my mind stills and the world quiets. I feel at peace.'

The aroma of Turkish coffee preluded Mrs Fischer's arrival. She placed a silver tray down between them, pressed a hand to Detta's cheek, and took her leave. Detta passed Forster a cracked cup. A stack of toast swam in a river of butter and she bit into a slice. 'And when your painting is finished? What then?'

He gave her a crooked smile. 'Then the world comes rushing back in again.'

She slowly nodded, delicately licking the butter from her fingers. Forster glanced away, pushing his glasses up with a knuckle, under the pretence that he was unaffected. He drank his coffee black, savouring the richness. Detta poured a swirl of cream-topped milk into hers. She brought it to her lips with a sigh. 'Once when I danced, I felt as you did. It was the sole purpose in my life, the very thing that granted me enjoyment, that quieted the voices in my head that whispered I should never amount to more. I danced with passion, with defiance. And when I stepped upon a stage, I became something greater. Then I entered Rothbart's Theatre of Enchantments and it granted my wishes before stealing my dreams.'

'After you told me to look the Theatre, I took it upon myself to pay it a visit.' She stilled. 'It's standing empty in York now but it's alive with rumours.' Forster hardly dared breathe. 'What happened to you there?'

Detta leant back, resting her cup against her leg. 'It is a lengthy tale.' She regarded him curiously and he found he could not look away. 'Though perhaps telling it will ease the weight upon my heart.'

'You have my full confidence. Anything you share with me shall never cross my lips to another.' Forster set his cup down.

'Then I shall spin you a story of magic and wonder, horror and cruelty.' She stood and fetched a nondescript album from one of the shelves, brushing the dust from it as she reclaimed her place beside him. She opened it, revealing old photographs of the Lakelys pasted inside: a woman and man with a curly-haired infant who grew into a girl with eyes that shone from the page, giving way to a young woman who stood with her mother, arms entwined around each other. Detta flipped past those pages as if they scalded, and Forster recognised that pinch of grief, as if you lingered too long on the face of your lost loved one, that sadness would work its way inside you, and you would never be rid of it. She skipped through it faster and faster, until she reached the end, where a newspaper review had been tucked inside the bindings.

She passed it to Forster. 'This was the first I heard mention of Rothbart and his Theatre of Enchantments. I was deep in the maw of grief when I read it, yet still I felt something calling to me. Tempting me. Later I wondered if the words themselves had not been bespelled, so irresistible they were to me. As if they had been lifted from my dreams, offering a wonderful escape.'

Detta's fingertips brushed against Forster's as he accepted the album. Their touch whispered through him. Perhaps he himself was bespelled. He lowered his eyes to the clipping he held and began to read.

The Theatre Gazette

16th May 1912

This spring witnessed the opening of another delightful offering from Rothbart's Theatre of Enchantments, fast becoming a must-visit attraction in York. As is this theatre's trademark, the debut of Twelve Dancing Princesses features a performance which combines the very best of ballet, acrobatics and illusions to spellbinding effect. It was adapted from the fairy tale by Rothbart, the proprietor of the theatre, who in addition to his choreographic prowess, is proving to be a master illusionist.

The story unfolds through the narrative ballet in an impressive three acts and fifteen tableaux. For aficionados of classical dance, there is plenty to admire from the twelve soloists who anchor the production in their elegant interpretation of the princesses for whom the show is named. Yet Rothbart's Theatre of Enchantments is not the playground of ballerinas alone; if one turned their gaze skyward, they would be met with the sight of the performance mirrored by twelve aerialists, swooping and leaping through the heavens.

At first the night appeared to belong to Penelope Petra, the young prima ballerina whose pas de deux with the soldier was deeply expressive, yet the true star became apparent when the audience were surprised with an unexpected rainfall within the theatre itself. Though fear not, the attendees' evening attire was not spoiled; upon contact, the water transformed to wildflowers, turning the theatre into a flower-flecked vision.

Another of Rothbart's stunning illusions at play, proving this man to be one to watch. A sorcerer among mortals.

Chapter Twenty-Five

Detta
1912

It was on a summer's day that I sought to change my life. I set off on a rambling cross-country train, licking the jam out of the tarts Mrs Fischer had baked for me. I was determined to distract myself from the sadness that filled every room of the manor I'd just inherited. A sadness so thick and suffocating I had begun to feel claustrophobic. On reaching my destination, a kind porter hailed me a taxi, where I sat beside my steamer trunk and carpetbag with my face pressed to the window as the horses trundled us over the little bridge over the river Ouse and into the wide street. There, the theatre proudly stood inside the walled city of York. It was grand with Prussian-blue columns, gold leafing, and overlarge gilded letters that spelt out *Rothbart's Theatre of Enchantments*. I tingled with excitement upon seeing it at last. A ticket for tonight's performance rested in my pocket and I kept reaching for it, checking that it was still there. Even in my secluded manor on a sleepy coast, I had heard the rumours. That Rothbart's theatre would steal your senses away, entrance you like fairy wine, ensorcell you with delight and wonder. There was a reason they called Rothbart The Sorcerer. Society gossiped that he was a genius, a prodigious talent turned to the business of entertainment. Tickets were hard to come by; no sooner had a new performance been announced than it was fully booked. It was a rare experience. And one that I was longing to attend.

The taxi swept me away and onto the lodging I had secured in advance.

When evening arrived, the proprietor obliged me, lacing me into my S-shaped corset before I dressed in my pearlescent Worth gown, pale-pink lace frothing down my arms and across my collarbones like cherry blossom. Pearls studded my ears and looped around the wrists of my satin evening gloves. I was finally ready to peek behind the veil of enchantments at the theatre. After a year marked with painful loss, I had come to realise the only way I might become happy was in the pursuance of my dream: to dance on stage. And there was no finer stage on which to perform than Rothbart's.

Pine-scented rosin, the tap of pointe shoes, and scurry of activity behind the velvet curtains made me ache for my mother. She had been my co-conspirator as we'd sneaked backstage to watch the dancers take their places, their tutus a-shimmer, whispering secrets and stifling giggles as they fizzed with giddy anticipation. A feeling I knew well was better than drinking a saucer of father's vintage champagne. As did she. Once, she had danced in the corps in Moscow before her family had decided to leave for England amid warnings of upcoming revolution. Here she no longer danced but still she adored it and when I came along shortly after her wedding my father, she named me for her favourite ballet. My earliest memory was seeing her face light up with inner joy when I landed my first pirouette on wobbling legs. She subscribed to the *Comœdia Illustré* for their special illustrated supplements that covered the dancers and costumes of Diaghilev's Ballets Russes in Paris but though she had been a great patron of the arts, she was less enamoured with my declaration that I wanted to leave home at an age she considered too tender. Thankfully, Mrs Fischer did not share her inclination. Or perhaps she knew me well enough to know that if she refused my sole request, I would have absconded in the night.

Now, I was ushered to my seat alone, the memory of my mother a permanent ghost that accompanied me. When the orchestra began, the air hummed with magic, a hushed excitement spreading among the sold-out audience. Something was creaking awake, alighting long-forgotten senses.

Time trickled away like warm honey and the performance began. It was a rendition of *The Twelve Dancing Princesses*, taken from Grimms' Fairy Tales and designed and choreographed by Rothbart himself. A fantasy in lavish sets, bejewelled colours, and music rich and delicate all at once so that hearing it was like biting into a mille-feuille. A delicious experience to be savoured. Just when I believed I could not be more entranced, with a shimmer and a flash, it began to rain inside the theatre. Holding out my hand to catch a raindrop, I let out a silent gasp when, rather than splashing onto my palm as expected, it transformed into a wildflower with dainty peacock-blue petals. A sigh of wonder rippled through the audience. The entire theatre now wore a petal-carpet. It was as if we were treading the same path as the twelve sisters on stage as they passed through a gossamer veil into a secret world where they danced the night away. When a hidden soldier spied upon them, following the twelfth and youngest princess into her boat that sailed across a silvered stage, a pair of swans flew out over the audience and vanished. As they exclaimed, I looked across to where the famed Rothbart stood in the wings. His face painted across the posters for *Twelve Dancing Princesses* outside had been beaming, jovial. I couldn't shake the feeling that that had been another performance as now, his face was devoid of a smile; owlish.

He met my gaze. In that moment, he was as luminous as the swans and I quite believed that he had created magic that lived and breathed. With a slight laugh, I dispelled the notion. His illusions were truly marvellous and I had fallen for them as the audience had. But Rothbart did not look away from me. His tawny eyes held a challenge within them as if he could read my thoughts and I knew that if I wished to dance for him, I would have to shine brighter than ever.

'I want to dance.'

I arched my neck, matching Rothbart's imperious stare, since it was he who had opened the stage door himself. Nondescript with peeling paint, the shabbiness of the back door was at odds with the grand sweep of the main entrance. Yet this was the door I had been instructed to find. 'I have travelled some distance to speak with you.' I was proud that my voice did not waver and betray me. I was still bewitched from the performance the previous eve and desperate to prove myself. He wore a fashionable purple double-breasted sack suit that I could not help noticing bore an uncanny similarity to his carpet. On anyone else it would have been outlandish yet Rothbart's presence was stronger than any outfit could hope to be. Intimidating. And I was painfully aware that he held my dreams in his hand. His to send soaring over the rooftops or crush in a fist. 'You must be lost, girl. I take only the best. The ticket office will open at midday if you wish to see another performance though we are fully booked this season.'

He had recognised me. This was emboldening. 'I am the best.'

He did not respond to this. Yet his scepticism was evident in those tawny eyes. There was a strange intensity to him. I refused to allow my confidence to tremble, to bow down before him. 'And if

I am not, then I refuse to rest until I am,' I added fiercely. My palm was slick on the small bag containing my pointe shoes. I gripped the handle tighter, desperate not to have to drag myself all the way home to the manor, weighted with rejection.

With a sudden jerk, he stood aside, holding the door open with an accompanying grand gesture. 'Then by all means, do enter.'

'Oh, thank you, I—' I bit off my words, unsure if he was making a mockery of me, and hurried inside. Whatever his motivations, I held my own. I would prove to this man that I was deserving of a place on the stage. That I belonged in his theatre.

'Follow me,' Rothbart boomed, striding off through a dark corridor that led to the beautiful great hall I had sat in last night with its shimmering crystal chandeliers and thick velvet curtains. Up on the stage, a lone ballerina performed an effortless string of fouettés. Spinning faster than a top, her leg whipped the air.

'Penelope is the star of my show. My prima ballerina,' Rothbart announced, observing her with no little pride.

'She is perfection.' I gazed at her slender form, her spangled tutu glittering as she span, her light-brown hair smoothed back into a bun. I recognised her both from the performance and the posters plastered everywhere in York; aside from Rothbart himself, she was the face of his theatre. But here, beneath the electric stage lights in an empty theatre, she was radiant. A vision of elegance, a dream of a dancer. I regretted my earlier self-vaunting even as I itched to dance, fretting that I would never be as great as her.

Whirling to a finish, Penelope curtsied in a classical révérance and vanished into the wings. The promise of magic seeped from the theatre with her exit. Rothbart switched his attention to me. He was standing closer beside me than I had realised, having been caught up in the ballet, and I noticed anew how oddly magnetic he was. His cheekbones were pronounced, his hair black as raven feathers and cut as fashionably as his suit. His moustache a graceful twirl. He clapped his hands together, making me jump. 'Now, *mon petit cygne*, the stage is all yours.' His voice deepened. Darkened. And I shivered to hear it. 'You possess a single chance with which to prove yourself. Impress me.'

I inclined my head. Walked slowly towards the stage. When I glanced back, rows and rows of crimson seating stared back at me. Their folds resembled hungry jaws and my confidence trembled for a moment as if they were feasting on it. I had prepared the Princess Florine variation from Tchaikovsky's *The Sleeping Beauty*, a succinct yet pretty sequence that bounced through a series of birdlike arabesques and tiny steps, spooling out into piqué turns with a liquid shimmer of arms. I had believed that it was the ideal piece with which to showcase my strengths, being a spritely and supple dancer, but after witnessing the magnificent performance last night, it was no longer sufficient. Not for the famed establishment that had drawn the patronage of the crown itself.

Ascending onto the stage, I determined to bid my old life farewell. To dance my way into my future, bright as a new moon. I felt Rothbart's gaze on me as he lounged back in one of the seats, crossing his legs. I had deep need of a dance powerful enough to seize his imagination and shake it to the core. To show him the dancer I knew I could be – would be – one day.

'What am I to play?' A pianist I had failed to notice earlier enquired in a slight French accent, his slender fingers taking their position to dance across the ivory keys in a duet with me.

A sudden conviction compelled me to respond with, 'Odile's Variation from *Swan Lake*'. Drawing up the dark swan's signature attitude, I allowed it to settle over myself like a costume. From the corner of my eye, I noticed Rothbart sitting upright at my words before banishing any consideration of him from my mind. Odile would not have cared what anyone thought of her and neither should I. Rothbart might have expected me to perform a pretty little variation but I wanted to throw his expectations out of the window; I might have lived as a princess but my life had been shaped by great loss. Now, that suffering was writ upon my very soul and I intended to channel every bit of it to summon the tragedy and power of this dance to life.

The opening strains of the coda stole across the stage. I regretted wearing my cornflower-blue dress that evoked the fluttering bluebird but I did not require black feathers to become the dark swan. I would carve a spell that ensured he believed it. The beguiling entrance sounded. And I entered the stage like a curse. Though the variation began on a seductive note, the darker edge of a fairy tale with its swan-like sweeping arms, slow pirouettes, and leg lifts, it soon transformed into a dramatic sequence of frenzied turns and leaps. I flew around the stage. Poured my heart into the soul of the variation, a heart aching for its deepest wish to be granted.

After the grand finale, when my skirts had settled back down, my breath heaving, I was certain I felt the spirit of Odile slip from me, as if my body had been possessed by the dark swan herself.

Rothbart's grin was calculating. 'It seems congratulations are in order.'

I exhaled, taking care not to allow the sudden relief to slacken my posture. Not within his presence.

'Welcome to my theatre.' He rose to his feet. 'Classes begin each morning at seven o'clock sharp. I shall have one of the girls show you to your room.'

✿

The theatre was known for its unique approach to performances, holding its own elite company within its grand stonework, where dancers, acrobats, and trapezists numbered among its students. Only Rothbart's performers reserved the right to flit across his famed stage. Still, I had not expected this. 'Oh, but I have already secured lodgings.'

'I require that all of my performers live onsite,' Rothbart continued as if I had not uttered a word. 'You shall find that my theatre is a truly magical place to work, and we are a close company more akin to family.' With that, his wide grin reappeared. I disliked it intensely. It was hard-edged, disingenuous. Lacking. A puppet mimicking human expression without the inner workings of that which makes us human. With another clap of his hands, a young girl scurried out of the wings. 'Show Miss . . . ' He hesitated, waving a hand at me.

'Kova. Detta Kova,' I said quickly. I wished to dance under my mother's maiden name as she had not left a legacy behind in ballet; she had left only me. And I was determined to shine bright enough for the both of us to be remembered forevermore.

'Miss *Kova* to her room,' he ordered, his sidled glance at me sly. As if he knew I had lied yet it was a ruse we were in on together. 'And then make arrangements with Mrs Windsworth for the rest of her belongings to be fetched here at once.'

Somewhat unusually, I found myself quite robbed of my ability to decline but I supposed it was a small matter, not worthy of a second thought. I had succeeded in dancing my way into Rothbart's Theatre of Enchantments after all. Once my luggage had been transferred to my new room, I might open the bottle of Taittinger I had stashed in my steamer trunk. Or take a stroll through the ancient crooked streets of York and purchase a cake, lavish with cream and powdered sugar. My mother had always imparted to me that every moment, no matter how little or seemingly inconsequential at the time, should always be properly celebrated. Life is made up of a thousand moments and if you do not mark them, you run the risk of losing them altogether. Thanking Rothbart, I followed the girl into the depths of the theatre, where a hidden staircase clambered up into several spacious dance studios, then up again to the living quarters and into my new life.

Chapter Twenty-Six

When Forster dragged himself from sleep the following morning, it took a moment to recall the previous evening with Detta. He had known he ought to bid her farewell and take his leave yet something deep within him had dug its claws in. As if by leaving the manor he would cross some threshold and lose everything he had discovered within those walls. Neither had Detta made any motion to stand though the light was fast withdrawing, the shadows sweeping in to claim them. Until she had spoken those sweet words: 'Perhaps you might stay?'

Now he leapt to look outside. His heart beat harder at the sight that greeted him: a thick blanket of snow. Detta would not have vanished in the night, rebound in her winged prison.

A knock sounded at the door.

'The snow has not yet melted,' Detta announced when he opened it. 'And the day is beckoning,' she continued before taking in the bedsheets he had clasped around his waist. 'I do apologise.' Her smile was slow, seeping mischief. 'I had not considered that you might intend to sleep the morning away.'

Forster cleared his throat. 'I'll be with you momentarily.' His cheeks warmed as her gaze dipped lower.

'Very well.' She glided out of the room.

Forster groaned and set about getting dressed. The guest room was large and comfortable, if a little worn. The grand fireplace had been hastily lit once it had been established that he was staying, and fresh sheets located to replace the stale ones on the canopy bed. Though the carpets were dust-flecked and the windows in want of a good washing, the view poured across to the clifftop and beyond that, the sea. The pipes groaned and rattled their protest each time he turned the taps but the water was piping hot and the bathtub generous. Once he was clad in the same knitted jumper and trousers he had worn the previous day, deciding there was nothing he could do about the stubble that graced his jawline, he made his way downstairs, failing to coax his curly hair into submission en-route.

Mrs Fischer was a hive of activity. Chopping, stirring, sautéing, baking, she whirled around the kitchen as if it were her stage. Detta was deep in conversation with her, idly dipping a finger into a bowl of batter and licking it off.

Forster stilled. A shaft of light was resting on Detta's seafoam-green day dress, toying with the gold-encrusted overlay. His fingers twitched, yearning to paint her. When she turned to him, she glowed like a fallen star and he burned at the sight. She had spoken of her mother's beauty last night yet he could never imagine a lovelier woman than Detta. For him, she was perfection.

Mrs Fischer flapped at him the moment she became aware of his loitering. 'Sit yourself down, I've already brewed a pot of fresh coffee.'

Setting his feelings aside, he obeyed.

Detta poured coffee into two delicate china cups, leaving his black. The aroma was rich and pleasing, calling to mind gently rolling hills, gingerbread-coloured and earthy, and faraway countries. He clasped his cup, savouring the scent, far removed from the instant coffee his flat's kitchenette was supplied with. She sat opposite him, where they had feasted on crêpes the previous morning, the moment already confined to memory. Before he had learnt how she came to be at Rothbart's Theatre of Enchantments, before he had decided to stay. 'Are you making preparations for another infamous party?'

'Heavens no.' Detta poured herself a second cup. 'Generally, I can only manage one each winter as it takes a great deal of preparation. I plan future events when I'm human and leave detailed instructions with a very trusted, bespoke concierge service who always manage to enact every desire I dream up, no matter how outlandish. When I return to my human form, I send word to them immediately and they spring into action.' She warmed her hands on her cup. 'I've always thought of them as my magical elves. I expect that the next shall be in December. Perhaps November. It feels rather fitting to host it on the first snowfall of winter so that I may celebrate my return to life. No, this is for a picnic.' She closed her eyes as she sipped her coffee, weak sunlight skipping over her face.

What must it be like to experience a scant few days, weeks at best, each year? He'd placed her at around twenty-nine as she'd been seventeen years of age when she had first joined Rothbart's theatre but he possessed no understanding of how her unique condition might have affected her age. He was unsure if she was biologically younger due to all those unlived days in her human life, or older than him now, an undesirable consequence of the swan's body having aged faster than a human one.

He glanced at the fluffy snow heaped up on the windowsills. 'Did you say a picnic?'

'Absolutely.' Detta opened her eyes and smiled. 'Why, it can never be too cold for a picnic. Besides which, we have one every year, it's tradition. And you must never break a tradition,' she said solemnly. 'I firmly believe that old ones are to be cherished and new ones cultivated as often as one feels inclined. Would you care to accompany us?'

Forster drank the remainder of his coffee, unsure if the invitation had been borne out of nothing more than common courtesy. He possessed no desire to infringe on their time together, not when they had so little of it. Even if the thought of lingering beside her warmed his cheeks.

'Oh no dear, I shall not be joining you this morning,' Mrs Fischer spoke before he could come to a decision. 'I'm not quite feeling up to it, I'm afraid the cold has seeped into my joints and these old bones are aching somewhat fearsome.'

'She may be a darling but she really cannot help herself, she's a relentless matchmaker,' Detta informed him as they wandered out into the snow together. Forster carried a picnic basket; Detta's arms were piled high with fluffy blankets. 'It's a vestige of her Victorian upbringing.' She let out a ragged sigh. 'And testament to the months she resides here along with nothing but her precious Austens to keep her company.'

Forster chuckled. 'She's a regular Mrs Bennett.'

'My my, artistic and well read.' Detta's eyes twinkled. A beam of raspberry-pink delight shot through Forster. 'You mustn't let Mrs Fischer find out; she'll barricade the doors in her efforts to prevent you from leaving.'

Forster laughed, trying not to reveal how everything was heightened in Detta's presence. Coffee tasted richer, his spirits soared, and his dreams were not tainted with the darkness his thoughts oft carried. These two days together had been a halcyon summer frozen over into a winter wonderland. Emboldened, he reached for Detta's hand, clasping it in his own. She offered him a shy smile, her hair falling over her face. Forster slowed, turning to tuck it back behind her ear. 'Thank you,' she murmured, her eyes searching his.

His fingers brushed against her cheek. 'I confess, I've always been a daydreamer but these days I find myself looking out of the window more and more, waiting for it to snow.' He lowered his hand.

This time, it was she who intertwined her hand with his. 'Yesterday I spent half the morning pacing the hall, wondering if you would remember. If you would come,' she admitted.

'I could never have forgotten you,' Forster told her, blushing. Everything about her flustered him and he wanted to spend the rest of the day learning more about her: from the colours rippling through her hair to her favourite book. He asked her the latter as they continued to walk and she told him, 'I am most enamoured with Fitzgerald's novels,' before their conversation ran on to other books and paintings they had enjoyed, to Howard Carter's startling discovery in Egypt a few years ago, and other things that Detta had missed in the months she had slumbered in swan-form.

During their discussion, they wandered through the snowy grounds to a small gazebo that stood surrounded by evergreens. There, they feasted on a fine picnic. Fresh bread baked with herbs in flower-patterns, each slice as pretty as a fairy garden. Little cheeses and slices of clementines. Honey tarts, every bite a mouthful of sunshine. They finished with thick slices of spiced cake, decorated with marzipan and frosted redcurrants, and cups of caramel-coloured tea.

'I simply cannot eat another bite.' Forster tossed half a slice of cake down, admitting defeat.

'Weakling,' Detta teased, licking the centre of a honey tart.

Forster's breath hitched. He sought a subject to distract himself with. 'What inspired your parties? The first one I attended—'

'That you remember.' Detta's smile was a devious creature. It did nothing to quell the heat gathering in his stomach.

'That I remember,' Forster echoed wryly, 'I thought I'd stumbled into some magical place. It had been far too long, longer than I care to admit, since I'd finished a painting. Until after that night. It stirred me.' She met his gaze. His voice ran deeper, huskier, straying into dangerous territory as he admitted, 'You stir me.'

Detta lowered her eyes. 'You forget that I am cursed.'

'I don't care,' Forster said roughly, 'I would endure a hundred curses if it meant I could do this.' He leant over and kissed her. Her lips were as soft as he'd remembered in his dreams. She kissed him tenderly at first then submitted to a deeper hunger as his hands ran up into her hair in a passionate embrace.

Detta suddenly broke apart from him. 'Forster, we cannot do this.' Her mouth was reddened, her cheeks flushed. Forster ached for her.

'I would argue that we're doing it very well.' He smiled with a boyish grin. Now that he had been lucky enough to kiss her more than once, he could no longer imagine not being allowed to do so again. He was burning for her. He bit his lip, awaiting her decision, her permission to close that distance between them, to reach out and pull her into his arms and kiss her until she forgot her own name.

Her pupils darkened, watching his mouth. 'Then you must promise me one thing.'

He inched closer, unable to stay away. 'Anything,' he vowed.

She leant in, her mouth a whisper-width from his. 'Never fall in love with me.'

'I won't,' he told her even as he wondered how one could stop such a thing. He had never been in love but he imagined it to be an unstoppable force. Then she fixed her lips on his and the rest of the world ceased to exist.

'Where are we going?' Forster laughed an hour later as Detta ran through the snow-blanketed gardens, towing him behind her.

She led him past the frosted weeping willow, down to the very edges of her grounds, where a small lake gleamed with ice.

Forster eyed it warily. 'I have a bad feeling about this—'

Detta darted into a small wooden hut nearby. She re-emerged with two pairs of ice skates that had seen better days. Her smile sharpened.

Forster shook his head. 'Those are practically rusted, I'm sure they'll send me to my death!'

Detta tossed two boots at him, forcing him to catch them in his arms. 'Live a little, Forster,' she teased, pulling on a pair and lacing them up tight.

With a good-natured grumble, Forster laced his own pair up. They squeezed his ankles and, when he stepped onto the ice, flew out from beneath him. He lay on the hard surface, the chill seeping into his bones.

With a sudden turn that sent ice flying from her blades, Detta stopped next to him. She pulled him up, mischief dancing across her face. Taking his arm in hers, she began instructing him until they managed a simple stroke and glide, stroke and glide. Side by side, they skated faster and faster until Forster laughed, half believing that they'd sprouted wings as they effortlessly floated along the iced lake. Detta set him free and soared onwards on one leg. Forster slowed, transfixed by her. Slowly raising her other leg behind, Detta stretched her arms out as if she might take flight, skating in great, looping circles before bringing her leg back down and spinning in place. Unaware he was watching, her eyes closed, a smile stretched across her face, free and beautiful. Yet Forster was haunted by the vision of the lake melting and she being cursed to swim on its waters as a swan. When she opened her eyes, still the vision lingered, even as he forced a smile at her, longing to share in her happiness of the moment, brief though it may be.

The sun set and still they skated. Until night thickened and stars spangled the heavens. 'It's not snowing anymore,' Forster whispered.

Detta span to a stop. 'The grounds are still coated in snow. I will be here until the last snowflake melts.'

'I ought to leave,' Forster glided to a stop before Detta.

She looked up at him. 'Why?' She slid her arms around his neck, pulling his mouth down onto hers. 'Stay with me, we still have more time,' she whispered between kisses.

Chapter Twenty-Seven

The next morning brought another stack of crêpes and a knowing smile from Mrs Fischer.

Though Forster had tossed and turned the night before, silently pleading with the sky, there had been no fresh snowfall. And the thick blanket that had lain over the grounds now thinned, revealing green patches. As the morning dwindled away, and Detta and Forster took an afternoon tea out to the gazebo, those green patches grew larger. Detta either did not care to notice or was determined to ignore it, setting out the little rose petal sandwiches Mrs Fischer had made, pretty as a picture, the buttery scones and pots of pillowy clotted cream and rich, sweet jam that glistened like a heart.

The past few days had been magical but now that spell had shattered, leaving Detta cursed to slip away at any moment. And Forster did not know when she would come back to him. 'Detta, I—' His voice cracked.

'Don't,' Detta interrupted him fiercely. Her hair was wild in winter's frozen wind and the look within her eyes set him aflame, and when her mouth sought his, deepening their kiss with a sigh, he did not know how he would survive not kissing her again until next winter.

'I'm sorry,' she whispered. The absence of their kiss was a thorn in Forster's side. 'This isn't fair to you. I am a cursed woman—' she evaded his searching gaze '—destined to be forever alone.' Glancing at the last melting spots of snow, her eyes filled and she turned her face from him.

'No.' Forster's jaw tightened. Catching her wrist, he gently pulled her towards him. She sunk into his embrace as if she had been made for his arms. He held her tightly as if he could keep her in her own skin. 'I refuse to believe that.'

When she spoke again, her voice was rougher. Filled with the wind-torn storm clouds of winter and the ragged screeches of the gulls that weathered them. 'I shall not drag you into this, Forster.'

'Sometimes a kiss is nothing more than a kiss,' he said, more concerned over losing this new understanding between them than he was whatever else their kisses may have meant.

Her mood darkened, a thunderclap of emotion rolling over her face as she stepped away from him. 'My life was ruined with a single kiss.'

Forster could scarce draw breath. 'Was it him? Rothbart?' Anger coloured his world in bleeding crimson. He'd had his suspicions since the day he had stood before the theatre and been told of the man who'd helped himself to his young charges. Forster did not want to think of how he had used his strange and wicked powers against Detta.

Detta's eyes were dark and bewitching. They told a tale he could not understand. 'It was.'

'Can it be undone?' Forster asked urgently.

Yet Detta fell silent. For Forster had failed to notice that the sky had altered. As they had taken afternoon tea, the air had warmed and the sky churned until it was thick with clouds, the stone-grey of disappointment. The soft pattering atop the gazebo roof was not snow but rain. Melting away the very last of the snow. He had been too lost in her to see it coming. Not until Detta shuddered and lost her clasp on humanity.

'No,' Forster cried out, watching her contort and shrink away until she was no longer recognisable.

He sat in the gazebo for longer than he ought, watching as the swan glided out on the watery lake. Then he slowly packed the basket, picked up Detta's clothes, and returned to the manor alone.

'Ah—' Mrs Fischer's knowing glance tightened Forster's chest '—no matter how long she stays, it's never enough, is it?'

He shook his head, placing the basket on the kitchen table. He couldn't stop dwelling on the rest of the year. It stretched out before him, a long and unappealing prospect without her. Maybe it would snow again in February or March. Perhaps October would carry an unusual chill. The notion that he may not see Detta again until near Christmas was unbearable, the time parting them too cruel.

'Before you leave, perhaps you might like to see this.' Mrs Fischer lifted down an old recipe book, bursting at the seams. She turned the pages with purpose, until she paused with a smile and removed a clipping. It was another newspaper review, though this time it was accompanied by a photograph of the cast. Mrs Fischer tapped a girl standing off-centre to the right, beaming at the camera. 'Look. My Odette. This was after her first performance on stage. The photographer instructed them not to smile but she never would do as she was told. Little rascal,' she said affectionately. Pretending not to notice the sadness Forster had dragged into the kitchen with him, she gently patted his arm and handed him the review.

The London Theatre Review

12th November 1912

As critical acclaim continues to grow for Rothbart's Theatre of Enchantments, the most coveted ticket this Christmas is set to be for the Sorcerer's unmissable interpretation of *The Nutcracker*. Though the press were invited to an exclusive early matinee, ticket sales have achieved a roaring trade the past several months despite the inaugural show not opening until late November.

With a delectable set of oversized sweets and edible confectionary spilling from the painted ceiling, which serves as a mid-show aperitif, this is a delicious performance that shall have you dreaming of chocolate for weeks to come.

Standouts included the troop of acrobats' graceful rendition of the Waltz of the Snowflakes, performed mid-air, and the bold energy of the Russian Dance, which marked newcomer ballet dancer Detta Kova as a notable talent.

Chapter Twenty-Eight

Detta
1912

I awoke with a start, uncertain where I was, the last of my dreams still haunting me. Voices calling from watery graves, the taste of brine on my lips as I rose from the narrow bed in my new room at the theatre. My mother's eyes stared back at me from the mirror, the mottled silvery blue of storms and great icebergs. Tugging a brush through my hair, I banished my nocturnal swim through my past. Stepped into my ballet dress and laced up my pointe shoes. The satin ribbon slipped through my fingers like seaweed, and I shivered.

It was a fierce struggle not to be disappointed. My new room was a far cry from my manor and, as I stood in the middle of it, a wave of loneliness threatened to overwhelm me, undercut with the dagger of grief. Mrs Fischer was heart-sore with missing my parents, but my heart had been ripped from my ribcage and torn asunder. A relic of an armchair sat dismally at the bottom of the bed and the thin carpet emitted a dusty sigh each time I stepped onto it. Perhaps the wallpaper had once been cream but now it carried a greyish hue as if the ghosts of the performers before me were entrapped within it. With several deep breaths, I composed myself. This was what I had fought when my parents had still been alive earlier this year. The singular purpose that had dredged me back up from the sea of grief

I had been drowning in after their deaths. The reason I wished to hide under the cloak of death in the public eye — so that I would have no need of a husband nor well-meaning relatives. I would dance into a future that was my very own. Rise to the rank of ballerina, a fairy tale in satin and tulle, a legend that would enrapture audiences as the great Pavlova currently was all over the world. Bolstered by the thought of one of my idols, I marched down to the studio with newfound determination.

When I entered, Penelope was warming up. As she stretched, she displayed such fluidity that envy slithered through me. Until she turned and offered a wide smile. 'Welcome to the theatre,' she said. 'This is Daisy and Ada.' She gestured at two other young women nearby. Both were petite in stature, a pair of sprites. Daisy with coppery hair and raven eyes that were so large and dark against the deep bronze of her skin they seemed to bespell you. Ada had high cheekbones, cream-coloured skin, and flaxen hair in a bun that perched atop her head like a nest.

They came over at once, peppering me with questions about where I was from and my history in ballet. I hadn't thought that taking my mother's maiden name would be an issue yet now I fretted that one of them might recognise it, unmasking my true identity. I didn't have to worry long. As suspected, my mother's career was too short, her stage too far away for her name to be known. I vowed anew that my story would be different. I would make certain that my mother's name was printed in newspapers and whispered in audiences around the world.

'You caused quite a stir when you turned up, determined to dance,' Penelope told me. 'We've been waiting to meet the girl who demanded an audition from Rothbart.'

Flushing, I cast around for something to divert their attention. The studio was of generous proportions and looked much like any other, a world of mirrors and barres, set upon wooden floors with a piano in the corner. Beside it, I noticed a thin woman with mottled shadows beneath her eyes and plump diamond earrings. 'Who is she?' I asked.

Daisy's mouth puckered. 'Edith. One of our soloists. She can be . . . difficult.'

Ava snorted. 'A raging nightmare, more like.'

Penelope sighed. 'Be kind. She's had a difficult start in life.' A wisp of sadness flitted over her face, her muddy green eyes holding secrets of her own. I had secrets I did not care to share so I had no desire to delve into hers. 'But none of that now.' She snapped back to attention. 'We're all very much interested to see how you bespelled Rothbart with your dancing. He never lets in just anyone.' A familiar gleam of competition lightened her eyes to emerald-green. I did not mind it; it was amicable and it had been some time since I had had friends. Grieving had been a lonely affair. I grinned at her as I began my own stretches.

That day, I began to dance. Harder than I had ever danced before in my short life. I may have once been under the tutelage of the finest ballet teachers my mother procured for me but I still had been groomed from girlhood to enter Society. Never had I danced under such a gruelling regime. But I was determined to make the most of this opportunity so I pushed myself, working hard to be as great as I'd dreamt I could be. My toes bled, shadows gathered beneath my eyes like bruised clouds and still I danced, faster and fiercer. Until my muscles grew ever tauter, leaner, stronger. Until I could stretch as deeply as Penelope, leap as high as Daisy, extend my turnout further than Edith, who sulked for a week upon noticing the fact. Yet no matter how great I shone, I was the glitter of a single star amid a galaxy of constellations. And so I remained in the corps. A swan flying with her flock in *Swan Lake*, one of the Wilis in *Giselle*. And I was proud of it. The corps were the body of dancers who anchored the performances, the true backdrop against which the soloists and acrobats sparkled. Yet still, I yearned for more.

Until the day a tragic illness spelled good fortune for me.

Being November, we were deep in rehearsals for *The Nutcracker*. Ada had promised me that sweets would fall from the painted ceiling and the entire theatre would be scented with chocolate for months to come. 'It's as if we upped and moved to a patisserie.' She glazed over like an iced bun. 'It makes you want to bite into the set.'

'Where's Edith?' Daisy suddenly asked. 'She's late and we're set to rehearse The Land of Sweets dances.' Edith was the soloist performing the Russian Dance alongside Ludwig, who was already warming up. Daisy and I were clad in the same glittering white as the troop of acrobats that were to whirl through the air for the Waltz of the Snowflakes, our presence only required as we were doubling up as understudies for the Russian and Spanish dances.

'I shall go and find her.' I rose from the floor where we'd been sitting together and wandered upstairs to locate my neighbour. Her door had been left open. I peered around it, noticing that we had one of the same photographs on our wall; of prima ballerina Marietta Stelle, who had set audiences ablaze with her raw passion on the stages of Paris and St Petersburg after being recruited during a particularly stirring performance of *The Sleeping Beauty* at the Theatre Royal in Nottingham. From the interviews I had read, she had claimed that the role of Aurora carried a special significance for her. I'd seen her dance several times and she had even taken the time to autograph my programme a few years ago in London when she'd danced alongside

Pavlova. Responsible for inspiring many a wide-eyed child with socks up to their knees to turn to ballet, all of Europe had mourned when she mysteriously vanished last year from the Paris Opera Ballet on tour in Vienna.

Not unlike my neighbour, Edith, who was nowhere to be seen. Her disappearance starting to spell concern, I marched along the corridor, knocking on doors until I had inadvertently raised a small search party.

Rothbart appeared as my worry grew tinged with panic. 'What is the meaning of all this?' he demanded.

One of the aerialists explained that Edith was nowhere to be found.

'Ah *mes petits cygnes*, I am afraid Edith has been taken ill.' His moustache drooped theatrically. 'She was removed to the hospital last night and is now under the care of her family. But the show must go on! Where is her understudy? You must take her place.'

One by one, the other performers' gazes fell onto me.

Rothbart eyed me with a peculiar expression. As he exited the room, he bent to whisper in my ear. 'This is your chance to impress me. Do not make me regret my decision now.'

Later that evening, I sat on my bed, heaped with fur-lined blankets which made me long for the comfort of home. In my hands were red pointe shoes. The Russian Dance was a high-kicking, heel-tapping energetic caper that demanded everything until I leapt into Ludwig's arms *al final*. Bold and dramatic, the costumes were candy-cane-red to match.

Yet guilt threatened to devour me. I never learnt what had happened to Edith or why she had disappeared without a sound that night. I never questioned why her first instinct had been to seek out Rothbart rather than one of us or the onsite ballet master, whose job it was to oversee us dancers. And I did not wonder why nobody was able to visit her to wish her well with bunches of flowers and cards that we had all written in. Instead, I took to the stage like a bird taking flight. And after I had jumped into Ludwig's arms for our final performance, we shared my celebratory stash of mince pies, dusted with sugar-snow, and glasses of dessert wine that tasted of caramel and warmed me better than a roaring log fire. Not long after, we shared my very first kiss, which was every bit as sweet.

Edith never returned. Yet I thought of nothing but my own good fortune when Rothbart promoted me from the corps. I was now a soloist. One step closer to my dream: being the prima ballerina.

That Christmas, I returned to the manor with my steamer trunk brimming with gifts for Mrs Fischer. Our first alone; much of the staff had already departed believing their services were no longer required after the tragedy. But it was of no matter, Mrs Fischer and I had already vowed to be each other's family. She seemed happy to take care of the manor and I paid her a handsome salary to do so. That Christmas, we celebrated my new position by feasting on puddings, which we each declared was the finest Christmas dinner we had ever tasted. Coffee and almond blancmange wobbled beside black cherry and rose jelly. Petit fours infused with brandy and a marzipan peacock with sugared almonds and meringues. I was sugar-hazed and mournful and content all at once.

I returned to York several days later with a secret promise to myself: I would become the best soloist that had ever graced Rothbart's stage.

Chapter Twenty-Nine

February was the coldest month. Temperatures plummeted to unseen depths on the thermometer, icing the watery veins of London and frosting over the streets, steeples, and domes. Still, it refused to snow. There was not a puff nor a wisp of cloud in sight. In the early hours, the sky was painted in a watercolour of robin's-egg blue, by midday it had deepened to a sapphire as bright blue as if Forster had squeezed a tube of oil paint over the heavens.

He slept leaning against his window, torturing himself with when he might see Detta again. Once, she had filled his dreams, but now he found himself trapped in a waking nightmare as the woman he longed to be with was lost to him. Rose and Marvin came and went, sharing more and more time together as their relationship deepened. Envy twitched her snakish tail inside him as he thought of a hundred little things he wanted to tell Detta each day and could not. Though he was happy his friends had settled into their courtship, it was a constant reminder of what he could never have with Detta. This monotony was broken by Vivian's increasing telephone calls as she checked on his progress and instructed him to deliver new paintings soon. But Forster could not think of completing canvasses and, once more, they stood empty, taunting him with their blank stares.

Eventually, Forster sought a distraction from his maudlin mood and tore himself away from his brooding to pay another visit to The London Library. There, he surrounded himself with yellow- ing newspaper pages, poring over reviews of Rothbart's Theatre of Enchantments.

He read about Detta's dancing like it was poetry. His hands tightening on the pages as one reporter described her beauty, another effusing her weightlessness in the air as if she had learnt the secret art of flight. Tearing his glasses off with one hand, he ground his palms into his eyes. He had not learnt more of the dark undercurrent that swept beneath the theatre, nor the mysterious showrunner himself. Rothbart. The name alone filled him with loathing. He was a spectre haunting Detta, ripping her life away from her.

'Excuse me.' A librarian was glaring at him over her counter.

Forster, who was clenching the papers in his fists, started. He smoothed their creases out, grabbed his hat, and left. He needed to think where he might find the next part of Detta's story.

And when his restlessness swelled, he began to paint again. Forster fell into his art like a man possessed and would not allow Marvin to distract him from his work. Dark, haunting manors with a luminous little swan dotted off to the side. He played with the quality of light in Caravaggesque ways. Manipulating shadows like a puppeteer, he showcased the swan in pearlescent white, drawing the focus.

Come the first week of March, he had memorised each of Detta's roles at the theatre and not much else. The Russian Dance. Ondine. Rapunzel. Snow White. The Sugar Plum Fairy.

Since their basement flat had once more filled with canvasses, he drove to Russell Square with a stack of them on the passenger seat.

'Yes, absolutely, yes.' Vivian flicked through them like a hungry bird, all eager flutters and beaky interest.

Her flat had been repainted in dark crimson since his last visit.

She pointed her silver cigarette holder at him. 'I am pleased to see that you have taken my advice on board.' She paused on a painting of a solitary ballerina dancing upon the surface of a storm-lashed lake, her dusky tutu holding the same light as the sky on the cusp of evening. Goddess-like in a weather-ravaged world, she walked en pointe across the water, the knowledge that if she slipped she might become lost in its timeworn depths plain to see as she stared out of the canvas. It stole Forster's breath each time he glanced at it. At her. Thinking of her alone on that lake, lost in her swan-self, was crushing.

Vivian slowly exhaled a ribbon of smoke. 'This one is especially magnetic, darling.'

'When might we hold an exhibition?' Forster asked. 'My paintings are selling better than ever and you know well I have more than enough to hang upon a gallery wall.' In fact, his paintings were selling rather nicely and the one that had lured a couple of wealthy Americans into a flurry of competing bids had paid for both Rose's old Ford and the Leica. Now he hoped to amass sufficient funds to rent a better flat. Perhaps even put a little money by so that one day he might be able to purchase a modest abode. This year he'd be thirty-two and most of his peers had already bought or inherited houses and started families of their own. Such was the price of pursuing a career in the arts.

Vivian surveyed Forster. Smoke hung like curls of chiffon between them. 'You're ambitious; I have always liked you the better for that. Yet you're not nearly a big enough name to warrant an exhibition of your own.' She lifted one shoulder in an elegant shrug but her expression was shrewd, gauging. Her jade dress, cut in the latest drop-waisted fashion, was edged with onyx beads that glittered darkly. She was unparalleled at hunting down sales with enviable connections to the most prolific collectors. And she had been a formidable force in the art world for longer than Forster had been alive. He waited respectfully. 'Leave it with me, I might be able to rustle something up,' she conceded after a lengthy pause.

Forster inclined his head. 'I would be most appreciative.'

Vivian tapped the end of her cigarette holder, speckling her parquet floor with ash. 'I am particularly enamoured with this one.' She indicated the first canvas he had painted after the last kiss he'd shared with Detta. The ballerina dancing on the storm-ravaged lake. He had been tempted to keep it for himself but it had only served to remind him of his loneliness. And he desired a better life. He was determined to carve it out himself, one brushstroke, one knifeful of gouache at a time. He felt as if he were on the precipice of something great. That *he* could be great if only he were presented with the right opportunity. Then he might be deserving of Detta.

'Keep it as a token of my appreciation,' he found himself promising her. 'I shall paint a thousand more like it.' He ignored the little voice inside those hidden dark recesses that dug its claws into him and whispered *but at what cost?*

Later that evening he still had not rid himself of that voice when Marvin returned home.

'I see you've been out,' Marvin observed in a flat tone.

'Yes, I paid a visit to Vivian. My apologies if, of late, I've been a little . . . Forster trailed off, unsure what he was apologising for or even if he needed to, only aware that he had emerged from his sustained period of creativity to discover this distance between them, strange and uncomfortable.

'Distant? Uncommunicative? Frightfully antisocial?'

Forster winced.

Marvin clapped him on the back. 'For a moment there I was afraid you were committing to becoming a recluse.' He looked in the mirror as he adjusted his tie. 'One of Rose's friends is throwing a party tonight, I assured her that we would both be in attendance.'

Forster's shoulders slumped when Charles and Nancy arrived. Charles was a pompous bore and an even more insufferable drunk with slicked-back blond hair that he was in the habit of smoothing down whenever someone else was speaking as if he couldn't bear to lose the spotlight. And Nancy, whose party it was, was a fellow Society friend of Rose's, yet where Rose was suffused with kindness and merriment, Forster discovered that Nancy was not. While her parents were holidaying in some fashionable resort, she'd taken the opportunity to host a grand affair in their London townhouse. It was an opulence of marble and old-world glamour and entirely soulless. The moment he crossed the threshold, Forster regretted his decision. He was aware he'd isolated himself of late and thought he had better spend some time with his friends yet now that he was here, he felt like a stranger. His mind wandered to other territories. Of girls with raspberry jam—sweet lips. Girls that grew feathers and flew away.

A bar had been assembled to serve champagne cocktails and a jazz band played in a dining room large enough to be a ballroom. Or perhaps it was a ballroom, he couldn't quite be sure. Disorientated, he came to a sudden, inevitable realisation: he no longer recognised his own life. He wasn't sure at which point over the past year he'd stopped fitting in at these parties but now all he desired was tangled up in a secret woodland, bound to a lake.

'You can hardly recognise her, she's practically wasted away, poor dear,' Nancy told Marvin in a stage whisper, the pair raking their gaze over the object of their discussion. Forster glanced at the woman, at her tight smile, the saucer of champagne trembling in her hand. 'She discovered him in bed with two other women and has been up to her eyeballs in laudanum ever since!'

Marvin slid a small notebook from his jacket pocket. 'And when did you say this happened?' His pencil scratched the paper, hungry to note down every salacious detail. 'And the women's names?'

Forster set his glass back down on the bar, feeling nauseous in a shade of bitter basil-green. It appeared he had not been the sole person who had changed of late. When had Marvin begun behaving in such a manner and how had he been too immersed in his own life to notice?

Suddenly weary, he made his way to the foyer where a valet returned his coat and hat. Before he might exit, Rose made her entrance in a swirl of rich crimson silks. 'Forster, what fortuitous timing.' She smiled as she shed her fur cape. 'I've been wanting you to meet with Charles again for some time now; did you know he's become an avid art collector?'

'Is that so?' Forster replied dryly. 'I'm afraid that we must talk some other time, I'm just leaving.' He did not add that he disliked her friends; that, even worse, he disliked his own friends here. That it was all horribly wrong and he no longer belonged and could not imagine how he ever had.

Rose's dimples vanished. 'Then I take it back, what terrible timing! I've barely seen you these past months. You must stop hiding away in your flat with all those paint fumes, it's awfully unhealthy.' She gave a delicate shudder before relenting. 'Though I daresay it's worth it; has anyone told you that you paint like a dream? Your latest canvasses are sublime, truly your best work yet.'

'You're too kind.' Forster lifted his hat as a valet held the door open for him.

Rose reached out for his arm. 'Must you go?' she whispered. 'I confess that I shall have far less fun in your absence.'

Forster looked up at the red-painted door. At the lion-shaped brass knocker that displayed too many teeth as it grinned back at him. 'Rose,' he softened, 'are you happy?'

Rose started. She made to speak but instead caught her lip between her teeth. 'I ought to say hello to Nancy—'

Forster frowned. 'You're evading the question.' One that he had not intended to even be a question. He'd merely meant to tell her that he could not stop thinking of a woman. That his thoughts were tangled in a dark and bewitching tale that he could not unravel. How his life in London didn't feel right anymore. But the words had got lost and instead of telling Rose that he was no longer happy in this city, he had stumbled upon her confession. His stomach twisted, concern growing like a frost along a windowpane.

'Is anyone ever truly happy?' Rose whispered.

Forster took her arm and guided her out into the night. After the valet closed the door behind him, he searched her face. 'What's the matter? What can I do to help?'

'It's Marvin. I'm starting to fear he's lost his way.'

'Have you spoken to him?' Forster asked. 'I know he cares for you deeply.' A lump hardened in his throat. It tasted like guilt. He ought to have noticed this shift in Marvin, this unhappiness Rose had been carrying alone.

'Not as much as he cares for his by-lines.'

'You're wrong,' Forster told her gently. But he could not be sure; he hadn't been present for months now, had been walking through life as if in a dream filled with cursed swan-women and enchanted theatres. 'But it does seem as if he's changed of late. That said, I know that if anyone can set him right, it would be you.'

Rose squared her shoulders, raised her chin. 'You're right. Must you leave now?'

His guilt sharpened but he could not summon the will to step back inside. And Rose was in a better position than he to speak with Marvin. 'I fear I must. But I'll send you a painting, how's that?'

'Only if it is your very best one.' Rose smiled and he knew all was forgiven as she walked back into the party. Leaving him alone on the street in the midnight hour.

Chapter Thirty

Spring whirled through the city in a lilac haze of wisteria and honeybees before surrendering to summer, ushering in both a heatwave and Forster's first exhibition at a fashionable London gallery.

'Darling, we ought to be at the seaside, cooling down and having a penny lick; the city is positively unbearable.' Rose sighed, fanning herself. 'That fountain is looking rather too tempting right now.' She sized up the stone water feature in the park outside the small gallery.

'Perhaps you ought to dive in.' Marvin's smile was wolfish.

Rose laughed. 'It might well come to that later.' She raised an eyebrow at Forster and Vivian. 'Who fancies joining me?'

'You can look elsewhere, I am far too advanced in years to cast off my clothes and dance in a fountain,' Vivian said. 'My body is a temple that my lovers may only worship at by candlelight.'

Forster did not have it in him to respond. His body was taut with nerves as if he were an overstretched string. One unwise movement and he might snap in half. A small crowd was gathering and he had already been congratulated several times. 'It's going to be a roaring success, I can feel it in my bones.' Rose flashed her dimples at him. He was gladdened that she and Marvin were there; after the shock of not realising Rose was unhappy, he had been making a renewed effort with them both, though not even their presence here tonight could erase his anxiety.

'Confidence, darling.' Vivian tapped him with her cigarette holder. 'In my younger exploits . . .' she petered off, casting Marvin a wary look.

He held his hands up in mock surrender. 'Your secrets are safe with me.'

'Hmm.' Vivian disregarded him in favour of a group of suited men that entered the gallery. They strode in with the kind of confidence that seemed to be baked into the wealthy and titled. 'Ah, Mr Wrenback, I had no idea you were attending tonight. Tell me, to what do we owe the pleasure?' She absconded with the men as Rose stared after her admiringly.

'She is a character, really too charming, darling.' Rose adjusted her evening dress; a dramatic black chiffon that plunged to daring depths on her back and glittered darkly with gold embroidery. As two fashionably dressed flappers entered the gallery, she looked a little melancholic, and Forster wanted to enquire why, if she was feeling happier yet, if she had mended things between herself and Marvin but Rose mustered a fresh smile and spoke first. 'Shall we go in then? You are the star of the event, after all.'

A sudden bout of paralysis struck Forster. His paintings were now open to public viewing. Each one an insight into the inner workings of his mind, his hiddenmost thoughts and deepest soul-aches. What if, after all this, what he had been working towards his entire career was not good enough? What if people did not care for these pieces of his soul, laid bare before them to scrutinise and comment upon? His anxiety churned in mouse-back-grey, turning his world to stone as he stood there, unable to take a step towards the gallery and the crowd within.

Marvin clapped him on the back. 'Buck up, old chap. Stiff upper lip and whatnot.' He pushed Forster in the direction of the doors. Rose hurried to take one of Forster's arms and the three of them entered together.

Inside, he was surrounded by a ballet of swans flying from canvas to canvas.

His nerves settled to a manageable level. His second glass of champagne did wonders to alleviate his anxiety. As did the patrons that were discussing his paintings in depth. To his exquisite relief, a couple had already sold. Forster wandered through the gallery, the walls hung with pieces of his soul. Detta's gaze following him through each twist and turn. A swan glowing in moonlight, a ballerina dancing on a molten silver lake, her hair a cascade of feathers taking flight. He stood before her, wishing summer would perish, wishing for snow and aching, aching, aching.

It had been six months since he had last seen Detta. He'd visited Wurthercliffe once in that time and Mrs Fischer had been happy to see him, pouring him a cup of black coffee and cutting him endless slices of cake, but it had been difficult to see the estate in full bloom, knowing Detta was missing it all. Tonight was harder still. There was so much he wished he could have shared with her yet winter seemed further away than ever. And time had slowed to a crawl. Now she stared out of painting after painting that Marvin had passed no remark on, the distance between them widening to a gulf as Rose's talk with him had had little effect. Marvin had spent the past few months bouncing from one party to the next, not returning home until sunrise, filling the pages of *The City Star* with debasing gossip that Forster had given up reading.

'Why don't you speak to him?' Rose appeared at his side. 'He is as uncomfortable as you are with this new strangeness between you.

Just because you have grown into different people does not mean you can't still appreciate the friendship you share.'

Forster's smile was strained. 'I was under the impression that you agreed with me on how Marvin's changed of late.'

'Our relationship has weathered a little change,' Rose admitted. 'And yours ought to as well. He's here to support you, is he not?'

Forster softened. 'Fine, consider myself persuaded. Where is he?'

Then came a cry. A crash. A man fell onto the wooden floor-boards, surrounded by broken glass. Pandemonium erupted. 'He's bleeding,' someone discovered as others rushed over.

It soon transpired he had been imbibing rather more than champagne. As he was removed, Marvin took down statements for *The City Star*, firing off a barrage of questions as Forster silently forged his exit, his mouth tight with disapproval. How aggravating that Marvin was more concerned with the salacious details for his ensuing story. It called to question whether Marvin had truly come to support Forster or if his attendance had been only for his own gain. With a long-suffering sigh, Rose grabbed a bottle and followed Forster.

Outside, night had fallen, cloaking the city in a starlit cape. It was thick with heat and the hum and buzz of night-flying insects and passing motors. Forster and Rose sat in the fountain together, passing the champagne bottle between them. 'What's the worst thing that can happen, you asked,' Forster hiccupped. 'I was concerned that my paintings might not be to their taste.'

Rose's laugh pealed out. She clapped a hand over her mouth, eyes wide. 'Oh Forster, I oughtn't laugh but really, this could only have happened to you.'

Forster nodded seriously.

Marvin exited the gallery, flipping through pages in his notebook as he strode over. 'Well, it seems that we've stumbled upon some excitement. It turns out that our over-indulgent patron was a member of the House of Lords and—' He looked down. 'What in the devil are you two doing in the fountain?'

'We're celebrating the death of my career.' Forster toasted him with the bottle and a bubble of errant laughter.

Chapter Thirty-One

It wasn't until a few months later, on the eve of his birthday, that Forster discovered why Marvin had been acting strangely of late. Forster stood there, clutching the little bottle of laudanum he'd happened upon in the cabinet while packing for their annual sojourn to the hunting lodge when Marvin entered the kitchen. His flash of guilt was like lightning. Illuminating. Forster was unsettled to the core as he stared and stared at the glass, a deep umber brown that matched his own disappointment. 'You don't take laudanum,' Forster said, puzzled, his thoughts skipping back to the scandal at his exhibition and the column inches Marvin had gained from the event. 'Please tell me this isn't what I think it is. That you weren't responsible for a member of the House of Lords's public collapse.'

'It sold your paintings well enough, didn't it?' Marvin leant back defensively against the doorframe.

Forster pinched the bridge of his nose. 'If I'd have known—'

'Do stop pretending that you're above this; we're of a likeness, you and I. Hungry to achieve our goals. I've seen the way you paint that ballerina, you are using her just as much as I used that man.'

'What you did was unethical, Marvin.' Forster slammed the bottle down onto the counter and picked up his case. 'Diabolical even. And there is no comparison; to suggest otherwise is as insulting to me as it is her.'

'We can debate that on the drive. Come on, Rose shall be arriving any moment.' Marvin pulled his coat on. As if a few words between them could erase this tension that had been bubbling over the past months. Forster had known their friendship was cracked but he'd convinced himself that they were like craquelure, the hairline cracks that appeared on old oil paintings after a time. Just a part of ageing and no less beautiful for it. But now he saw that he was wrong, for those cracks had splintered, giving way to a ravine. Deep and unpassable.

Forster pushed past him and slung his case into the passenger side of his Tin Lizzie. He pushed up his glasses with a shaking hand. He was angry, humiliated, and overwhelmed with sadness. Suddenly he doubted if his exhibition would have been as successful if Marvin had not dedicated his column to the scandal. Now, he would never know if the paintings he'd sold had been to admirers of his art, collectors who recognised something of worth or beauty within them, or merely those who wanted a piece of the scandal, a talking point for their next dinner party.

Rose parked beside his motor, calling out from behind the steering wheel, 'Happy almost-birthday, dearest. Are you ready to go?'

'I'm not going.'

Rose's happiness soured. 'What have you quarrelled about now?'

Forster hesitated beside his motor as she got out of hers and came over. 'Did you know?' he asked her quietly. 'About the laudanum, did you know?'

She winced.

'I see.' Forster sat down, slamming his door shut and starting the engine.

'Darling, wait, I had no idea at the time. I merely discovered the

172

fact afterwards and I was wracked with uncertainty if I ought to tell you or not—'

Forster was not in the mood to hear any of her justifications. Hitting the accelerator, he tore past her, tyres screaming as he sped out of the city as fast as he could. He did not drive to the hunting lodge. He was unsure if Marvin and Rose would have even gone themselves and, either way, he did not wish to reconcile with them, not yet. Instead, he spent his birthday wandering through the woods in Wurthercliffe, where the trees were crowned with fire and a single swan swam on the lake. Forster sat on its wooded shores and told Detta the whole sorry story, wishing more than ever that she might respond and offer him some advice, a pearl of wisdom, a sympathetic ear. But she could not and Forster felt more alone than ever.

✿

When the snow fell in early November, Forster was home alone, painting. Marvin had departed with Rose an hour earlier in a haze of cigarette smoke but Forster had declined his half-hearted invitation in favour of the stack of hot buttered toast and mug of instant coffee he had just made. The world stilled around him as he painted, calming the whorl of activity within his brain to a distant hum. Their disagreement over Marvin's scandalous antics at his exhibition had not been resolved and since Forster's return from Wurthercliffe, they had been dancing around each other, with Forster taking long walks when he knew Marvin would be home, and Marvin going directly from work to his many social events, returning when Forster was abed. They had hardly seen each other. The gulf was widening.

The basement flat deepened into a thicker silence. The light slanting across Forster's canvas lightened from dark pewter to dove-grey.

When he glanced out of the window, the skies reflected the brilliant white of his canvas.

The first snowfall.

There came a knock on the door. When Forster opened it, a paper boy handed him a paper bag with a doff of his cap then scampered off before Forster might pass remark. He peered inside the bag. There were three apples inside. The first, a bright green which was painted with, *hero?* Forster's pulse thundered. With a soft exhalation, he pulled the second out. Shiny scarlet, painted with, *villain?* Then the third, a glossy purple-black like a ripened heart that simply asked, *or lover?*

Forster pulled on his finest suit and raced through the frozen streets of London. He roared past shopfronts bedecked in Christmas cheer, electric lights strung across grand buildings, little carts selling hot roasted chestnuts, and the tallest fir tree he had ever seen, glittering with baubles. Until he hit the open roads and finally was on his way to her. It had been ten long months since they'd been together but this last hour was the sweetest anguish yet.

Chapter Thirty-Two

Forster tore both doors to the manor open at the same time when he arrived.

The party was in its earliest stages; dusk was settling around the manor like a velvet gown flecked with snowflakes. Large lanterns cut through the centre of the hall in a path that led to the ballroom. And standing in the middle of it, was Detta. Awaiting him. Her curls loose, burnished by candlelight, her gaze burning with a hundred feelings as she watched him. Forster's chest tightened at the sight of her, even more beautiful than the memories he'd been holding onto tightly the past year. She wore a dress that might have been cut from the night itself. From her hips to her hems she trailed ink-dark feathers. It ended with daringly short wisps that frothed at her knees as she slowly walked towards him.

'You came.'

'Did you ever doubt I would?' Forster's smile stretched wider until she fell into his arms, her mouth seeking his. He lifted her, deepening their kiss until she let out a shuddering gasp and whispered his name. Heat pooled in his stomach. It was an effort to remember where they were and he reluctantly loosened his hold, setting her back down on her black pointe shoes.

'Your suggestion inspired tonight's theme.' Detta performed a slow revolution, revealing the gauzy black wings fluttering behind her. 'I have been secretly planning it since you mentioned it. Carabosse, at your service.'

'The wicked fairy godmother?'

Detta's eyebrows had been darkened, their arches accentuated. She raised one, lowering her voice. 'Don't you know it's *always* more fun to play the villain.' Her eyes were painted with black feathers as if she were wearing a mask, her lips golden to match her headdress.

Forster took in his surroundings for the first time, eager to see how she'd breathed life into the theme. Inside the great hall were steamer trunks that might have been shipped from a Parisian atelier, brimming with silks and satins in extraordinary shades. Vine-green to rose pink, silvered with sequins or encrusted with gold. Between the shimmering fabrics, Forster glimpsed antlered headdresses and delicate briar crowns. A Chantilly lace gown, fine as cobwebs. An emerald velvet suit, fit for a king of the forest. More and more guests were arriving in droves, dipping into the trunks for costumes and slipping into their fairy-tale personas.

But Forster only had eyes for Detta. 'Then I take it you would not care for me to be your Prince Charming?' He grinned, enjoying the way she lingered close, as if she too did not wish to be parted after their long separation. Despite the burgeoning crowds and lively chatter, she did not leave his side.

'I would not.'

Forster replaced his jacket with a Lincoln-green hooded tunic and leather wrist guards, slinging a cachet of arrows over his shoulder. 'Then I shall be Robin Hood and wreak havoc and mischief throughout the night.'

Detta clapped in delight. 'Superlative. Now have a taste of this.' She plucked a pair of golden flutes from a nearby table, freshly ladled from a bubbling cauldron. She held one out to him, golden bracelets weaving up her lace-clad arms, her fingers ornamented with rings in winged shapes. Raspberry champagne. Sweet and strong. She laughed at the expression on his face. 'Drink up. The more you drink, the sweeter it tastes and the stronger the magic becomes.'

Eager to please, Forster gulped it down and Detta laughed again and led him outside.

A castle stood in the grounds.

It had been carved from shimmering ice. A few guests were already wandering through its frozen terraces and clambering up cut-ice stairways to the turrets. Light winked from little lanterns hanging along the crenelations and glass globes were set onto each step and window, each one lit with a rose-scented candle that twinkled away, perfuming the night.

Forster allowed himself to be led into the little ballroom inside. There, music played and roses clambered over a table that supported platters of elegant morsels befitting a fairy queen: Mountains of hot-house berries, airy pastries piped with thick cream, flowing fountains of molten chocolate, surrounded by stacks of flower-studded sugared biscuits for dipping. A sprinkling of white petals surrounded the food and more raspberry champagne bubbled in a giant cauldron. Familiar red and green apples were stacked everywhere, the red ones carved with *villain*, the green with *hero*. No *lovers* though.

'That one was just for you.' Detta appeared to have read his thoughts.

'Good,' he told her. He hadn't dared to presume she might wish him to stay again but there seemed to be no question of it now. In such a decadent affair she had clearly worked hard to organise, she had not left his side once. He couldn't stop watching her, the sight of her more intriguing than the ice-hewn castle they were standing in.

'How the devil did you manage all of this on short notice?' Forster couldn't fathom it.

Detta looked delighted. 'Well, I cannot share all of my secrets with you,' she said in a lower tone that slunk between them. 'I shall require far more champagne for that.' She refilled their goblets. Forster discovered that the petals were sugar in a burst of fizzing sweetness that melted on his tongue. Detta's gold-painted lips curved as she took his hand, leading him into the heart of the dance.

Under an ice-sculpted candle chandelier, between the beat of the drums and the press of her hand in his, Forster was lost to the night. When Detta's arms reached around his neck, he drew her tighter. The music reverberated through his bones. Primal and ancient. It spun tales of faerie hills and wild creatures that crept beneath the blanket of the midnight hours until they became the wildness. The cauldrons of champagne never emptied and Forster spied Mrs Fischer stealthily topping them up at one point. She threw him a wink and vanished with a swirl of her witch's cape. The dancers multiplied, princesses and princes, hunters and wolves.

Detta clasped Forster closer and the dance whirled faster, the fairy-tale ice castle weaving its spell on them. 'That champagne of yours is rather a potent brew.' Forster spun Detta, her whisper-thin wings brushing against his chest. He was lighter than a snowflake, unable to believe his luck that he was the one whose arms she sought. He never wanted to let her go.

Her smile was dark with mischief. 'Ah, but it is no ordinary champagne. It's a love potion.'

Forster's heart thrummed harder. 'A love potion?'

Another twirl, faster this time, left her leaning against his chest. Breathing faster, he slowly reached out to slide her hair back from her face, tucking it behind her ear. His fingertips skimmed her cheekbone, coming away dusted with shimmering powder. As if she truly were a magical creature and he himself had been ensnared.

'Why, of course. After all, there's nothing more dangerous than love.' She looked up, her breath catching. 'You might find yourself losing your wits entirely. Or worse, your heart.'

Forster swallowed. He had not forgotten what she had told him almost a year ago. *Never fall in love with me.* Yet the thought of life without her was intolerable and he was slipping, teetering on the edge of that dangerous brink, poised to dive straight in.

Detta glided out of his arms like a ribbon of silk to pour them more wine and then they were strolling past the glittering lantern-lit ice and out of the frozen castle. The strumming, beating, and dancing faded into the background, leaving the crunch of their tracks across the snow the sole sound in the hushed winterscape.

Detta's golden-embroidered ballet slipper caught on a hidden stone edge and she tripped, her laugh ringing out.

'I have you.' Forster almost toppled over with her, splashing her neck with his champagne.

She shrieked as the icy liquid trickled down her dress, darkening the gauze in its path. 'My apologies, allow me—' Forster located a bench secreted away in the shadows and foraged in his pockets for a handkerchief. He gently patted Detta's neck as she sat beside him. It was satin-soft, her glass beads tinkling as she unclasped her necklace. Feeling her gaze resting on him, he raised his eyes. Forster recognised the look in her expression. The wanting. He gave into temptation and buried his hands in her hair, pulling her onto him, their kiss urgent under the midnight skies. Champagne and desire fizzed through his veins as she pressed herself harder against him, her tongue seeking his. Snow fell on them until Detta's hair grew damp and he worried she would catch a chill. 'We ought to return to the warmth,' Forster murmured into her neck. Detta sighed, her hand falling to rest on his thigh. His willpower almost melted away. 'Come.' Forster pulled her to her feet, brushing the snowflakes from her hair, her eyelashes.

She watched him with those deep blue-grey eyes. 'Tiring of the snow already?'

He paused. 'How could I when it brought me you?' She dipped her chin to hide her smile. He offered his arm and she took it as they returned to the manor and the fairy tale spilling from its doors.

Forster stole through the crowds, golden platter in hand. Not a soul paid him a lick of notice. Not when Detta was performing Carabosse's Curse in the centre of the ballroom. Inside the ballroom was a forest of ice-sculpted trees. Red and green apples hung from each one, inviting guests to bite into them and discover their fairy-tale destiny: hero or villain? Mist slithered over the floor and cauldrons bubbled with more of Detta's potent love potion. Yet all eyes were on Detta. Her dancing commanded one to watch. The piece was dramatic and powerful and Detta wielded the role like a dagger, enjoying playing the villain as she feigned cursing the crowd, much to their delight. Pointing an imaginary wand at the crescendo, she threw down a handful of blossoms. On impact with the marble floor, they erupted into a thick column of smoke, leading the nearest guests to hastily step back. When the smoke cleared, Detta had vanished.

Forster smiled to himself, adding jewel-toned jam tarts and red-tipped chocolate mushrooms to his plate. Detta had forewarned him of her plans to experiment with some parlour tricks. He topped the platter with a curl of a cream cake, glittering with sugar, before he turned towards the stairs.

'You've purloined quite the feast there.' Marvin intercepted him out of nowhere. He wore a smoke-grey furred cape and wolf ears. Painted bronze leaves danced down one cheek. 'And here I was under the impression that you did not wish to socialise tonight.'

Forster's thoughts were hazy at the edges. Each time he attempted to consider one, it darted out of his way. Mischievous sprites, the lot of them. 'I had a change of heart. Excuse me, I—' He gestured at the platter.

Marvin's tone grew colder. Calculating. 'Do you mean to tell me that you're not interested in finding her?' He gestured at a single, lingering feather of smoke.

Forster made a noncommittal noise.

'Well then, Rose and I shall search for her. Probably for the best if you concentrate on whatever it is you're doing here.' Marvin eyed him shrewdly.

Had his smiles always been laced with ice? Forster blinked but the image vanished. The champagne cocktails must have been the culprit. Devil knew what Detta had spiked them with. He nodded and wandered back through the ballroom, certain that he did not wish Marvin to witness him ascending the stairs. He had to protect Detta from his gossip rag; nobody could learn her secrets.

Chapter Thirty-Three

Forster waited until Marvin was otherwise occupied with Rose to slip upstairs unwitnessed. There, he sequestered himself away in Detta's private drawing room to wait the last dregs of the party out.

Her room looked much the same as it had when he had taken it upon himself to snoop for clues some years ago. Like an iced cake in pink and cream and gold. Now, a fire roared away in the hearth, the antique French mirror reflecting its crackle and shine, and the plump settees perched either side of it had been scattered with cushions. It was a stark contrast to the rest of the manor with its plush carpets and vases of hothouse roses. A stack of old theatre programmes with illustrations of ballerinas on the covers rested on a little table next to an almost empty bottle of perfume. They had not been there when he had stolen in before. He itched to look through them, to see if Detta danced through their pages, wanting another glimpse of her.

'Mrs Fischer takes care to maintain my drawing room.' Detta appeared in the doorway. 'My bedroom is situated on the other side of the adjoining door.' She nodded at a closed door beside a shelf of framed photographs of ballerinas and her discarded ballet slippers. 'This is the most private wing in the manor and the one that Mrs Fischer prioritises. She sleeps a few doors down so that she might listen out for me the nights that I spend here.' Her face softened.

'I could not survive without her.' She sat on one of the settees and reached for a jam tart. It glistened in the firelight as she bit into its gleaming heart.

'Was I hallucinating on your ridiculous cocktails or did I see Mrs Fischer earlier?' Forster looked around as if she might pop up from behind one of the chairs.

Detta's laugh was bright. 'Of course you saw her; she attends every party. Costumes do make for a wonderful disguise and Mrs Fischer is of the persuasion that magic does not belong solely to the young.'

Forster sat beside her and ate several delicate rose petal sandwiches before his champagne-haze lifted. He was fortunate that Mrs Fischer had not happened upon him on either of the occasions he had broken into the manor. Though that did explain the ominous creaking; it had not been haunted by the spectre of Detta but her fierce protector. He gave her a crooked smile, picturing Mrs Fischer hiding behind a door, rolling pin in hand.

Detta reached out a hand and stroked his cheek.

'What?' he asked, setting his sandwich down, self-conscious.

'You've grown a beard. You look different.' She stared at him for a moment before deciding, 'It makes you look rugged, like you'd be at home in the wilds and woodlands.'

'Is that a good thing?'

Detta removed her hand, sitting back to survey him better. 'Of course. You forget I spend most of my days in those woodlands.'

Forster shook his head. 'That, I could never forget. Being away from you this last year has been like living with a part of myself missing.'

Her darkly painted eyes were seductive. They drew him in until he lost himself in their depths. 'I missed you, too.'

The space between them was charged. Forster was suddenly aware of his hands, his breath, how close Detta sat beside him, her legs crossed, her chest rising and falling as fast as his.

Forster wished he might hold onto the hands of time, eke out this moment between them forevermore. 'Are you certain that you don't wish to return downstairs?' he whispered into that space. 'Or need to supervise? You are the host after all.'

Detta lifted one shoulder in an indolent shrug. 'Mrs Fischer can take care of all the necessary arrangements. I'd prefer to be with you.' Forster ran a finger along her hand, needing to be closer to her, to touch her. 'Besides which, I find it preferable to mysteriously vanish after I have performed my variation. Otherwise the odd partygoer or reporter may be awaiting my reappearance. Vexing me with questions I do not know how to answer and the kind of attention I do not care for. Once, that served me well, allowing me to stir the cauldron with my own rumours. But now they've grown into something bigger than myself. It was never my intention to create such gossip, you know,' she confessed. 'I merely wished to celebrate returning to myself and live as if it was the only day I had for another year, which, sometimes, it is.' She sighed. 'But people do love to solve a mystery.'

'Yes, I suppose they do.' Guilt nipped at Forster as he thought of Marvin and his quest to reveal her identity. Of his own quest to solve the mystery of Detta's life, her past, her curse.

'I wasn't referring to you,' she said softly.

'You weren't?'

'No.' She reached for a blanket and pulled it over both of them. Soft and thick as a cloud, it warded off the chill gnawing at Forster's bones. Her leg rested against his and he stilled, aware of how close they now were. That they were alone behind a closed door. Detta plucked a handful of chocolate mushrooms from the platter resting on a little end table before them. She nibbled at one, revealing a praline-core to her faerie-ring of chocolates. 'I know that you care for me.'

The air between them seemed to crackle. 'I do. Deeply.'

Her glance at him was dark and stormy. 'I have been thinking and—'

'You can tell me anything.'

She lowered her eyes, digging her fingers into the chocolate. 'I had believed that this curse was a death sentence. I never imagined I would find—'

'What?' Forster whispered.

She took a deep, dragging breath. 'Something that made me want to live again.'

Forster couldn't speak for a moment. He did not dare to imagine she might be referring to himself. 'Then you must hold onto it and never let it go. Never stop reminding yourself what it means to feel this way.'

Detta set her chocolate down, unfinished. 'It's not enough,' Detta whispered. 'It would not be fair to you to wait for me.'

Forster took her hands in his. 'I don't care,' he said gruffly, warring with hope and fear. 'I will be here. Each and every day it snows, I am yours.'

'I want to see the bluebells carpet the woods, bathe in sunlight and swim in the lake when it's warm and golden with summer, and dance through fields of wildflowers with you.' Her eyes darkened. 'But that will never happen. It is an impossible dream. And I shall not have you condemned to a life of waiting for snowfall.'

'Then we must end this curse.' Forster could not help pressing her hands a little tighter, hoping that she would agree, that she would trust him with this, that she would want to at least try. That this would not be an ending between them but a beginning. Their first step into spring.

'I cannot ask you to do that.' Detta withdrew her hands. 'I have never needed a man to save me and I do not intend to start now.'

'This is not a usual situation, Detta,' he told her. 'All of us must learn to accept a little help now and then. If Mrs Fischer were taken ill, would you not care for her?'

She gave him a terse nod. 'Well . . . ' She hesitated before speaking again, reluctant to voice her thoughts. 'If there was a way out then only Rothbart would know.'

'Then I will track him down and bring him back here,' Forster vowed.

Detta suddenly stood. Began pacing. 'That may prove harder than you might think.'

'Let me try,' Forster pleaded. He stood, catching her mid-pace and holding her. Her cheek rested against his chest. Kissing her forehead, he repeated, 'Won't you let me try?'

Yet she did not answer and another terrible thought snagged his focus. 'Detta,' he raised her chin with a finger, frowning at the agony he saw behind her eyes, 'do you not wish to be un-cursed?'

She wrenched herself from his grasp. Turned to look out of the window at the frosted landscape that was reflecting the first hint of sunrise. 'You do not know much about me, Forster. Perhaps I am deserving of this punishment.'

He started towards her. 'No, that cannot—'

'I have accepted my fate,' Detta said. 'And I must ask the same of you.' Her eyes shone brightly, questioning. 'If you care for me, you must do that.'

'If that is what you wish.' He told her the words she wanted, needed to hear, even if saying them felt like coming apart, like admitting to himself that this curse would never end.

She slid her arms around his shoulders then, fitting herself perfectly against him and, as his grief sharpened to a dagger's edge, he lost himself in her.

As morning dawned, Detta helped herself to a handful of chocolates, tucking her feet up beneath the blanket they'd both cosied under. 'Now, I wish to hear all about your exhibition. Tell me everything I have missed.'

As Forster told her the whole sordid tale of the gallery and Marvin's underhanded scandalous antics, his attention drifted back to the stack of magazines. From here, he could see that Detta was indeed on one of the covers. As was Rothbart. For who else would not concede the spotlight to his performers but crave it himself? Forster seethed, disliking his dramatic stance, the twirl of his moustache that seemed to quiver with excitement, and, above all, his owlish stare at the lens that betrayed a keen intelligence yet failed to match the glee in his grin. He did not know what could have happened that Detta considered her curse a justified punishment. The very notion curdled his stomach, had him clenching his jaw at the man who had done this to her. He needed to fix things, to save Detta, but he battled the urge, vowing to himself that he would stay true to her wishes.

When Detta excused herself to change out of her costume, he searched for her through the pages. He had not expected her name to be printed beside another's, the two women leaping towards each other as if in battle.

✹ ✹ ✹

Dancers Magazine

23rd May 1913

Penelope Petra and Detta Kova:
A Tale of Two Ballerinas

It appears as if the illustrious Rothbart's Theatre of Enchantments has a new ballerina at its helm. In an unusual turn, the principal role of Ondine, the theatre's summer offering, has been interpreted by both previous prima ballerina Penelope Petra and current soloist Detta Kova, whose rise through the ranks of ballet has been stratospheric.

Over fifty years ago, Fanny Cerrito and Marie Taglioni danced the same programme in Milan, causing a rift within the city as the press wildly debated sides. Do we have a similar rivalry on our hands? For those fortunate enough to have secured tickets for both performances, were your hearts captured by Petra's refined classical steps or seized by Kova's soul-aching intensity?

Though the question on everyone's lips may be which ballerina was the greater Ondine, we at Dancers Magazine implore you not to overlook the rest of the show that

Rothbart has created this summer. With all the theatricality and parlour tricks at play, Rothbart's theatre elevates his productions into an unmissable experience where the show seeps out into the audience itself. One instance of this was when soloist Daisy May Smith pirouetted through the air on invisible cables, releasing a stream of golden fishes that swam through the audience as if the air had turned to water. Is this the most magical stage in all of Europe? Something tells us it may well be . . .

Chapter Thirty-Four

Detta
1913

Some days Rothbart's Theatre of Enchantments was a castle you might have stumbled upon in a book of fairy tales, other days a Russian forest, snow-flecked and crackling with wild magic. Danger lurked behind those frosted trees as I danced and danced, oblivious to its ominous presence. And in the distance, the threat of war snarled a little louder. A beast creeping through the forest.

With the arrival of spring came the theatre's performance of Perrot's *Ondine*, where the stage rippled in underwater scenes and our ballet dresses were seafoam-green and deep sapphire, befitting our status as water sprites. When Penelope danced the principal role of Ondine, Rothbart transformed the backdrop into a shimmering waterfall that swept over our pointe shoes before wisping away into mist that poured off the stage in waves. During opening night, he turned all of our hair cerulean and I could not understand how he had bewitched us so.

Edith had not reappeared. And when Ludwig was absent for rehearsals one morning, I worried afresh for them both.

'I'm sure that he's simply returned home to Lübeck and was loath to admit his departure to him,' Ada said when I voiced my concerns to her. *Him* was always a reference to Rothbart. The acrobats worshipped him, the trapezists seemed bemused by him but the dancers, they regarded him in awe. And more than a little fear. The illusions he crafted were so all encompassing that it was difficult to know where the magic ended and the man began. The façade he presented was merely that, an act of his own. The great showrunner. Another character in one of his cleverly devised performances with his villainous moustache and jovial grins. We did not know his true name, only what we assumed was a stage name. Rothbart. He was charismatic, compelling, and unpredictable.

Penelope agreed with Ada. Yet it was in the way their eyes slid to the side as they stated the fact, the curt nod and avoidance of further conversation on the topic that betrayed them. They did not believe their words to be true.

As spring ripened, I began to attract notice. My name was printed in the illustrated programmes that were sold in the foyer before performances. Penelope remained the prima ballerina, the theatre's star attraction, besides Rothbart himself, of course. She sparkled with an energy that might have led me down the path to envy if she had not been so welcoming. Quick to grace me with one of her wide smiles or bestow some gentle advice as I learnt my way as the newest soloist. Never wavering in her kindness or support. And as trees burst into cherry blossom, showering the streets of York with their fragrant mauve bounty, more often than not, we were in each other's company. Our friendship had bloomed into the kind of closeness I'd only read about in *Anne of Green Gables*, cherished and dear. We were kindred spirits.

Our days were framed with ever more rehearsals and classes. Yet the nights belonged to us. Long after sunset, we often stole up to our favourite spot in the theatre: a tiny room nestled up in the eaves of the roof, packed with antique steamer trunks. Each time one of those trunks was opened, the trappings of another character poured out in shimmering fabrics and glittering beads: old costumes that had been discarded. Those nights we dressed like queens. Penelope liked to invent a tale for each one: This one a rich silk brocade from the eighteenth century, embroidered with peach blossom and tied with a hellebore velvet ribbon for wandering old fairy paths in the woods, basket of wild strawberries in hand. That one a carefree Edwardian dress in marine-blue with matching parasol and delicate lace filigree for strolling along the Italian coast. Or an empire-waisted Regency gown in ballet slipper–pink, for dainty slices of almond cake in a rose garden. When we tired of this, we whispered our secrets to each other, a single candle melting away the hours. Penelope alone knew my real identity. She was the sister I had never had, and we soon grew inseparable. Sometimes we'd steal into the kitchens, still wearing the loveliest silks in macaron-hues, as Penelope baked her favourite lemon-drizzle cake and I twirled in endless pirouettes before the sun rose.

When the talons of grief dragged me down into the black surface of my old nightmares and below, to those freezing depths, I opened my eyes to Penelope shaking me awake. Holding me until I stopped shivering. And in return, I kept a vase on her dressing table filled with hothouse apricot peonies, the kind she had once lingered outside a florist to gaze upon yet never bought herself.

✿

Towards the end of spring, I was meandering up the corridor for my final ballet class of the day, flanked by Ada and Daisy, when a single word ruptured our easy conversation.

'No.'

It was laced with panic and enough fear to still my feet.

'That sounded as if it came from his office.' Ada glanced at Daisy, whose expressive face might have been carved from ice.

'There's nothing we can do.' Daisy's throat bobbed up and down as she swallowed. 'It would be better to ignore it.'

But I could not ignore it. There was no nightmare I would not have plunged into to drag my sister free from its grasping claws. I marched over to Rothbart's door.

Ada snatched my arm. 'Please, Detta, think,' she warned. 'It would be better not to draw his attention onto you.'

Daisy lingered in the corridor, cast into misery. I knew she wanted to help but her fear of Rothbart's wrath was overpowering her, leaving her helpless.

Pulling my arm free, I threw the door open. It was lighter than I'd anticipated and thudded into a bookcase. Penelope was standing inside, lines etched down her cheeks where the path of her tears had eroded her face powder. Rothbart reclined on a Chesterfield, one leg casually slung over the other in a pin-striped suit. 'Ah, Detta,' he said, his voice silken as one of his enchantments. 'What a pleasant surprise. Though I do not recall summoning you.' His smile was cheerful with a touch of condescension. At once I disliked what I witnessed in his eyes. Something animalistic that gave me shivers.

'Deeply sorry to intrude like this—' I feigned a pretty smile, conjuring an air of confusion and general helplessness '—but I'm afraid I require Penelope's assistance with, ah, a small matter. At once.'

Penelope looked to Rothbart. I bit the inside of my cheek in an effort to maintain my calm. I sensed the only way to face Rothbart would be to quietly manipulate him and so I played the girl he expected me to be. I stole a wide-eyed glance at his office, pretending to be impressed. Mahogany bookcases were stocked with leather-bound tomes and curios collected from Rothbart's travels: an ivory carving, a marble statuette of Hecate, an ornate box that once appeared to have framed two golden keys yet now held just the one. And photographs: Rothbart standing outside the theatre as his gilded sign was winched into position, staring straight down the lens of the camera; a crumbling castle cradled by jagged mountains; standing beside a man with bright silver hair and unusually pale eyes.

'Why, whatever could be wrong, *mon petit cygne*?' Rothbart said amiably. His hand, stretched out along the back of the settee, was rigid.

Penelope's smile wavered. She looked strangely vulnerable, her hair loosened from its bun and escaping onto her face. Seeing her like this had my warning bells clamouring. Because I had never seen Penelope look small before. She was strong, strong enough to jeté clear across a stage, to execute as many fouetté turns as Pierina Legnani had in *Cinderella*, and strong enough to be the kindest person I had ever met.

'Take a seat.' It was not an invitation. 'Can I offer you a drink?' Rothbart stood, wandered over to one of his shelves, and poured himself a generous measure of cognac. It scented the room with its rich spice.

'No, thank you.'

'We were discussing my next performance. How I intend to make it magical beyond belief. Perhaps you yourself would be interested in learning a few of my . . . tricks.' Rothbart's hand trailed onto Penelope's shoulder, where it tightened. She blanched. And I realised I needed to hasten with my ruse to get her out of here. I stumbled forward, catching myself on the back of an overstuffed chair in a hideous purple silk. Pressing a few fingers to my mouth, I moaned as if I were about to spill the contents of my stomach over said chair.

Rothbart leapt up at once. 'You cannot be taken ill now,' he snapped, 'I have invited the press to attend tomorrow's matinee and I fully intend on sending them into raptures.'

'Sorry.' I affected a groan that made Penelope wince. 'I had requested Penelope—'

Rothbart whirled around and ordered Penelope, 'Put this girl to bed at once and see to it that she recovers in time. I have immense plans looming on the horizon and nothing, nothing I say, shall interfere with them.'

'You shouldn't have done that,' Penelope whispered to me as I marched her past Daisy and Ada and upstairs, to where our living quarters nested high inside the theatre, their slanted windows allowing the sun to beam down on us. I ushered Penelope into her room as I voiced the first of many questions that scorched my throat in their urgency. 'What happened? Did he behave in an untoward manner towards you? I know he possesses a certain charm but he is in the position of authority here. He cannot take whatever he wants for himself merely because he owns the theatre.'

Framed programmes of the ballets she had starred in gazed down at us from the walls. I knew them all by heart. We had whiled away many an evening in here, both of us lying on the narrow bed, exchanging confidences.

'You ought to report his behaviour to the police; no career is worth this,' I naively told her, viewing the world as if through the lens of a camera; rendered in black and white.

Penelope sank down onto her bed. 'Detta, you don't understand of what you speak.'

Sitting beside her, I clasped her hands in mine. 'I understand that it must be a frightening prospect. Would it help if I were to accompany you to the station? Think of all the young girls that sleep beneath this roof; we must protect them.' I might have been one of the youngest performers on stage but there were younger students of ballet and acrobatics attending classes, preparing to take their turn on what the papers had dubbed 'the most magical stage in all of Europe'. Rothbart preferred to train them young, ensuring that he would never be without an unending river of talent. My blood chilled.

'It isn't that.' Penelope interrupted the macabre twist my mind had taken. 'Rothbart's never taken liberties with me. He's . . . something more.'

I frowned at that. 'I'm afraid I don't follow.' I took pains to keep my tone gentle, undemanding. Penelope was trembling like a caught moth and I worried she would be taken ill, overwhelmed by the shock.

'All I know is that dancers disappear. We never see them again.'

'What do you mean?' I whispered, picturing Ludwig with his sweet manner and sweeter kisses. Edith. 'Do they not return home?'

Penelope gave a slow shake of her head. Her eyes were fear-bright, a hunted deer. 'Wherever they go, we never hear from them again. Our letters go unanswered. They just vanish. And Detta?'

I squeezed her hand. It was as cold as my own, despite the sunshine puddling on her bed. My worry gave way to dread. 'Yes?'

'I think that whatever becomes of them was about to become my fate. He told me it was for the good of the show.'

That fire licked up my bones. I took her face in my hands. 'I won't let him,' I told her fiercely.

'I doubt that you could stop him,' Penelope whispered.

'Then you need to leave before it's too late,' I told her, ignoring the sadness that thought conjured. Dancing without Penelope would feel hollow, I had grown accustomed to seeing her in the studio, on the stage beside me. I lived for the nights when we were not too tired to bake lemon-drizzle cakes together, eating as many slices as we could before the other performers caught the scent of sugar in the air and descended upon us like a swarm of hungry bees. My stomach clenched at the idea of her leaving.

But Penelope shook her head again. 'I have nowhere else to go,' she said fearfully.

That night, I bade Penelope sleep in my room. We curled up together on my little bed, two crescent moons curved against each other, battling to shine through the blackest of nights. When dawn coloured the sky fondant-pink like a freshly iced petit four, I smiled to see Penelope sleeping beside me. We dressed and attended our first class of the day. I stayed with her until it was time for me to practise my solo variation, for which she assured me she would be watching in the wings. But those were the last words she spoke to me. When I had finished my rehearsal, she was no longer standing there.

And she never returned.

The following day, I stepped into her satin slippers as the new prima ballerina. My greatest achievement, the desire for which had coloured my dreams were tainted with guilt that I hadn't been able to save Penelope. I began to list other cities I might consider escaping to, other ballet companies whose names were as lustrous as the Theatre of Enchantments had once been to me. For now I knew there was a darkness at its core that I could not comprehend.

Chapter Thirty-Five

Some hours later, Forster dreamt of ballerinas leaping and spinning on a glittering stage as a fierce snowstorm with shadowed eyes and ice-teeth howled about them. Try as they might to dance, their satin slippers slid on the snow, and each time one fell from a pirouette, the storm-beast devoured them whole. Forster awoke with a start, certain that he would set eyes upon a panicked swan, trapped within the drawing room. But Detta was lying on his chest, their limbs entwined. She was deep in sleep and he stayed still so as not to disturb her slumber.

They breakfasted on crêpes that shimmered with sugar and fluffy vanilla cream that melted on Forster's tongue. Each of the manor's many windows glittered in white. As if the Snow Queen herself had passed by, freezing the world over in her wake. After Forster aided Detta and Mrs Fischer in restoring the house to its original state – the décor and debris had already been cleared by the same firm that Detta employed to create her fanciful events – he fetched a sketchbook and set of watercolours from his motor, and set them up in the library. There, he painted. A sky still rose-pink with dawn and two young girls hidden in an attic. Detta and Penelope, taking tea in white gloves and empire-waisted Regency dresses. Sherbet-lemon for Penelope, tangerine for Detta. Bright flowers. Before the gathering darkness stole them away into the raven-feathered shadows. In the background, something old and Russian played on the gramophone, one of Detta's mother's favoured classical compositions, wilful and romantic. Each time Forster glanced up from his painting, he found Detta's eyes on him. She was standing on a low stool in the adjoining drawing room, ensconced in a frothery of tulle and satin with Mrs Fischer clucking over her measurements. Surrounded by boxes that had been shipped from London and Paris. A Redfern coat, dark as a starless sky, trimmed with jacquard silk. A ruby-red woollen suit, tailored to fit. He gave her a slow smile, watching her lips curve in response.

He couldn't stop thinking about last night.

Forster painted Detta with a lover's attention to detail. The soft peach her cheeks had glowed as she'd come undone in his arms. Her rosebud mouth, full and ripe. 'Stay with me,' she had told him in the midnight hours. 'Stay with me and kiss me until I forget to watch the snow melting away.' Then Forster had claimed her mouth with his and they had not spoken again until dawn. Unable to resist any longer, he looked back up, through the open doors.

Detta, wearing a short Lanvin lace dress with real pearl earrings that glimmered like mermaid treasure, gave him a smouldering look. The air between them blazed, catching their fire. Detta caught her bottom lip with her teeth and he blushed, raking a hand through his curls as his thoughts snapped back to how she'd bitten him last night.

'Oh, for heaven's sake, just talk to him,' Mrs Fischer grumbled aloud. 'You're barely in another room.' She lifted a cloche hat in dreamy lavender from a box, holding it up for Detta's consideration.

'Have you ever painted a live model before?' Detta nodded at the hat and it was set aside with the others. Her gaze turned suggestive.

Forster cleared his throat, his imagination set aflame. 'I have not.'

'I think I had better take my leave then.' Mrs Fischer gave a hearty chuckle and creaked to her knees.

'No, I—' Forster's face warmed.

Mrs Fischer winked at him. 'Behave yourself.' Detta hopped down from the stool and strolled into the library. While Mrs Fischer made herself scarce, Detta examined Forster's painting. 'You captured her spirit so well.' She ran a wistful finger over Penelope's face, turned towards Detta's, the secret smile they shared. 'Would you paint me now? I want to see myself the way you see me.' She faced him then, running her hands up his forearms, kissing his neck, his jaw.

'You want to know how I see you?' Forster's voice turned husky. Detta's mouth was swollen from grazing his stubble and he couldn't stop looking at it, at her. 'When we are together, all I can think of is you, and when sleep comes, I dream of you.' Detta had stilled yet he continued, unable to stop. 'And when we're apart, I ache for you. Missing you is a physical pain that I cannot rid myself of and nor would I ever choose to because there is no sweeter pain than that which reminds me of you. You are my everything.'

Detta pushed his hands away. 'You cannot mean that.'

'Why?' Frowning, he caught her hands, kissing them. 'Is it so wrong that I want to spend all of my days with you?'

'You promised that you would never fall in love with me.' Detta's gaze turned searching.

Forster hesitated, uncertainty warring within him.

'I'll break your heart,' she whispered.

'It's mine to risk,' he told her.

As the evening deepened, Forster unwillingly tore himself away from the sweetness of Detta's embrace to fetch a fresh canvas. As she reclined on the chaise, he prepared his palette. Her dress was the colour of the sky before a storm. Its pale-grey bodice was scattered with seed pearls like raindrops, its lace skirt touched with purple and blue like ripe clouds. The oak-walled library was buttery in the candlelight, and with a fire flickering in the grate, Detta's hair showed hints of red. Like a velvet cape he longed to sink his hands into. Instead, he filled his bristles with colour and began to paint. She was silent. Watching him watch her. Again and again, he touched his brush to paper, bringing her to life on his page. Outside, the night came too fast, sweeping over the woodland, thick as thieves. Yet here, they were suspended in time.

And there began the oldest story. Of a heart that quickened. Its owner, unaware.

Detta stayed human for an entire week. A week where there seemed to be no question that Forster would remain by her side. Their days together fell into the most pleasing rhythm. Of breakfasting together, taking long walks in the snow, skating when Forster could be cajoled back onto the ice, picnicking when he demurred, and evenings spent painting and dancing and talking deep into the night. Those twilight hours were the ones he had come to cherish the most.

Until the week drew to a close, finding them drinking champagne in the gazebo at sunset, watching the last of the snow melt as the sun painted them gold.

'This last week with you has been——' Forster shook his head, words failing him. Everything he wished to tell her veered into forbidden territories between them. And he could not comprehend that tomorrow he would wake and she would not be here. For how could he continue without her now; surely the sun would refuse to rise, the moon relinquish her tide, so impossible was a world without Detta in it.

Detta's emerald velvet dress sighed as she moved. 'Don't do that,

Forster.' She downed the rest of her champagne as he turned to evaluate her. A sealskin coat poured off her shoulders in thick and luxuriant fur, and delicate shoes that were entirely unsuitable for the weather clothed her feet in cherry-red silk.

'I'm sorry,' he said, uncertain what he was apologising for.

'Don't say goodbye to me, don't you ever say goodbye.' She poured herself another glass with trembling fingers. It clinked against the bottle, ringing out in a sharp note.

Forster gently took it from her hand and poured it for her. 'There are no goodbyes for you and I. The moment it snows again, I shall be here. I will always be here.'

Detta let her coat trail further down her shoulders, puddling around her feet. She slipped off her shoes. Setting the trappings of one life aside for another. She presented her back to Forster. 'Will you unbutton me?'

He set his glass down on the gazebo ledge and slowly unbuttoned the line that ran down her spine. Revealing her silky white chemise beneath. 'Do you swear that you will return?' she asked, facing away from him. Staring across to the woodlands that were about to claim her.

'Always.'

She nodded once, her back to him still. 'Then I want you to find him for me.'

Forster's hands paused on her shoulders, hardly daring to breathe. 'Do you truly mean that?'

'Yes.'

'Why the change of heart?'

She bit her lip, trembling. 'These days we've spent together have been perfect,' she said softly. 'And so are you, Forster. Nobody has been here for me the way that you have. And now . . . well, now I wish to be here for you, too.' She cast him one last, anguished look as she began to shiver. And Forster held onto her as she cried out with the change, until he could hold her no longer. 'I will find him if it's the last thing I do,' he vowed, though she could no longer hear him. 'I'll scour the earth until I dig him out of whatever hole he's hidden in so that he may bring you back to me.'

The sunset poured colours across the sky until it looked like crushed berries. And beneath it, a lone swan.

Forster turned his back and walked away, leaving his love gliding along the lake.

Chapter Thirty-Six

Forster dined in silence with Mrs Fischer that evening, unable to face leaving the manor just yet. She looked paler than usual, her eyes sallow, mouth pinched. As if she had not slept in a decade. 'Sit with me a while,' she bade Forster when he re-entered the kitchen. He acquiesced, realising that they shared the same sorrow. This eased his loneliness a little. She poured him a cup of coffee the way he liked it, pushing leftover biscuits his way: brandy snaps filled with whipped cream and coconut pyramids. She sat opposite him at the table, scrutinising him with a hawkish intensity. 'I can't help noticing that you've been spending a lot of time with my Odette of late.'

'I admire her greatly,' Forster said cautiously, accepting a coconut pyramid.

Mrs Fischer fixed him with her stare, and he had the distinct feeling that she saw straight through his skin, his bones, to the heart that beat and bled for Detta alone. 'Has she spoken to you of her past?' Her hand tightened around her teacup. 'She will not confide in me about her days at the theatre; it is the one, the only subject she refuses to share with me.'

Forster wondered what Detta had shared about him. 'I know a little. But before she became trapped until the next snowfall, she asked me to find Rothbart.'

'Good.' Mrs Fischer crumbled with relief. 'And will you?'

'I will not rest until I've tracked him down and brought him back here to undo this terrible curse.'

'Thank you.' Mrs Fischer reached out to press his hand. 'Thank you. I need to know that my girl will be taken care of. Will you promise me that you will care for her?'

'You have my word.'

He stayed another night at the manor though he did not sleep, having already been awoken from the dream he'd shared with Detta. Snapping him back into a reality that was colder, greyer, without her. Mrs Fischer cooked him a generous breakfast the following day before bidding him goodbye with the rest of the biscuits, a heap of assorted sandwiches for the drive home, and a chocolate sponge she had baked that morning to 'keep his strength up'. As they parted, she pressed his hands tenderly. 'I know well the toll this burden takes on you,' she told him. 'And the weight of sadness is not an easy one to bear alone. You must take care of yourself as well.'

When Forster stepped back inside his flat later that afternoon, it seemed smaller. Letting his weekend bag fall to the floor, he went in search of coffee. There, Marvin was awaiting him. 'Been gone almost a week,' he remarked, patting his pockets. He pulled out a pack of Prince Charming Cigarettes with a grimace at the popular Prince of Wales beaming on the packet, the image used to ensnare a predominantly female clientele. 'Rose,' Marvin said by way of explanation. 'So. Anything to report? Where've you been?'

Forster poured himself a cup of coffee. Bitter and black, it tasted like sadness. 'Nothing out of the ordinary. The usual lot, photographing, sketching. The party you also attended.'

'Yes, how did you find out about that? I searched for you to share the news but you'd already left. For the party, it transpires.' Marvin struck his lighter and lit his cigarette.

Forster gave a nonchalant shrug. 'Our paths must have just missed.'

'See, I find that hard to believe. I know you—' Marvin's eyes bored into Forster's '—and I know well when you're attempting to conceal something. You're lying to me, Forster.'

Forster forced a laugh. 'Well, I wouldn't be the first of us to hide something.'

'Still holding onto that?' Marvin's words were dagger-sharp.

'It's not as though you ever apologised for it,' Forster retorted, his frustrations mounting. 'Or made any attempts to mend your ways. You've become impossible to be around of late since you've dedicated yourself to digging through other people's lives, hunting for secrets that might be their undoing.'

Marvin's answering smile revealed too many teeth. 'Why Forster, am I making you nervous?' He did not shift his gaze. It was an uncomfortable intensity that made the back of Forster's neck prickle.

'Why should I be nervous?' he answered coolly.

Marvin leant back in his chair, one foot resting on his knee. 'Only a man with many secrets of his own would behave in the manner you are.'

'Is that so?' Forster was dizzy with anger at Marvin's behaviour, his fierce protectiveness for Detta overwhelming any consideration he held for the man who had once been his closest friend. 'Then I am thrilled to inform you that I am not the sole person offended by your recent behaviour. It wasn't all that long ago that Rose confessed she was unhappy with you, also. So what does that tell you about your relationship?' he snapped.

Marvin shot up out of his chair. His neck had violently reddened.

'You just lost any sympathy I might have held for you. Now I'm seriously going to enjoy discovering if my suspicions prove accurate.'

'Then we are finished.' Forster exited the room, slamming the door behind himself.

In his bedroom, he sat on the bed and threw a despairing look around. At the window set high into the wall, the sunlight forsaking him as shadows nestled around the room. At the thin mattress and rickety furniture that might expire if you so much as sneezed in its direction. At how the door did not quite close, allowing a draft to seep in beneath it. He spent a scarce few days at the manor each year and yet it was ruining him. After bathing in Detta's luminous glow and hunger for life, he was lacklustre without her. She was colour and life and wonder, and when she returned to her cursed state, he was plunged into living within the reel of a film; cast in black and white and silent. And now Marvin was unrecognisable to the man he had first met, his loneliness threatened to overcome him.

But it need not be this way forever.

He grabbed his coat and hat and left the flat in search of one of the new red phone boxes that had been sprouting up over London since Giles Gilbert Scott had won the recent design competition. It took half a dozen telephone calls before his rather unusual request met a willing participant.

'Come next Wednesday,' the man told him after a lengthy hesitation. 'And bring the one I mentioned with you.'

*

One week later, on a bright and cold November morning, Forster made his way to the neo-Gothic Public Record Office on Chancery Lane that had been built some seventy years or so earlier. A young man was awaiting him, his natural black curls cut short, his suit sharp. A felt bowler sat atop his head at a fashionable angle. He strode forwards, extended a hand. 'Mr Sylvan, I presume? I'm Roger, we spoke last week.'

Forster shook his hand. 'Thank you for meeting me, Roger. I appreciate this more than I can say. I have the piece you requested here.' He handed the canvas over. It was a jewel of a painting; a lake in rich turquoise and teal that revealed mermaids in its hidden depths, their scales flashing in golden hues, mirroring the sky above, deep with stars. A pearl palace, a moon bitten in half, and a swan that allowed herself to be stroked by a precocious mermaid that had wandered up to the surface.

'Ah, my girl will love this.' Roger smiled, his face alight with affection. For a moment, Forster envied him, dreaming what it would be like to return home, knowing Detta would be there. 'She read about your paintings in the paper and has been wanting one since. Just wait until I surprise her with this tonight.' He laughed and Forster's envy dissipated. It was impossible not to share their happiness. 'I located your Daisy May Smith.' Roger passed a slip of paper over. 'This is her address according to the last census. That was four years ago now though, so you understand it's not a certainty.' He spread his arms.

'I know, I'm willing to take my chances.' Forster stared at the paper. At the neatly penned address. Northampton. His mood turned smoke-dark. 'Thank you, Roger. Thank you.'

'Mind you don't tell anyone about this,' Roger warned as he clamped the canvas under one arm and bid him farewell. 'And good luck now, you hear.'

✫

'Had a good morning?' Marvin asked Forster when he returned home a few hours later, finding his flatmate in their excuse for a kitchen, despite his best attempts to avoid him.

Forster slowly set his hat down. 'It was fine. And yours?' It was hard to imagine that they had once been close as brothers when now the distance between them took on a physicality of its own. Filling their little basement flat day by day until he feared it would suffocate them both.

'Fine. Did you happen to go anywhere interesting today?' Marvin averted his focus, pouring himself a cup of tea and offering Forster one.

Forster declined. 'I spent the day with Vivian,' he lied.

Marvin lowered his cup too fast. It clattered into its saucer, spilling tea down his hand. 'Dammit.' He reached for a cloth and swiped angrily. 'Then I suppose I'm incorrect in thinking that I saw you outside the Public Record Office earlier today?' He tossed the cloth into the sink, his murky blue eyes fixed on Forster. Clouded with suspicion. And not a little hurt.

Guilt caught Forster in its snare. 'Vivian asked me to run some errands for her.' He shrugged, tasting the bitter-almond taint of the lies he was spinning. 'Since we are no longer friends, I wasn't aware you required me to account for every minute of my whereabouts.' His heart stuttered with frustration and guilt as they stared each other down.

A shrill noise caught them both unawares.

Marvin walked into the hallway, picked up their newly installed telephone, and spoke to the operator. 'I'll fetch him at once. Who will I say is calling?'

Forster glanced out of the window. It was becoming habitual, these wintry evaluations of the weather. It was a cold, clear day, edged with pewter clouds towards the horizon. His speck of hope guttered. Then a single flake of snow wandered down.

'A friend?' Marvin raised his eyebrows at Forster.

Forster strode over and signalled for the telephone, his hope flaring, lighting him up from inside with the possibility that it could be her. His Detta.

'How frightfully mysterious . . .'

Marvin demonstrated no signs of feeling inclined to pass the receiver so Forster reached out and liberated it from him. But the voice he heard was devoid of the life and colour it painted his life with for a few rare and precious days each year. Leached to the pale grey of timeworn rocks on a storm-lashed shore.

'Forster, are you there? I need you.'

Chapter Thirty-Seven

Detta was standing outside the manor when Forster leapt from his Tin Lizzie. Her Russian-inspired peasant dress was far too delicate for the snow drifting down and she looked fragile, her face pale and intense. A winter's evening had set in and she stood beneath an infinite onyx sky with snowflakes caressing her hair, her bare shoulders. She did not seem real. She was a vision from a story book, a kind of magic that was impossible to understand. Forster strode towards her and gathered her in his arms. His euphoria at hearing her voice only one week after he had parted with her had been short-lived at learning the circumstances.

'She was all that I had and now she's gone,' Detta sobbed into his chest.

Forster opened Mrs Fischer's biscuit tin and made a pot of tea. He brought both over to the kitchen table where Detta had folded herself onto a chair. 'You need to eat something.'

She toyed with a silver spoon. It caught the eye of the electric lights overhead, sending spangles shooting around the room. 'She has—had—a cousin in town that visited her often while I was indisposed. Gladys. She was the one to discover her. Apparently she suffered from a weak heart.' Detta gave a bitter laugh. 'I never knew.

She was far too busy taking care of me to concern herself with such matters.'

'You couldn't have known.'

'And yet I should have known.' Detta's voice cracked. 'She was already lying in a grave when the first snowflake fell from the sky. Did I tell you that? I missed her funeral. Returned to an echoing house and a headstone.' She abruptly fell silent, laid her head in her arms, and wept.

Forster went and sat at her side of the table, gathering her into his arms and resting his cheek on top of her head, wishing that he could take her pain away. His heart ached at Detta's grief-stained rage at the world. At one of the brightest stars that had suddenly and unfairly winked out of existence. At the injustice that Detta had sustained losing her parents, then herself, then the single person she had left to rely upon. He held her and listened.

'The manor was locked when the snow fell. That was my first sign that something was amiss but I could never have imagined this.' The shaky words poured out of her like tears, course and salty. 'She used to monitor the temperature and weather forecasts, did you know that? So that whenever snow was possible, no matter how distant a chance it may be, she could fling the doors open and fill the kitchen with my favourite foods and wait for me.'

'How did you get inside?' Forster asked softly.

'We have several spare keys hidden in the grounds. I used one of those,' Detta sniffed. 'Forster, I let her down.'

'What? No, that's not possible,' he said firmly.

Her tears fell faster. 'I did, I did not know she was ill, I was too concerned with my own pitiful situation to ever think of what she may be suffering through. I was selfish. Condemning her to live alone for most of the year.'

'You are the least selfish person I have ever encountered,' Forster told her, gently wiping the tears from her eyes with his thumb. 'She loved you and nothing made her happier than the time you shared. Put all other thoughts out of your mind for that is the only one which matters.'

Detta nodded and then they walked down to the graveyard and laid lilies as white as snow on Mrs Fischer's final resting place, beneath a gnarled blackthorn that would flourish with life in spring and scatter its blossoms on her deep slumber.

'Detta?' Forster tapped his knuckles against her bathroom door. His stomach was churning with worry; she had refused to eat any of the biscuits he'd tried to tempt her with earlier, and since she'd sequestered herself away, claiming she wished to take a bath, the sun had set on her silence.

She did not answer and, possessed by a swift tide of panic, he gently pushed the door open. She was sat in a clawfoot tub, hugging her legs to her chest, her head resting on her knees. Her hair was trailing in the cooling water, her eyes swollen, plum-bruised with grief, and his heart splintered to see her so. Forster knelt on the floor behind her and reached for her bottle of shampoo. Working up a lather, he tenderly washed Detta's hair. After wrapping her in a thick towel and helping her into bed, he fetched her a mug of warm milk with a pinch of nutmeg and honey and as she drank it, he told her of his decision to stay as long as the snow held.

✳

The end of November snowed into December and still, Forster stayed. Taking up residence in the guestroom that had become somewhat his, concerned that if he left, Detta would return alone to an empty home. Yet the snow showed no signs of abating. Mrs Fischer's absence was palpable. A wound too sore to press. The kitchen a painful void, cold and barren. Forster could not bear for Detta to lose that warm heart of the manor, for her happy memories to be tainted with grief forevermore, so in the hopes of nourishing both her and the manor back to life, he had taken up cooking.

He soon discovered that the culinary arts required an alchemy not entirely unlike painting, wherein a palette of ingredients or colours might result in a masterpiece. It also did not take long for him to learn that studying recipes alone was not an adequate substitute for experience. But his greatest find was that within Mrs Fischer's meticulous recipe books was an entire life recorded. Through them, he felt her presence. Shrewd and discerning and caring. Wildflowers pressed between pages, pithy observances of the townspeople, notations on how to make rations last or what to subsidise when food shortages ran rampant during the Great War. Letters from a long-lost love that he did not read out of respect, and records of Detta's transformations, which he did. Most merely noted the days in which she had been human and the length of hours. Though the year of 1919 bore a longer, more disturbing comment:

The temperature is well below freezing but my girl has already left us. It seems it is no longer sufficient for it to be winter, now she must be surrounded by snow for her to maintain her body.

214

Forster snapped the book shut with trembling hands. In a hurry to rid himself of unbidden thoughts that crept forth, his mind swelling with fear thick enough to cut with a blade, he began seizing ingredients from the larder and preparing the oven.

'According to the wireless, it is nearly Christmas,' Detta said that evening as she nibbled at the pie he'd baked. Flames danced in her pupils as she stared into the hearth. 'It is strange to me, that these days have all melded into one indistinguishable haze. I usually pay such detailed attention to each and every hour I am lucky to enjoy but now they all seem lost to the same darkness.'

'Give it time,' Forster told her, re-entering the kitchen with an armful of firewood he'd become accustomed to chopping himself. 'But yes, Christmas is three days away.' He stamped snow from his boots. The manor was echoing and draughty and a blizzard howled outside.

'You ought to leave if you wish to celebrate the season with your friends.'

He glanced up from the fire. 'You were wrong when I answered your call, when I arrived.' She laid her fork down, waiting for him to elaborate. 'Mrs Fischer was not all you had, not anymore. You have me and I shall not go anywhere, not while you have need of me.' The fire flared, devouring the log he'd fed it.

'You do not need to be my carer, Forster,' Detta said quietly. 'I realise that I have not been myself but I don't wish you to stay out of any obligation you feel—'

'It's not obligation, dammit.' Forster brushed the snow from his hair. 'I can't think of anyone I would rather spend Christmas with than you.'

'Then stay.' Detta's smile warmed him more than the fire. 'Stay with me and let's celebrate together.'

✳

Their Christmas was quiet and cosy. Spent curled up before the fire as a blizzard besieged the manor. On Christmas Eve, Forster vanished for an hour and returned the proud bearer of a small fir he had cut from the woodland. As the gramophone spun Tchaikovsky's Nutcracker Suite, Detta hung delicate glass baubles on the branches. When she tossed a smile over her shoulder at Forster, his chest swelled.

His hands ran up her arms, gently sweeping her hair onto one shoulder. Planting a soft kiss on her neck, he removed her gift from his pocket and fastened it around her neck. Her eyes widened as she clasped the necklace. Silver with a crystal snowflake pendant, it twinkled next to the Christmas tree. 'Merry Christmas, Detta,' he told her huskily.

Turning around, she placed her hands on either side of his face, looking up into his eyes. 'I hope you know how precious you are to me.' She kissed him before he could respond, then kissed him again and again, until he silently gave thanks to the stars above that she was here, in his arms, this Christmas.

PART FOUR

1926

'The princess shall indeed prick her finger with the spindle, but she shall not die. She shall fall into sleep that will last a hundred years.'

—JACOB AND WILHELM GRIMM, *Sleeping Beauty*

Chapter Thirty-Eight

The blizzard had raged through Christmas. Snow tumbled past every window, as if the manor was at the heart of a snow globe. And still it continued to snow as the calendar tipped them into a fresh year.

When the afternoon was on the cusp of evening, that velvet hour when the world seems a little softer, Forster set down a golden brown pie before Detta, accompanied by a generous portion of roast potatoes and vegetables. A hint of a smile toyed with her lips. 'You are improving at this,' she joked.

Seeing her smile again tugged at his heart. 'I only burnt one and I still maintain that wasn't my fault.' He laughed.

Forster lit a roaring fire in the hearth yet despite that and the heat emanating from the oven, a chill hung in the air. The manor was too vast for one person alone. Especially one person that spent most of her year lost to the lake. He had known Detta for both years and just a handful of weeks at the same time. And during that dichotomy of time, she had eclipsed everyone else he knew to become his closest, deepest friend. And moreover; she was the only one who truly understood him in life. They had been fortunate the snow had lasted this long but he couldn't chance it melting, couldn't trust their precarious time together as it might be snatched away at any moment, leaving important things unsaid. No, he had to speak his mind tonight.

'Tell me about your family,' Detta said as they dined. 'We have set the world to rights, you and I, many times over, yet them you barely mention.'

That old ache curved around his bones. The last time his mother had spoken to him. Her words that had seared through him like an arrow, leaving him with barbs lodged inside his ribcage. His heart snagged against those barbs. Then, a touch of his hands. 'It's all right,' Detta told him, 'you can tell me anything.' She was gentle and caring, a Botticelli maiden in soft blush tones.

'It hasn't been the same since the death of my father,' Forster admitted. 'Grief is like a well: you can never truly leave it but the walls grow wider and wider until one day you look up and realise that you can see the sky again.' Detta was listening, running her thumb along the back of his hand as she did so. This gave him the strength to continue. 'My father died in the war. I wasn't permitted to fight. Flat feet, they told me.' His laugh was wry. 'I'd never heard of such a thing yet suddenly I was at home with my mother and my elder sister while my father—' His voice splintered. Detta held his hand tighter. Forster dragged in a breath, trying to steady himself. 'My father, who had the soul of a poet, who lectured at university and never passed a garden without picking a rose for my mother, departed for the trenches. My brother-in-law fought too. Hell, even Marvin did. It didn't take me long to leave for the war too. I ended up volunteering for the British Red Cross Ambulance Corps. Driving around, unable to help anyone, not the soldiers nor the doctors and nurses. My grandfather was a doctor; even in his senile years he would have been more use than me. But there was nothing more I could do.' He glanced down at his watch, out of sight beneath his jumper sleeve.

'None of that was your fault,' Detta said softly.

'I know. Though knowing that never quite eases the sting, does it? I wish I had been by his side when, when he—'

'I know.' Detta did not stop stroking his hand. 'You can tell me anything, Forster. Let it all out.'

Forster's thoughts turned to his mother; the vault he kept her locked within had burst open, letting his past spill out. 'We all grieved him. My sister Beatrice and Mother didn't say anything but I felt as if they blamed me in some incalculable way. That if I too had fought, perhaps that would have satiated the beast of war enough to not devour our father.'

Detta's headshake was gentle, sad. 'That is not the way of war.'

'No. Seeing it for myself, I am well aware of that. But it turned my mother against me. Things became worse and worse between us until they broke down altogether, severing what remained of our relationship. She told me that it should have been me who died. That she wished it had been. That my death she could have borne.'

Detta inhaled sharply, her hand tightening on his, a reminder of her support.

'That was the last time I saw her.'

'Oh, Forster—'

'I had already left home for London by then so I returned to mine and Marvin's flat that night. Marvin was out late that night; actually it was the first of your parties he'd attended—' Forster exchanged a wry smile with Detta '—but when he eventually came home, though he was exhausted and more than a little drunk, he stayed up the rest of the morning with me. That was the moment I saw him as more than just my flatmate, the first step in our journey of friendship. Little did I know then that we would end up like brothers, the closest thing I had to a family.' Forster paused, his sadness a creeping villain, threatening to overwhelm him. 'Anyway, I was fortunate that that same grandfather was from a wealthy family and thanks to him, I receive a modest stipend that's paid my way thus far. It isn't much but it has gifted me time. I drew and painted until I improved then improved again. Until it became not just a distraction but my lifeline. Though sometimes I wonder if I have pursued a selfish want, more of an indulgence than a career.'

'Never,' Detta exclaimed passionately. 'Art is a pillar of human culture. There is a reason we seek to preserve it during warfare.' Forster made to speak but she forged on. 'Whether that art seeks to inform or entertain is of no consequence, it is part of our human experience and carries immeasurable value.'

Forster's throat clogged with emotion. 'Thank you,' he managed. He was met with one of her incandescent smiles that left him a little stunned. Day by day, he lost himself a little more to her. Until this morning, when he had awoken to realise that she carried his entire heart, without knowing.

They ate for a while in an easy silence that settled around them like a blanket, warm and comfortable. When Forster glanced across at Detta's plate, it had been half emptied. After eating his fill of roast potatoes, their insides melting like butter, he broke their silence with a blade of truth. 'I have something to say that I do not think you'll welcome. Yet you and I, we have always been honest with each other, no matter the subject.'

Detta turned wary. 'Go on.'

'You need to hire a custodian. Someone who will take care of the manor in warmer months.'

She set down her knife. 'Mrs Fischer was unique in understanding my situation. Imagine a housekeeper who did not. What would they think when I appeared at a godforsaken hour, out of nowhere with no fair warning and nothing but the skin on my back? Not to mention they would not know to check my rooms in the event that I had shifted back and become trapped inside. Or what if the unthinkable happened?' Her blue-grey eyes darkened as her voice lowered, delving into the waters of the lake of secrets they held between them. 'What if they were to witness me changing? Not many people would have reacted in the manner which you did, Forster.'

His heart slid further down his chest. She was right.

'Not unless that person was you.'

He stared at her. 'I am not a custodian, I know next to nothing about maintaining an estate of this grandeur. Nor am I a house-keeper. Besides, as much as I hold you in the highest of esteem, I have no desire to stop painting.' And worse, he had fallen in love with her. A secret that burned within him, but a truth too far. One that she could not learn, not until he had hunted Rothbart down and restored her life to her.

She gestured with her fork. 'You cannot tell me that you're content where you live now. I know that your friendship with Marvin was not what it once was. And can you honestly tell me that you possess sufficient studio space and light in that basement? I'm certain you must be inhaling fumes. You have a motor car, your art dealer in London may be at your disposal still. And you would have all the inspiration you require here, at your fingertips. Besides, I own more rooms than I know what to do with.' She spread her hands.

'I have no need of your money,' Forster said quietly.

Detta's sigh was laced with exasperation. 'And nor would I assume so. It would be a mutually beneficial arrangement with no financial transaction. Why not live and paint here in exchange for providing me with peace of mind that the manor shall still be standing the next time it snows?' Her gaze softened. 'This isn't charity, Forster, it is but an idea. You know well how I'm prone to wild, grand ideas.'

He did know. He knew *her*. And this was the first occasion since Mrs Fischer's death that she had been ignited with a familiar spark. Yet he did not know how he could live in her manor knowing that he was falling more in love with her each day. To do so would be the height of foolishness. But love makes fools of us all. And she was right, he had lost the relationship he once had with Marvin. It was not as cruel and final a parting as Mrs Fischer's death, or his own family's abandonment of him, but he had grieved the loss all the same. It had been some time since he'd belonged in London. The idea took root. Perhaps it would be a mistake. But, it could be wonderful. 'If you're truly certain?'

'I have never been surer of anything in my life.' Detta toasted him with her crystal glass. 'At the eve of the previous year you declared that I would never be alone again. Well, Forster, neither shall you.'

Chapter Thirty-Nine

'You're moving out?' Marvin stared at Forster. 'Whatever for?'

'I have ruminated at length and decided to move to Wurthercliffe,' Forster told him. After the gale of tension that had recently swept through their little flat, he took care to keep his tone breezy. He had no wish to spark another storm. He continued packing his belongings into the battered trunk that had contained his entire life when he had first boarded the train to London, clutching onto it as if his hopes and dreams coursed through its cracked leather. Marvin watched, leaning against the doorframe, cigarette in hand.

'I know things have been a little . . . awkward of late, but we're family, Forster. You don't leave your family without good reason. You've already been gone for well over a month and, well, I worried for you.'

Forster was unable to hold his tongue a moment longer. 'The truth is I don't feel like I fit into this life anymore. Too much has passed between us and I believe we would both benefit from some space. Besides, you know well how the environment in Wurthercliffe has inspired my art more than London ever did and it's far more economical to live there, too. I can easily drive back here whenever I wish. This is just what I need right now.'

Marvin's silence did not assuage his guilt. Forster carried his trunk outside and into the passenger seat of his motor, which groaned its protest. When he hurried back inside to begin the more laborious task of packing his materials and canvasses, Marvin dragged on his cigarette. The epitome of casual indolence. 'This has something to do with her, doesn't it?'

'I don't have the slightest inclination what you're insinuating.' Forster wrapped a painting in brown paper and tied it with string. 'I've left next month's rent beside the decanter; it will tide you over until you've replaced me, though you might wish to speak with Charles. Last I heard, he was making enquiries for lodgings in Chelsea.'

'Have you informed Rose of your plans?' Marvin asked. 'I was not the only one who has missed you this past month.'

'Not yet.' Forster's conscience twinged. He did not intend to linger in the city; though he was in a rush to return to Detta while she was still human, he already had another stop along the way. He could not lose more time. It was too precious, like water trickling through a closed fist, the tighter he attempted to hold onto it, the faster it squeezed out.

'Look, I'm sorry, Forster,' Marvin suddenly said. 'I know you have not agreed with certain decisions I've made lately and if this rift between us is down to my actions, then truly, I apologise.'

'I appreciate your contrition but I'm afraid it changes nothing. As I said, London is no longer the right place for me, and the space between us will do us some good. I need a fresh start,' he said honestly.

Marvin stubbed out his cigarette and came to assist Forster with the last of his belongings. 'Very well,' he said ruefully. 'You know, birds always find their way home, no matter the distance. Perhaps you will, too.'

Chapter Forty

It wasn't until he had left London that calmness descended upon Forster, duck-egg blue and light as a blossom-sprinkle of springtime. Until he did not wend his way along to Detta but drove to the Midlands instead, hoping that his little detour would give him a promising lead to return to Detta with. He stopped in Northampton and made his way across to The Drapery to the Bisou café and tearooms. It was curious, returning to the town of his birth. He oft caught himself glancing about, as if he might catch sight of his family, treading these familiar streets. Truth be told, he wasn't certain he would recognise his nieces and nephews if he did. Beatrice had three children now – or was it four? Though he sent the odd gift their way – a painting of a shimmering fairy grotto; a fine porcelain doll with a turquoise bow in her hair; a little Hornby engine that steamed and sputtered – and now and then received a photograph or short letter back, their lives chugged along on different tracks and the thought no longer pained him.

He was ushered to a table inside, where a woman in her mid-thirties awaited him, stirring a teacup.

'Miss Smith?' Forster removed his hat and sat opposite her when she nodded.

'Though it's Mrs Wilson these days.' She laid her spoon down on the saucer with a hint of a smile. Perhaps the article Forster had read of her pirouetting through the air had enflamed his imagination but she appeared to him like a sprite with her petite stature, finely spun copper hair, and near-black eyes. 'I was pleasantly surprised when my mother passed your letter onto me. I haven't spoken to Detta in an age; do tell me how is she faring? Does she still dance? Would you care for some tea?' She filled his cup from the teapot before he had a chance to answer, her questions tumbling from her mouth faster than his thoughts.

'She is well. Though a little . . . indisposed, hence her unavailability today.'

'Milk? Sugar?'

'I take it black, thank you.' He accepted his cup. 'She's been telling me stories from her time at Rothbart's Theatre of Enchantments, and I confess, I'm quite compelled to learn more of it. Which brings me to my purpose of visiting you—'

Daisy leant forwards. 'You wish me to tell you all the most salacious gossip that Detta is far too well-mannered to share?'

Her mischief was infectious and Forster laughed despite himself. 'I will gladly hear all that you have to tell. How long were you a dancer at the theatre?'

'Just four years. I started a few years before Detta arrived and left shortly after we toured in Paris.' Her countenance darkened with her mention of the city and Forster paused, surveying her over his cup.

'What happened in Paris to make you leave?'

Daisy's eyebrows drew together. 'You know, for a man, you're remarkably perceptive. I wish my own husband would notice certain details. Take last night for instance, we had scarcely arrived home when the sink—'

Forster buried his smile in his teacup.

But Daisy herself was unusually perceptive; this nourished his tender hope that she might be able to tell him where Rothbart was now.

'Ah, I'm getting off topic, aren't I?' She gave him a rueful look. 'Rupert tells me I have a habit of doing that. Well, Paris.' She sighed. 'Paris was an experience. Wonderful at times but well, too wonderful, if you know what I mean? Our time there shone too bright, bright enough to dazzle us all and bright enough to make us forget what happened in the shadows. And nobody glowed more than Detta. Oh, she loved Paris, she did.' Daisy's smile was bittersweet as she continued, 'It was beautiful to see after how hard she'd taken our friend Penelope's departure. And the city loved her back. For a while, at least. But Rothbart didn't take kindly to sharing his stage and it didn't take long for the pressures of orchestrating the greatest, grandest performance ever to show their cracks. Our rehearsals doubled and his expenditures tripled but for a brief moment, we were soaring to new heights. At the very top.'

'Then what happened?'

Daisy set her teacup down. 'Nobody stays at the top forever. Rothbart grew greedy, demanding more time from his performers, more funding from our patrons, larger stages.' Her voice faltered, her lips tightening as if she was suppressing an unsavoury memory, and Forster wanted to ask what had truly happened there but he did not know this woman well enough and then it was too late and she had gathered herself. 'His demands couldn't be met and so we returned to York, to perform on our home stage while planning the next tour. Vienna and St Petersburg it was to be, I believe. But I'd already left by then.' Another falter. She was omitting something, smoothing over the cracks to make her story more palatable for company but there was no avoiding the pinch of grief in her face. Something significant had happened in Paris, triggering their departure, Forster was certain of it. And more than a little curious.

'Several performers had succumbed to illness or injury in their attempt to keep up with Rothbart's frenetic schedule and I had no interest in being next,' Daisy continued. Someone had vanished in Paris, Forster was certain of it. Someone that Daisy had been close to.

'And Detta . . . well, after Paris, she wasn't herself. The city changed her.'

'How so?'

'I believe that the fame and attention were too much for her,' Daisy said carefully. 'After all, the spotlight is both a blessing and a curse.'

Forster inclined his head, not pressing her for details. He would prefer to hear the story from Detta herself, all too aware that he was hearing this version from someone who did not know and could not guess at the sinister truth lurking beneath Rothbart's Theatre of Enchantments. 'I don't suppose you happen to know what became of Rothbart?' His throat tightened as he spoke, finishing his tea in an effort not to betray the tremble in his heart and the desperation in his soul to find this man. The only man that could restore Detta's life to her.

'No.'

Forster forced the ensuing tide of hopelessness down, trying to pay attention as Daisy continued speaking.

'I saw in the papers that he was under investigation but had fled and I presumed there would have been another story if he'd been found but there never was and well, life goes on, doesn't it? I stopped dancing, got married, had children. All of that seems like it belongs to a different life now. Another world.' She shrugged and poured them both another cup of tea.

The taste was beginning to sour. Like old disappointment.

'I'm sorry I couldn't be of more use. Though I did bring you this. This was when Detta danced Snow White, the first role that Rothbart created for her.' Daisy slid a photograph over the table. 'It was taken before opening night, her first as a prima ballerina.'

In the photograph, a younger Detta beamed with pride and exuberance. It pained Forster that he had not known her then; it seemed as if she had always been in his life, impossible to imagine the days he had lived without her.

'You may keep it. I thought Detta would like the memento to remember old times.'

'Thank you.' He slipped it into his breast pocket where it rested, against his heart. 'Do you know where I might find out more? If someone else knows more about Rothbart or the theatre or even Detta herself?'

Daisy cast him a curious look. 'You said that you're her friend?'

'Her closest.'

Her half-smile was knowing. Touched with pity. 'Does she know that you're in love with her?'

Foster ran a hand roughly over his jaw. *Unusually perceptive indeed.* 'I'm not sure. It's complicated,' he admitted.

'Ah, matters of the heart so often are. Well, you may wish to pay a trip to Théâtre Magique in Paris.' Glancing at her pearl-edged watch, Daisy exclaimed and finished her tea in a hurry. 'Sorry, Forster, I must dash but this was a lovely stroll down memory lane. You and Detta must join us for dinner sometime soon.' She stood, pulling on her cream woollen coat. 'Provided things become less *complicated*,' she added with a hint of mischief.

'Thank you. Can you tell me what's at Théâtre Magique?' Forster left payment on the table and stood, too, churning with anxiety for the last of his questions to be answered before she left.

'It was where we performed there. Look for Jacques, the owner.'
Daisy began fastening the buttons on her coat.

'Was he close to Rothbart?'

'Yes.' Daisy hesitated, meeting his eyes. 'And he was Detta's first love.'

✶

Tree-lined roads, salted breezes, and glimpses of the blustering sea cleared Forster's head as he came to terms with Daisy's revelations, curious over what had happened in Paris and with Jacques. As he neared Wurthercliffe, the first delicate flakes of snow landed on his windscreen. He grinned with relief that it was still snowing and sped along the snow-carpeted roads until he'd reached the manor. There, he stopped for a moment, staring up at the grand estate, its vast roof frosted in white. How peculiar that this was to be his new home. He was half grateful, half disbelieving of the fact.

After parking, he shucked off his driving gloves and cap and entered the manor with his own key, feeling as if it were the key to some great secret. Treading through the pages of his own fairy tale, laced with a heady cocktail of enchantments and curses. His footsteps echoed as he made his way upstairs, seeking Detta.

'I'm in here,' she called out cheerfully.

He was greeted by a cloud of steam as he opened the door. Detta was reclining in her clawfoot bathtub, covered by a mass of pink bubbles and sipping a saucer of champagne. Slowing, he drank her in. Detta stretched one leg then the other with pointed toes. His head swam. She watched his reaction, his hunger, and sat forwards, the bubbles slipping down her naked form. Slowly revealing herself to him. 'Why don't you join me?'

Forster tugged his jacket and shirt off in a hurry as Detta's gaze darkened with desire. Something rasped against the material. Forster pulled the photograph Daisy had gifted him from his shirt pocket, glancing at it by rote.

'What is that?' Detta asked, reaching for the bottle of champagne and pouring a second saucer for him.

'Just a photograph—' Forster frowned at it. A younger Detta stood before a snarl of forest, her dress swan-white, her hair pouring down her back the way he liked. But when he'd first looked at it, he'd been too prepossessed with Detta to notice the shadowed background and the ruined castle which stood there. He squinted at the ruins, wondering why they had struck him with familiarity. Then, a flash of insight. One of the photographs he had taken from Rothbart's fireplace had captured the same ruins: Snow White's castle.

✻ ✻ ✻

The Times

18th October 1913

Rothbart's Theatre of Enchantments takes on Snow White

In his latest offering, the great showrunner Rothbart has adapted the classic fairy tale Snow White into a Gothic masterpiece. The lead role was created for his newly appointed prima ballerina, Detta Kova, who brings a delicate intensity to the titular character, dancing at turns with a fierce defiance, demonstrated through powerful leaps and jumps, before paring back with raw vulnerability. This is exaggerated by the costume designer choosing to dress Kova in white, ensuring that she presents a stark figure against the overwhelmingly shadowed set design.

The performance itself takes a dark turn with Snow White's palatial home recast as medieval ruins and live trees that march through the theatre, seemingly by themselves. Rather unexpectedly – though we have surely learnt by now not to attend a Rothbart production with expectations – the use of puppets is utilised for the first time on this theatre's stage with startling effect.

Their uncanny movements and silence lend an eerie note to the show, as does the slow-falling snow which softly coats the audience as Snow White succumbs to the poison apple.

Chapter Forty-One

Detta
1913

Being promoted to prima ballerina came with the blistering heat of the electric spotlights and the envy of my fellow performers. And Rothbart. Always there, in his box, in the wings. The great show master. His attention now turned keener, unnerving me as he watched me dance.

With the first bite of autumn, I donned my favourite picture hat, with its boysenberry sash, and departed the theatre. I had taken the liberty of chasing down Penelope's former address. It led to a modest dwelling in Lime Street, Hungate. Walking past an outside water pump, I knocked on the door. Penelope had preferred to speak of her future rather than her past, only revealing little glimpses that she'd had a difficult upbringing: the way she'd saved her earnings rather than squander them on prettier dresses or a thicker coat to buffer her against the stinging winters. Why she had pressed the apricot peonies I had surprised her with, so she might keep them forever. She had auditioned for Rothbart at a young age without having been to a single ballet class, only knowing that she desired nothing more than to learn. Even then, he had recognised her aptitude for dance, propelling her to stardom. Though she had never allowed her fame to sweep her away, tempting her to fritter her money on silly luxuries, she was too practically minded for that.

My knock went unanswered, her former residence appearing vacant. Yet as I turned to leave, weighed down with regret, I caught a figure watching from a neighbouring flat. I strode over at once to make enquiries.

'Always had such aspirations, she did.' The woman peered at me from beneath a nest of pigeon-grey hair, her hands red-raw, eyes as golden as an autumnal sunset. 'She and her mother with their ambitions too grand for the likes of us. They resented being here.'

'Have you seen Penelope lately?' I asked.

'No.' The woman shook her head and shuffled off.

'What of her mother?' I called after her.

'She died years ago. I reckon she'd been dying of a broken heart the moment she'd got here. It wasn't really a surprise, sickly thing like her.' The woman banged her door shut.

Reluctant to return to the theatre without answers, I stayed until the sun sank lower in the sky and the narrow alleys played host to a myriad of shadows. It was to no avail, nobody had seen nor heard anything. Whatever had become of Penelope, she had certainly not returned to her former home. My secret glimmer of hope that she had, darkened. But I would not give up searching for her. I had always thought that when I became a prima ballerina it would fulfil me, but success without anyone to share it with was lonelier than I could have imagined. I pondered if I ought to leave the theatre like I had instructed Penelope to do before she vanished but leading the company for the first time was intoxicating and I resented the idea of stepping down into a lesser role at another company. And so I stayed.

All too soon, another opening night dawned on Rothbart's Theatre of Enchantments, and stepping into the glittering spotlight in a dress as white as fallen snow was me. Rothbart's *Snow White* was reminiscent of Stravinsky and Diaghilev's *The Firebird* ballet, which I'd seen with my mother three years ago in Paris. Those costumes had been designed by the painter Chagall and everything had been eerie in a surreal, fantastical manner. With *Snow White*, Rothbart summoned the spirit of the forest within the theatre, with lavishly painted sets, a haunting score, and real snow that fell as we danced. Rothbart had ordered additional rehearsals until everything was perfect, demanding more and more from us until he was satisfied that opening night would bring a show-stopping performance. Most performers grumbled at this but it seemed to cost Rothbart the most; there was a marked change within him and as his preparations escalated, his hair greyed. The rest of the company whispered about this, that he expected too much, but my own ambition growled to life, driving me to dance more than ever, to practise until I sparkled every bit as brightly as the star of the show ought.

That evening, I twirled in pirouettes, alone on stage. Behind were imposing pine trees that had picked up their roots and marched in when the curtain lifted. And behind those, lurked the seven dwarves. Unlike the Broadway play that had debuted an ocean away last year, with seven dwarves that had charming if odd names like Flick, Glick, Snick, and Quee, Rothbart's dwarves were silent, ominous creatures. Puppets. Their strings guided by invisible hands beyond the spotlight's reach. Though the puppets' expressions were fixed in varnished wood, I was certain that their eyes trailed me as I danced between the trees. The music whipped faster as I lashed my leg out in fouettés, spinning and leaping through the little clearing, the evil queen closing in on me.

Rothbart leant closer in his box seat, his moustache twitching with excitement as I folded down onto the stage, the poisoned apple tumbling from my hand. The entire theatre was suddenly scented with tart apples and as I watched from half-closed eyes, gnarled branches grew over the walls, doors, and ceiling. Plump rosy apples dangled down, tempting the audience to reach out and take one. Daring them to bite into its juicy flesh. After a carefully choreographed pause, to allow the audience to exclaim and delight, I was laid to rest in my glass coffin. Though it was not real, my thoughts spiralled to dark and darker places. To Penelope and where she might be resting at this moment. The coffin may have been glass but I was trapped, my pulse quickening as I stared up into the boxes. I may have been the one locked within a faux coffin yet Rothbart appeared on the verge of death. His face was waxen and he appeared to be muttering to himself with closed eyes. I did not know how illusionists worked but, to me, this looked like some dark incantation at play. Perhaps he was succumbing to his own hubris, his ambition taking too great a toll. Before I might observe more, my prince arrived.

A honey-gold light beamed across the theatre like sunlight, wild and warm. It set my glass coffin a-glittering. And as the audience gasped, I realised it was not a coffin of glass at all but one of sugar that was melting beneath the warm light. It liberated me and I stood, performing my pas de deux with the prince in the glowing forest as the sinister dwarves retreated into the shadows.

In perhaps one of his greatest illusions yet, the ruined castle that Snow White had fled from suddenly let out a deep grinding sound. Breaking from my performance, my partner's hand tightening on mine in warning, I whirled around.

It had been painted on wooden boards and assembled on stage yet now the stonework groaned to life. A slow awakening. Rothbart continued to manipulate it, forcing it to repair its missing gaps, to grow taller. The cast and audience were silent, caught in Rothbart's spell. We watched as one. Until the castle had overtaken the entire stage like an invasion. Now sparkling new and crowned with turrets.

Suitable for a queen. Its doors snapped open and I did not have to feign Snow White's delight as I danced inside.

When the curtains closed on us with a velvet sigh of relief, Rothbart had vacated his box. We performers waited for him to materialise on stage, to take his customary first bow, soaking up his adulation. Yet he did not come. I did not see him until several nights later, when he appeared outside my bedroom.

Having heard the creak of floorboards outside my door, I opened it. At once, my courage seeped from me at the way in which he regarded me. Curious and cautious. And most worrisome of all, silent. He had stepped out of his character as a snake sheds their skin. His owlish face was fixed upon me, his tawny eyes glinting with something that resembled hunger. As if he were a man tempted by something that he knew he ought not to be. I stood there, feeling as if I had been tossed into the ice-water of my nightmares, my fear of this man a singular shock. We did not exchange a single word before he turned and walked away.

That was the moment when I knew that the whispers were right. Rothbart must be responsible for the disappearing performers. Concern for Penelope washed over me and returning from the spotlight to an empty room, devoid of her light and leftover slices of lemon-drizzle cake, felt wrong. An uneasiness was settling inside my ribcage.

But when I closed my eyes that night, I dreamt of the applause the audience had showered upon me, the roses that had been flung onto the stage, the way the other performers had congratulated me. I was Snow White, Rothbart's theatre my cursed apple. And I had already bitten into it.

Chapter Forty-Two

After a few days together, which were entirely too brief, the snow melted away, and so too did Detta.

In her swan-skin, she had followed Forster through the grounds, across to the thicket. When they reached the lake, cast over in the thick gloom of the burgeoning evening, he yearned for her, wishing that he had kissed her one last time, told her everything she meant to him. But she slipped into the water and floated away until the mist claimed her and he could see her no longer.

Forster distracted himself by roaming the manor, seeking a place he might call his own. It was of little use; his mind pirouetted faster and faster, his anger the bright red of the nutcracker soldier's jacket. Detta deserved more than this half-life. And they had already exchanged a lifetime of goodbyes, his heart splintering a little more each time she shuddered and shook apart. Night had fallen, thick and fast as a storm, by the time he'd moved his belongings into his new rooms. They consisted of a small bedroom with an adjoining bathroom that had been modernised perhaps a decade ago, a cosy drawing room which would be easy to heat and furnish himself, and a larger, airier room with views that stretched to his lake. This would be his very first studio.

It didn't take long for Forster to settle into his life at the manor.

His routine was slower than it had been in London, allowing him space to breathe, to think, to paint. He took his coffee in the library overlooking the woodland, before strolling down to the lake-edge to visit Detta. A visit that never failed to exacerbate his loneliness. He'd moved down here to be closer to her yet now she was further away than ever. Unreachable. Tearing himself away from her, he proceeded to spend the remainder of the day in his studio. Having a studio to call his own was a revelation and each time he wrote to Vivian, appraising her of his progress, he mentioned what a difference it had made to his work. He painted until the light dwindled and the sun yawned, its mouth gaping across the sky in violet sunsets before it slipped into bed. Then came a stroll to the nearest shop for supplies, the local grocer's stock determining what would be for dinner, followed by further experiments from Mrs Fischer's cookbooks, the measurements adjusted to cook for one. And finally, an evening walk to the lake. Where Detta sat atop the mirror-smooth water, resplendent in silken moonlight. He often sat beside the lake, telling her the little moments that had framed his day and how he missed her dearly. How she had become the axis around which his world rotated. When warmer weather arrived, removing even the faintest hope of snow, he would take his leave for France, to pick up the thread of his investigations. Until then he busied himself with making enquiries into Théâtre Magique and the mysterious Jacques, so that they might meet upon his arrival in Paris.

When the clotted cream-cloud sky next whipped up a batch of fluffy snow in February, Forster was delighted it brought Detta back to him. They found themselves sitting before the hearth in the drawing room, Detta nestled in his arms beneath a cashmere shawl, a cup of hot chocolate warming her hands. Having just emerged from her clawfoot tub, her hair was wilder than usual. A single ringlet rested against her cheekbone and Forster was idly winding it around his finger. He'd been wandering alongside the lake when the first flakes had fallen. Dropping his mug of coffee, he'd raced around the shore until he'd found her, feathers falling away as she gasped, beak turning to blue lips, frozen together. 'Are you warm yet?' he murmured into her ear, securing the shawl tighter around her.

'Don't fuss so, Forster.' She leant back to kiss his cheek. 'I told you, I never feel the cold.'

He scoffed doubtfully, resting his chin on the top of her head and pulling her closer against him. Trying not to glance out of the window where he knew what he would see; the light flurries falling onto grass where they promptly vanished. It wasn't cold enough. 'I know it isn't setting,' Detta said and Forster closed his eyes, silently pleading with the fates not to let the snow melt.

'I told you not to fuss.' Detta sighed impatiently. 'It doesn't help matters.'

'Fine.' Forster fell silent, sulking a little.

But Detta poked him. 'I know what will distract you,' she murmured. She turned to face him, climbing onto his lap and fastening her mouth onto his with an urgency that stole his breath away. Her kiss hot and fierce, her tongue seeking his, she tugged at his damp shirt with a desperation that resonated through him, wanting nothing more than to lose himself in the woman he loved before she was gone.

Some hours later, Forster ran his hand up and down Detta's back as they lay before the dying fire. 'Have you decided upon the theme for this year's party yet?' he asked.

He felt her smile against his bare chest. 'I most certainly have.'

Forster could not help smiling in return. 'And are you planning on divulging it to me?'

She considered for a moment, glancing up at him as her expression turned mischievous. 'I think not. Perhaps I shall banish you from the manor while I have it set up.'

Reaching out for his cooling hot chocolate, he flicked some cream at her. 'Tease.' She scooped it up with a finger and licked it. Forster groaned and pulled her hand to his mouth, trailing kisses along her fingertips. Too many nights she pirouetted through his dreams, appearing as if she had walked from the canvas of a pre-Raphaelite painting with those unbound curls and dresses as light as cloud matter and now that she was here, he couldn't stop reaching for her, holding her, worshipping her.

'Yes, it shall be a surprise,' Detta decided, watching his lips pressed against her hand. 'Though I'm certain you shall appreciate it. And perhaps—' she swallowed and he hesitated, meeting her questioning gaze '—perhaps it could be the last party I hold. Have you made any progress in finding Rothbart?'

A life was so fragile, spun from magic impossible to understand, yet hers weighed heavily on him. The promise he had made her, heavier still. 'You would not wish to continue the tradition?' he asked instead, cursing himself as her brows drew together.

'If I could be that lucky, if my destiny was not bound to the lake, then I wouldn't need to wring every drop from life on just a few days or weeks each year. Instead, I could just . . . live.' She whispered the final word as if it were impossible to believe.

'Regretfully, I haven't found him yet. But I've had a promising lead.' He hesitated, not wishing to give her false hope. 'Though it would be useful if you were to tell me what happened to Penelope,' he said, softer, burying his other question deeper within himself. He could not ask why she had not left, saved herself, not when he already knew the ending to her dark tale. 'Did you ever find her before the company travelled to Paris?'

Detta rested her head back down on his chest. He stroked her hair. The firelight had lent it a russet-gleam and he longed to paint it. 'I did not. When we performed in Paris I was worried about Penelope, about Rothbart, and I was not myself at all. Perhaps if I had been, I would have noticed how perilous my own situation was, but that too, I did not realise. Not until it was too late.' Detta's sigh was rueful. 'But before we left for Paris, I did see Penelope one last time.'

Chapter Forty-Three

Detta
1913

Final performances were always a spectacle to behold at the theatre. Rothbart's illusions would pour across the stage, wilder and more sensory than ever until we performers almost believed that his magic was real. On the eve of the finale of the *Snow Queen*, rather fittingly, it snowed. Flurries whispered down onto the spires of York, nestled against the ancient city walls and melted in the Ouse with a sigh. Of course, when you are on stage, night reigns eternal so we did not notice the early snowfall. Not yet.

As I pirouetted through the night in a pearl-white tutu, embroidered with gingerbread-brown boughs that glittered darkly, the forest began to march across the stage. Trees picked up their roots and scuttled forward, surrounding the cottage in which I had sought sanctuary. Eyes blinked open on their trunks, through which the Snow Queen spied upon me. It reminded me of how Rothbart had fixed me with that terrible look that night outside my bedroom. Ever-there, ever-waiting. Above, trapeze artists whirled through the air like snowflakes. And with a great cracking, frost crept through the entire theatre until the audience gasped and shivered, their breath frozen as they exhaled in wonder.

As I danced in little bourrée steps, seeking an egress from the cottage, my arms reaching for freedom, an almighty roar shook the electric chandeliers. Several screams sounded. I faltered in my arabesque as, rushing up the frosted central aisle of the theatre, the Snow Queen stood in a sleigh crafted from ice, harnessed to two living, breathing polar bears. Faster and faster they came until they were upon me. Though I knew they were but an illusion, my knees weakened as their breath huffed onto my face, hot and rank with meat as if they had just feasted. Unable to breathe, my scream died in my throat. We never rehearsed with Rothbart's illusions. He claimed it kept our reactions authentic but in truth, I believe he preferred us awed and, increasingly of late, terrified. His illusions were growing more dangerous with each show and I feared where it would all end. With a frightened whimper, I closed my eyes. And the theatre whipped out from beneath me. Snapping them back open, I found myself soaring above the audience in one of the acrobat's arms. Holding my own arms out en couronne, my fingertips meeting above my head, I watched as the polar bears stiffened and glazed over, becoming snow statues as the audience rose to a standing ovation. I smiled at the storm of applause, my fears subsiding as euphoria set in.

After the audience had trickled away and the theatre belonged to us once more, we celebrated the ballet's success in the grand foyer. Still in our costumes, we glittered with sequins and the wind-rush of adrenaline that had whipped in like a gale the moment we took our bow. According to the reviews, the *Snow Queen* had been one of our most enchanting ballets yet. Rothbart, or The Sorcerer, as the broadsheets were fond of declaring him, had exceeded himself. Yet as he fetched a crate of vintage champagne, the bottles dusty with age, I noticed how haggard he was. His dark hair had silvered, his moustache drooped, his cheekbones hollowed. Perhaps he had taken ill. He had certainly over-expended his energy during the ballet's run, falling prey to his own ambition, and I did not pretend to understand how time-consuming his illusions must be. Those polar bears had been uncannily lifelike and I was still suffering the after effects of the adrenaline that had screamed through my veins upon being confronted with them. It had left me shaken and scared and I felt most peculiar. I still had my list of other cities I might like, but I was reticent to leave when I was enjoying such success, my name, my mother's name, glowing in the reviews. Neither was I keen to surrender my holidays spent with Mrs Fischer, the last vestige of my family. Instead, I drank another glass of champagne.

The cool sweetness of my glass did nothing to quench my thirst for those halcyon days when Penelope and I had picnicked in a nearby park. Sitting beneath the oldest beech tree on a woollen carpet, we would stay until the day ran into night and we had neared the end of a bottle of some delicious wine I had procured for the event, the sandwiches and lemon-drizzle cake she had made us long since eaten. Her laugh still pealed in my ears as we finished this spiced-blackcurrant Cabernet or that apple-crisp Riesling and my words muddled together like squashed grapes.

'I hear he has a vault beneath the theatre where he keeps his private stash of luxuries,' Daisy whispered to Ada, rousing me from my sun-dappled memories back into the theatre, where the temperature was plummeting as if the Snow Queen herself was prowling by.

Another cork popped. An errant cannon. It was met with a ring of laughter and then the sudden exclamation of, 'Why, I don't believe it – it's snowing!' Nothing unusual for November but then we were giddy with success and the coincidence of the weather playing along with our production felt immense. As if the whole city had transformed into our stage. I rushed to peer out of the windows with the others.

The crooked streets of York looked like they had been dusted with confectioner's sugar.

The doors flung open. I failed to recognise the woman that had entered through them; she was waifish with dirty hair clinging to her face and a torn dress. A current of murmurs swirled around her. The woman did not seem to notice or care that she was barefoot. Outside, the snow carried no trace of footsteps. A brackish aroma clung to her. Then she fixed her stare on Rothbart and I saw past all of that, finally recognising her.

The foyer faded in and out. I blinked away the darkness, the thousand stars that followed. My glass shattered beside my foot, soaking my pointe shoes with champagne. 'Penelope?'

She did not respond to me, nor look my way. Her eyes were swollen moons. Staring, drifting on a tide I did not understand.

Rothbart had paled to ice. Yet ever the showman, his trademark grin appeared, forced onto his face as if he were some grotesque puppet or clown. 'Always a pleasure to see you, *mon petit cygne*.'

The rest of the cast were still watching, though some began to pour themselves second or third saucers, their attention beginning to divert. I could not look away. Daisy's fingers locked around my wrist as she stood, motionless at my side.

'Undo it,' Penelope said, her voice weak, as if she had been resting on the bottom of a lake, a long-forgotten water sprite, abandoned there ever since she had vanished dancing the part of Ondine. 'Please, I beg of you.'

More eyes averted. Her pitifulness a stain against the ivory satin and crystal glasses. Her truth too painful to confront, to forsake this precious dream for. And I, standing there as guilty as the others. Rothbart's brightest star, ignoring the darkness that surrounded me for my chance to shine. Or perhaps I shone brighter thanks to that.

Prising Daisy's iron hold from me, I stepped towards her. 'Penelope, where have you been? I've been searching for you—'

'Let us adjourn to my office,' Rothbart interrupted, sweeping his arm out grandly. 'Resume your celebrations, for tonight shall be ours!' he called out to a roar of appreciation.

I bit the inside of my cheek until I tasted copper. Something was wrong with Penelope. There was a wildness wisping over her skin. She had gone and returned as something else, something raw, something I could not comprehend. Her expression was haunted, a woman crawling out of a fairy tale just as it was reaching its dark and bloody conclusion. I had feared never seeing her again, I never once had considered I might do so and yet find her unrecognisable. I fretted as to what had become of her. I reached for her but she was unreachable and Rothbart was already whisking her down the corridor and into his office. As he closed the door, something knowing glimmered across his face. And a darkness slinked behind his eyes. Despair seized me in its talons.

Behind me, the cast launched themselves back into their celebrations. If their laughs were overbright, they drowned them in champagne until it did not matter. Succumbed to their forced joviality until it became real and they forgot that behind that closed door, there was being writ a story of suffering. But I could not forget. My mind whirled after witnessing Penelope's sudden reappearance and strange behaviour. I had to find out what was happening. And *he* could not be permitted to be alone with her.

As the grandfather clock's hands inched towards the witching hour, the snow ceased to fall, and I strode up the corridor and pressed my ear to the door. While Rothbart prided himself on his masterful creations and decadence, backstage, the illusion shattered into thin walls and doors, scratchy carpets, and a theatre that was falling into disrepair as he threw more and more money into his performances. I ought to have been able to hear an entire conversation from the other side of the door. Finally learn the ending to the story I never wished to read. Nothing but silence crept into my ears. Panic bubbling in my veins, I burst into Rothbart's private office.

He was sitting on his Chesterfield. Beside him was a swan. Rothbart was stroking the creature's feathered back, again and again, his ministrations lulling it into a hypnotic trance.

I stilled. Penelope had faded into the night and once more, disappeared.

'Ah, Detta, what brings you to my side of the theatre?' Rothbart toasted me with his glass. 'A stellar performance tonight, *mon petit cygne*, perhaps worthy of a greater stage than York.'

As much as it pained me, his distraction was effective. I wanted what he was offering. Craved it. To dance into fame and greatness across the world. Shaking the temptation away, I soldiered on. 'I wished to speak with Penelope. Where is she?'

He lifted one shoulder in an elegant shrug, gestured at his large, well-appointed quarters. 'I am afraid you were too late, she has already departed. Though it appears I was wrong about her.' His sigh was loud, theatrical. It was kindling for my burning hatred of him. 'She does not possess what it takes to dance upon my stage.' His gaze bored into me as he continued to stroke the swan. 'I do hope I am not wrong about you.'

My stomach clenched. 'I didn't see her leave,' I said stubbornly.

That peculiar expression stretched across Rothbart's face once more. As if he was playing host to an internal war. On more than one night I had heard him standing on the other side of my door, my heart entrapped in an ice coffin as I'd listened to his breathing. One hand on the dagger-sharp hat pin beneath my pillow as I'd wondered if that night would be the one when my door handle would turn. If I would finally learn where the performers vanished to. If it was my turn to tread their path. 'I've instructed many a girl upon my stage,' he continued, setting his glass down, 'and if I have learnt one thing it is that you all tend to be rather flighty. You are not to blame; you cannot help being impressionable creatures, plagued with an imagination too great for your sensibilities. Why, you girls might claim to see or hear all sorts of things that you simply dreamt.'

I had believed that I was marching into a confrontation. Now I knew that I had walked into a nightmare. My step backwards was involuntary.

Rothbart's laugh was too high, something igniting in his eyes. 'You might dance like a dream, Miss Lakely, but you are far too wilful. A ballerina must make sacrifices to truly be great.' His voice lowered, intensified. 'I could make you great.'

I was torched with fear and indignation and, worst of all, temptation. Had Penelope paid one of those sacrifices? 'Nobody shall be making any sacrifices,' I said firmly, even as my heart fluttered and a whisper teased my thoughts: *you are making a mistake.*

A wave of fury swept across Rothbart. He stood, the movement sudden, violent in the still room. His mask slipped away and for a moment, I glimpsed the true man beneath; arrogant and unbearably cruel. The swan was in his arms now.

My fingers curled into my palms, tight enough to leave a row of crescent moons embedded there. 'What are you doing? Put that poor creature down.'

'Ah, that is the problem with wilful girls,' Rothbart mused. 'You are far too vocal about that which matters to you. And do you know what?' His voice dropped to a dangerous cadence. 'It betrays your weaknesses.' He reached down and grasped the swan's neck and before I could move or shout, he twisted. There was a sickening snap.

In a display more callous than breaking the swan's neck, Rothbart allowed its body to tumble from his arms. It hit the floor with a dull thud. I stared at it, horrified. 'I don't understand,' I whispered.

Rothbart dared to laugh. It was thin and unfeeling and my hatred of him swelled a hundredfold. 'Oh, but one day you will. One day, you will.'

I ran from the room. Cold as river-water, I slipped out of a side door and into the dark night, where I called for Penelope until my voice hoarsened and my tears were spent.

Chapter Forty-Four

Forster paced, looking out of the iced library window for the hundredth time that morning. It was just a fortnight after he'd last exchanged farewells with Detta and the world had frozen over. He kept the window open, breathing in the wintry air, filled with the scent of snow yet to appear. When the first flakes fell, he ran downstairs, wrenching the double doors open as Detta forged a path towards them. Back to him. He ran to meet her, lifting her in his arms and whirling her around as she laughed and he kissed her neck, her cheeks, her lips. 'Forster, Forster,' she protested, pulling back to look at him. 'What month is it?'

'It's late February, you've only missed a few weeks,' he assured her, beaming as she laughed with glee and kissed him harder.

'Oh,' she faltered. 'I missed my birthday. I'm thirty now, how strange. Why are you giving me that peculiar look?'

Forster carried her back inside the manor and shut the doors behind her. On a side table rested a large box. 'Because, I have a surprise for you.' He lifted the lid from the box, watching Detta's face as she reached inside and drew out the dress he'd ordered from Lanvin. Vintage blush lace with matching silk slippers. 'Why, it's beautiful,' she murmured, stroking its fabric as Forster failed to hide how pleased he was that she admired it. He lifted it over her head and fastened it, his touch lingering on her back.

'Where do you keep your warm clothes?' he asked, pulling on his boots, coat, and a hat.

Detta laughed. 'You forget Forster, the cold does not bother me.' She slid on her silk slippers and ran outside. When Forster followed, he took a snowball to the face. 'Now tell me, why did you bring me out here?' she asked as he spluttered and wiped the snow from his glasses.

'Well, we haven't had a winter picnic in some years,' he told her. 'And I don't recall us ever having built a snowman together which must be put right. What would Mrs Fischer say?' He gave her a crooked smile. She stepped up on tiptoes and kissed him. Her lips soft, her curls carried the scent of snow and chocolate, setting his soul aglow in the warmest tones of honeyed gold that would linger in his dreams.

Hoping she suspected nothing, he led her towards the large pond where they'd ice-skated together last year, watching her as they rounded a great oak and his surprise came into view. She pressed a hand to her mouth, stifling a soft gasp.

A hundred white roses were arranged in vases atop a large table. Fur blankets were draped over a bench to keep them warm when they sat and dozens of candles flickered between the roses. Forster's smile grew as she noticed the cake he'd spent the past two days working on, ever since he'd learnt it was forecast to snow. He'd known his preparations could have ended with nothing but disappointment and rain, but he'd hoped and dreamed and wished, and it had come true. She had been returned to him. Gingerbread with cinnamon cream cheese frosting and decorated with glittering sugar snowflakes. 'Did you do all this for me?' Detta turned to him, her eyes glimmering.

'Yes,' he told her, a little gruffly. 'And this—' He pulled the small notebook from his pocket and gave it to her. 'Happy birthday, Detta.'

She opened the notebook, casting him a curious glance. 'What is this? Oh, you've written inside it.' She turned one page, then another as he shuffled in the snow, his nerves clustering that it was too much, too little, that he had poured his heart out on those pages and she would not care for it. 'These are letters you've written me,' she said slowly. 'And they're dated—'

'One for each day we've been apart since our first kiss.'

Detta stared at him. His heart fluttered, his throat tightening. 'You see, sometimes I find myself wishing I could tell you all the little things that have happened in my day. Or a song I've heard on the wireless that I think would interest you or a new book I've loved or an artist I've discovered—'

She shook her head, stepping closer to him. 'You are the sweetest man I've ever met.' When she kissed him, he felt tears on her cheek.

He pulled back, surveying her. Caught a tear on his finger. 'I hope these are happy?' he murmured.

'The happiest,' she declared. 'Now can we cut into the cake? I'm famished.'

When they had devoured slices of cake, and Detta had read many of his letters, she danced away over the snow, calling for Forster to follow.

Forster's boots left deep impressions in the snow. Detta appeared to have flown over it. When he caught up with her, she had vanished inside a lopsided gardener's hut. It was nestled out of view behind the manor, its wooden bones slumped over to one side. Detta unearthed a sledge from its weary depths. 'My grandfather gifted me this one Christmas.' She rested a hand on it, nostalgic. 'He carved it by hand himself. When I was a slip of a girl who still wore my hair in a plait down to my waist, my grandparents liked to boast that I never cried. Until the day that I refused to go home after they'd taken me sledging, that is. Then, I stood in the snow and howled.' She gave him a wicked grin and he laughed and hoisted the wooden sledge up onto his shoulder.

They whiled away the rest of the afternoon plodding up a nearby hill and sledding down. Forster suggested they take turns but Detta insisted they both pile on the little sledge, weighing it down so that they might soar downhill faster. The carved runners wove deep tracks down the hill, a rush of cold air whistling past, then the dash back up, Forster's boots sinking into the snow, the sledge pressing him deeper. Still, he would have carried it up a thousand times for those few precious minutes of wrapping his arms tightly around Detta on the descent.

As the afternoon deepened into evening and the moon yawned and peered down at them, the sledge curved on its path, tipping them both off. Detta laughed as Forster fell on top of her, then abruptly stopped. Looking up at him, she bit her lip. He nearly came undone at the sight. 'Forster.' She sighed. 'Oh, how I wish—' Maddeningly, she selected that moment to fall silent. Snowflakes fell on her eyelashes. On her delicate dress and bare arms. She was a creature of ice and winter and she was not his. 'It will stop soon,' she said instead, her voice catching in her throat. 'Melt away entirely.'

'It may still snow into March,' he said. 'There will be plenty of days of snow to share yet.'

'I may not see you again until November,' she whispered and his lungs filled with ice.

'I would gladly wait a hundred months for a single day like this,' he told her.

He picked up the sledge and they walked back up the hill, hand in hand. Two figures battling against the darkening which claims each day.

Chapter Forty-Five

'Oh, Forster, do come quickly.' Detta's cry was laced with urgency and Forster at once abandoned his sketchbook and perch on the library's window seat to answer her call.

He found her standing on the threshold of his bedroom, wearing a simple cream knitted jumper and high-waisted trousers that suited the early March morning. She did not appear troubled. 'Whatever is the matter?'

She heaved a sigh. 'I apologise terribly for my actions.'

He scarce had time to frown in confusion before she had planted both hands on his chest and, with a surprising amount of force, pushed him into the drawing room and closed the door after him. A click sounded. When he attempted to open the door, his suspicions were proven correct; she had locked him inside. 'Detta? What the devil are you playing at?' He laughed.

'I did apologise,' her voice returned, light and playful as a sprite. 'I left you supplies and plenty of firewood so you cannot think too badly of me, dearest.'

'But—'

'All shall be revealed in time,' came the mysterious response before her footsteps skipped away.

A plate of sandwiches, a jug of water, and a flask of hot cocoa had been deposited on one of the side tables. A white suit on one of the wing-backed chairs bore the note: *wear me*. A short while later, the crunch of wheels on gravel beckoned him to the window where he saw several vans pulling up outside the manor. One of which was marked with the now-familiar: *Watchers Private Security Est. 1884.*

It was a peculiar feeling, being on the other side of the curtain for Detta's grand events when, only a few years ago, he had been scouring the streets of London, desperate to find an encrypted invitation. It robbed him of the magic. So too did the mottled shadows beneath Detta's eyes. She had walked back into the manor two days ago, only one week after they had celebrated her birthday together, and Forster's sudden delight had cracked like frost, giving way to a creeping concern as he'd noticed how slight she felt in his arms. Her collar bones jutting out, bird-like, the bruising that shadowed her back where her wings had been. But she refused to entertain his worries and he suspected that he had partly been locked away so that he could not see the toll this was taking on her.

Detta's voice floated up to his window but the snow was falling heavily, the wind whipping it up into an icy frenzy, and he could not determine what she had said. He settled for opening the book he had been reading, *A Passage to India*, and making a start on the sandwiches. After he had read the same page five times, he set the book back down. Kneaded his forehead with a knuckle as he stared into the glittering depths of the fire. *It could be the last party I hold.* Detta's words whispered around his head, heady with hope. He and Roger had exchanged a flurry of letters as Roger had searched through a trail of records, hunting for Rothbart. As thanks for the man's time, Forster had sent him several more canvasses for his wife: a ballerina whose jeté had her fingertips skimming the moon; a forest rich with greenery and a shy dryad who hid amongst owls in the upper branches of a great oak; a witch stirring a cauldron glistening with beaks and claws and the deepest darkest red hearts. But, as suspected, there was no record of the man anywhere. No taxes, nor census nor marriage or birth certificate. Not even a death certificate. Whoever Rothbart was, his name was his own invention. The sole light in this endless night was resting in his bedside drawer: a ticket to Paris. He would go this May. When Paris blossomed with spring and snowfall was a distant dream.

As Forster reread the latest missive from Roger, the key at last turned in the lock. Stuffing the letter back into his pocket, he stepped out into a world painted white with winter's brush. Gossamer veils draped down from above, separating the manor into gauzy layers like a slice of mille-feuille. Ice swans preened here and there, little tables heaved with mountains of cream cakes and white glittery tutus fluttered from the vaulted ceilings. And everywhere Forster looked, he saw his innermost feelings, his heart painted onto canvas, staring back at him. His paintings lined the great hall and ballroom.

A row of ballerina waitresses clad in ivory sequinned dresses twirled past, their porcelain trays loaded with snow-white cocktails and choux-swans, bursting with fresh cream and dusted with sugar. Guests were entering, in suits and gowns as pale as the first morning frost. White rose petals began slowly drifting down.

'Detta, I'm quite speechless.' Forster returned his gaze to her. 'How ever can I thank you for this?' He wished that his words held the same colour as his paintings. That she might look upon them and understand that she was the reigning queen of his heart. Though perhaps she did see and simply did not love him back. A thorn lodged inside him at the thought. 'I have a few suggestions.' Detta smiled at him, pressing a hand on his white jacket sleeve and leaning in closer to whisper in his ear. 'Perhaps I shall show you later, when we're alone.' She bit his earlobe playfully and he shivered, wishing they were alone now but before he could tug her back upstairs and into her drawing room, she sauntered off to attend to her event, her satin gown gleaming like a pearl.

Mere hours later, the ballroom was swollen with guests. Magnesium camera flashes sparked outside but there was a guard on the doors, prohibiting entry to all photographers, an additional service now provided by Watchers Private Security, after Detta's parties had started to attract the attention of the press. Each time the doors in the great hall opened, the manor inhaled more people. One of them was particularly disgruntled. 'Have you been colluding with another art dealer, darling?' Vivian, dripping in diamonds, eyed Forster with suspicion.

'I assure you, nothing could be further than the truth,' he reassured her.

'Then I trust you shall tell me everything later. Though I have my theories, of course.' Her mischief twinkled brighter than her diamonds.

'I'd expect nothing less,' he said, amused, before she strolled off, greeting other guests by name and a wave of her fingers, adorned with her famed collection of engagement rings from men she had never married.

As he wandered through the icy dreamscape of the manor, he heard mentions of his own name sprinkled in among the usual rumours that snowed down about the exquisite ballerina, whose very name remained a mystery. Though it was as busy as ever, Forster noticed that the clientele were slightly different; invitations appeared to have been targeted to art collectors and tastemakers, and there were several prominent figures that he recognised from the art scene.

'Interesting that our host has chosen to host an exhibition in March this year, what do you make of that? I wonder who exactly this Forster Sylvan is?' one woman in white chiffon asked another as Forster happened by. They were both pondering one of his paintings with which he was less than pleased: a dancer who ran barefoot through the woods, her blackberry-hued gown furling to raven feathers. He had not managed to achieve the right tonal palette for the trees and it looked a little muddy as a result. 'I mean, judging by this, he doesn't seem the most adept,' the woman criticised, and Forster closed his eyes for a beat. He would never grow used to people picking apart his work.

'Oh, Dorcas, you do ask such peculiar questions.' Her companion let out a long-suffering sigh that curled Forster's lips with amusement. 'I happen to think he's rather accomplished and I've already bid on one of his pieces. Now have another cocktail and leave me be.'

The exhibition whirled on, the last of Forster's works sold, and Detta performed her namesake's variation from *Swan Lake*, bringing the inspiration of the paintings to life. Forster could hardly bear to watch it. Her movements were too swan-like, the orchestral music too playful that it felt a cruel parody of her other, hidden life. She intended it a farewell to that life. Her hope a precious, delicate thing that had curled around Forster's limbs and hardened there. Each step he took was weighted. Her life, his to save. Yet with one glance from her, he knew he could bear the weight of the world if only to see her smile again.

The snow had begun to fall last week and after spending two long weeks fretting that he had seen the last of Detta until next winter, longing to know what she had been on the verge of telling him earlier that year, *Oh, how I wish*, he felt the wicked pinch of time.

By the time the guests had left the exhibition and the paintings removed to be packed and sent, Forster had fallen into a peculiar mood. 'What made you decide to do all this?' he suddenly asked Detta. 'We have such precious little time together, so few days in a year that I hate the thought of you going to all this trouble and sacrificing our time together.'

When she replied, her words were delicate, forlorn. 'I had hoped you would appreciate my efforts.'

'I do, of course I do, but I would rather have been alone with you!'

Detta took a while to respond and his chest tightened, regret sinking down in a morose grizzle-grey. 'This estate is expensive to keep,' she began quietly. 'I wanted to secure you more funds in the event that we are not able to find Rothbart and the manor passes to you in my will. Which it shall. I have already written to my solicitor, appraising him of the fact.'

Forster blinked, stunned. 'Why would you do that?'

'Don't you know by now, Forster?'

But Forster was lost at sea, trying to follow her logic without drowning in the deep pool of fear and sadness her actions had triggered.

'That I am in love with you, you fool,' she cried out. Stunned twice over, Forster stared at her. She gave him a slow shake of her head before crossing the room, continuing the tidy-up.

He came back to his senses with a start. Chasing after her, he reached for her arm and pulled her to face him. 'You love me?' He swallowed. 'Why have you not told me before? You bade me never to fall in love with you but you know that I have been yours alone for a long time now, and you—' his throat threatened to close '—you've kept this part of yourself locked away for years.'

'Because you deserve better.' Detta's smile was laced with sadness. And not a little pity. Forster was uncertain if it was for herself or him but he disliked it.

'Then you are the fool, not me.' He released his hold on her. 'For all I want, all I could ever need, is you.'

'Forster, be reasonable,' Detta told him. 'I spend most of my days on that damned lake, where I can't remember my own name, let alone yours. I cannot leave you forever waiting for snow. That is no life. But this—' she gestured at the stacks of canvasses they had been slowly packing up together '—this, I can do for you.'

Forster's voice turned gravelly. 'You don't believe I will find Rothbart, do you?'

Detta sucked in a trembling breath. 'We have to consider that as a possibility. That we may not have the life together we've dreamt of. And in that case, I do not wish to cost you your freedom.'

Forster sighed, pushing his hair back roughly. 'This argument between us growing old and I am tiring of it. I have no need for money or a manor; I would be perfectly content living in a hut so long as I had you by my side. You know that I love you a thousand times more than any reason you could give for why we ought not be together. There is no other possible future for me than you. I would sooner die than stop loving you,' he growled.

They stared at each other, their chests rising and falling in unison. 'Then you had better make sure you find Rothbart because I'm not letting you go after a speech like that.' Detta's jaw was held high, a stubborn gleam in her eyes.

'That was never an option.' Forster suddenly tugged her forwards and kissed her hard.

As the night thickened like whipped cream, the snowfall grew thin and the moon blinked wearily down on them, visible once more between the waning clouds.

Detta slipped out of their bed and Forster followed. She stumbled downstairs and outside and he ran to her, supporting her weight as she shuddered. 'What is it, what's wrong?' he cried out. There was still snow on the ground, a delicate lacework over grass and stone and roots.

'I don't know,' she gasped, her hair silvering as the final flakes fell. 'I don't think it is enough.'

'I have you, I'm here.' He slung one of her arms around his neck as she looked at him miserably.

'Oh Forster, I'm far from ready to leave,' she whispered. 'I just wanted another day.'

Silken down rippled along her arms and she inhaled sharply, making him consider for the first time that this strange and elegant and cruel magic might come at a greater cost than he'd known. She was in pain. The realisation tortured him and he wished he could take her place, for he would rather undergo a hundred shifts than allow her to suffer one.

'Please, do not leave me,' she begged.

'Never,' he promised her, lifting her into his arms and striding towards the woodland. Returning her to the trees that concealed the dark fairy tale of her life. With each step, the thorn in his heart dug in deeper, splintering him apart. 'We will be together again soon, my love,' he whispered into her feathering neck. Yet as he lowered his arms, he saw that she was beyond hearing. He waited until she swam out onto the lake, constellations winking into view as the last cloud-wisps melted away. The water twinkled with star-glitter.

As Forster trudged back to the manor, its blazing lights a beacon on the clifftop, he felt a hundred years older. Desiring nothing more than to recline on the settee before the fire in his drawing room, he re-entered the great hall alone, ringing with silence after the peaceful rustle of trees and call of birds taking wing between the lake and the trees and the stars. He needed to puzzle out why Detta had suddenly transformed, why she had turned swan when there was snow on the ground still. How it had happened that her human days, already too few, too precious, had constricted again. He needed answers. It was time to go to Paris. As soon as the last chance for snow had passed.

Chapter Forty-Six

Forster busied himself for the rest of March shipping out the canvasses he had sold during Detta's swan-themed exhibition. As he bid them farewell, one after another, the manor was besieged by a particularly violent set of storms. Rain lashed down the windows and Forster sequestered himself in the old library. There, the fire burnt brighter and, from the window seat, he could spy the lake, cloud-dark, and listen to the faraway roar of waves battering the cliff. His star was hurtling upwards. Thanks to the exhibition and recent sales, his snowscapes and swans soaring away on silvered wings to sprawling country estates and smart townhouses. Illuminating little sitting rooms and adding a touch of whimsy to children's playrooms. The thought ought to have been comforting. Instead, it reminded him of his own loneliness. He was thirty-three, living in a rattling manor, isolated both from his previous life and the one he longed for. It was strange and unsettling that whilst he sat beside the fire, warmed with flames and the scent of old leather-bound books, his heart was battling the bluster and howl of the storm. Each day he fought his way to the lake, through the creaking trees and sea-flecked wind. Trod the worn path under the deep gloom of sky, the storm raging as if ancient battles between gods were being waged above.

Detta was a lone speck of white. Weathering the lake's chop

and sway. He fetched her food – a tangle of worms and nutritious lake-weeds – ensuring that she had sufficient sustenance. And there he stayed, watching over her for as long as he could bear. Until his fingers grew numb, his lungs iced, and he could almost hear the crackle of magic from a world that was wilder and fiercer and ravaged with dangerous curses that might steal the object of your heart away.

April ushered in gentler skies, deceptive in their soft pastel blues and daffodils that sprung up around the lake, waving as one with the wind-ripples of the water's surface. The temperature did not warm and Forster hardly dared sleep for fear of missing a fleck of snow. He wrapped himself in thick woollen blankets and painted outside. Filled canvasses with a series of water sprites: dancing over the lake; collecting raindrops for thirsty snowdrops; harvesting the morning dew by dusky moonlight. When light rain turned to sleet, Detta began to flicker in and out of her human skin.

Forster returned her to the manor. Warmed her with the softest blankets and hot cocoa when her curls poured down her back and she shivered at the knowledge of humanity, her awareness taking root. Maintained his distance when she slipped back into her wilder, cursed skin. Several days passed in such a pattern, the sleet too thin, too wet to take shape as snow, too cold to pass for rain, leaving Detta trembling on the verge between man and beast until they were both disillusioned and exhausted.

'Why can I not stay?' Detta cried out and Forster held her, calming her ravished cries, steadying her. Only when she was swan did he slump over, cradling his head in his hands with the deep sigh of wearied souls, heart-sore at the torment the woman he loved was forced to bear. If he could, he would have borne it for her.

He had not been aware he'd drifted off until he was roused by Detta, night having fallen. She was pale and weak, her hair knotted.

'Forster,' she murmured, reaching out for him. She had dressed in a forest-green velvet dress and all he could think was that she wore the colours of the woodland, that it had marked her, awaiting her return. 'Are you awake?'

'I'm here.' Forster sat up, searching for the glasses that had fallen from his face. 'Is it snowing?' Finding them, he slipped them back on and Detta came back into his focus.

Her smile was slow, touched with sadness. 'For the time being, yes. Though it is not setting and I'm uncertain how long it shall last.'

'At least now we might speak a while.' Forster made to stand; he had slept on the floor before the hearth, his back propped up against a settee, but Detta quieted him. 'Thank you.' Her blue-grey eyes sought something within his.

'You ought to eat something—'

'You were there for me,' Detta interrupted. 'In a manner nobody else ever has been.'

Forster caught his lip between his teeth. Her gaze dipped to his mouth and he near lost his composure. 'I will always be here,' he said simply. 'I love you.'

'And I love you,' Detta whispered.

She then turned swan once more and Forster closed his eyes, tired of dragging himself through day after day without her. Since it was already spring, it was unlikely he would see her again now until late autumn, leaving him facing the prospect of those long months ahead without her.

✿

A couple of days later, in a bid to distract himself, Forster set off on a long walk around the estate, drawing the budding life that peeped out of the soil, butter-yellow, ballet slipper–pink, and dreamy lavender coloured petals unfurling under pale sunlight, the grey drizzle turning the gardens green once more. On his way back, he picked up the post, pleased to see a thick envelope had arrived from Rose. She'd sent him the latest issue of *The City Star* along with a heart-felt letter which filled him with foreboding:

Darling Forster,

It is with the utmost sadness that I must write to tell you this but our dear Marvin has continued down a tangled path and I am starting not to recognise him. To be quite frank (for you, my dearest friend, know all of my deepest secrets), his latest actions have forced us apart. I am nurturing a fierce hope that this separation shall not last as I am determined to confront him on the error of his ways, but I cannot, in good conscience, hide this from you. Do not be too angry, darling, for you left him in a state of great injury and I believe that his hurt and confusion have festered and led to this. You are a good man, kind and forgiving, and I must ask of you to be the better man now.

Oh, and do pay me a visit soon, won't you? I miss you greatly and could use your friendship now more than ever.

Your dearest friend,

Rose

Forster paced up and down the library. Until the words he had not yet read taunted him with what-ifs and what-could-bes and he succumbed, unfolding the newspaper. It was the headline on the front page:

Hostess of Society's Most Elusive Event a Fraud! Read the full story, as uncovered by Marvin Kembles, inside.

Once finished, he marched downstairs and telephoned his old flat in Chelsea with shaking hands, Rose's letter quite forgotten. 'I had thought you wanted to be a reporter, not a vitriolic leech spewing rubbish about the intimate details of an innocent woman's life.'

'Are you still going to pretend you have no connection with the woman?' Marvin taunted gleefully and Forster clenched the receiver. 'All's fair in love, war, and reporting, old chap.'

'Having the indescribable good fortune not to be on the *Titanic* does not amount to faking your own death,' Forster growled at him.

'Ah, but that doesn't quite have the same ring to it, does it?' Marvin said cheerfully.

'And what about the accusations you levelled in my direction?' Forster uncrumpled the paper and read aloud: '"The up-and-coming artist Forster Sylvan is also guilty of participating in this charade, having colluded with society's most elusive fraud to further his career."' Forster threw the paper in the bin with more force than was necessary. 'Did our years of friendship mean nothing to you?'

But Marvin seemed undeterred, even when confronted with his bitterness and betrayal. 'I say, why don't you drive down and we'll have a drink and discuss it face to face?'

'You must be out of your goddamned mind. You're the last person I want to see.' Forster slammed the receiver down and resumed his pacing.

In the weeks that followed, the telephone rang constantly. A bevy of enquiries and accusations beleaguered Forster after Marvin's blistering exposé. As did the numerous people who turned up at the manor, knocking on the door and peering in the window in the hopes of gleaning something scandalous. After Detta's swan-themed exhibition, Forster's name had become entwined with hers and he heard it now, shouted through the thin panes of glass as the rumours swirled, fiercer than a storm, outside.

April was a terrible month for Forster. Though, according to Vivian, he was earning a substantial sum from sales and commissions from new patrons, ironically in part thanks to Marvin's story, life in the manor had become stifling. Hiding from the outside world's attention by day, walking to the lakeside by eve, a singular thought percolating all the while: the moment this month breathed its last, the moment the storms ceased to carve their might across the lake, he would be crossing the Channel for Paris, to resume his hunt for Rothbart. And he would not return without an answer. For Detta was running out of time.

Then, a parcel arrived. Wrapped in brown paper and tied neatly with string, it bore a note:

Forster,

I came across these reviews that covered our time in Paris. Hope they prove useful to you.

Regards,
Daisy May

25th November 1913

Rothbart's Theatre of Enchantments dazzles on the Parisian stage!

After a dazzling performance like none other, Rothbart and his theatre have firmly won the hearts of their Parisian audience. Taking yet another beloved fairy tale, this time Rapunzel, and spinning it into his own whimsically choreographed show, performed by his resident cast of dancers and acrobats, Rothbart has ensured that the city of love is not likely to forget his Parisian tour any time soon.

Debuting on the first of December, this is a show that will steal your senses away. From the troop of aerialists fluttering by on feathered wings to the pure white deer that appeared from thin air and proceeded to sleep on stage, to the river of chocolate cream that twined through the audience, prepare to enter a world like none other.

Prima ballerina Detta Kova follows her success at dancing Snow White at the theatre's home stage in York with the lead role of Rapunzel. It speaks volumes that although Rothbart's signature illusions will have you near believing in magic, Kova battles his charms for attention, performing a remarkable thirty-five fouetté turns, breaking the current record, and bringing the audience to their feet in a richly deserved ovation.

Chapter Forty-Seven

Detta
1913

Paris in winter was insatiable. It glittered with life. As did I, strolling along the Champs-Élysées, feasting on a box of pistachio macarons from Ladurée. Rothbart had imposed a company rule forbidding his performers to socialise with anyone outside of our own, tight-knit clan while on tour, and it galled. I wanted to sit in a café and philosophise with a handsome stranger and wander the most fashionable ateliers with some of the French ballerinas I had only exchanged pleasantries with. Anything to distract from Penelope and the last memory I held of her: vanishing in front of me. The way she had stared straight through me with those haunted eyes. I had so adored Penelope's wide smile, carefree as a posy of wildflowers, yet she had left and returned as something else. And now Rothbart's prowling attention was fixed on me. Still, I did not leave. I had considered it, turning back to my list of cities that I was eager to see and finally writing to ballet companies there. Their responses were fast and disappointing; they all had other prima ballerinas and soloists already filling their spotlights. If I left, I would have had to step back down into the corps, and I had come too far for that. This was my dream. And when I could not help remembering that bone-snap of the swan Rothbart had ended, there was always another bottle of champagne to crack open. I breakfasted on hothouse peaches and crystal saucers of Moët in a silk peignoir before our mandated retinue of classes and rehearsals began. My tastes running more extravagant until I dreamt in sequins and ballgowns. Forgetting was sweeter than any dessert. I ordered a new wardrobe from Poiret and Worth, wearing gossamer gowns merely to swish into the patisserie down the street to purchase a chocolate cake. Intoxicating myself with couture until my cage glittered, distracting me from its bars.

Still, the nights were my own.

And the later the hour, the brighter Paris sparkled. Unable to sleep for fear of seeing my door handle slowly turn, I stole out into the city under the cloak of night, where Rothbart's rules couldn't follow me. Drowned myself in champagne and a few needles of morphine I'd illicitly sourced in a smoky nightclub until sleep reached out and dragged me into unconsciousness.

Checking my little Cartier watch, I stopped for café au lait in a china cup delicate as spun silk, and a pain au chocolat, buttery and flaky, filled with rich chocolate that melted on my tongue like satin. I could have stayed in Paris forever. If only to evade Rothbart and keep dancing on a stage. To not have to suffer the return journey, to never again feel that boat bucking and rolling beneath me, threatening to send me down into those unfathomable depths, the water claiming me as it had my parents. I lingered at that café for as long as I could before I had to hurry back to the Théâtre Magique and the first full dress rehearsal of Rothbart's latest enchantment: *Rapunzel*.

As ever, even our dress rehearsals were missing its most vital component: Rothbart's illusions. Keeping us in constant suspense as we could not yet predict how the theatre would tremble and alter before us on opening night. It would have been a welcome distraction from the rehearsal, which was unusually gruelling. Coming to Paris had set something aflame within Rothbart. His eyes sparkled with a manic energy, his voice boomed louder, his gesturing grew more grandiose than ever. His ambition was a wild force. And it whipped us into a frenzy. I danced longer and harder than the days when I was first trying to prove myself, consumed with the picture Rothbart painted, of the grand city falling at its knees before us. Of the audiences that would adore us and cry encore. I deserved this. For each day I danced for Rothbart, I risked it all.

On opening night, we shone fiercer than ever, the trapeze artists flying from greater distances, the dancers' leaps reaching for the clouds. As I performed my first variation, in front of the tower within which I was set to be imprisoned, the stage glowed mint-green and shoots pushed through the wooden boards, blooming into roses with midnight-petals and pink orchids, each one larger than my head. Moss rippled up the tower's stonework as the garden swelled to exaggerated proportions and an earthy brown stream bubbled up from between two stones and twisted through the audience. With a murmur and a gasp of glee, the attendees dipped fingers into the stream as one discovered it did not run with water but chocolate cream. As I began my pas de deux with the witch who unlocked the door to the tower, a pure white deer ran from a shadowed alcove and into the audience, a basket of bell-shaped cakes on its back. The audience helped themselves, dipping the little cakes into the chocolate stream as the deer returned to the stage where it curled up into itself and sweetly fell asleep.

I might have been enchanted had I not been infused with ambition of my own.

As I entered the tower, the set piece revolved to display its open back and within, me. When it span on its axis, so too did I. The choreography demanded a string of twenty-five fouettés. My own hubris demanded more. My ambition smouldered in my veins. I passed twenty-five without slowing, burning for more, burning to be *great*. Then twenty-eight, thirty. I felt rather than saw the audience tighten in their seats. I held their attention now. When I reached thirty-five before placing my foot down, the audience roared to their feet. My skin crackled with lightning like I had been touched by a god. I *felt* like a god. Incandescent with power.

When we took our final bows, applause rained down on us, scattering the stage with roses. And as I walked in stylised ballet steps into the wings, my arms full of blooms, I found Jacques awaiting me, leaning against the wall with his shirtsleeves rolled up. The owner of Théâtre Magique, he was tall and broad and a decade older than me with an accent that curled my toes. We had been exchanging long and longer glances since I'd arrived in Paris and he had first seen me dance. A renowned balletomane, Jacques made no secret of his admiration as he observed me from the wings. Rothbart knew, too. It was not a coincidence that he had announced the new company rule of no fraternising after spotting Jacques lingering. But to forbid a thing only enhances its allure. And the temptation was as deliciously exquisite as the de sévigné chocolates I'd been buying by the boxful. I craved him.

After my performance, I ached to sit down, the breath tearing from my lungs after I'd exited the stage, shortly followed by Daisy, who gave Jacques an appraising look. 'I suppose you won't be joining us to celebrate opening night then,' she whispered into my ear as I batted her away. She giggled and ran away with Ada, their pointe shoes clacking against the wooden floorboards. They were followed by a rush of other performers, predominantly dancers, as the aerialists and trapeze artists that had chirruped and soared through the air on feathered wings had ascended up, flying past the tower and into the painted clouds when the curtains fell. Jacques and I stood there, suspended in an immoveable silence, our gaze locked as the world fractured into noise around us. And when the stage had at last emptied and Rothbart was nowhere to be seen, he led me to his private rooms, where we finally kissed, as hot and fiery as I'd imagined it would be.

Though I was headlining the best performances of my career in Paris, by night Penelope haunted my dreams with waterlogged hair, a selkie emerging from the depths. By day, I danced and danced until I shone brighter than a thousand stars, illuminating the dark underbelly of my thoughts, my memories. I lost myself, one fouetté, one standing ovation, one saucer of champagne at a time. I did not pause to consider that the more I dazzled on stage, the more the shadows banded together, growing ever stronger, ever darker. Or that I was not the only one living in those ink-dark ripples. And once I left the stage, I stole through the theatre by moonlight, fleeing to the comfort of Jacques's arms and admiration, which proved intoxicating.

'Tell me what you liked today,' I ordered him, each night, as he poured me a glass of blood-red wine.

'Your pas de chats were delightful, quick and nimble,' he said one night. Another, 'When you sank to the stage, overcome with Rapunzel's pain, it was unforgettable.' Inevitably, he would pour me a second glass, then a third, before requesting that I dance for him. I pirouetted slowly in his bedroom, feasting on his attention, as he sat back and watched me, pouting at him when he critiqued my performance, a director in his own right. I had not yet realised that he was a mirror. The man I believed I loved was nothing but a reflection through which I saw only the best of myself. I was Narcissus.

But Daisy knew that none of it was real. We shared a room and nothing eclipsed her. 'Does it make you rest easier at night?' she asked me one day, moving a hatbox aside so she might sit at the window in our little bedroom. Busy lacing up my darling new boots, their syrup-brown leather buttery soft, I frowned at her. 'Going to sleep surrounded by all of this?' Daisy continued, picking up a rogue earring from the carpet and examining it.

'Yes, it does,' I told her. She did not respond to this. 'I can practically taste your disapproval, you know,' I added. 'It's coming off you in waves.'

Daisy laid the earring in an over-filled jewellery box. 'I'm sorry, it's not my place to judge.'

'No, your god will do that for you, won't he?' I laughed bitterly.

Daisy stood. Her face soured as if she'd bitten into a lemon. 'Yes, he will.' She left our room.

I closed my eyes and rubbed my temples. I was beginning to sober and I disliked the feeling of reality pressing against me when I was not numb enough to face it. After another minute, I dashed out to find Daisy. 'I'm sorry,' I burst out. 'I'm sorry. I just——' My throat felt peculiar and I stopped speaking. When I touched my cheek, I was surprised to find it wet. 'I miss Penelope,' I whispered, confessing to whatever forces of fate might be watching. 'And I worry he will come for me next but I cannot leave. Anyway, you've seen his rules in Paris, who knows if he will even allow me to leave? He is not a man to cross. And——' I hesitated, half afraid to admit the guilty secret lurking at the heart of my reason for staying '——I love dancing in the spotlight. I cannot walk away now; I need it too much.'

Daisy folded me into her arms. 'I know,' she murmured into my ear, holding me tightly. 'I know. But you must be careful, Detta. Some days I hardly recognise you anymore. I fear that you are treading a dark path.'

'Is that not precisely how Rothbart prefers us? Veering on the edge of darkness. Becoming great and greater until we slip into that eternal night like wraiths. Or whatever fate he has in mind for us.'

'You are too great to disappear into that night.' Daisy gave me a little shake, bringing me back to my senses. 'And I won't hear you talk like this again.'

I nodded, my throat too swollen to continue. To say what I ought to have said; that I might have been bathing in champagne and couture to forget it all, but Daisy was living in denial.

That night, as the stars began peeking out over the horizon, they found me lying in a pile of silks with Jacques, our gaze turned skyward. 'Do you think Rothbart would let me stay in Paris?' I asked.

'That's a dangerous thought,' Jacques told me. 'He does not seem like a man that would let his biggest talent walk away.'

This brought my thoughts to the edge of that which I did not wish to confront. It was no small task to walk along that edge of knowledge. My breath quickened. I lifted my hand to admire the cocktail ring I had purchased earlier. A diamond-shaped gold frame held a green onyx, cut in a square with tiny diamonds winking around it like star-glitter. I stared at it until my thoughts calmed and cleared. Jacques lifted himself up on his elbows, watching.

'Do you like it?' I asked but he did not answer. 'Will you miss me when I've left?' I tried instead.

'Of course, but such is life. We are all birds in a wide, wide sky. Oftentimes we might fly alongside another but we must each soar on our own current.'

I frowned, unsure if it was due to his English or my own wine-muddled head that I hadn't understood. Before I could ask again, he lowered himself atop me, kissing me until all my fears melted away like snow. Until nothing existed but he and I and the city lights that guided our lips, our hands, as we lost ourselves in each other.

✶

We were booked at the Théâtre Magique until the first bloom of spring, when the chestnut groves blossomed, perfuming the boulevards. The thought of Paris reawakening gave me hope that I could navigate a path through my recent troubles. Yet it was not to be. For before the New Year was ushered in, Daisy roused me from Jacques' bed, her copper hair falling from her ribbon where she'd tugged at it in desperation: Ada had been summoned to Rothbart that night.

She never returned.

On Rothbart's sudden orders, we stole out of Paris under the shine of a watchful new moon. Abandoning our sold-out performances and leaving the company in financial strife, a move that would make Rothbart's patrons furious and give rise to rumours that his Theatre of Enchantments was unreliable. As we crossed the deep waters that led home, I fell into a nightmare of feathered wings and snow.

Chapter Forty-Eight

Forster snapped the newspaper closed and laid it down on the café table at the same time that a man approached him. He was somewhere in his forties, dressed in a blue wool cassimere suit, his salt-and-pepper hair trimmed short. 'Monsieur Sylvan, I presume?' he enquired in an accented English, perturbing Forster, who had fancied he resembled an artfully tousled bohemian from the Left Bank and not, as he now suspected, a mere tourist. 'Yes.'

'Jacques Laurent. A pleasure to make your acquaintance.'

'Likewise. What will you have?' Forster gestured at a waiter who conversed with Jacques in their native tongue, which further disheartened Forster, who was lost in a sea of words that curved and coiled like waves dashing over his head.

Jacques gave a self-deprecating smile which was filled with knowledge of the fact. 'I am afraid I am somewhat particular when it comes to my wine. But, do not fear!' He tapped his nose. 'I have a nose for fine wine; you will enjoy it.'

Forster began to nurture a dislike of the man. Suspecting envy was at play, he attempted to set it aside. 'Whatever you prefer. I'm grateful for any assistance you can offer me in the matter we discussed.'

'You wish to hear of my relationship with Detta.' Jacques's

smile reappeared, this time touched with curiosity. 'Is it a matter of jealousy?'

'Not at all.' Forster hesitated as the waiter appeared with a bottle of burgundy. 'In fact, we need not speak of Detta at all. My concern is primarily focused on Rothbart.' *Rothbart.* That drum-beat of his heart when Forster spoke his name, anger and hate and hope all twined together. 'I need to locate him and I've been given to understand that you managed Théâtre Magique when his Theatre of Enchantments toured there; surely you had some communication with the man?'

'I did. Though—' Jacques sighed and spread his hands '—that was then. We have not spoken since. There was some peculiar business with one of his ballet dancers and I did not care to embroil myself in that. It was bad enough that they left so quickly, in the middle of their season. His reckless abandonment cost me a fortune and I have not forgiven him.'

'But perhaps you have some details of how you might contact him again?' Forster pressed. 'Or know of who else I might turn to next? Who else was close to him?'

'Regretfully, I do not know.' Jacques swirled the dregs of his wine without meeting Forster's eyes. His lips and teeth were stained as if he had feasted on a handful of berries, ripe from the brambles, or, in the fading light, blood.

One day later, Forster's frustrations had doubled. He could not decipher whether Jacques was unable to recall a shred of information or simply unwilling. Forster had travelled to Paris to meet with him, his sole remaining lead. If he did not change his mind, if Forster could not convince him to share what he appeared to be hiding, this had been for nothing. Meanwhile, he feared that back in England,

Detta continued to deteriorate. Forster wandered Paris as if in a daze, a man caught between the tides of two very different worlds.

But the French capital was a beacon for art and culture, and each time he left his hotel, he experienced something new that sought to challenge and delight him. He explored the streets strewn with pretty pastel blossoms, wide green parks sprinkled with tulips, and little hidden cafés. He hopped from gallery to gallery, taking in Picasso's latest ground-breaking works in blocky shapes and colours, alongside other revolutionary artists practising Surrealism and Cubism, which tore the very idea of art apart, reforming it into something bold and bright and new. Art Deco infiltrated every creative avenue and Diaghilev's Ballets Russes were crowned the kings of the cultural world. Forster took copious notes of it all. A fortnight in Paris lifted his spirits and gave him his appetite for life back. He indulged in long, luxurious lunches, expensive wines, and zesty little cheeses that he scooped up with the baguettes he bought each day. And as the sun set, he did not return to his hotel. One evening he watched Josephine Baker singing to a packed audience, her voice an extraordinary experience he never wanted to forget. Another, he was invited to philosophise at a literary salon by a fellow artist who recognised him in a café. Then there were the jazz clubs. Alive with the shimmying and leg-kicking new dance they called the Charleston.

Paris kept his sadness at bay and there was a part of him that did not wish to leave. But as his trip drew to an end, his thoughts returned to home.

When he closed his eyes at night, he dreamt of Detta as Snow White, a forestful of foes stalking her steps. Owlish eyes following her every which way she turned, capturing her in sugar as if she were to be devoured alive.

Chapter Forty-Nine

On his last night in Paris, after he'd enjoyed an entire fortnight there, Forster was ruminating on how Jacques had kept his secrets locked within himself and if he ought to have pressed harder on that lock. Filled with regret in the darkest of blacks, he paid his tab and made to leave his hotel bar, down the street from Harry's New York Bar, drinking playground of Hemmingway and the Fitzgeralds. Before he exited, he heard a familiar voice. He hesitated at the door. 'Rose?'

She looked up with a start. It had been some time since he had last seen her. Whereas Detta grew more fragile, ethereal, each time he saw her, forever on the verge of melting away into the woodland, leaving only feathers in her wake, Rose was much the same as ever. Her amber eyes bright and wide, her chocolate-coloured hair in its trademark flapper bob, couture dress skimming her Rubenesque curves in a fondant-pink shade reminiscent of a strawberry macaron. He slowly removed his jacket. Sat beside her at the polished teak bar. 'Fancy seeing you here. It's been quite some time since we last spoke; I meant to write back to your latest letter, but this is even better. What a happy coincidence running into you. Might I buy you dinner?'

'Forster, darling, where have you been hiding over winter?' She gave him a delighted smile, pressed a kiss to each of his cheeks. 'I was beginning to think that you had started hibernating like a bear!' She laughed and stood. 'Since you're offering, let's go next door. They've got steak frites that are positively to die for.'

They strolled next door and found a little table in a corner of the bustling bistro. It was moody inside, with live jazz playing and clouds of cigarette smoke. Forster removed his hat, continuing their conversation. 'I'm afraid I've been holed up in my new studio. What brings you to Paris?'

'Oh, this and that. Tiresome engagements and social appointments I shan't bore you with,' she said airily, smiling at the waiter as he delivered their order, sizzling and dripping with herb butter, a 75 cocktail for Forster and champagne for Rose on the side.

There was an awkward lull to their conversation, a gaping hole they were both skating over that now loomed, threatening to drag them into the tumultuous black waters beneath. Forster was first to plunge into it. 'And Marvin? Have you resumed your relationship with him again?'

'I have.' Rose shook her napkin out and dove into her dinner. Catching Forster's shifting mood, she exclaimed, 'Oh, don't . . . don't let this ugly business with Marvin and his story come between us. It did not come from a malicious place and he has mended his ways since realising how it affected you so. And myself. He has apologised time and again since he realised how he had also hurt me through his actions. We would not be seeing each other again if I did not believe he was truly sorry.'

Forster stabbed a frite, disliking Rose's easy forgiveness of Marvin. 'He knows not of what he writes.'

'I daresay that's true,' Rose examined him. 'But we . . . I have missed you. And I understand that you're loyal to your employer;

your loyalty is one of the things I admire most about you. But you have forgotten your loyalty to us.' She paused and glanced down, rearranging her napkin on the bar. 'Once we were the closest of friends, Forster. And you and Marvin were like brothers. I understand how badly he betrayed you, but he is trying to change. Perhaps we could take a little trip to the hunting lodge like old times? I'm certain that once you speak to Marvin again you will see the difference in him.'

'Rose—'

'It takes two people to drift away,' Rose interrupted him with not a little sternness, setting her cutlery down on an empty plate. 'And you two were drifting apart long before all this mess with the story. Marvin is equally to blame, he let you go. But you saw that he was veering off on an ill-advised path and you didn't help him either. You only watched as he lost himself.'

Forster pushed his unfinished plate aside, his stomach knotted with tension. 'You're right. Of course, you're right. How is he?'

'Why don't you ask him that yourself?' Rose asked softly.

'Because he behaved despicably, Rose.' He took a large mouthful of his cocktail, catching the aroma of dry gin and apple brandy. 'And I don't know that I can forgive him for that.'

'I understand. This was a bad error in judgement on his behalf, I'm not mitigating that,' Rose told him. 'But people make mistakes every day. That doesn't mean that we're not good enough or not worthy of love. It means that we're human. And anger is nothing but a festering wound. You think you're punishing Marvin with this anger but, really, you're hurting yourself by allowing this rotting thing to live inside you.'

Forster's sigh was long, pained. 'How did you get to be so damned smart?'

Rose's dimples appeared. 'I've always been the smartest one, which is how I've known for years that you're in love with that ballerina. Odette. A pretty name for a dancer, very fitting. Will you marry her?'

'I—' Forster's laugh was short, surprised. It ended with a pinch of wanting that near choked him. If only. If only life ran to simple rhythms and their love story could be just that. A beautiful story they could tell each other, over and over again; *I fell in love with you when I painted you and you danced in a shaft of golden light and that light poured into my heart and I knew in that moment that my life would be forever changed.* The kind of story that they would embroider together throughout their lives until their twilight, when they would trace the threads that bound them together, marvel at the tapestry of their life, and tell it to their grandchildren at bedtime.

Instead, Forster had fallen in love with a cursed woman.

Rose grasped his hand. He read the pity on her face before he felt his salted cheeks. 'Do not give up on her, you must follow your heart.'

'What do you do when love is no longer enough?' he whispered. For he knew Detta loved him but that did not write their story a better ending. Not when he had failed to find the lead he had been counting on in Paris.

'Why, Forster, I never thought I would hear you say such a thing,' Rose exclaimed. 'You're a man who loves freely and paints with his soul and is courageous of heart. You more than anyone ought to know that love is always enough. There is no greater force in this world and nothing it cannot do.' She sipped her champagne. It sparkled under the moody lighting, a red imprint of her lips marking her glass.

Forster laid his cutlery down. Having finished his dinner, he was now digesting her words.

Rose dabbed at her lips with a napkin. 'That was positively delightful. Now, I must make my way to a little party on the Left Bank, would you care to join me?'

'I shall have to pass, I have somewhere else to be,' Forster suddenly decided, leaving a pile of francs on the table as he kissed Rose's cheek and bid her a fond goodbye.

He walked out into the night alone.

An hour later, Jacques entered the hotel lobby. Forster motioned to a pair of overstuffed armchairs that stole into the secrecy of an alcove. 'Thank you for meeting me here tonight.'

Jacques inclined his head. 'You made such an impassioned plea on the telephone I felt I had no choice. But as I have already told you, I have no further information to give you. I cannot help you, Forster.'

'Detta was young when you first met her—' Forster nursed a glass of gin '—and already so talented she was the darling of the press. Even though she had just lost her parents.'

Jacques blanched. 'I did not know this.'

'No, I imagine not. But you suspected something, didn't you? Some inner darkness that had taken root in her?' Forster set his glass down, leant forwards as Jacques hesitated, then nodded, just once. 'And then there was Rothbart. Enigmatic, charismatic, talented too but there was something about him that you couldn't pin down, that you instinctively disliked. It was not his choice to leave Paris but yours, wasn't it? You told him to leave your theatre after you heard the rumours that danced around him.'

Jacques's posture slackened. 'It's true. I was a coward. I did not want my reputation to be tarnished by his and so I bade him leave, end his season early, which was a considerable expense, but I could not risk the scandal of being linked to Rothbart. That poor ballet dancer of his was never found and to this day she haunts me.'

Forster's suspicions when speaking with Daisy had been proven correct: someone *had* vanished. 'Tell me what happened to Detta in Paris.'

Jacques removed a silver case from his jacket pocket and lit a cigarette. 'The Detta I knew was fragile. Not physically, you understand – in that respect she was stronger than any man I knew then or since – but in her mind, her heart. She was too ambitious. She hungered for the spotlights, would have wrecked her body to fly across the stage.' His pause was significant. 'And she was plagued with nightmares. Terrible ones that had her crying out in the blackest nights. She drowned her tears in champagne and worse, until she was a lost soul, yet still, the nightmares came.'

Forster swallowed the noxious envy that bubbled up in him like a sulphurous gas. This man, with his casual remarking on the nights he had shared with Detta, did not know that Forster spent his alone.

'What were they about?' he asked instead, already knowing.

'That she did not share with me.' Jacques exhaled a ribbon of smoke. 'You must understand that what we shared was not a true relationship. I knew that Detta only used me as a distraction, that she liked me for how I admired her dancing, her beauty. She never once shared her mind with me.' He gestured with his cigarette. It left a silver-grey trail behind. 'Besides which, Rothbart had forbidden any such liaisons; his company were prohibited from spending time with anyone not in their group. Another way for him to maintain his control over them, I see that now, but at the time, it added a certain thrill.'

Forster's jaw tightened.

'I enjoyed our brief affair. That was all she was to me, an interest-ing *divertissement*. But you, I see now that you truly love her. After you telephoned tonight, I placed a call to another of the performers from those days. The Delightful Daisy we used to call her. She informed me that you have already met her. Charming but a bit shallow, no?'

Forster passed no remark.

'She mentioned that she'd spoken to you in person and assured me that you held no ill will towards Detta, so I returned to meet with you one last time. You were right, I did dislike Rothbart. There was something not right about that man. Before he came to Paris I asked around about him but it was as if he had appeared from nowhere. This protected his identity when the police came searching for him in York, as I later learnt.'

Forster closed his eyes for a beat. It was as he had fretted; nobody knew the man behind the illusion. And it was impossible to track an illusion; you could no more hold back the wind from gusting.

'Ah ah, do not despair yet.' Jacques stamped out his cigarette on an empty plate. 'Rothbart might have come from nowhere and nothing but this meant that he could not fund his beloved theatre himself. He needed patrons. Wealthy ones.'

'And these patrons will know where he is?' Once more, Forster's hopes began to lift, a slow sunrise in clementine and lavender.

Jacques gave a Gallic shrug. 'Perhaps. Speak to Sir Henry Forth, he was the first. And the richest. And Forster?'

'Yes?' Forster was already rising to his feet.

'I wish you luck.'

Chapter Fifty

In summer, Forster returned to York to make fresh enquiries. He drove down Museum Street and parked, switching his driver's cap for a boating hat that suited the warmer clime and leaping over the side of his Ford. Wearing a loose white shirt that fluttered like a summer's breeze and a pair of tweed trousers, he strolled into a redbrick, granite-columned gentleman's club. Affecting an air of entitlement, he strode past the would-be gatekeeper by feigning a greeting to someone in the recessed cigar lounge.

Once inside the upper echelons of society, he tugged the brim of his hat low to disguise his face and made himself at home on a leather armchair. Smoke drifted through the room like mist, scenting everything with tobacco and old leather. Forster selected a cigar from a wooden box, trimmed the end and avoided the sceptical gaze from the attendant who lit it for him. Puffing on his cigar, he looked around the room, redolent with mahogany and dark Victoriana décor, and listened in to the three men sat behind his back. One of which was the man he'd hoped to meet: Sir Henry Forth. The men he sat with possessed reputations as some of the richest, most politically influential men in the north, leaving Forster curious to eavesdrop on their conversation. Perhaps learn a nugget of information that might prove to be valuable when he questioned Forth. They appeared to be mid-discussion on a dancer who may or may not have been involved in a love affair with a former prime minister's wife.

'—She was in the Cult of the Clitoris, was she not?' an older gentleman with an outrageous moustache asked.

'Oh?' the other enquired. 'And which Greek god was that?'

Forster almost choked on his cigar smoke.

Sir Henry Forth, a stout man in his late sixties with thinning hair, bellowed a laugh and excused himself. Forster waited five seconds after Forth passed his chair before standing and following him into the facilities.

'Pardon the intrusion, Sir Forth, but I was hoping to have a word with you.'

Forth eyed Forster warily. 'What is it? Make it snappy, I do not have all day.'

'You were a patron of Rothbart's Theatre of Enchantments, were you not?'

Forth's mood darkened at once. 'Whatever do you mean, coming in here and accosting me like this?' He reddened, fastening his jacket. 'This is a well-regarded gentlemen's club and you sir, do not belong here.'

'Forgive me.' Forster stepped forwards. 'I only mean to ask you a question—'

Forth bristled. 'I refused to be harassed in my own club. Kindly leave, now.'

'If you could just tell me where I might find Rothbart—'

'*Now.*' Forth raised his voice. An attendant opened the door. 'Is everything all right, gentlemen?'

'This man is harassing me and I demand that you escort him out of this club at once. I would wager that he does not hold membership here and is trespassing.' Forth's moustache trembled with rage as he issued his instructions and though Forster ought to have been overcome with frustration, his question had not merited this response. Which could only mean one thing: Forth was hiding something.

'Come with me, sir.' The attendant held the door open for Forster to exit. 'You must be a member to enter these premises.'

'This is all a terrible misunderstanding,' Forster said calmly. 'I meant no harm, I only wished to ask Sir Forth a simple question.'

Forth drew himself to his full height. 'Remove him or call the police to remove him for you. I want him out of my sight. Immediately.' He turned an alarming ruddy colour. Forster froze, unsure what to do as he watched his singular opportunity vanish. The attendant suddenly turned on Forster. 'Who are you?' he demanded. 'Tell me your name this instant.'

Forster hesitated. 'Really, this has become entirely overblown—' but the pair were no longer listening to logic and with a frustrated sigh, he left the club.

✫

'When I told you that there was nothing love couldn't do, this wasn't exactly what I had in mind.' Rose surveyed Forster leaning against a lamppost. He'd attempted to leave York in a hurry after Forth had commanded the full weight of his title against him but, to his dismay, his motor had had other ideas and had broken down around the corner from the gentlemen's club. After arranging for it to be towed for repairs, Forster had then realised that he hadn't sufficient funds for a train ticket nor hotel on his person and had had to telephone Rose.

'I've parked it behind the—' Marvin rounded the corner and fell silent.

'Marvin.'

'Forster.'

Rose sighed. 'Is that all you have to say to each other? Really, darlings, this has gone on long enough.'

'Thank you for coming so quickly,' Forster told her, his appreciation tempered by her meddling attempt to force a reconciliation between him and Marvin. It had been a long, infuriating day and, to cap it all off, a headache had taken root just above his left eye.

'It was nothing,' Marvin said quietly, reading Forster's discomfort. Even at odds, Marvin knew him better than anyone, save Detta.

'It most certainly was not nothing.' Rose's tone filled with indignation. 'Why, it took us near an entire day to motor up here and you had to beg off work to accompany me.' Marvin rubbed the back of his neck as Forster evaded either of their gazes, hot shame slinking down the back of his neck. 'The least you could do is buy us dinner,' she finished.

Dusk was settling in to York now, lending a rosy glow to the honeyed stone streets. It reminded Forster that he had not eaten in hours. Bracing himself for the awkwardness that was sure to follow, he nodded. 'I would be glad to.'

Chapter Fifty-One

Through the wending streets, the large, crooked windows of The Shambles peering at them as they passed by, Forster, Rose, and Marvin walked in an uneasy silence. Forster's thoughts kept perambulating like an old clock, turning back again and again to Detta. She was finding it harder to shift back into her true self and his nightmares were swollen with the notion that, one day, she would simply remain swan. Unless he found out what Forth was hiding, what had turned him defensive and overbearing on hearing Rothbart's name.

Rose led them into a nook of a restaurant dripping with Deco brass fixtures, its walls painted a fashionable shade of viridian green. The three of them sat in a booth at the back, where the lighting was at its dimmest and Forster felt as if he were sitting in some underwater cave. For a moment, he imagined sitting there with Detta, his muse more myth than life. He would have painted them conversing over a table of golden sand, a mischievous crab sneaking a pincer towards the salt. Tiny fishes with luminous sparks for scales darting through the water around them. And Detta. A river sprite that belonged in emerald depths, her eyes haunted with the shadows of the past. But she was not there. Instead, Rose and Marvin sat opposite him, their curiosity palpable.

When a waiter appeared to take their orders, Forster asked for a Turkish coffee, having decided he could not manage a single bite. Between his despair at his encounter with Forth and lingering frustration with Marvin, his stomach churned.

'I'll take the same,' Marvin said, tossing his menu onto the table, apparently unable to eat either. This brought Forster a modicum of satisfaction; at least Marvin was suffering, too.

'And for you, miss?'

Forster gestured to the menu. 'Please. Order whatever you like. Champagne, a cocktail?' As much as he could not forgive Marvin, not yet, he owed the pair for leaping to his assistance.

Rose's fingers opened and curled shut, a pale-pink shell reaching for something beyond its grasp. Forster knew what she wished to say. 'Just the rose and pistachio cake for me.' With an acquiescent nod, the waiter retrieved the menus and vanished.

Forster waited.

'What happened?' It did not take Rose long to speak her mind now that their silence had been fractured.

'Rose said that you'd mentioned an altercation with an esteemed gentleman? Sir Henry Forth?' Marvin asked. 'What the devil did you want with him?'

'Searching for your next scoop, are you?' Forster said tightly. Having forgotten he'd mentioned Forth in passing on the telephone, he was annoyed with himself; he ought to have known Rose would home in on the fact. Though not as irritated as he was with Marvin.

'I'm sorry.' Marvin held his eye contact. 'I did not realise how much she meant to you or I would never have—'

'So, exposing an innocent woman would have been fine if I hadn't been in love with her?'

Their order arrived.

Forster sipped his coffee, midnight-dark and strong. Marvin

tipped a couple of sugars into his and stirred it, his jaw working as he stared down at it. Rose took a delicate bite of her cake. The slice was pale meadow-green, blushing with frosting and crowned with chopped pistachios and candied rose petals. A flower fairy's dream.

'No, it wouldn't have been fine.' Marvin's words were tentative, hesitant. One hand slipped under the table and Forster knew if he were to look, Rose would be holding onto it, lending him strength. 'I admit I got carried away; I became lost in the thrill of the chase, in discovering the secrets that twisted through society, the deeper truths responsible for the ripples on the surface. It took me too long to see how I had become reduced to hunting down what amounted to gossip or malicious rumours.' He paused, his knuckles white against the handle of his coffee cup.

'He's establishing himself a new role in the paper now.' Rose radiated with pride. 'Exposing corrupt politicians and the like. Using his knack of discovering sordid little secrets to hold those in power accountable for their crimes.' She laid her fork down. 'Now, it's your turn.'

'My turn for what?'

'To share whatever's been burdening you. We can see it, darling. You walk through life as if you're Atlas, holding up the weight of the world on your shoulders, when perhaps if you shared it with those who care about you—' she indicated herself and Marvin '—it would not feel as heavy.'

Forster reached for his coffee, hiding the prickle in the back of his throat. He could not stop remembering how Detta had struggled to change between forms. Desperate and clawing to be human, to stay, as her life slid through her fingers like water. In his darkest moments he relived the wicked heart of her curse; how her bones cracked and bent, how she cried out in pain. The bruises that mottled her skin after shifting, how she grew paler and more fragile with each year that passed. And the things that whispered in his thoughts of a night-time, the things he could not bear to voice aloud. That she was never destined to be his, not when the lake and the woodlands were waiting for her. 'I cannot share it,' he began and Rose sighed with vexation. 'Even if I wanted to—' he shot Marvin a cautious glance '—even if I decided to give you my trust once more, it is not my secret to share.'

Rose drummed her fingers on the table. 'Would you tell us if we happened to guess it?'

'Rose.' Marvin gave Forster a half smile, the kind they would have exchanged when it had been just the three of them against the world and Rose had uttered something amusing or nonsensical. 'We're not going to turn this into a parlour game.'

'Thank you,' Forster interjected. Rose rolled her eyes and resumed eating her cake, though she was struggling to disguise her pleasure that the two men were on speaking terms once more.

'That said—' Marvin turned serious once more '—Rose is right; whatever is going on, this has gone on long enough. Clearly you need help.' Forster made to protest but Marvin held a hand up and continued, 'You don't need to confide the entire story in us for us to lessen your load. Why don't you tell us a small part of it instead, something we could assist with? Perhaps why you sought out Henry Forth. Then we could aid you without having to learn this great secret you've promised to keep, for Odette, I presume?'

Forster nodded, considering. Marvin had access to a sea of resources, vastly greater than his, and it was imperative he learnt what Forth knew. If he didn't, there was no saving Detta. And there was nothing he would not do to save her. 'I'm looking for a man called Rothbart.'

Rose almost dropped her fork. 'Rothbart? Of Rothbart's Theatre of Enchantments?'

Forster nodded again and Rose pointed her fork at him. 'My father accompanied me to one of their performances once. Snow White. It was unlike anything I've ever seen since.'

'Odette once danced there.' Forster ignored the trickle of guilt that seeped through him. He wasn't sharing the secret at the heart of this mystery, just a small part of it. And who could ever guess at the real story of curses and swans and a man whose fingertips crackled with terrible magic? 'And for . . . certain reasons, it is imperative that I locate this Rothbart. Only it isn't his real name and he's proving impossible to find.' Forster raked through his hair, his curls snagging on his fingers, the short pulling pain cathartic as Detta's face swam through his thoughts. 'I recently learnt that this Henry Forth was one of Rothbart's original and wealthiest patrons. If anyone knows where Rothbart might be hiding, it would be him. However . . . '

'You tried to ask him and he panicked and you were required to leave in a hurry?' Rose asked wryly.

'You're surprisingly astute at times,' Marvin told her.

Rose dabbed her lips with a napkin. 'Please. How often do I have to tell you that I'm always right?'

Forster smiled to himself, surprised that their bickering had cheered him. That though he could not quite forgive Marvin yet, all was not lost between them. And he believed Marvin when he'd declared that he was finished with the side of journalism that had led him down an increasingly twisting path. That had ended with the fissure between him and Forster splitting into untraversable ground. The Marvin that sat before him now had not been untouched from that experience. And if his old friend valued him enough to race up to York to give him a ride home, to start down a new path, Forster

300

owed him the same courtesy. To start forging a bridge back towards friendship.

'Rose is right. Which to me indicates that Forth is hiding something as I was hardly pestering the man enough to drive him to lose his temper.'

Marvin looked thoughtful. 'I would agree. Then how do we approach him now?'

Forster started. 'We?'

Marvin's roguish grin reappeared for the first time in an age. 'Well, we can't very well let this Henry Forth get the better of you, can we?' Forster hesitated and Marvin continued, 'Let me make amends by helping you. Please. I want to prove to you that I am here for you, that you may rely on me as you once did. I cannot bear this distance between us; not us, not when we used to be as close as brothers. It pains me, Forster.'

Forster pushed his hair back roughly. 'It pains me too,' he admitted gruffly.

Rose let out a delighted squeal. 'Oh, we should have got champagne, this calls for a toast!' She lifted her cup of coffee instead. 'To old friends reunited and new plans hatched.'

The three of them clinked their coffee cups together.

And for the first time in an age, Forster's burden lessened some of its crushing weight as he looked between Rose and Marvin and smiled. Perhaps he did not need to struggle through this unbearable loneliness after all.

Marvin considered the menu again and grinned. 'Now that we've cleared the air, shall we order properly?'

Chapter Fifty-Two

Despite Forster being in the midst of his hunt for Rothbart, he returned to the empty manor for a short spell. It echoed with ghosts and grief. He slept each night alone, his dreams haunted with silvery ballerinas that pirouetted until they grew feathers. And as one week without Detta stretched to the next, he painted. Until his studio filled with paintings of her, his loneliness a cloud he could not escape, following him from one room to the next with its chill. Frustrated with his lack of answers, with being alone, forever alone, he walked out to the lake.

There, Detta swam.

It had been five months since she had turned swan and stayed that way. Trapped in her feathered form. The seasons had slinked through the year, unspooling one after the other like a rainbow of paint spilling from a tube and again; she would miss each and every one. Spring had unfurled in petal-fine days, a budding of life in yolk-yellow daffodils and a rainbow of tulips. Then came these silky summer days when the breeze was like an enchantment, heady and wild, thick with the scent of wildflowers. Soon the fiery spell of autumn would blaze through the woodland, painting the trees alive in vivid shades of garnet and tangerine, when Forster would turn thirty-four years old. Last year, he had marked the changing months. Saved acorns that he had painted with delicate scenes of forest fairies and rainstorms. Pressing the flowers that held the prettiest petal-patterns between *Anna Karenina*, the thickest volume he owned. Setting a canvas aflame with the richness of an autumnal day. He had not showed her any of these things. He'd swept them away into a box, fearing that they would only bring sadness.

Both Marvin and Rose had offered Forster a place to stay while their investigations progressed, keen for him to return to London. But Forster had declined. He needed to be beside her. Standing on the shore, the water lapping at his feet, he didn't want to leave. Couldn't bear the thought of returning to the chilled halls of the manor where he would eat dinner alone before going to bed by himself. Instead, he decided to circumnavigate the entire lake on foot.

Beating his way through the branches and wild tangle of over-growth proved satisfying. When he reached the far side of the lake, he stared back at the manor, that ancient sentry looming in the distance. Where the best and worst moments of his life had happened. He whiled away the evening there, his thoughts deep and murky as lake-water. There, the oaks and yews embraced above him, keeping the woodland as dark and mysterious as the background of a Rembrandt painting. And on the lake, Detta remained swan. Though the sun beamed down on her, glazing her feathers brilliant white, Forster was iced with fear that he would not find Rothbart soon enough. Time was a devious creature and he, its helpless prey.

An idea suddenly presented itself to him. Before stopping to consider it, he dropped to his knees on the lake bank and began tearing out weeds and nettles with his bare hands.

✷

'Just here?' The builders that Forster hired two days later regarded him as if his sudden conviction to live beside the lake was as wild as he had suspected.

'Yes, that's correct.' He looked at the patch of bracken and weeds he had cleared. Pulling out a sketch he'd drawn with nettle-stung hands, he framed his new home with words for the first time.

In mere days, the structure began to take shape. A small wooden cabin that perched over the periphery of the lake on thick stilts. It was well hidden from view and boasted a generous deck that stretched out over the water so that Forster might always be beside Detta, even as she whiled away months of her life at a time. He bought a small rowing boat and painted it cherry-red before tying it to the deck. A chimney appeared, along with the promise of crackling fires in winter's frosted reign. Next, large windows that peered out across the lake.

When it was finished, Forster stood inside the cabin and surveyed his new kingdom. Pine-scented and rustic, surrounded by water and woodland, it was akin to a crooked cottage in the depths of some forested fairy tale. Rather fitting for a man in love with a cursed swan-woman.

He moved in at once. Now he never needed to leave his love.

Chapter Fifty-Three

Summer passed in the flutter of a dragonfly's wing.

Forster enjoyed witnessing it from the deck of his new cabin rather than being confined to the manor. Standing and painting outside as a fat bumblebee wove lazy patterns through the air, he wondered if the countryside was the birthplace of art. There was something about being surrounded by trees and water that calmed him from within.

Until the telephone rang during Forster's evening check of the manor.

'I've got him,' Marvin said eagerly.

Forster tightened his hold on the receiver. 'You are absolutely certain? We can't have him slip through our fingers again.'

'He's a wily creature, I'll give him that.' Marvin's tone was grim. 'It took me far longer than I'd been expecting to pin him down. But it turns out the old man was having an affair. I've sent a telegram instructing him to meet us at Rose's hunting lodge tomorrow at midday. That should ensure that there are no direct links between you and him. If things turn nasty, he doesn't know your name, or where you live.'

Forster exhaled, heady with relief. 'Marvin, thank you. I owe you—'

'Consider it repayment for my poor behaviour last year,' Marvin said lightly.

'It's already forgotten.'

✿

The three ogee gables of the old hunting lodge rose from the forest like a familiar story. And before them, Rose lounged against her sunshine-yellow Rolls-Royce, its roof folded back to soak up the summer. Forster halted and jumped out of his motor, striding over to envelop her in a deep embrace. 'Hello, darling.' She smiled. 'Isn't this rather thrilling?' She wore a gauzy chiffon dress with a single long strand of pearls dancing down her low-cut back.

'You find everything thrilling,' Marvin called out, exiting the hunting lodge with a folder in one hand.

Rose looked a trifle indignant. 'Well, I've never engaged in blackmail before.' The beaded fringe of her dress clattered as she turned to him. 'Are those the photographs? What shall we do if he arrives with a police escort?'

'He won't,' Marvin assured her. 'I made it perfectly clear that these—' he raised the folder '—would be released to the press if that was the case.'

'He ought to be here at any moment.' Forster checked his grand-father's watch.

Rose twisted up a bullet of lipstick, coating her lips in blood-red armour, before sliding a pair of tortoiseshell sunglasses on. Marvin regarded her with no little amusement. And a deep warmth that pleased Forster to see. Yet before either of them could comment on her sense of theatricality, another motor sounded, crunching up the worn forest track.

Sir Henry Forth ground to a stop, slammed his door shut, and marched over. If Forster had thought he had been defensive and angry on their last encounter, he was positively apoplectic with rage now. 'You again?' he sputtered upon spotting Forster. 'Why you have some nerve—'

'Actually, I was the one who placed that telephone call.' Marvin stepped forward. He raised the folder with a jaunty wave. 'I believe this will be of interest to you.'

'I am not interested in baseless accusations.' Forth's nostrils flared as he raised his voice. 'I came only to instruct you that I shall be filing a legal suit against you all at once.'

Rose looked down her tortoiseshell sunglasses at him. 'How uncouth,' she commented. 'I don't believe your poor wife would enjoy seeing those photographs splashed over the papers.' She gave a delicate shudder.

Forth scoffed in disbelief. Though his eyes skittered down to the folder. 'I do not believe you possess anything more than what amounts to a calculated bluff.'

With exaggerated finesse, Marvin slid one photograph free. He passed it to Forth, who blanched. With a single terse nod, he sank into silence. Marvin jerked his head at Forster.

This was it. His last chance to free Detta from the curse that had claimed her. Each time he considered the man who had committed this crime, it stirred something within him that thrashed about in his stomach like a fanged snake. Anger. He let it rise to the surface now. 'Tell us where Rothbart is.'

At first it did not seem as if Forth would speak. As if he were battling some inner instinct against it. Forster's jaw tightened but Marvin gave him a steady look and he held firm.

Forth relented. 'Nobody has spoken of that scoundrel in years.

He just absconded one day. Up and left, leaving his precious theatre to rot on the pavement. Took all our investments with him as well.'

'Where did he go?' Forster asked.

'If I knew I would have hunted him down myself. The man owes me a veritable fortune.'

'No. *No*,' Forster growled. 'A man of your means does not allow his assets to wander away. You must have had someone search for him.'

'Well, there were rumours at the time—'

Forster stepped closer. 'What rumours?'

'Rumours that he was helping himself to the girls under his care. Rumours that ensured I wanted nothing more to do with that man, regardless of what he owed me.'

Behind him, Rose let out a shocked gasp.

Forster shook his head, pushing his hair roughly back. 'His location. You must have some idea where he could have gone. I have it on excellent authority that the two of you were close; you must know *something* of use.'

'I know nothing,' Forth said. 'I merely wired him the money.' But the slight upturning of his mouth, the subtle sneer, spoke volumes.

It coloured Forster's world in darkest vermillion. He knew his desperation was evident but he had no intention of letting Rothbart slip through his fingers once more. He would hunt him down. Even if he had to become the kind of nightmare that prowled under the velvet cloak of night, fiercer than any enchantment or curse. That fanged snake snapped its jaws and Forster reached out and grasped Forth's lapels, shaking him. '*Tell me.*'

Rose exhaled and Marvin crossed his arms yet neither moved.

'There is a castle,' Forth whispered, the whites of his eyes turning milky. Forster loosened his hold on him at once, guiltily realising that he had been half strangling the man. 'I heard Rothbart refer to it once as his true home but he bade me never to repeat that to another living soul.'

A castle.

Forster's laugh was tinged with mania. He slumped to the forest floor. 'That godforsaken castle!' His head fell into his hands. He did not hear Rose running over, nor Marvin dispatching Forth, his wheels skidding over the peaty drive in his hurry to get away, yet suddenly there they both were, kneeling either side of him. His flare of anger, of frustration, burnt hot. 'For years I've had in my possession a photograph of that castle but upon learning that its likeness had been used to create the set of *Snow White*, I dismissed it. Never once paid it a lick of notice. Of course, it's ended up being the bloody key to the entire mystery.'

Chapter Fifty-Four

Time seemed to drag its feet until finally November arrived and, with it, a deep chill that entombed the land in frost. Forster took to drinking his morning coffee at his window seat overlooking the lake. Watching and waiting. The temperature gauge he had affixed to the glass plunged lower and lower. Forster painted, chopped firewood to feed his hungry little log burner, and slowly roasted good things in his oven to make bowls of hearty soups that warmed him from the inside. He learnt how to bake bread. And all the while, he read books on castles in England, in Germany, made enquiries on the telephone, and kept a watchful eye on the lake. As soon as spring arrived, he would scour the country to drag Rothbart out of whatever rotten hole he had crawled in to hide for the past decade, but until then, he could not risk being away from Detta, afraid she might cry out for help that never came. He could not bear the thought of her suffering alone. But November froze into December and still the skies remained a stubborn cerulean, refusing to grant a solitary flake of snow.

Forster decided to celebrate Christmas in the company of a bottle of cognac. And when the telephone in the manor house rang and offered him an alternative, his initial thought was that he could not leave the lakeside.

'Darling, you simply must come. Why, it's Christmas! And it has been an age since we last celebrated it together. Marvin and I are hosting a little party and it would mean the world if you were to come. We are family and we ought to be together at Christmas, now that we've put the past behind us. Besides, you're garnering quite the reputation as a hermit, sequestered away in the middle of nowhere. This will be good for you,' she said firmly. He winced, knowing that he had terrified the both of them that day at the hunting lodge. That they had pressed him to allow their help but he had refused, fleeing back to the solace of his cabin alone.

'Rose, you live in London, you consider the rest of the country to be in the middle of nowhere,' Forster told her, turning his gaze to the wooded copse sheltering the lake. The sky was a bright-blue roof over the world. The kind of crisp winter's day that capped the lake with ice.

'It will do you good,' Rose repeated stubbornly. 'Oh, do say yes! I've invited all my favourite people to celebrate with us; you'll learn why if you come.' A devious twinkle entered her voice.

Forster closed his eyes. Christmas without Detta had turned him maudlin and his mood bleak but Rose had offered a lifeline and he needed to take it. 'All right, all right. I will come.'

'Oh, superlative. I must dash now but I shall be seeing you soon. Come to . . .' She rattled off a new address before tacking on a *Ciao, darling!* and hanging up before Forster could respond. He cast the receiver a bemused look and replaced it before dashing back to his cabin to change.

✿

London sparkled with Christmas cheer. The address that Rose had given Forster led him to a modest but smart Georgian townhouse in South London with a neat row of black railings and a shiny green door, festooned with a wreath. Though Forster had been prepared that Marvin was no longer living at their old flat, the change still surprised him. They were well and truly cleaved now. But with those changes had come so much good that he could not fault the changing topography of their lives.

Marvin opened the door. As it swung open, there was a flash of emerald floor tiles in geometric patterns, a large vase of flowers and a pretty lamp that gave off a soft glow. But Forster's gaze landed on the golden band on his ring finger.

'It seems congratulations are in order.' He handed over the bottle of champagne he had carried in from his car.

'Thank you.' Marvin took it awkwardly. 'It was a quiet, private ceremony. We were—' his ears reddened, much to Forster's amusement '—in a bit of a hurry,' he confessed, and Forster's smile stretched wider. 'Do not let Rose know you know.' Marvin lowered his voice. 'It was meant to be a surprise. Anyway, I'm glad you've managed to tear yourself away from Wurthercliffe; it meant a lot to Rose to have you for our first Christmas at the new house. It means a lot to me,' he added.

And with that, Forster caught a glimpse of his future with Marvin. Sharing the kind of memories that old friends dipped into at leisure, over a glass of good wine, a long dinner, a winter's evening frozen into a night with no place to go but beside the fire, warming your hands on the flames, your hearts filled with nostalgia. When Forster had left Northampton in search of something to devote his life to, Marvin had taken him in. Their friendship had been forged somewhere between the fires of rejection and first gleam of success and now, standing there in the hallway of Marvin's new house, it all came roaring back to him. He could not deny that when he looked at Marvin, he saw a brother.

'I couldn't have missed it,' he told him.

Rose's clattering heels preluded her arrival. Wrapped in red velvet with a matching gold ring adorning her hand, she clasped Forster in a tight hug. 'I thought I heard voices. Oh, I'm so happy you made it, darling. Dinner shall be served in one hour, do come and join us in the drawing room.' She left by the same door she had appeared from. A waft of warm laughter, a pinch of spice, and a tickling of piano keys that faintly resembled a carol escaped. Yet when one is lonely, the sounds of distant merriment only exacerbate that loneliness, leaving you more alone than ever. Forster felt as blue as the last final strains of sunset. A blue so deep and dark it could hide the stars. He was suffering an acute pang of homesickness for the home he yearned for yet did not have. For though he lived in a cosy cabin, taking care of a manor rich with history, it was silent as a bated breath.

Marvin's gaze, too, was lingering on where Rose had exited. He roused himself with a laugh, unexpected and loud. 'She's entirely bewitched me,' he admitted before resting a hand on Forster's shoulder. 'Now come.' He guided Forster into the drawing room. 'We have some news to share and you must swear to feign surprise.'

The drawing room welcomed him like a warm embrace. Wooden floors slinked out in a herringbone pattern, cosied up with Persian rugs and a grand fireplace. A Christmas tree sparkled in one corner, illuminated with electric lights and decorated with golden baubles and red ribbons, tied into cheering bows. A cut-glass chandelier dripped icicle-like from the high ceiling and a mirrored cocktail cabinet was being put to good use as Rose mixed Vivian a drink.

Forster was heartily welcomed and introduced to another couple that shared a settee; an old school friend of Rose's and her husband.

Marvin took his place at Rose's side as Forster sat beside Vivian, who patted him on his knee and passed him a saucer of champagne along with a promise to visit his new cabin soon.

'Now, before we dine, we have some news to share,' Marvin announced. 'Please raise your glasses to my lovely new wife and—' Marvin paused for dramatic effect and Rose blushed prettily, swatting him with affection. Though he shared in their happiness, Forster swelled with envy at the ease of their relationship. How Marvin did not have cause to fear each time the weather turned. Then Rose's hand dipped lower to cup the curve of her stomach and he forgot all else. 'The newest member of our little family!' Marvin finished.

The room erupted in delight, clinking glasses together and congratulating them as Marvin's grin turned sheepish and he spoke of the son they had wished for – before Rose interrupted to declare that she was simply positive they were having a girl. 'Love is not an easy matter, is it?' Vivian said quietly to Forster.

'No. It is not.' He downed his champagne and stood to offer his own congratulations. Marvin shook his hand before pulling him in for a hug, which Rose joined. 'Thank you for sharing this moment with us,' she whispered to him.

'I wouldn't have missed it for the world,' Forster swore and they both held him tighter. And just like that, even as it pained him that he might never have a future like this with Detta, he had his family back again. And that was no small comfort.

Chapter Fifty-Five

Forster dreamt that he was flying. Soaring through the night on stolen wings, wondering if this was what it felt like to turn into a swan. Then a storm set in and he fell from the sky. Startled, he awoke in an unfamiliar bed, his heart racing before he realised where he was; in Rose and Marvin's guest bedroom after having stayed up late the previous evening, celebrating Christmas with the newlyweds. It was still dark outside though according to his grandfather's watch, it was already morning. Slowly, he dressed. As his gaze wandered past the mirror to the window, he was struck with a single, agonising realisation.

The street was white with snow.

Travelling home was no gentle journey. Worsened by the weather sending everyone into disarray and the smoke-grey storm of desperation that thundered within Forster. He motored towards Wurthercliffe in haste, cursing at the remnants of snow dripping from tree branches. It was already melting. Forster slammed his hands against the steering wheel. He should never have left. A damson dawn was crowning the sky as the odd flake fell, each one weighing on Forster's heart. He pleaded with the fates that he would not be too late.

As he screeched to a halt before the manor, a few flappers stumbled out, laughing in jewelled headdresses, their ostrich-feather fans fluttering at each other. Forster rushed inside, aching to set eyes on Detta. To see her pirouette in the great hall, catch an echo of her voice. He stepped on a carpet of crushed petals and lotus blossoms. His frown deepening, he fretted that she had shifted back into her skin without knowing the month, the year. She must have been confused without him there. Upset that he was missing. The familiar guard on the door nodded to him but Forster could not question him for fear of acting suspiciously. Pyramid and scarab motives abounded and golden platters bore cakes shaped into the likeness of crocodiles. No music played and the ballroom held just a few lingering guests. He and Rose and Marvin and Vivian had all missed the clue, the invitation, Detta had sent out. Christmas Eve must have interrupted the chain, several key links having journeyed elsewhere to celebrate with loved ones. He cursed himself for leaving the lake.

Forster ran upstairs, taking them two at a time, searching through the rooms for Detta. For her curls swinging as she walked, for those blue-grey eyes that had so transfixed him four years ago. Years of finding her only to lose her once more. Each time she transformed, it cut a deeper welt on his heart.

He found it resting atop his bed. A folded note that carried her perfume. Of snow and frozen lakes and the wild sweetness that he had tasted on her breath the last time she had kissed him.

Forster. I am sorrier than you
know to have missed you.
Until the next time, my love.
Yours, Detta.

He closed his eyes in despair, crumpling to the floor.

PART FIVE

1927

'Love is like death, it must come to us all, but to each his own unique way and time, sometimes it will be avoided, but never can it be cheated, and never will it be forgotten.'

—JACOB GRIMM

Chapter Fifty-Six

In January, the first snowdrops sprouted. Pushing through the frozen ground to offer a glimmer of hope that life was burgeoning beneath. And with them, came Detta. A short snowfall, a single night. Detta barefoot as she ran towards Forster. She had found his deck, wrapped around his new home, a bridge between the lake and himself, and the blanket he had left draped over one of the posts, waiting for her.

The moment Forster caught sight of the first snowflake whispering past his windows, he leapt up and tore open the door. And there she was. The blanket slipping from her shoulders as she sought sanctuary. He stepped out into the snow and she flew into his arms.

'When you were not here at Christmas, I was beside myself,' she said. 'I thought you had left me, feared you had grown tired of this cursed existence. That I might never see you again.'

'Never,' he vowed fiercely. The snowfall grew heavier yet still they stood there, locked in their embrace.

'I love you, Forster; whatever the future may hold for us, I want us to face it together,' she whispered.

'I will never leave you.' His heart swelled. 'It's you, Detta. For me, it's always been you.'

She raised her face and kissed him.

It was wild and windswept, filled with the months he'd yearned for her, loved her, and the time that had wrenched them apart. A sweet agony to feel her lips on his after so long apart. When she pressed herself harder against him, he lifted her into his arms and walked back into the cabin. Lit with warmth, its windows were a twinkling beacon across the lake. He kicked the door shut behind them, his glasses steaming up as he hesitated, looked at her, the bruising that marred her collarbones where her breastbone had sunken, the feather that still clung to her hair, the blue tinge to her lips. 'Are you certain—?'

'Take me to bed, Forster,' she murmured, biting his ear.

He obeyed.

Her gaze was as raw as her lips, leaving him bare before her, body and soul. And as they moved as one, he watched her come undone beneath him, her curls tumbling across his pillow. He had never seen such a beautiful sight; she was poetry in motion and he longed to spend an eternity with her. To worship her forevermore.

As she lay with her head on his chest, tracing teasing paths with her fingertips, he gently stroked her hair. 'When did you have this built?' she asked.

Forster glanced around his cabin. It was one large room. They lay upon a four-poster bed hewn from pine, knots staring out like beady eyes. Nearby was a clawfoot bath, the kind Detta favoured, set beside another great window, overlooking the trees, now clad in snowy capes. A kitchenette tucked into one corner, dough rising under a cloth, awaiting the oven. A loveseat nestled before the central fireplace, framed with over-stuffed bookcases. And walls bursting with art. All woody, smoky, and turpentine-scented. 'In the summer,' he told her. 'I needed to be closer to you. It's been a hard year without you.' His arms tightened around her as if he could hold onto her forever, keeping her beside him and safely in her own skin.

'I'm here now,' she said softly, running a hand down his chest. 'Do you think our love story shall be one of the greats?' she asked.

'The greatest,' he promised.

She lifted herself on an elbow, turning to look at him. Her hair was wild, her cheeks rosebud-pink, making his heart beat fiercer. He grazed a hand against the velvet of her neck wondering at the fates that had granted him her. 'You oughtn't say that, you know,' she told him. 'The greatest love stories are the ones that cut the deepest.'

Her melancholic streak set his thoughts a-flame. He reached for her, kissed her deeply. 'I refuse to let you be another Juliet or Anna.' He whirled Detta around until he rested atop her.

She looked up at him. 'Do you truly believe anyone could have stopped that train?'

'I would sooner die than allow such a thing to happen to you.'

Their second time that evening was lazy and languorous. As if they possessed an ocean of time. A lie. As the snow pattered down on the roof, the trees sighing outside the wooden walls, the fire roaring within, Forster and Detta spent the night learning each other a-new.

'Have you made any progress in your search?' Detta asked some hours later.

'I have.' His statement was soft, one he almost wished Detta would not hear for he did not care to give her false hope, wanted to find Rothbart before he could slip through Forster's fingers. Or perhaps he was the one afraid to hope. It was inconceivable that such a time had ever existed when they had not been Detta-and-Forster, two halves of one whole for the rest of time and he could not lose her now. She took so long in answering that he half-believed she had not heard. But when he glanced down at her, her smile was as beautiful as the sliver of moon, peeking through the clouds. 'Good,' she told him.

'I have chosen to believe that everything shall turn out as we wish it. Returning to the manor without you there made me determined never to take your love for granted. I'm grateful for each day that I see you, each moment you wrap your arms around me and tell me how you love me. You give me the strength to battle how hard the changes have become, how much weaker I feel.' He held her tighter at this, his throat prickling as he listened to her speak. 'Meeting you is the greatest thing that has ever happened to me. So, I shall hope and dream of a better future because we deserve it, Forster. And I trust that if anyone can find a way to restore me to my rightful self, it will be the man who knows me better than anyone, the man who loves me.' His emotions spilling over, Forster ran his hands up Detta's neck and onto her face, kissing her tenderly. She took a deep breath, meeting his gaze. 'I am ready to hear what you have found.'

Forster nodded. 'I located one of his old patrons and pressed him for information. I believe that Rothbart is hiding away in the ruined castle he used for the set design of *Snow White*.'

'You truly found him?' Detta clenched the bedsheets in her hands. 'Where is this castle?' Her gaze wandered over to the stacks of books beside the fireplace.

'That I do not know,' Forster confessed. 'But I'm close, I know it.' He could almost sense Rothbart out there, hiding away in his castle, awaiting Forster.

Detta went to examine the titles. '*Great English Castles, An Exploration of Castles and Palaces throughout Europe . . .* ' She glanced up at him. 'You have been researching. There must be, what, thirty books here?' They were piled up on the floor, on the crooked little table he had attempted to make himself.

'Twenty-seven,' he corrected. 'Did he ever mention anything about the castle to you?' He watched Detta pick up the photograph, her forehead a map of creases he could not read. 'Or anything that could be of use at all? Something that might be a clue?'

Detta's sigh was rough. 'He never shared anything of himself with us. He was far too dedicated to the persona he had crafted. Every day was a performance for him until my last day, when he revealed himself at last.'

'What about the things that he didn't say?' Forster pressed. 'Did he ever use a local idiom or speak in an accent, perhaps possess a fondness for food or drink from another region? Any sounds or smells—what is it?'

Detta had turned to him, her fingers rigid on the photograph. 'I had forgotten entirely. But once I overheard him speaking to himself in his office.'

Forster stood. 'What did he say?'

'I couldn't understand it, it was in another language.'

Forster inhaled sharply. 'Please tell me you recognised which one.'

Detta's smile eased his flayed nerves. This was it, the final clue to the mystery he had spent years working away on. His to solve at last, his prize greater than any other imaginable.

'He was speaking Welsh,' she said. 'I remember because it was the only time I heard him talk in a different accent. At the time I wondered if it could have been his native one.'

Forster's hopes illumed like a shiny moth's wing. 'When the weather grows warmer and I know it shall not snow again for some time, then I will travel there. I will scour the entire country for him if I have to.'

'You can leave sooner if you prefer,' Detta offered.

'No.' Forster closed the distance between them, enclosing her in his arms. 'I am as impatient as you to find him but your safety is my priority and I never want to be away when you come back to me again.'

In the early hours, before the sun had yet crested the horizon, Forster put the bread into the oven to bake for lunch before assembling a breakfast tray to bring back to bed. A pot of excellent coffee and crêpes, following Mrs Fischer's recipe until her memory was conjured amid the grated lemon rind and puffs of sugar that set the air a-shimmering. And as they feasted on crêpes, they shared stories. Of Forster's adventures in Paris, of Marvin and Rose's news, and Detta's memories of returning to England, where things took a darker turn.

Chapter Fifty-Seven

Detta
1913

By witnessing Rothbart killing a swan, I had voyaged into the darkly glittering heart of his theatre. Had glimpsed the cruelty behind those velvet curtains, hanging thick and silent as a threat. Paris had distracted me. Too much. I had plunged headfirst into the glitter and glamour, the spell that Jacques's adoration had spun on me, until I lost more and more of myself. Now we had returned to York, Penelope shone brighter in my memories than any spotlight. After Ada's disappearance in Paris and our sudden departure, I doubted Penelope had left the theatre of her own accord the night she had returned. I worried I was doomed to be next but Rothbart would never have let me leave his stage. After I had broken the record number of fouettés performed, his ambition was a hungry beast I could not satiate.

That Christmas, I danced the Sugar Plum Fairy from Tchaikovsky's *The Nutcracker* to a sold-out theatre as brightly wrapped sweets tumbled from the galleried ceilings. Each one a sugared jewel, its flavour a fantasy. Emerald praline fir trees that melted on your tongue as the aerial artists waltzed through the air, snowflakes belonging to the Land of Snow. Amethyst-marzipans that conjured the sweet memory of being a child on Christmas Eve, toys and magic awaiting beneath the tree. Golden chocolates that were the creamiest thing you ever would taste and were held responsible for the unaccountable fits of glee that several members of the audience succumbed to. Lollipops and sugarplums and iced gingerbread hearts and candy canes. A Christmas that promised to enchant you forevermore.

But I did not share those sentiments.

I performed the Dance of the Sugar Plum Fairy wishing that I might fly away on my gauzy violet wings, over the grey ribboning streets of York and farther, until I felt the wind billow over the clifftops and tasted salt upon my lips. Since we had returned from Paris, I had been reduced to a paler, thinner version of myself. Before I walked on stage, Ivy, our newest soloist promoted from the corps, had tutted and painted my eyes, lips, and cheeks in brighter colours until my exterior sparkled as fiercely as my fairy-gown. A façade I struggled to maintain. Daisy had departed soon after our return to England, unable to avoid the truth any longer: a dark and prowling fate was hunting us down, one by one. And though we all knew his face, his name, none would speak of it.

Our finale fell on Christmas Eve.

When children were awaiting Father Christmas, noses pressed to frosted windows, and families were to feast together after the matinée. When the magic ran deeper and darker than ever. When everyone's mood was bubbling with laughter and gaiety and the cast seemed to have forgotten its lost members. As I had too, just weeks earlier. The fact of which now marked me with guilt. The Dance of the Sugar Plum Fairy appeared light and delicate yet the playful leg-flicking variation required deep reserves of strength. As I pirouetted, the emerald forest of Christmas trees began to light, one by one. Glittering pinpricks alighted on their branches. Whilst I span around the stage, faster and faster, to the caramel-sweet melody, the pinpricks took flight. Up they flew, to the painted ceiling, where they formed a shimmering silhouette of Clara's Nutcracker Prince. He remained there, twinkling away until the culmination of the ballet when there sounded a crack as if the theatre had been torn in two, and down spiralled hundreds of tiny nutcracker soldiers. A souvenir for each member of the audience to take home. It was magic. But I was no longer under its spell. Numb to the enchantment, I reached out and caught one of the last falling nutcracker soldiers. Its face had been modelled after Ludwig's, the dancer who had been my very first kiss before he'd disappeared. The cruel irony was a knife twisting in my back and I could bear it no longer.

After the curtains fell, before changing out of my Sugar Plum attire, I sought out Rothbart. 'Tell me the truth of what happens in this theatre,' I demanded.

He had been pouring himself a snifter from his decanter. His back to me, it stiffened before he turned. His tawny eyes glinted in the firelight, the space between us too intimate, leaving insufficient room for his oversized stage persona.

'I cannot live with not knowing what happened to Penelope,' I continued, knowing I was treading a dangerous path yet unable to heed the warning, to turn back. 'To Ludwig, to Edith, to all those performers that vanished in the night. Ada. Penelope—' My voice cracked. 'Why do they never return? What did you do to them? What is it that draws you to linger outside my door on those moonless nights?' Ada who had possessed an extraordinary kind nature, sweet Ludwig who had been the most considerate dance partner, and Penelope who had been so much more. The kind of friend that burrows into your soul and loves you like a sister. They deserved to be more than a memory. And I deserved to learn the truth.

'Forget this now.' Rothbart downed the contents of his glass before slamming it down. It cracked against the wood and I flinched. 'Our next season will be our biggest yet, I have booked us in to perform somewhere you've always dreamt of dancing.' His mouth curved into a smile.

I swallowed. 'Where?'

He spread his arms wide. 'Where else? St Petersburg, of course.' He came closer, his voice dropped seductively. 'Imagine dancing upon the stage of the Mariinsky Theatre, the spotlights trained on you, an audience roaring to their feet in a standing ovation, showering you with bouquets as they did in Paris. Imagine Imperial Russia falling in love with you.'

The temptation was a siren call. To visit the land of my mother's family. Tread the stages in a city where she had danced. Yet my mother would not have taken pride in the woman I had become. 'No. I forgot Penelope once and I will not, I cannot, forget her again. There will always be another stage, another performance, but I have danced my last in this company.'

Rothbart's eyes clouded over. Even as I feared the storm to come, I forced myself to stand still. To not seek refuge and hide. 'This is the last time I shall warn you, put this out of your mind,' he growled.

Still, I held firm. 'I cannot,' I whispered. 'You may consider this my official notice. I will leave at the end of the season.'

'You forget yourself,' he snapped and I flinched again, my veins sparking like an electric current was racing through them, shocking me. My nerves a live wire. I watched him prowl closer to me, his stage persona peeling off, revealing the fury beneath. 'Do you know what you would have been without me? Nothing. I took you in, gave you a position in my theatre, and this is the appreciation you show me? I made you great.'

I raised my jaw and glared at him. 'I am great because I worked myself to the bone to become so. And do not pretend that you hired me out of any charity on your behalf, not when my dancing brought in such substantial ticket sales.'

He whirled around and swept a vase off his shelves. It shattered into a hundred pieces. 'Why must you feel the need to challenge me?' he thundered. 'Why did you have to go ahead and ruin everything!' His roar shook the study. My feet were rooted to the carpet, my breath coming in tiny gasps as he unravelled before me. 'You are right. You were the star of my show.' Disappointment crested across his face.

His words were unnerving. Frightful. Shaking my head, I let out a laugh that did not sound as if it belonged to me. 'No, *you* are the star of the show, which is why you have never feared ridding yourself of your prima ballerinas, your finest performers. You know that there will always be another one, younger, hungrier, stepping into their pointe shoes. But you? Nobody can do what you do and that is what sets your theatre apart. And that is why we do not truly matter to you.'

He offered a rueful smile but there was a greed in his eyes, a glint of wickedness that chilled me more than his shouting or throwing things. 'Ah, Odette.'

My true name was a spell. It roused me to my senses, forcing me to stare into the cracked looking glass of my recollections, my memories sharp and wicked. The bone-snap of a swan's neck that had haunted my darkest thoughts until I had drowned it in expensive champagne and haute couture. Little delights, spattered like starbursts over a deep galaxy of hurt. I suddenly feared I was confronting the same fate which Penelope had met but I did not know whether I could fight against whatever was coming or if it would devour me whole. I trembled. Staring at him, I noticed afresh that his haggardness had only exacerbated since our return to York, his cheekbones hollowing as December marched by.

Rothbart's voice was a sinister crawl, a creeping terror. He considered me with a hunter's stare. 'I regret to inform you that, once again, you speak of matters which you do not understand. You are the stars, all of you. You shine in exchange for the magic I extend to you all. You are all part of something greater than yourself.'

Horror trickled down my spine at the implications of what he was voicing. 'Are you telling me that you *sacrifice* your performers?'

'In a way.' Rothbart stepped closer to me and I ran to the door, tugging at the handle only to find it locked. My horror swelled, panic screaming inside my head.

'I demand you let me go this instant,' I shouted. 'You are seriously disturbed; nobody's life is worth taking for the sake of a petty illusion!'

'If only it were but an illusion.' His laugh was hysterical, his head rocking back from the force of it. A clump of hair fell near my foot and I shuddered, revulsed. 'Then I might work my enchantments every night without cost. Yet magic demands a price.' His grin was a nightmare made flesh. 'Take heart, Odette, this way you will shine brighter than even your dreams.' He lurched for me, grasping my face in his hands and kissing me.

It tasted like night and poison and fear.

A kiss from the darkest of fairy tales. One that felt as if he was sucking my soul from within me, a thin wisp which I exhaled from my mouth like a little lost cloud. Rothbart inhaled it as if it was the most delicious morsel. When he released me, I stumbled back on my pointe shoes, desperate to claw as much distance from him as I could, my despair growing until it swallowed me whole. He had done something irrevocable to me. But I was too intent on fleeing to pause to consider why he should be observing me with such a particular expression upon his face. A face that gleamed with life and youth, magic crackling at his fingertips. Perhaps I ought to have. Or perhaps another moment of not knowing my fate was sweeter. For scarcely a second before I placed my hand on the doorknob, it began. A deep rushing through my blood. The sense of something indefinable becoming untethered.

I fell to the floor, unable to stand upon my own legs as I slipped away from my body on a murky current of fear. A cresting wave of panic washed over me as my humanity slid away. One sole thought remained; this was what it must mean to die. I had become his latest sacrifice. Gasping for breath, I drowned in the terror of losing myself forever. I was nothing but a worn patchwork of broken thoughts, interlaced with thin, silken strands that struggled to contain me. When I could hold on no longer, the silken strands snapped and I was but a suspended promise in the air. A promise of memories, dreams and experiences. I swirled weightlessly in that liminal space, a place that was nothing and yet everything. The universe contained in a single sigh. Then, I began to fall. Downwards and backwards and sidewards and frontwards and falling and falling until I hit the very bottom and was reborn into my cursed life.

Chapter Fifty-Eight

Forster did not trust himself to speak for a spell. It was still dark; they had almost waited out the night together. Detta traced her name in candle smoke. As he watched, the letters grew feathery, floating away on invisible wings.

'That was the moment when I understood what had truly happened to Penelope,' she told him. 'Odette . . . ' She lingered on her name. 'Do you believe that the fates are laughing at their cunning? A girl named for a swan that became a swan herself.'

'I refuse to believe that this is your fate.' Forster stood, walking back and forth.

The floorboards creaked as she padded over to the window. He joined her and she wrapped her arms around him. They gazed out at the lake to which she would return when the last flake of snow had drifted away. 'Oh, Forster, do be careful,' she pleaded. 'Rothbart is unpredictable and the very thought of you confronting him pains me. Perhaps it would be better to leave him be. After all, we have each other, we're already luckier than most. Why risk it all?' Her voice was breathless, as if strings of lakeweeds were slipping down her throat, stealing the air from her lungs, drowning her in their ropey grasp.

Forster clutched her arms, bending to look into her eyes. 'Because I could not live with myself if I did not try everything I could to break this curse. You deserve everything in this life, more than I am able to grant you, but if I may do one thing for you, let it be this. Let me find the man who tore your world apart and bring him to justice so that you may live again.' His hands slid down her arms, clasped her hands within his. 'And you can wake each and every morning in my embrace.'

'I used to wonder if I deserved this curse. If I brought it upon myself for craving attention on the stage, generous and idolatrous enough that I might wrap it around myself like an expensive fur coat. Now I know that I did not. Your love has made me realise many things but the greatest gift it brought with it was teaching me how to love myself again. But I may never deserve you, Forster,' she admitted.

'No,' he told her fiercely, tilting her chin up and looking deep into her ocean eyes. 'You deserve more. But I shall never stop trying to give you everything. For you, I would cut the stars from the sky.'

Her eyes stormed with waves of longing, passion, and ambition. 'I miss my old life, Forster,' she whispered, and his heart ached for her anew. 'This body is ageing and I am starting not to recognise myself. I worry how much time I have left; the magic is exacting a heavy toll upon me and each time I return, I grow weaker and weaker. Do you truly believe that even if you find Rothbart, he will reverse this curse on me?'

'You are every bit as wonderful as the very first day I met you—' he pulled her closer to him, holding her against his chest '—and I won't rest until I have found a way to persuade him.' He didn't confess that Detta had voiced one of his secret fears, put it out of mind for now. After all, he still had to find the man first.

She smiled at him. Soft candlelight danced over her sharp cheekbones and, with a sudden whim, he placed a record on the hand-crank gramophone he had bought for the cabin, which did not have electricity. As the ragtime jazz began to play, as the sunrise flooded the lake in strawberry-pinks and caramel-golds, he taught Detta how to dance the Charleston.

✿

The following week brought more snow, yet Detta remained her swan-self. And as Forster agonised whether to stay beside her or leave in pursuit of Rothbart, he combed through his books with greater urgency. But his photograph was charred and difficult to make out and the short descriptions of most of the castles impossible to discern whether or not they were a match. Defeated, he pushed over the nearest stack and slumped back in his armchair. An envelope addressed to himself caught his attention. Cursing himself for not noticing it earlier, he snatched it up. Detta's note was short and unexpected and he wished there was more of her contained within it.

> Forster, do not underestimate Rothbart. I fear you have become so caught up with the notion of finding him and asking him to reverse this curse that you have not considered the very real possibility that he may refuse. Or worse. Be careful, my love, and heed my warning. I am already too familiar with loss but I would rather live an entire life as a swan than lose you, too.

Detta's words galvanised Forster into action, desperate to have more answers for her the next time she returned to him. Something she could hold onto and hope with. He strode to the manor and began making enquiries on the telephone, being connected through to archives and history departments at universities, requesting assistance and chasing leads until he struck gold: there was a librarian by the name of Miss Thomas working in Cardiff Library, who happened to be a brilliant amateur historian. And she was confident she could help him identify Rothbart's castle.

That afternoon, Forster sat on the dock as the sky darkened, papery grey clouds bruising into night. Detta the sole swan lingering on the iced lake. Her head was bowed as she slumbered, her elegant neck looped over her body. It reminded Forster of all the times he had witnessed Detta curl up on a chaise, her feet tucked underneath. Snowflakes began spiralling down, blanketing the woods, leaving Forster pacing with excitement for her to return so that he might share his latest good news with her, yet she stayed locked within her swan-self.

Recalling Mrs Fischer's notes on Detta's transformations, he suddenly realised with a bite of guilt in deep carnelian-red that he ought to have been maintaining them. He wanted to scream at the skies, at the snow for not holding sufficient magic, at Rothbart for condemning her to this life. Sadness pierced him like a barbed thicket. He ran back inside the cabin and foraged through one of the bookcases until he found what he was seeking. Back on the dock, he sat at the precipice of the lake and began to read from an age-darkened volume of fairy tales.

If he could not protect her then he would turn her dreams to magical stories, of gallivanting elves, princesses falling in love by moonlight, dashing heroes, and everything ending happily ever after.

Chapter Fifty-Nine

Towards the end of January, Forster was sitting outside on his deck, bundled in blankets on the crisp winter morning as he watched over Detta and read the latest issue of *The City Star* out loud to her. It was filled with snatched photographs of the Bright Young Things. Their escapades were a thousand miles from his secluded lakeside cabin and though Rose had been smiling at someone out of frame in one of the photographs, Marvin's by-line was noticeably absent from the gossip columns only to reappear on the political pages, attached to a small yet thoughtful piece on the troops that Britain had just dispatched to Central China. Forster's sable paintbrushes were drying nearby, as was the canvas perched on an easel overlooking the lake. It was a slow afternoon and Forster had just wandered back inside for another mug of coffee when he heard someone stride inside the cabin. His hands fluttering around the mug, he turned. 'De—'

Vivian was scrutinising him. 'You have lost weight since Christmas, darling.' Dressed in a rich shade of emerald, she was a bright flower against the muted tones of his woodland home, all caramel-pine and honey-oak.

Forster forced his disappointment down, chastising himself. Of course it was Vivian; he had been expecting her since they'd arranged her visit at Christmas. He was gladdened to see her and she was keen to see what he had been painting as there were several interested parties pursuing his work. He kissed her cheek, offering her coffee or tea. 'I shall take a champagne since I have practically travelled to the furthest reaches of this island.' She cast a disparaging eye around. 'So, this is where you have sequestered yourself. You are establishing quite the reputation as a hermit, you know. Though I support you cultivating a level of mystique, I cannot help but worry that you're isolating yourself. Perhaps—'

'No,' Forster said, popping open a bottle of champagne and obliging Vivian with a saucer. Jan Garber crooned 'Baby Face' on the gramophone in the background as he ushered Vivian to seat herself. Though she would be aghast at the very notion of him knowing that she was far older than the years she claimed, she took it gratefully. 'Just one tiny gallery.'

'No,' he repeated, more firmly. 'My paintings are selling well, whether or not I am in attendance, and that is enough for me.' He could not leave Detta's side, not while she was struggling to change when it did snow. And when snow was no longer a possibility, then he would resume his hunt for the man that possessed the power to right what he had wrought. And he would not take no for an answer.

'Very well.' Vivian tapped a finger against her saucer. Her many engagement rings tinked against it. 'I am a trifle concerned for you though.' She peered at him. He stood, leaning against the fireplace, drinking his coffee.

'I can assure you that I'm perfectly fine.' He raised his coffee mug as if to toast her.

'Is it an unrequited love perhaps?' Vivian pressed. Before he might answer, she continued, 'Or something entirely different altogether?'

'The latter,' Forster admitted, 'but do not ask me to explain for I cannot. I am bound to secrecy.'

337

Vivian's eyes twinkled. 'Ah, now that I understand. I am well versed in inadvisable love affairs, I'll have you know.'

Forster's laugh surprised them both. 'You shall be the very first I enter into my confidence,' he promised her. 'Now, would you care to see my latest painting?' He led her out onto the deck as she clutched her fur stole tighter against herself, drawn towards the canvas the easel offered.

It was Forster and Detta. He had painted himself as a creature born of the forest, the woodland's ancient rhythm beating through his heart with vines in place of veins, his hazel eyes lanced through with the green sword of spring. And Detta, clouds and feathers, on the verge of floating away to where the sky thinned and great birds made their passage to other lands. To where the stars shone their brightest and winged creatures flitted across moonbeams. Painted-Forster had wrapped his hand around her ankle, attempting to pull her back to earth. Yet if one looked closely, you might see his heels lifting from the earth as she sent his muse soaring to fresh heights.

'I cannot sell this.' Vivian's voice was hoarse.

Forster turned to her with a slight frown. He had, perhaps fool-ishly, considered this his finest work yet. 'You do not care for it?'

'Oh, my darling boy, it is precisely the opposite. You have painted your heart and I cannot take your heart away.'

Forster's throat thickened. Vivian's hand found his as they both gazed at the painting.

After a strong mug of Turkish coffee and several slices of the Victoria sponge cake Forster had baked earlier that morning, he carried a stack of canvasses to where Vivian's driver awaited them, outside the manor. She turned to him in a whirl of Chanel No.5. 'We are going to have some very happy buyers with these; watching you develop as an artist is exciting,' she told him before pressing a hand to his cheek. 'But do take care of yourself, too. Especially that heart of yours.'

After Vivian departed, Forster paced back and forth in his cabin. He knew he needed to leave at once; Detta was declining at an alarming rate. Yet he had promised her that he would never leave her side in the event that she needed him. Until a sudden snowstorm struck that eve, leaving Detta gasping for air on the deck, somewhere between swan and woman, beautifully grotesque in her distorted form, and he realised he no longer had that luxury. Detta was running out of time and he could not afford to wait for spring.

Chapter Sixty

Forster motored to Wales that night, arriving as the sun rose and gilded the sky. He had not visited Wales since the family holidays of his youth, yet the emerald hills, giving way to cloud-scraping mountains and moss-green valleys, were just as he remembered. En route to Cardiff and the librarian he had spoken to earlier that January, Miss Thomas, he stopped at a cosy, thatched-roof inn for a pot of strong coffee and a paper bag of Welsh cakes, fresh from the oven. He drank several cups of black coffee in quick succession, rousing himself from the nightmare he had been plunged into the previous night with Detta, caught between two worlds. Half-woman, half-swan. She had fought to be with him until she'd surrendered to the moonlit lake, unable to battle the curse sighing through her veins. It was a sight likely to plague his darkest dreams forever. Taking his glasses off, he pinched the bridge of his nose and forced himself to concentrate on the map before him. His route already marked to his first destination: the majestic old library in Cardiff.

'It's unusually formed, do you see?'

Miss Thomas, to whom Forster had previously spoken, had proved easy to find and he'd been pointed to her desk straightaway. Enthusiastic to solve a historical mystery, she'd immediately asked to see the photograph and was now bent over it with a magnifying glass, her black bobbed hair swinging around her face. 'Undoubtedly – that mountain ridge resembles a dragon's spine – and then see these thick walls?' She lowered the glass and tapped the walls in question. 'I'd say that's a medieval stone keep castle. You're probably looking at it having been built sometime in the twelfth century, if I were to hazard a guess.'

'Excellent.' Forster exhaled in relief that Miss Thomas was as proficient as the faculty member he'd spoken to at the history department in The University of Wales had promised. Wales may not appear large at first glance, but its endless valleys and mountains and wending coastlines would be impossible to traverse by himself alone. 'Now where would I find this castle? As I mentioned before, I want to pay it a visit myself.'

'One moment, please.' Miss Thomas held up a finger and scurried away.

Forster glanced around Cardiff Library. It was a grand affair, rising from the street in stories of honey-tinted Bath stone and Portland stone columns with beautifully tiled corridors beneath arched ceilings. Forster drummed his fingers against the oak counter, restless to move on, to pin Rothbart down like the squirming worm he was.

'Here.' Miss Thomas made her triumphant return. She heaved an oversized book down between them. *A Photographic Tour of Medieval Welsh Castles*. 'We ought to find it amongst these pages.' She did not wait for Forster to open the book. With a spine that creaked and shuddered as she opened it, she began turning the pages with a zealous interest that kept Forster captive despite his increasing restlessness. Miss Thomas hesitated on a page. She swivelled it towards Forster. 'Is this not the castle you have been seeking?'

Forster laid the photograph against the larger one in the book.

They both leant closer to examine it. It was a perfect likeness. Both held the same peculiar mountain ridge, the same castle that threatened to tumble down into the valley below, the same shaped walls and towers and stones. 'I can't believe it,' Forster breathed, taking it all in. 'At times I thought I was never going to find it.' He grinned at Miss Thomas. 'I can't thank you enough.'

She beamed back at him. 'I'm happy to have been of assistance; I always enjoy when people consult my talents as a historian. Now, according to this, your castle is located in Ceredigion, which narrows your search down to almost seven hundred square miles but fails to pinpoint it exactly.' She reached for a pencil and paper and began writing an address. 'I suggest that you pay a visit to an old friend of mine, Gwynfor, who shares my interest in history. He is based in Ceredigion, in Aberystwyth, and is a veritable fount of local knowledge; if anyone will know the location of this castle, I can assure you that it will be him.'

Forster took Gwynfor's details and his photograph and left in a hurry, thanking Miss Thomas so profusely that she blushed.

It wasn't until mid-afternoon that Forster reached Aberystwyth. The little port town's promenade was a curved half-moon as if once the sea had taken a great hungry bite from it. Coco Chanel and the French Riviera set had recently started a vogue for suntans but their beaches were golden, touched with summer's kiss year-round. Here, on certain streets, the wind-rush swept off the sea like a great seabird, catching you unawares in its wings as you struggled for footing. Forster held onto Miss Thomas's paper tightly, until he'd located the pastel-blue house facing the water, which matched the address she'd penned for him.

'*Noswaith dda,*' Gwynfor boomed cheerfully upon opening the door.

'Good afternoon,' Forster replied, 'I've just come from Cardiff where I met with one of your acquaintances, Miss Thomas, on a matter of local history. She helped me immensely and—'

'Ah, how is Miss Thomas?' Gwynfor enthusiastically led Forster inside. 'Come in, come in, tell me how you came to meet her and what's brought you all this way to my neck of the woods.'

Inside Gwynfor's house, it was small and lit with gas lamps but warm with hand-knitted blankets. Wide windows offered a roaring view of the sea, its grey-tipped waves crashing onto the promenade itself. Eager to keep moving, Forster condensed his story and pulled out his photograph quickly, hoping against hope that this had been more than a wild goose chase. That the fates were not laughing at him and Detta after all but perhaps tweaking their spools at this very moment, guiding them onto a better path together. 'Oh yes, I know this one!' Gwynfor exclaimed upon examining the photograph and Forster nearly crumbled with relief. 'It's not much of a tourist site, mind.' He looked doubtful but nothing, nothing could subdue that relief, running through Forster as if it had a mind of its own. 'I don't mind one bit.' He grinned at the confused man, who shrugged and offered him a cup of tea, which Forster declined, thanking him as he hastened back to his motor.

Perhaps Forster could be the hero of his own story after all.

Later that afternoon, when darkness fell like a curtain, revealing a backdrop of glittering stars above the twisting roads, hanging like plump diamonds he might reach out and pluck, Forster finally set eyes upon it.

Rothbart's castle.

Chapter Sixty-One

Though Rothbart's castle looked even more dilapidated since the photograph had been taken, it was the same unmistakeable shape: thin and high with a single turret remaining. An iron-bolted door secured the ground floor. Forster stiffened, bracing himself for the encounter, his thoughts wheeling like gulls. Soon he would confront the man they called The Sorcerer in the flesh. The man who had cursed his great love, her future resting in his untrustworthy hands.

Forster left his Tin Lizzie concealed to one side and walked up the incline, his heart thrumming in his chest. Harder and harder until he could feel it pounding against his ribcage. Both from Detta's stories and his own research, he knew that Rothbart was a man at the mercy of his own ambitions, whose need for others to worship and exclaim over his creations was his driving force in life. And he could not imagine that such a man could bear to see his reputation, his glittering accolades, stripped from him. Forster planned to use this against him. And if it failed, well, Rothbart was a wanted man, in hiding from the police. He was certain he would not wish to exchange his castle, however damp and moth-eaten, for a jail cell.

Summoning his courage, Forster reached out for the door handle. It was bronze and peeling, unassuming. The iron bolts running across the door reminded him of a vampiric lair from the kind of horror films Rose had dragged Marvin and him to. Little had he known back then that the world contained actual horrors rippling beneath the surface. That curses were real and magic, greater and more terrible than he could have imagined, truly existed. Gulping back his fear, he pushed the door. And almost fell inside. He hadn't expected it to be unlocked. Yet the man that Detta had painted a picture of was a man filled with hubris; a man that would never expect another to triumph over him. Hatred and fury reared up inside him, fanged and longing to bite. It devoured his fear. Pushing his glasses up, Forster entered the castle.

The stone halls were cold, echoing with the ghost of history. Forster shivered, sensing a dark presence at play. Half-rusted suits of armour followed him with their iron stare. He crept deeper inside the castle, his tread soft. Almost expecting to see a dragon rise from the crumbled stones as if he were a knight of long ago, walking towards a desperate fate to save the woman he loved. Ascending a spiralling staircase, the stones smooth and sloped, his heartbeat stuttered. It had grown warmer up here; someone was heating this portion of an upper floor. His anger swelled like a ripe blackberry. A deep, rich heliotrope-purple. How dare this man, this sorcerer, have seized Detta in his wicked claws. He had used her like a tool with which to wield his enchantments, yet on the stage, Detta had spun her own magic that was greater and purer than anything this man could have conjured. His anger governing his head, he marched along the stone passageway until it crooked to one side and Forster stumbled upon a haggard man.

'Who might you be?' he asked, not ungenially. He stood before Forster in a room that was barely more than an alcove, hollowed out from the thick walls. Stacks of plays and theatre programmes, their pages browned with age like a rancid apple, towered around them.

345

A sliver of a window, wide enough for a single arrow to poke through, looked down the mountainside.

Forster stared at him. If one peeled back the years, you could see the man Rothbart had once been, his photograph having adorned magazines and newspapers that Forster had pored over, searching for clues. Learning his foe. Yet those had only been taken some fourteen years ago. The period of time did not account for his wizened state. 'Are you Rothbart? Of Rothbart's Theatre of Enchantments?' he bit out.

The man spread his arms. 'The one and only.' His pride was evidenced in his tone though he was unkempt in ragged clothes and grey hair, his moustache grown too long and thin.

'You're a monster,' Forster growled.

Rothbart's pride snapped into suspicion. He peered at Forster. 'Who are you and why have you sought me out?' His suspicion grew, his tawny irises sharpening in the cloudy pools of his sclera. 'Precisely how did you find me here? I told not a soul where I lived. There are no records to trace me here.' He stepped back, then back again, one arm sneaking back, reaching for something.

Yet he was old before his time and Forster was fuelled with rage and love. *Do not underestimate him*, Detta had warned. Rothbart might have been wizened but he was still deadly. Forster launched himself at the man, clamping his hands around Rothbart's throat and pinning him in place.

'Wait,' Rothbart yelped. 'Tell me who you are.'

Forster's glare burnt into him. Hatred was bubbling inside him at the thought of this man putting his hands, his mouth, on Detta. 'I am here on behalf of someone you have wronged.'

Rothbart's owlish mannerisms turned wild. Fearful. Forster couldn't tell if his powers had faded, leaving him vulnerable, or if this was just an act to lower Forster's defences.

Forster's voice rose, echoing around the alcove. 'You were a dark sorcerer masquerading as a harmless illusionist, stealing your performers one by one and condemning them to live a cursed life.'

'Who survived?' Rothbart croaked.

'You sound surprised.' Forster did not remove his hands from the man's throat, unwilling to chance leaving himself unprotected. Detta had told him all the stories he'd read were real, of polar bears and trees that marched across a stage, castles that grew as if by themselves and rain that turned to flowers. If this man wielded such powerful magic, he was dangerous enough to leave his door unlocked, a greater match than anyone who might wander through. Sweat turned his palms slick. Before his grip slid, he tightened his hands on Rothbart. He may appear an old man but this was the villain of darkness and curses, an enemy with a poison-kiss.

'It is unfortunate but that is the nature of my curse.' Rothbart's sigh trembled. 'None of them live longer than a few years. Though perhaps that is a blessing in their state.'

'What?' Forster stared at him in confusion and horror. He did not know how Detta had long surpassed the others' lifespans as swans, only that it was more important than ever that Rothbart returned with him.

'Who are you here to avenge?' Rothbart's tone took on a patina of boredom. 'Was it that lovely girl on the coast last year? Or perhaps the young man with the soul of a poet I found exploring the castle walls several winters ago?'

'You sicken me.' Forster's words shook with anger. 'How dare you speak so casually of the lives which you have ravaged! You must be held accountable for your crimes.'

'Perhaps. Though that is hardly your prerogative.' Rothbart was far too dismissive considering he stood with Forster's hands tightening around his throat. For a moment, Forster struggled with himself, his fury bleeding into his thoughts, tempting him to squeeze those hands until Rothbart choked and turned as blue as Detta did each time her feathers peeled back to skin. 'I could kill you this very moment,' he told Rothbart, his jaw tightening as he stared the man down. He had never known how powerful hatred could be until he'd set eyes on Rothbart in the flesh. The force of it was overwhelming. 'And nobody would mourn for you, nobody would even notice you were missing, and if they did? They would rejoice to be in a world without you.' For the first time, fear entered Rothbart's eyes. Forster was grimly satisfied to see this; the more he could rattle Rothbart, the more his threat would hold and he could bend the man to his will. 'Your once grand life would end here in the rubble and you would know that, in the end, none of what you did truly mattered. In the end, you were nothing.'

'What do you want with me?' Rothbart croaked.

'Did that disturb you?' Forster was locked in place, the importance of what came next too great to move, to look away, to lose this power he had stolen. 'You're a man who spends his time polishing his own ego like gold,' he continued. 'Who surrounds himself with the legacy of his theatre, his productions, the accolades he once achieved.' The alcove was littered with awards and newspaper clippings of his own prowess. The same ones Forster himself had collected, learning Detta's past. One bore an old photograph of her. This gave him the strength to continue, to battle the numbness spreading through his hands as he clenched them around Rothbart, preventing his escape, his retaliation. 'Imagine if the press could see you now. An old man, reduced to living in rags and ruins. His reputation rendered to base accusations, a man unworthy of any respect, his awards stripped from him. Soon to be remembered for his crimes alone as he is condemned to rot away in a high-security prison.'

Rothbart's silence was like glass. Sharp and fragile.

'I shall leave you with your freedom on one condition.' Forster's chest tightened, squeezing his heart until it fluttered with fear. 'That you un-weave the curse you wrought upon Odette Lakely. Or Detta Kova, as she was known as a ballerina.'

Rothbart started upon hearing her name. 'Odette?' he whispered. 'She lives still? How is that possible? It must have been over a decade—'

Forster stepped closer to him, his hands hardening around his throat until Rothbart gasped. 'Yes, over a decade of her suffering,' he growled. 'Can you imagine what sorrow and loss she has grieved over all those years? You will grant her life back to her. Her freedom in exchange for yours. Do we have a deal?'

Rothbart's laugh was high. 'If only one could survive for that long, of course it was Odette,' he rasped. 'After I had taken my fill of her, my enchantments grew ever more potent. Being at the helm of that theatre was draining me of my life essence. I needed more, vast quantities of it.' His gaze turned retrospective, greedy. 'Odette was magnetic, it was a shame to lose her but once you sip another's soul, you develop a fierce craving. Silky and beautiful and delicious, ah, I could only resist hers for so long. But what I made with hers was *magic.*'

Fury stormed through Forster. 'You shall undo it,' he snarled. 'At once. Or I swear to god, I will make your life a living hell until you fall down on your knees and beg me for the sweet release of death.'

'I will, I will, I swear it!' Rothbart yelped, his lips turning blue.

They exited the castle together. Outside, the evening was raven-dark and full of eyes. Forster placed a firm hand on Rothbart's hunched back and pushed him towards his motor.

They drove through the night in silence. The mountains great hulking beasts that gave way to tamer hills as they neared the border. It was there that Forster noticed it was very finely snowing. He drove like a man possessed, never once loosening his grip on the wheel as he motored back to the woman he loved, his hope as tentative as the first rays of sunrise that glowed over the horizon as they reached the manor.

Forster's wheels skidded on the driveway beside the fountain. He had no intention of inviting this despised man into his woodland sanctuary. Ushering Rothbart out of the motor, he fumbled in his pocket for his key to the grand front doors. Yet there was no need; they swung open of their own accord. And there, framed by the electric chandeliers sparkling behind her, stood Detta.

Chapter Sixty-Two

'Odette Lakely, what a treat to be graced with your presence after so many years. Or do you still go by Detta Kova?'

Forster regretted bringing Rothbart directly to Detta's door. His fingers curled at his sides as he longed to leap between them, to shield her from his presence yet, much as he was loath to admit it, they had great need of this man. He was the sole person who might grant Detta her life back. And, for that, Forster would tolerate anything. Even the man who had stolen it from her.

'He has sworn to right the wrongs he inflicted upon you,' Forster explained quickly as Detta still did not move. 'In return for not handing him over to the proper authorities and reducing his reputation to tatters.' She looked frail, her wine-red velvet dress loose about her shoulders, and he hated that she had suffered the change alone. Had she cried out for him as her bones broke and reformed, battling the pain of becoming human once more?

Rothbart rubbed his throat. 'And for keeping my skin,' he muttered, peering inside the manor. 'My, how you do live well, *Detta*. Whatever drove you to leave all this for my humble theatre?'

Detta drew her poise up through her spine as if she were about to pirouette. 'Nothing you could ever hope to understand.'

'Ah, but there you are wrong, *mon petit cygne*. Once, I understood you better than anyone else in this world. After all, we are not so dissimilar, you and I, both our hearts beat harder when we are worshipped and adored, our stomachs growling with our appetite for ambition. I am sure that you have heard I am the villain of this little convoluted story yet the truth is rarely as it seems and your great love is more culpable than she would care to admit.' He gave Forster a pointed, triumphant look as Detta blanched. But Forster knew everything there was to know about Detta and nothing this man could say would shock him or change his mind about her.

'You are the only villain I see here.' Forster threw Rothbart over the threshold and slammed the manor door shut. The wind had picked up outside and was howling, sending snow whirling past the windows. Heavy and thick, it was blanketing the grounds and emboldening Forster. This was it. It was too cold to lose Detta to the melting snow and she was too weakened to endure another change. 'You will return Detta to her true state tonight,' he informed Rothbart.

Rothbart's gaze travelled around the great hall. 'Very well. I shouldn't imagine it shall take but a moment.'

Forster's lungs filled with ice. 'Then you have never attempted this before?'

'Not to worry, I assure you it shall be far more arduous on myself than your beloved Odette.' A shadow danced over his face. 'What you are requesting of me is immense.'

'Then you may have the day to prepare. But no longer,' Forster snapped. He had not slept in two nights now and his temper was slipping out of control, aggravated by spending too much time with the man who had harmed Detta. 'Or a jail cell will start to look cosy and welcoming compared to what I have in mind for you.'

Rothbart fell silent.

'Lock him in a distant room in the upper floors as I do not wish to set eyes on him until he is removing the curse,' Detta said crisply. She turned to Rothbart. 'And as long as you are beneath my roof, you are not to wield your magic.' Her pause glittered with danger, her gaze dipping to where Forster had wrapped his hands around Rothbart's neck, finger-shaped bruises emerging. 'Or I shall finish what he started.' With that, she stalked away.

Forster deposited Rothbart in a disused drawing room that was dusty and distant enough from Detta's wing so as not to disturb her. 'You may have whatever items you require but be warned—' Forster allowed a vein of fury to bleed into his voice '—you have until tonight only.' He shut and locked the door behind himself before Rothbart could respond.

Downstairs, Detta handed him a large cup of coffee. She cupped another in her hands. 'We cannot trust him, Forster,' she said when he reached her.

Forster removed his glasses to clean them, blinking wearily as the world softened around the edges, the lights swelling into shining orbs. 'You and me both. I shall keep him under lock and key until he undoes this curse. And I believe you should telephone Watchers Security too; let's arrange for them to post their private guards inside the room with Rothbart so that we have eyes on him at all times. I will be taking no chances with your salvation.'

Detta hesitated. 'Forster?'

He braced himself when he caught the worry twining between her brows. 'What is it?'

'I very much doubt that Rothbart has had cause to take back what he has wrought before. There is a chance it may not be successful.' She glanced down, toying with her snowflake necklace. 'You heard him, he has never attempted this before. I had been so caught up with the notion of actually finding Rothbart, of fearing his dark and strange magic, that I had assumed he knew how to perform this un-cursing. What if he does not?'

He caught her chin with his fingertips, gently raising her face to his so that he might kiss her. 'He will. He dislikes not being the one who holds the power, that is all, so he must find some way to frighten you, to steal a little back for himself. But pay him no heed, for this is what we've been working and waiting for, this is our time at last. And I shall be at your side throughout.' He kissed her protests away. 'Now, ring the security firm and arrange for them to drive over at once, then wait half an hour before following me home. I have a surprise for you.'

Her blue-grey eyes twinkled. 'What kind of surprise?'

'Now that—' he drank the rest of his coffee and stood, setting the cup down '—would be telling.' He walked off before darting back to bestow more kisses on her lips, her neck, the tip of her nose, until she laughed and batted him away, archly informing him, 'You have only twenty-nine minutes left now.'

It was now snowing more generously than Forster had witnessed in an age; it had coated the grounds in the space of minutes and his boots were already sinking into feather-white mounds as he exited the manor and strode towards his cabin. His heart swelled. Soon, Detta would no longer leave him the moment the snow melted. They would share entire seasons; springs that bloomed into summers sweet as orange blossom macarons. Autumns as rich in colour as blackberries gleaming in a piecrust. Soon their life would be more than snatched moments.

On entering his cabin, Forster opened a large box and hurriedly set to work, pleased that he had thought ahead and left it out for when Detta next returned instead of getting rid of it when he'd faced celebrating Christmas alone. He hung forest-scented wreaths, with plump garnet berries crowning them like jewels. Placed frosted candles on every surface, surrounding them with cloud pine until the cabin resembled an elven-dwelling woodland. All emerald green and twinkling with the light of a hundred candles. When he had finished, he smoothed his shirt down, tied his curly hair back, and, with a shaken breath, slid a small box into his trouser pocket.

With a flurry of snow, Detta entered on time. She'd added a little fur-trimmed cape atop her dress, and it was dusted with snowflakes. Her laugh was soft, gleeful as she admired his efforts, and Forster's heart tripped to see her so happy. 'Oh, Forster,' she exclaimed, 'this is beautiful. What's the occasion?'

'You are.' He walked towards her. 'It was just over four years ago now that I first saw you and I have thought of little else ever since.'

Her smile faded a little. 'Do you ever regret it?'

'Never,' he said fiercely as he reached her. 'You are extraordinary, and I could no more regret meeting you than the sun could regret her shine.'

Her smile trembled. 'Do you know, for the very first time I feel as if I am not spinning wildly from one snow-filled moment to the next, losing days as one might lose single breaths or beats of their heart?'

Forster could not tear his eyes from her. Rothbart had invited the most dangerous element of all back into his life. Hope. He was aflame with it, and it had gilded Detta, too.

'For the first time in years, I may embrace the possibility of a future once more,' she whispered.

'Good,' Forster said roughly. 'Because I do not care for any future that doesn't include you. You, Detta, are my everything and I plan on loving you for a very very long time to come.' He reached for her hand, clasping it tightly within his as he knelt before her.

She let out a soft gasp, her other hand pressed against her heart. 'Odette Lakely, my darling Detta, would you do me the honour of becoming my wife?' He opened the box from his pocket. The ring beamed up at them both. Pale peppermint-green beryl, enlaced with a diamond border, on a delicate gold band.

'Nothing could make me happier.' Detta smiled through her tears.

Forster slid the ring onto her finger. 'A perfect fit.'

'Did you ever doubt we were?' Detta teased.

'Ah, I believe you were the doubting one, actually.' Forster grinned back at her.

She dropped to her knees before him and wrapped her arms around his neck. 'Not for a long time now and never again,' she murmured. 'You are my everything.' She pulled him onto her lips, welcoming him into her future that had begun to gleam and dazzle once more.

Chapter Sixty-Three

A few hours later, Forster roused himself from a deep nap to visit Rothbart. A guard unlocked the door as he juggled a bowl of porridge and two mugs of Turkish coffee, black as the storm-clouded sky he'd re-awoken to. It was hard to believe it was still morning; half the lights in the manor were lit. The weather was blustery, tossing great flocks of snow around and he welcomed it. Detta seemed in no risk of turning swan before Rothbart could work his magic upon her.

'Ah, come to keep an old man company for a while?' Rothbart asked upon sighting the second mug.

'I wish to speak with you.' Forster locked the door after himself and sat down on the settee before the unlit fireplace. A second guard stood next to it, surveying Rothbart coldly. Forster wondered what Detta had told her trusted security firm.

Rothbart spooned greedy bits into his mouth, gesturing at Forster. 'Speak away, there is precious little else we may do. If your plan is to bore me to death in the interim, it may well work. He—' Rothbart gestured at the guard '—doesn't talk much, does he? Or have you bade him not to? No fraternising and all that?'

Forster clasped his hands around his mug for warmth. 'Tell me where you learnt your magic. Such a craft can't have been easy to come by; were you born with this power or did you make yourself a student of it?' If Detta was soon to brush against it once more, he wished to understand it better himself. His surreptitious glance at the guard showed the man had not reacted to his questions as he had assumed he would; Detta paid them a generous sum for their discreetness.

'Ah.' Rothbart perked up. 'Now there is a fine story. One I was suspecting that I should never have the opportune moment to tell.' Animated, he set his bowl down and leant forwards. A show master with fresh material at last. 'You see, we happen to live in a world of doors yet so very few possess the keys.'

'Metaphorical doors, I presume?' Forster took a deep swig of his coffee, bracing himself for Rothbart's winding and no doubt dramatic explanation.

'Not at all. I am referring to tangible doors through which we might find ourselves in any number of different, wondrous places. Yes, I was as surprised as you when I first learnt of this myself.' Rothbart chuckled at the expression on Forster's face. 'Though I first discovered the doors when I was a young man, and upon being presented with the physical evidence of this phenomena, it becomes much easier to grasp. I understand the notion of it alone must be a slippery thought, one that your innate comprehension of logic and physics in this world is at this very moment attempting to dismiss.'

'You forget that I have witnessed first-hand the effects of what your magical experiments have exacted upon Detta,' Forster said coldly, disliking the man's superior tone, his lack of remorse more chilling than the snow stealing along the windowpane.

Rothbart shrugged and gulped half his coffee in one. 'Seeing a woman transform into a swan is child's play compared to the things which I have experienced in my time. When I first stepped into another world . . . ' his tawny irises glazed over ' . . . it was greater than anything I could have ever imagined. Then I crossed paths with a stranger. Once a doctor, turned toymaker, who possessed vast reserves of power. I was intrigued and begged him to mentor me. Being of like minds, we became acquaintances and he attempted to teach me a little of his magic though I regret I did not have the same propensity for it as he did. What I learnt amounted to little more than parlour tricks, the playground of illusionists and magicians. Still, it was useful. After a time, I learnt of this curse and its most beneficial side effect; sapping another's life force so that my magic might grow grander, my life filled with the days they would never live to see.'

Forster's jaw pulsed, his teeth clenched. His voice trembled with the anger coursing through him, gathering like the snowstorm outside. 'You stole their lives. You're no better than a common murderer.'

'You're an artist, are you not?' Rothbart gestured at the paint staining Forster's trousers and dried on his shoes from deep cerulean to the palest periwinkle-blue, as if he had strolled across the lake. Forster nodded. 'Well then, I created art. That you cannot deny. Only my creative pursuits demanded a higher sacrifice.'

'You will be reversing the curse on Detta tonight. Tell me what magic you intend to subject her to,' Forster demanded.

'Ah, that.' Rothbart seemed to crumple in on himself. He looked as worn as the settee he rested on, his skin the hue of old parchment. 'I have changed my mind,' he said. 'I would rather rot in a cell than run the risk of attempting such dangerous magic.'

Forster stood, his anger deep and relentless as an ancient ocean. It crashed over him, making it an effort to maintain civility. To manipulate Rothbart to his will. 'How curious. I had not thought you of all people would doubt your own abilities.'

The wrinkles on Rothbart's forehead deepened. 'It is not doubt, merely a healthy dose of realism—'

'Are you not the same man the papers declared a sorcerer, the greatest illusionist to grace the stage all over Europe?'

'I was more than an illusionist,' Rothbart growled, creaking to his feet.

Forster jabbed a finger at his chest. 'Exactly. You wielded such powerful magic in front of their noses, made your fame and fortune. And you are telling me that you are incapable of reversing a single curse on one woman?'

'I would not say incapable, only that I have never put it to the test.'

Forster hesitated, his words were not having the desired effect on Rothbart. Mindful of how pale Detta looked when he had left her slumbering in their bed, how little time they had left, he switched gears. 'You're right.' He frowned in pretence. 'This is untested magic and you are clearly not as powerful as you once were. Perhaps I have acted in haste, assuming that you were strong enough—'

'I can do it,' Rothbart interrupted, glaring at Forster. 'I am not the old man you are making me out to be, I have powers beyond your wildest dreams. Though that does not mean that I am willing to sacrifice my own life for another.'

'Your death is not a certainty,' Forster said softly. 'Not unless you break our agreement now.'

Rothbart eyed him warily. 'You do not have it in you to kill me. No matter how much you think you want to, actually committing such an act is beyond you. You are, at your core, a lovesick man. Nothing more.'

'Perhaps you are right.' Forster leant in closer. 'But there remains the small matter of your unpunished crimes.'

'A jail cell is better than death,' Rothbart interrupted.

'Who says your fate is jail? You're wanted for investigation into several unusual disappearances,' Forster parried back. 'And murder carries the death sentence.'

Rothbart remained staunch, though he began to look waxen. 'I did not kill those performers and there is not one bit of evidence that might indicate such a thing.'

'An innocent man does not run,' Forster snapped. 'And you not only ran from the police, you fled from a monumental debt, owed to some of the most influential figures across the country, no less. The kind of people whose word shall mean far more than yours. Don't you think they would like to see you hang?'

Judging by Rothbart's silence, he agreed they would. Forster took care to hide his satisfaction. 'If you return my Detta to me, then I will allow you to scurry back to your castle rather than face the noose.'

'Fine.' Rothbart nervously stroked his moustache. 'Sunset ought to work well. It is then when the veil between the worlds runs thinner, allowing our world to crackle with a little more magic than other, ordinary times.'

Forster cast a look out of the window. The sky held unfathomable snow in its clouded arms. 'Sunset tonight then.' Fear fluttered weakly within his chest at the fate which Detta would shortly be confronting.

Detta was outside the cabin, building a snowman. As Forster neared, she speared its face with a carrot. 'I have decided that Geoffrey here shall be our witness.' She crowned him with a faded top hat at a comical angle and stepped back to survey him, hands on her hips. 'Just the ticket, wouldn't you agree?'

Forster rested an arm around her shoulders. 'I do. Rothbart has decided that sunset shall be the opportune time.'

'Very well.' Detta's smile was slow, sweet as caramel. 'Then let us marry before sunset. Marry me then and I shall not fear surrendering to Rothbart's magic once more.' Forster stilled, hardly daring to dream that he had heard her correctly. Her smile slipped. 'That is, if you wish to marry me so soon?'

He kissed her smile away, kissed her harder until her lips parted and she sighed. Then he swept her up into his arms and strode into the cabin. 'I would marry you a thousand times over, Odette Lakely. Until the moon falls from the sky and the stars no longer glitter.'

Chapter Sixty-Four

That afternoon brought a whorl of activity to the manor as they hurried to prepare for their upcoming wedding celebrations. Fortunately, the storm had abated, and Detta had parted with a fortune to tempt her contacts to battle the snow. Forster ducked beneath a strawberry-red-and-white big top that five men were slowly raising in the ballroom then evaded a tray of caramel apples being carried at head-height by a man on stilts as he forged a path to the telephone.

'Hullo? Marvin? It's Forster,' he called over the chaos. Running the show was Detta, who chose that moment to stroll by and blow him a kiss. His thoughts stuttered and ground to a halt. She wore a form-fitting woollen dress in an evergreen shade that complemented her ring and he could not believe that, before night fell, she would swear to be his forevermore.

'Forster? What the devil is that noise?' Marvin drew his attention back to the receiver he held.

He cradled it, attempting to shut out his surroundings. 'Apologies, it's a circus over here,' he said with a bite of dark wit. 'Listen, Marvin, there's to be a party tonight at the manor. One of Detta's grand themed ones. Do say you'll come, the both of you.'

Marvin's chuckle was low. 'You're forgetting something, old chap.

While you've been holed up in that cabin of yours, it has grown less easy for us to travel. We only have a few months longer to wait now.'

'Is Rose faring well?' Forster asked anxiously.

'Marvellously so.' Marvin's exhale was warm with pride. 'Rose insists that when the time comes, you are to be an uncle. She's also determined that the little one shall be named Marigold and is already planning a wardrobe for her from Paris.'

Forster chuckled. 'That sounds about right. Well, then, I understand you may not be coming but you ought to know, we will be making an announcement tonight.'

'An announcement, eh?' Marvin sounded like he was smiling. 'You have me intrigued. In that case, I'm sure I could persuade Rose to make an appearance.'

They exchanged their goodbyes and, as Forster replaced the receiver, his mood began to shimmer as brightly as a new moon.

As he walked through the manor, trapeze artists cavorted along a highwire that grazed the electric chandeliers. An acrobat dived through the air above, ribboning down on a stream of silk, glistening in seafoam-green; a lost mermaid who had mistaken the skies for her sea. Shouts came from the front doors as several men carried through an elephant-shaped cake, true to size in cloud-grey fondant. He forged his way outside, to where dancers rode upside-down on horseback in the snow, and little red-and-black-striped stalls offered paper bags of cinder toffee or roasted, sugared nuts. The air was warm with caramel. Forster itched for his paintbrushes, the scene reminding him of an old painting by an unknown artist, of the Frost Fair on the Thames. It had been a while since he had attended one of Detta's lavish affairs and this, the party to announce their wedding, to celebrate her becoming un-cursed, promised to be one of her most spectacular yet.

Forster exited the manor and strolled over to the cabin. Here, the world was hushed and glittering white. Light from the windows cast honeyed puddles on the snow and the cabin looked like it had appeared from the pages of a storybook. The perfect place for a fairy-tale wedding.

Chapter Sixty-Five

When the clouds blushed petal-pink that evening, Forster stood between two fir trees that framed the entrance to the wooden gazebo. They preened beneath their sparkling glass icicles. Boughs of evergreen were pinned along the hexagonal gables above, with little lanterns hanging down. As the snow-clotted sky darkened a shade, Forster had lit the candles until the gazebo twinkled like its own constellation.

Forster's breath caught in his throat as Detta walked through the snow. Her moon-white silk dress poured off her shoulders and down to her satin ballet slippers, embroidered with shimmering snowflakes. As she approached him, clasping a bouquet of white camellia flowers and pinecones, the delicate pearl crown she wore on her head marked her as the reigning queen of winter. When she reached the wooden steps, dusted with snow, he stepped down to take her ivory gloved hand in his. 'You're looking rather dapper tonight,' she told him, her gaze lingering on his tuxedo.

'Detta, you,' he swallowed, 'you are a vision.'

They exchanged their vows before the registrar and one of the guards, acting as both protector and silent witness. And as the snow continued to fall from a rose-gold sky, they became husband and wife. Sometime later, the registrar and witness melted away and Forster took Detta in his arms. 'Are you happy?' he murmured, drawing her towards him, fascinated with her soft red lips. 'Incandescently.' She sighed into his mouth, curving her body against his. It pained him not to sweep her to their cabin, to pull away to ask, 'The sunset is almost upon us; are you ready to become uncursed at last?'

Rothbart, the sorcerer, the villain of their little fairy tale, stood before them. Closing his eyes, he brought his fingertips together with a fizz of magic. Detta, still resplendent in her wedding dress of molten moonlight, was opposite him. Forster watched on, his nerves clamouring at him in a sickly yellow. He longed to gather Detta close to him, to hold her tightly and protect her from the world's cruelties. Instead, his love faced a monster in a battle he could not fight for her. And he, helpless on the side.

'A kiss for a kiss,' Rothbart declared, stepping towards Detta and pressing his lips to hers.

Forster clenched his hands behind his back. Waiting. Hoping.

With a sudden gasp, Rothbart pulled away, clasping his chest, and Forster could not look away, entranced by the silvery pale mist that flowed from Rothbart's heart into Detta's. Detta closed her eyes, spreading her arms like wings as the force lifted her up onto her toes. Her dress was ruffled like feathers, her hair flying around her. Forster stepped closer, reaching for her, panicked that she may soar up and away into the snow-filled sky. He clenched his hand shut before he could touch her, too afraid to meddle with the magic that swirled into her.

Perhaps if Forster had not been so enraptured with the notion of waking each and every morning in his new wife's arms, he might have seen Rothbart blanch, the pain that rippled over his face. The way his lungs began to crackle with each breath, a breath that turned cold and colder until it became ice. Shards of ice that fell to the snow, Rothbart's lips tinged the deep blue of the oldest part of a glacier.

Yet Forster did not see this. Not until the crack that sounded, ripping apart the night. The silvery mist snapped back into Rothbart and Detta fell to the snow.

A ringing silence followed.

'No,' Forster whispered, running to Detta. 'No!' Fearing the worst, he could hardly breathe until she sat up and turned to him, pale as ice. 'Did it work?' she shivered. 'Oh Forster, I can feel the cold again, look.' She stretched out her arm, showing him the hair that rose along it, the goose bumps puckering her skin. 'How beautiful to feel it again at last. I wonder how the sunshine will feel come spring. I haven't seen the seasons in so long, I hardly dreamed I would again.' Her smile was hypnotic, entrancing Forster as he stared at her in wonderment. Delighted that all his planning and hoping and investigating had finally given Detta her life back again. A life they could now fully share. 'I feel changed,' she told him. She shivered more violently, and Forster removed his jacket in a hurry, but before he could put it around her shoulders, she cried out with pain. 'Something's wrong.' She bit her lip, holding herself together.

'No.' Forster ran his hands over her, searching for the source of her pain. 'Don't worry, Rothbart can fix whatever it is; he can make it right.' Yet he did not realise the thorned truth until Detta shook her head and wrenched his hands from her and told him, 'Look', her voice splintering.

Time slowed, the space between them filled with spiralling snow as Forster twisted round and saw at last.

Rothbart had frozen.

It was grotesque. An uncanny sight that Forster shuddered at, even as he rushed to aid him, seeking a way in which he might thaw the man as Rothbart's eyes rolled from side to side, holding a silent scream of terror within them. Another loud crack sounded and in one terrible moment, Forster realised what was making that sound: Rothbart was splitting apart. Forster could see the space where the man's heart had once beat in its bloody cavern. It was dark blue, and it had shattered. A cobweb of cracks had spread from it and the ice groaned and creaked as Rothbart's eyes rolled back in his head and he succumbed to the eternal night. Then shattered apart into a thousand tiny crystals of ice.

Detta screamed. Years of pain and anguish rang through it, and it hurt Forster to hear it.

He threw himself in front of her, his body a shield. Shards of ice flew into his back, his shoulders, but it was his heart alone that felt their impact. It sang with pain. Then Detta screamed again, high and thready and primal, and Forster nearly collapsed under the weight of his grief. Detta crumpled to the ground and wept. And as her tears fell to the snow and froze like diamonds, she began to silver. 'We were too late,' she sobbed as her hair turned to white and feathers sailed down her back. 'Oh, Forster, we were too late.'

He sank beside her, the snow gently falling on them both as he held the woman he loved as she came undone in his arms. 'Stay with me, Detta,' he told her through his tears. 'Please don't leave me, I can't bear a world without you in it; you're the love of my life and nothing makes sense without you. Stay with me. Just stay,' he whispered until her feathers were soaked with his tears and his throat was too ragged to speak another word.

Forster did not know how long he had been lying in the snow. He couldn't even feel the cold for it did not matter anymore. He was dimly aware of glittering lights exploding high above him: fireworks.

Guests were arriving at the manor for Detta's celebration party. He could hear their shouts of joy accompanied by a band playing in the distance. But Detta was still trapped as a swan and Rothbart was still gone, perishing along with Forster's last hope.

'Forster? Forster?'

He heard his name called but did not possess the strength to speak out. 'Nothing matters but her,' he murmured to himself.

'Oh god, there he is.' The hazy figures of Rose and Marvin came into view, peering down at him.

'She's gone,' Forster told them. He could cry no longer, his tears were spent and his chest hollow; his heart had been ripped from it. A pleasing numbness was spreading through his limbs and he thought that if this was what it felt like to die, it would not be so bad after all. Less painful than existing without his wife, his reason for being, his heart. She was his everything and now that she had gone, he could no longer imagine how the sun and the moon would rise and fall on a world he could not share with her. Their storybook had closed too soon.

For a true fairy tale never did end happily.

Epilogue

The story always started the same way.

When the nights deepened, swallowing daylight by the hour. When winter whispered its frozen song across the land. When the promise of snow could be tasted in the air.

Then, and only then, would the reclusive artist living beside the lake be reunited with his swan-wife. Only then would she shed her wings for her human skin and walk back into his life. Yet those days were few and fewer and he dreaded the day when she could no longer shift back, when she would be a swan forevermore.

Their love was a thing of legend, as if two stars had collided and set the sky itself aflame. The woman who wore a cursed cape of feathers and the man who spent his days painting her.

Their story woven from the darkest of fairy tales.

Acknowledgements

Upon a Frosted Star is the hardest book I've tried to write so far. It's also my oldest idea and one that I was forever saving until I was a 'good enough' writer to do it justice. Until Thérèse Coen sold this book and I couldn't put it off any longer! Thank you Thérèse for being a wonderful agent and friend, and for loving this idea and encouraging me to write it.

Thank you to my brilliant editor, Katie Seaman for believing in it from the start and being my guiding starlight, forever patient and wise as I stumbled my way through those difficult first drafts!

To my Team Unicorn at HQ Stories, I'm so appreciative of all you do for my books (and me). I feel so special being one of your authors. Special thanks to Kirsty Capes and Sarah Lundy in marketing and publicity, Georgina Green, Brogan Furey, Angela Thomson and Sara Eusebi in sales, Angie Dobbs in production, and everyone at HQ who's been involved in any way, you're all magical. And of course, a huge sparkly shoutout to Charlotte Phillips, who has created another showstopper of a cover that I am obsessed with.

Being an author can sometimes be lonely but not when you have excellent author friends like Vic James, Kate Weston (and Angus), Rachel Rowlands, Stacey Thomas, Lee Newbery, and the Swaggers, who are my favourites to procrastinate with. Thank you all for always being there to chat about anything bookish or otherwise.

To all my friends that have spent the past few years listening to me talk endlessly about this book, (which may or may not have had the affectionate working title of Problem Child), I can't thank you enough! Christine Spoors and Amy McCaw, who show up for me every single day, Jonathan Norman and Evangelos Palaiologou, for your friendship and many many excellent boardgame nights. Alex McGahan, who is always there for me, and Sarah Hackmann, sorry about the lack of ferns in this one! Polis and Chris Loizou-Denyer, for all your lovely support, here's to many more double dates at Coco Tang! And of course my Shakespearean Sisters, who I couldn't do without.

I'm hugely grateful to all the bookshops, booksellers, bookstagrammers, bloggers and booktokkers who have supported me across many books, especially Helen Tamblyn-Saville at Wonderland Bookshop, Lauren Cassidy, Dan Bassett, Gavin Hetherington, Jess Deacon, Georgie Nicole, and all of the lovely people at Waterstones Nottingham and Waterstones West Bridgeford.

Thank you to everyone in my family that have showed up and supported me, particularly my mum, who always has time to chat about my books (both the ones I'm reading and writing!), my babcia for filling my freezer with pierogi, Jane and Chris Brothwood for being a second set of parents to me, and Jill Biddulph, who was a grandmother to me and who I miss.

I could never have written this book (and rewritten it several times) without Michael Brothwood, my husband and best friend, who never stops believing in me and encouraging me to follow my dreams.

Finally, I am so grateful to anyone who has ever picked up one of my books or posted lovely reviews and content about them across social media. You are all the best and I hope you enjoyed stepping into this fairy tale with me.

Curl up with another spellbinding book from M. A. Kuzniar — a magical fairy tale retelling of *The Nutcracker*

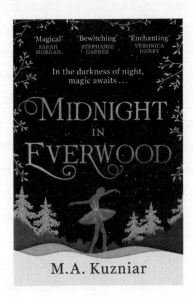

In the darkness of night, magic awaits . . .

Marietta Stelle longs to be a ballerina but, as Christmas draws nearer, her dancing days are numbered — she must marry and take up her place in society in the New Year. But, when a mysterious toymaker, Dr Drosselmeier, purchases a neighbouring townhouse, it heralds the arrival of magic and wonder in Marietta's life.

After Drosselmeier constructs an elaborate theatrical set for her final ballet performance on Christmas Eve, Marietta discovers it carries a magic all of its own — a magic darker than anyone could imagine. As the clock chimes midnight, Marietta finds herself transported from her family's ballroom to a frozen sugar palace, silent with secrets, in a forest of snow-topped fir trees. She must find a way to return home before she's trapped in Everwood's enchanting grip forever.

ONE PLACE. MANY STORIES

Bold, innovative and
empowering publishing.

FOLLOW US ON:

@HQStories